중간고사 완벽대비

적중100

영어 기출 문제집

중2

능률 | 김성곤

Best Collection

구성과 특징

교과서의 주요 학습 내용을 중심으로 학습 영역별 특성에 맞춰 단계별로 다양한 학습 기회를 제공하여 단원별 학습능력 평가는 물론 중간 및 기말고사 시험 등에 완벽하게 대비할 수 있도록 내용을 구성

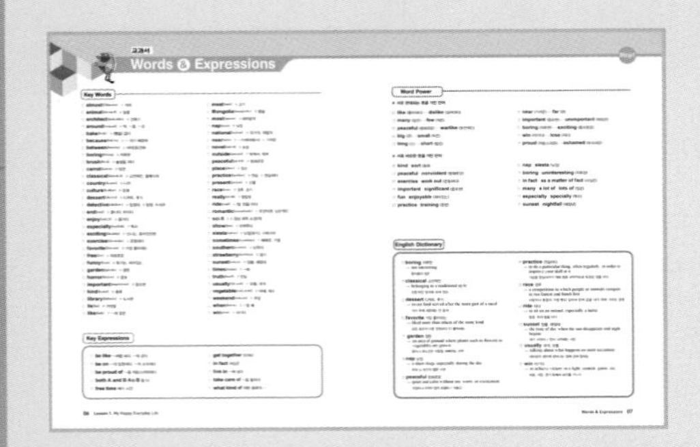

Words & Expressions

Step1 Key Words 단원별 핵심 단어 설명 및 풀이
Key Expression 단원별 핵심 숙어 및 관용어 설명
Word Power 반대 또는 비슷한 뜻 단어 배우기
English Dictionary 영어로 배우는 영어 단어

Step2 실력평가 단원별 수시평가 대비 주관식, 객관식 문제풀이

Step3 서술형 대비 학업성취도 및 수행능력평가 대비 서술형 문제풀이

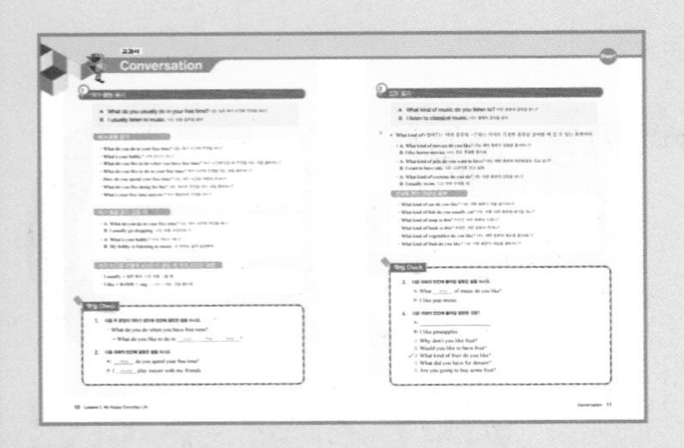

Conversation

Step1 핵심 의사소통 의사소통에 필요한 주요 표현 방법 요약
핵심 Check 기본적인 표현 방법 및 활용능력 확인

Step2 대화문 익히기 상황에 따른 대화문 활용 및 연습

Step3 기본평가 시험대비 기초 학습 능력 평가

Step4 실력평가 단원별 수시평가 대비 주관식, 객관식 문제풀이

Step5 서술형 대비 학업성취도 및 수행능력평가 대비 서술형 문제풀이

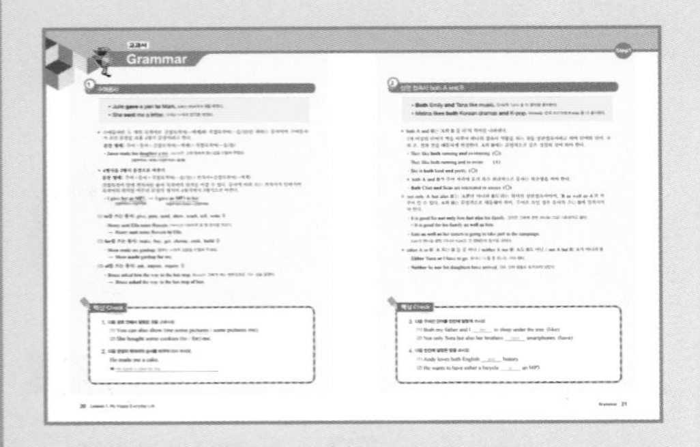

Grammar

Step1 주요 문법 단원별 주요 문법 사항과 예문을 알기 쉽게 설명
핵심 Check 기본 문법사항에 대한 이해 여부 확인

Step2 기본평가 시험대비 기초 학습 능력 평가

Step3 실력평가 단원별 수시평가 대비 주관식, 객관식 문제풀이

Step4 서술형 대비 학업성취도 및 수행능력평가 대비 서술형 문제풀이

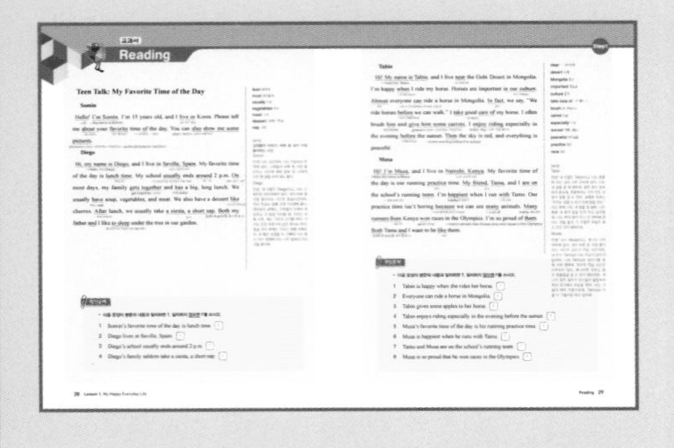

Reading

Step1 구문 분석 단원별로 제시된 문장에 대한 구문별 분석과 내용 설명
확인문제 문장에 대한 기본적인 이해와 인지능력 확인

Step2 확인학습A 빈칸 채우기를 통한 문장 완성 능력 확인

Step3 확인학습B 제시된 우리말을 영어로 완성하여 작문 능력 키우기

Step4 실력평가 단원별 수시평가 대비 주관식, 객관식 문제풀이

Step5 서술형 대비 학업성취도 및 수행능력평가 대비 서술형 문제풀이
교과서 구석구석 교과서에 나오는 기타 문장까지 완벽 학습

Composition

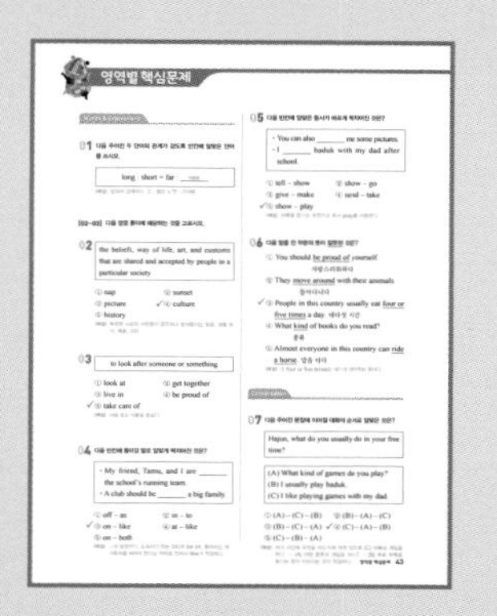

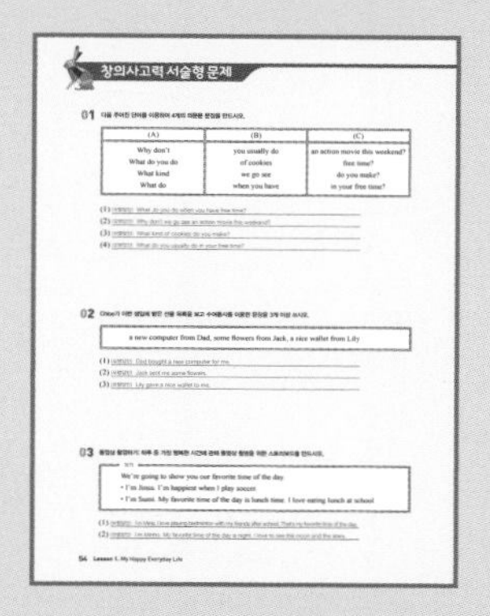

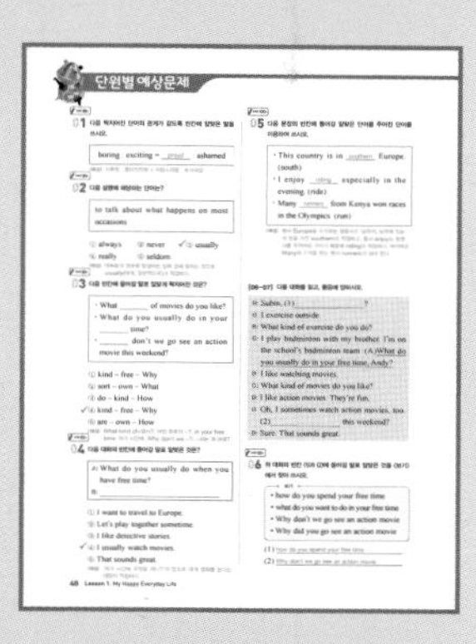

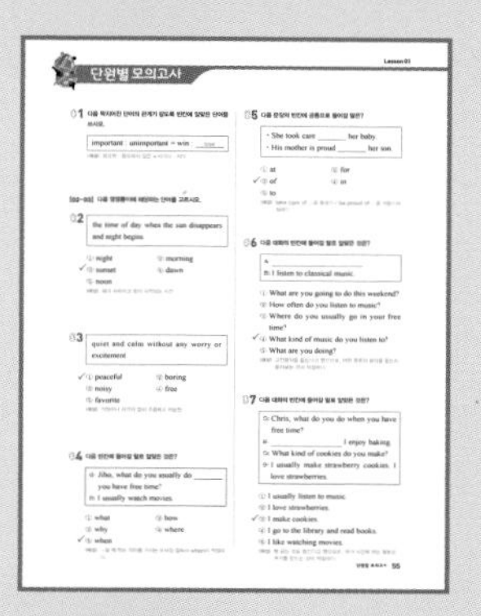

|영역별 핵심문제|

단어 및 어휘, 대화문, 문법, 독해 등 각 영역별 기출문제의 출제 유형을 분석하여 실전에 대비하고 연습할 수 있도록 문제를 배열

|서술형 실전 및 창의사고력 문제|

학교 시험에서 점차 늘어나는 서술형 시험에 집중 대비하고 고득점을 취득하는데 만전을 기하기 위한 학습 코너

|단원별 예상문제|

기출문제를 분석한 후 새로운 시험 출제 경향을 더하여 새롭게 출제될 수 있는 문제를 포함하여 시험에 완벽하게 대비할 수 있도록 준비

|단원별 모의고사|

영역별, 단계별 학습을 모두 마친 후 실전 연습을 위한 모의고사

교과서 파헤치기

- **단어Test1~2** 영어 단어 우리말 쓰기와 우리말을 영어 단어로 쓰기
- **대화문Test1~2** 대화문 빈칸 완성 및 전체 대화문 쓰기
- **본문Test1~5** 빈칸 완성, 우리말 쓰기, 문장 배열연습, 영어 작문하기 복습 등 단계별 반복 학습을 통해 교과서 지문에 대한 완벽한 습득
- **구석구석지문Test1~2** 지문 빈칸 완성 및 전문 영어로 쓰기

이책의 차례

Contents

Give a Helping Hand

의사소통 기능

- 도움 요청하고 답하기
  A: Can you help me move these books?
  B: Sure. / I'm sorry, but I can't.
- 제안하기
  Why don't we donate our clothes to the community center?

언어 형식

- 목적격 관계대명사
  The little black dress **which** she wore in a movie is famous even today.
- 감정을 나타내는 과거분사
  She was **shocked** because their lives were very difficult.

교과서

Words & Expressions

Key Words

- □ **accident** [ǽksidənt] 명 사고
- □ **alive** [əláiv] 형 살아 있는, 존속하는
- □ **beauty** [bjú:ti] 명 아름다움, 미(美)
- □ **blind** [blaind] 형 눈 먼, 장님의
- □ **carry** [kǽri] 동 나르다, 운반하다
- □ **collect** [kəlékt] 동 모으다, 수집하다
- □ **donate** [dóuneit] 동 기부하다
- □ **elderly** [éldərli] 형 나이가 지긋한
- □ **fame** [feim] 명 명성
- □ **favor** [féivər] 명 호의, 친절
- □ **feed** [fi:d] 동 먹이를 주다
- □ **fire** [faiər] 명 화재
- □ **following** [fálouiŋ] 형 (그) 다음의
- □ **goodwill ambassador** 친선 대사
- □ **grass** [græs] 명 풀, 잔디
- □ **hold** [hould] 동 열다, 개최하다
- □ **homeless** [hóumlis] 형 집 없는, 노숙자의
- □ **honor** [ánər] 동 예우하다, 존중하다
- □ **international** [intərnǽʃənəl] 형 국제적인
- □ **item** [áitəm] 명 항목, 물품
- □ **kind** [kaind] 명 종류, 유형
- □ **luckily** [lʌkili] 부 운이 좋게도, 다행스럽게도
- □ **medicine** [medisn] 명 약
- □ **mission** [míʃən] 명 임무, 사명
- □ **moment** [móumənt] 명 순간, 잠깐
- □ **nursing home** 양로원
- □ **plant** [plænt] 동 (식물을) 심다
- □ **praise** [preiz] 동 칭찬하다
- □ **raise** [reiz] 동 들어 올리다, (자금을) 모으다
- □ **realize** [rí:əlàiz] 동 깨닫다, 알아차리다
- □ **respect** [rispékt] 동 존경하다
- □ **return** [ritə́:rn] 동 돌아오다, 반납하다
- □ **saying** [séiliŋ] 명 속담, 격언
- □ **serve** [sə:rv] 동 (음식을) 제공하다
- □ **spirit** [spírit] 명 마음, 정신, 영혼
- □ **statue** [stǽtʃu:] 명 조각상
- □ **support** [səpɔ́:rt] 동 지지하다, 원조하다
- □ **survive** [sərváiv] 동 살아남다, 생존하다
- □ **turning point** 전환점
- □ **volunteer** [vὰləntíər] 형 자원봉사의 명 자원 봉사자
- □ **walk** [wɔ:k] 동 산책시키다, (사람 · 동물을) 걷게 하다
- □ **worldwide** [wərldwaid] 형 세계적인

Key Expressions

- □ **all the time**: 늘, 내내
- □ **be going to** 동사원형: ~할 것이다
- □ **be in a hurry**: 서두르다
- □ **break one's arm**: 팔이 부러지다
- □ **clean up**: ~을 치우다, 청소하다
- □ **fall down**: 넘어지다
- □ **give a hand**: ~을 돕다
- □ **hand out**: 나누어 주다
- □ **have to** 동사원형: ~해야 한다
- □ **help** 목적어 (**to**) 동사원형: …가 ~하는 것을 돕다
- □ **hold a party**: 파티를 열다
- □ **in need**: 어려움에 처한
- □ **pass away**: 죽다, 사망하다
- □ **raise money**: 돈을 모금하다
- □ **search for**: ~을 찾다
- □ **take care of**: ~을 돌보다
- □ **thanks to**: ~ 덕분에
- □ **What[How] about** 동명사 ~?: ~하는 게 어떨까?
- □ **what kinds of** ~: 어떤 종류의
- □ **Why don't we** ~?: ~하는 게 어떨까?

Word Power

※ 명사 – 형용사

□ **beauty**(아름다움, 미(美)) – **beautiful**(아름다운)

□ **favor**(호의, 친절) – **favorable**(호의적인)

□ **respect**(존경) – **respectful**(존경심이 가득한, 존경하는), **respectable**(존경할 만한)

※ 서로 반대되는 뜻을 가진 단어

□ **alive**(살아 있는, 존속하는) ↔ **dead**(죽은)

□ **luckily**(운이 좋게도) ↔ **unluckily**(불행히도)

□ **beauty**(아름다움) ↔ **ugliness**(추함)

※ 서로 비슷한 뜻을 가진 단어

□ **following**((그) 다음의) : **next**(다음의)

□ **thanks to**(~ 덕분에) : **because of**, **due to**(~ 때문에)

□ **collect**(모으다) : **gather**(모으다)

□ **pass away**(죽다) : **die**(죽다)

※ 사람의 성격을 묘사할 때 쓸 수 있는 형용사

□ **nice**[**kind**/**friendly**](상냥한, 다정한)

□ **funny**(재미있는)

□ **honest**(정직한)

□ **polite**(공손한)

□ **creative**(창의적인)

□ **wise**(현명한)

□ **patient**(끈기 있는)

□ **generous**(관대한)

□ **curious**(호기심 많은)

□ **gentle**(온화한)

□ **lively**(쾌활한)

English Dictionary

□ **accident** 사고
→ a sudden event that causes damage
손상[손해]을 유발하는 갑작스러운 일

□ **blind**: 눈 먼, 장님의
→ not able to see anything
어떤 것도 볼 수 없는

□ **collect**: 모으다, 수집하다
→ to put things together in one place
한 장소에 사물들을 함께 두다

□ **donate**: 기부하다
→ to give something to help people
사람들을 돕기 위해 무언가를 주다

□ **fame**: 명성
→ the state of being famous
유명한 상태

□ **honor**: 예우하다, 존중하다
→ to treat someone with respect
존경심을 가지고 누군가를 대하다

□ **international**: 국제적인
→ involving more than one country
하나 이상의 나라를 포함한

□ **mission**: 임무, 사명
→ a special task to be accomplished
달성되어야 할 특별한 일

□ **moment**: 순간, 잠깐
→ a particular point in time
시간 상의 특정한 시점

□ **nursing home**: 양로원
→ a place where people who are too old or sick to take care of themselves live
너무 나이 들거나 병이 들어서 스스로를 돌볼 수 없는 사람들이 사는 장소

□ **praise**: 칭찬하다
→ to say nice things about someone
어떤 사람에 대해 좋은 점을 말하다

□ **realize**: 깨닫다, 알아차리다
→ to suddenly know something
갑자기 무언가를 알다

□ **respect**: 존경하다
→ to admire or look up to somebody
누군가를 존경하거나 우러러보다

□ **statue**: 조각상
→ a sculpture of a person made from stone or metal
돌이나 금속으로 만든 사람의 조각품

□ **support**: 지지하다, 원조하다
→ to provide with assistance
도움을 제공하다

□ **survive**: 살아남다, 생존하다
→ to continue to live after something bad happens
어떤 나쁜 일이 일어난 후에 계속 살다

□ **turning point**: 전환점
→ a time when a huge change takes place
큰 변화가 발생하는 때

□ **volunteer**: 자원 봉사자
→ someone who is willing to do a job without getting paid
돈을 받지 않고 기꺼이 어떤 일을 하는 사람

01 다음 중 성격이 다른 하나를 고르시오.

① creative ② generous ③ lively
④ lucky ⑤ passionate

[02~03] 다음 빈칸에 들어갈 말로 가장 적절한 것을 고르시오.

02

Please don't ______ the animals in the zoo.

① feed ② blow ③ cost
④ fall ⑤ find

03 중요

This box is so heavy that I can't ______ it alone.

① carry ② wear ③ play
④ try ⑤ break

[04~06] 다음 밑줄 친 단어와 바꿔 쓸 수 있는 것을 고르시오.

04

I bought these items at a low price because they are used ones.

① sites ② stops
③ goods ④ markets
⑤ views

05 중요

He died at the hospital last night.

① passed over ② passed away
③ got over ④ gave up
⑤ got back

06

I want to meet many people and travel all over the world.

① nationally ② internationally
③ worldwide ④ global
⑤ variously

07 중요 다음 중 밑줄 친 부분의 뜻풀이가 바르지 않은 것은?

① I'd like to make an international call. (국제적인)
② Her mission was to establish schools for children. (임무)
③ The man keeps his family's tradition alive. (살아 있는)
④ She's gone but her spirit is right here with us. (정신)
⑤ They will raise money to help the poor. (들어 올리다)

[08~09] 다음 영영풀이에 해당하는 단어를 고르시오.

08

a time when a huge change takes place

① turning point ② schedule
③ timetable ④ moment
⑤ honor

09 중요

a particular point in time

① second ② plan
③ moment ④ motive
⑤ respect

01 다음 짝지어진 두 단어의 관계가 같도록 빈칸에 알맞은 단어를 쓰시오. (주어진 철자로 시작할 것)

luckily: unluckily - a__________ : dead

중요
02 다음 밑줄 친 부분과 의미가 가장 가까운 것을 주어진 철자로 시작하여 쓰시오.

We'll never forget his soul.

➡ s____________________

[03~04] 다음 빈칸에 공통으로 들어갈 말을 쓰시오.

03

- Can you drive faster? I'm ________ a hurry.
- I helped the people ________ need.

중요
04

- The kind girl ________ some money to the poor old man.
- He came to us and ________ a hand.

05 다음 빈칸에 알맞은 단어를 〈보기〉에서 골라 쓰시오. (형태 변화 가능)

보기

break hand search take

(1) Please ________ care of my son while I'm not here.
(2) He ________ his arm a week ago.
(3) Santa Claus ________ out gifts to the children last Christmas.
(4) Would you help me ________ for more information about these?

중요
06 우리말에 맞게 주어진 단어를 바르게 배열하시오.

(1) 네 충고 덕택에 기분이 나아졌다.
(thanks, advice, I, to, your, feel, better)
➡ ____________________

(2) 그녀는 지난달에 세상을 떠났다.
(month, passed, last, away, she)
➡ ____________________

(3) 정부는 노인들을 후원할 계획을 세웠다.
(the, the, planned, support, government, elderly, to)
➡ ____________________

(4) 그는 부와 명예 둘 다 얻었다.
(gained, fame, both, he, and, wealth)
➡ ____________________

07 다음 영영풀이에 해당하는 말을 주어진 철자로 시작하여 쓰시오.

(1)

not able to see anything

➡ b____________________

(2)

to continue to live after something bad happens

➡ s____________________

(3)

to treat someone with respect

➡ h____________________

교과서

Conversation

1 도움 요청하고 답하기

A Can you help me move these books? 이 책들 옮기는 거 도와줄 수 있어?

B Sure. / I'm sorry, but I can't. 그럼. / 미안한데 못할 거 같아.

- 상대방에게 도움을 요청할 때는 'Can you help me ~?'로 시작하는 문장으로 표현할 수 있다. help me 뒤에 동사원형이나 to부정사를 써서 구체적으로 어떤 도움이 필요한지를 밝힌다. 'Can I ask you a favor?'나 'Can you give me a hand?' 등의 표현도 쓸 수 있다.
- 이에 대한 긍정의 대답으로는 'Sure.' 등을, 부정의 대답으로는 'I'm sorry, but I can't.'나 'I'm afraid, but I can't.' 등을 쓴다.
- 도움을 요청할 때 can 대신 would나 could를 써서 'Could you help me ~?'나 'Would you help me ~?' 라고 말하면 공손하고 정중한 느낌을 준다.

도움 요청하기

- Can[Could/Would/Will] you help me (to) 동사원형 ~? (내가 ~하는 거 도와줄 수 있어?)
- Could you please 동사원형 ~? (~해 줄 수 있니?)
- Can you give me a hand to 동사원형?
- Can[May] I ask you a favor? (부탁 좀 해도 될까요?)
- Can[Could] you do me a favor? (부탁 좀 들어 주겠니?)

도움 요청에 답하기

- 수락하기: Sure. / Okay. / Certainly. / No problem. / Go ahead. / All right.
- 거절하기: I'm sorry, but I can't. / No, I'm afraid not.

핵심 Check

1. 다음 우리말에 맞게 대화의 빈칸을 채우시오.

A: Can you do me a ________? (부탁 좀 해도 될까요?)
B: Okay. ________ ________. (문제없어요.)

2. 다음 주어진 단어를 이용하여 대화를 완성하시오.

A: ______________________________? (help, can, wash, you, the dishes, me, to)
B: Sure.

2 제안하기

Why don't we donate our clothes to the community center? 우리의 옷을 지역 문화 센터에 기부하는 게 어떨까?

- 특정 행동을 함께 하자고 제안할 때는 'Why don't we ~?'로 시작하는 표현을 쓴다. 'How about ~?'이나 'What about ~?' 등의 표현도 쓸 수 있는데, 이때 동사 형태는 'How about donating our clothes?'처럼 전치사 about 뒤에 동명사를 쓰는 것에 유의한다.
- 'Why don't you + 동사 ~?'는 함께 하자는 것은 아니고 상대방에게만 권유하는 것이다.

제안하기

- Why don't we + 동사원형 ~? (~하는 게 어떨까?)
- How[What] about (동)명사 ~?
- Let's 동사원형 ~. (~하자.)

- 상대방의 제안에 응할 때는 'Sure, I'd love to.', 그렇지 않을 때는 'Sorry, but I can't.'로 대답할 수 있다. 허락을 요청하는 말에 거절하는 경우에는, 보통 간단히 이유를 덧붙인다.

핵심 Check

3. 다음 대화의 밑줄 친 부분과 같은 의미가 되도록, 주어진 단어를 이용해 문장을 만드시오.

> A: <u>How about having some ice cream?</u>
> B: Sure, I'd love to.

➡ (Why) ______________________

(What) ______________________

(Let's) ______________________

[4-5] 다음 주어진 어구를 배열하여 대화를 완성하시오.

4.
> A: ______________________? (the movies, we, tomorrow, why, to, don't, go)
> B: That sounds good.

5.
> A: ______________________? (school. about, after, how, soccer, playing)
> B: Okay.

Conversation 교과서 대화문 익히기

Listen & Talk 1 B

B: Hey, Minji! ❶What's wrong with your leg?
G: I ❷broke it last week.
B: Really? What happened?
G: I ❸was in a hurry ❹to catch a train. But I ❺fell down in the street.
B: Oh, that's terrible! ❻Is there anything I can do for you?
G: Well, ❼can you help me carry this bag?
B: Sure.

B: 민지야! 너 다리에 무슨 문제가 있니?
G: 지난주에 부러졌어.
B: 그래? 무슨 일이야?
G: 기차를 타려고 서두르고 있었어. 그런데 길에 넘어졌어.
B: 오, 정말 끔찍하다! 내가 너를 위해 해줄 게 있니?
G: 음, 이 가방을 드는 걸 도와줄 수 있니?
B: 그럼.

❶ 'What's wrong with ~?'는 상대방의 안 좋은 일에 대해 묻는 표현으로 '너 ~에 문제가 있니?'의 뜻이다. 'What's the matter with ~?', 'Is there anything wrong with ~?', 'What happened to ~?' 등의 표현과 바꿔 쓸 수 있다.
❷ broke는 break(부러지다)의 과거형이다.
❸ be in a hurry: 서두르다
❹ to부정사의 부사적 용법 중 목적(~하기 위해서)의 의미로 사용되었다.
❺ fall down: 넘어지다
❻ Is there anything I can do for you?는 '내가 너를 위해 해줄 게 있니?'의 의미로 도움을 제안할 때 쓰는 표현이다. 'Can I give you a hand?', 'May I help you?', 'What can I do for you?', 'Do you need my help?' 등으로 바꿔 쓸 수 있다.
❼ 'Can you help me ~?'는 상대방에게 도움을 요청할 때 사용하는 표현이다. help me 뒤에 동사원형이나 to부정사를 써서 구체적으로 어떤 도움이 필요한지를 밝힌다.

Check(√) True or False

(1) Minji broke her leg last month. T ☐ F ☐
(2) The boy will help Minji to carry her bag. T ☐ F ☐

Listen & Talk 2 A

G: ❶What kinds of volunteer activities can we do?
B: ❷Why don't we clean up our town's streets?
G: All right! ❸Let's do it.

G: 우리 어떤 종류의 봉사 활동들을 할 수 있을까?
B: 우리 동네 길거리를 청소하는 게 어때?
G: 좋아! 그러자.

❶ What kinds of ~: 어떤 종류의 volunteer: 자원봉사의; 자원 봉사자
❷ Why don't we ~?: ~하는 게 어떨까? clean up: ~을 치우다, 청소하다
❸ 'Let's 동사원형 ~.'은 '~하자'의 뜻으로, 어떤 일을 제안할 때 사용한다. 'Let's 동사원형 ~.' 외에도 'Why don't we ~?'의 표현을 쓸 수 있다.

Check(√) True or False

(3) They talk about volunteer activities to do. T ☐ F ☐
(4) They will clean up their town's streets. T ☐ F ☐

Listen & Talk 1 A

B: Mia, ❶can you help me move these books?

G: Sure. ❷What are you going to do with them?

B: ❸I'm going to ❹donate them to a children's library.

❶ 상대방에게 도움을 요청할 때는 'Can you help me ~?'로 시작하는 문장으로 표현할 수 있다. help me 뒤에 동사원형이나 to부정사를 써서 구체적으로 어떤 도움이 필요한지를 밝힌다. 'Can I ask you a favor?'나 'Can you give me a hand?' 등의 표현도 쓸 수 있다.

❷ 상대방의 계획에 대하여 물을 때는 'What are you going to do ~?'로 물을 수 있다. (= What will you do ~? = What are you planning to do ~?)

❸ 'What are you going to+동사원형 ~?'에 대답할 때는 'I'm going to+동사원형'으로 말할 수 있다. 내용상 주어가 바뀔 경우 그에 따라 'be동사'를 바꾸어 써야 한다. be going to 동사원형: ~할 것이다

❹ donate: 기부하다

Listen & Talk 1 C

B1: Wow! These dogs are so dirty. Jay, can you ❶help me wash them?

B2: Allen, ❷I'm sorry, but I can't. ❸I have to feed the cats now. ❹Why don't you ask Nicky?

B1: Okay! Nicky, ❺can I ask you a favor?

G: Sure, Allen. What is it?

B1: Can you help me wash these dogs?

G: Sure. But I have to ❻walk these dogs first. After that, I will help you.

B1: All right! Thank you.

❶ help는 불완전 타동사로 '~이 …하는 것을 돕다'의 의미로 사용되었다. 목적격 보어로 to부정사와 동사원형을 쓰는 준사역동사이다. 그러므로 목적격 보어 자리의 wash 대신에 to wash도 가능하다.

❷ 상대방의 요청을 거절할 때 쓰는 표현이다. (=I'm afraid I can't.)

❸ have to 동사원형: ~해야 한다 feed: 먹이를 주다

❹ 상대방에게 함께 ~하자고 제안이나 권유할 때에는 'Why don't we+동사원형 ~?'을 사용할 수 있다. 'Why don't you+동사원형 ~?'은 함께 하자는 것이 아니고 상대방에게만 권유하는 것이다.

❺ 상대방에게 도움을 요청할 때 'Can you do me a favor?'(나 좀 도와줄 수 있니?)라고 말할 수 있다. 상대방이 도움을 주겠다고 하면 'Can you (please) help me ~?' 등의 표현을 통하여 구체적인 내용을 말할 수도 있다.

❻ walk: 산책시키다, (사람 · 동물을) 걷게 하다

Listen & Talk 2 B

G: Good morning, students! ❶As you know, there was a big fire in Mapletown. ❷Why don't we raise money and help the people there? Come to our special event ❸at the school grounds on May 3! Please ❹bring your items and donate them. We will sell your items. Then, we will ❺give all the money to Mapletown. Please ❻give a hand to people in need.

❶ as: (접) ~과 같이, ~하는 대로 as you know: 아시다시피 fire: 화재

❷ Why don't we ~?: ~하는 게 어떨까? raise money: 돈을 모금하다 raise와 help는 접속사 and로 연결되어 있다.

❸ at+장소: ~에, on+날짜: ~에

❹ bring과 donate는 접속사 and로 연결되어 있는 명령문이므로, 동사원형이 되어야 한다. them = the people in Mapletown

❺ give+간접목적어(~에게)+직접목적어(~을, ~를) = give+직접목적어+to+간접목적어

❻ give a hand: ~을 돕다 in need: 어려움에 처한

Listen & Talk 2 C

B1: Next Wednesday is Volunteer Day. We ❶cleaned up the park last time. ❷What are we going to do this time?

G: ❸Why don't we visit a nursing home and clean it up?

B2: That's not a bad idea. But I want to do something fun. Why don't we ❹hold a party for the people there?

G: That's a good idea. What can we do at the party?

B1: We can ❺serve some food.

B2: And ❻how about playing some music? I can play the piano.

G: And I can play the cello.

B1: It sounds like a good plan.

❶ clean up: ~을 치우다, 청소하다

❷ What are we going to do this time?: 이번엔 뭘 할까?

❸ Why don't we ~?: ~하는 게 어떨까? nursing home: 양로원 clean up은 구동사이다. 구동사는 동사+부사(up, on, off, over 등)로 이루어져 있다. '동사+부사+목적어'의 어순이나 '동사+목적어+부사'의 어순 둘 다 가능하다. 하지만 목적어 자리에 인칭대명사(it, them)가 올 때는 반드시 '동사+목적어+부사'의 어순으로 쓴다.

❹ hold a party: 파티를 열다

❺ serve: (음식을) 제공하다

❻ 'How about (동)명사 ~?'는 특정 행동을 제안할 때 사용할 수 있는 표현으로, '~하는 게 어때?'의 의미이다.

Conversation 교과서 확인학습

● 다음 우리말과 일치하도록 빈칸에 알맞은 말을 쓰시오.

Listen & Talk 1 A

B: Mia, ________ you ________ ________ move these books?

G: Sure. ________ ________ you ________ to do with them?

B: I'm ________ ________ ________ them to a children's library.

해석

B: Mia, 이 책들 옮기는 거 도와줄 수 있어?
G: 그럼. 너 이 책으로 뭐 할 거야?
B: 나는 이 책을 어린이 도서관에 기부할 거야.

Listen & Talk 1 B

B: Hey, Minji! What's wrong ________ your leg?

G: I ________ ________ last week.

B: Really? What happened?

G: I was in ________ ________ to catch a train. But I ________ ________ in the street.

B: Oh, that's terrible! ________ ________ anything I ________ ________ for you?

G: Well, ________ ________ ________ me carry this bag?

B: Sure.

B: 민지야! 너 다리에 무슨 문제가 있니?
G: 지난주에 부러졌어.
B: 그래? 무슨 일이야?
G: 기차를 타려고 서두르고 있었어. 그런데 길에 넘어졌어.
B: 오, 정말 끔찍하다! 내가 너를 위해 해줄 게 있니?
G: 음, 이 가방을 드는 걸 도와줄 수 있니?
B: 그럼.

Listen & Talk 1 C

B1: Wow! These dogs are so dirty. Jay, ________ ________ ________ me ________ ________?

B2: Allen, I'm sorry, ________ I can't. I have ________ ________ the cats now. Why ________ ________ ask Nicky?

B1: Okay! Nicky, can I ________ ________ ________ ________?

G: Sure, Allen. What is it?

B1: ________ ________ ________ me wash these dogs?

G: Sure. But I ________ ________ walk these dogs first. After that, I will help you.

B1: All right! Thank you.

B1: 와! 이 개들 정말 더럽다. Jay, 이 개들 씻기는 거 도와줄 수 있니?
B2: Allen, 미안한데 못할 거 같아. 지금 이 고양이들에게 밥 줘야 해. Nicky한테 물어보는 게 어때?
B1: 알겠어! Nicky, 나 좀 도와줄 수 있니?
G: 물론이지, Allen. 뭔데?
B1: 이 개들 씻기는 거 도와줄 수 있니?
G: 그럼. 근데 나 이 개들 산책 먼저 시켜야 해. 끝나고 나서 도와줄게.
B1: 그래! 고마워.

Listen & Talk 2 A

G: What ________ ________ ________ activities can we do?

B: Why ________ ________ ________ ________ our town's streets?

G: All right! Let's do it.

G: 우리 어떤 종류의 봉사 활동을 할 수 있을까?
B: 우리 동네 길거리를 청소하는 게 어때?
G: 좋아! 그러자.

Listen & Talk 2 B

G: Good morning, students! ________ you know, there ________ a big fire in Mapletown. Why ________ ________ ________ money and help the people there? Come to our special event ________ the school grounds ________ May 3! Please ________ your items and ________ them. We will sell your items. Then, we will give all the money to Mapletown. Please ________ ________ ________ to people in ________.

해석

G: 좋은 아침입니다, 학생 여러분! 아시다시피, Mapletown에 큰 화재가 있었습니다. 우리 돈을 모금해서 그 곳 사람들을 도와주는 게 어떨까요? 5월 3일 학교 운동장에서 열리는 특별 행사에 오세요! 물품들을 가져와서 그것들을 기부해 주세요. 우리는 여러분의 물품들을 팔 것입니다. 그리고, 모든 돈을 Mapletown에 기부할 것입니다. 어려운 사람들에게 도움을 줍시다.

Listen & Talk 2 C

B1: Next Wednesday is Volunteer Day. We ________ ________the park last time. What are ________ ________ ________ do this time?

G: Why ________ ________ ________ a nursing home and clean ________ ________?

B2: That's not a bad idea. But I want ________ ________ something fun. Why don't we ________ a party for the people there?

G: That's a good idea. ________ can we do at the party?

B1: We can ________ some food.

B2: And how ________ ________ some music? I can play the piano.

G: And I can play the cello.

B1: It sounds ________ a good plan.

B1: 다음 주 수요일이 봉사 활동 날이네. 우리 저번에는 공원을 청소했지. 이번엔 뭘 할까?
G: 양로원 가서 청소하는 건 어때?
B2: 나쁜 생각은 아니야. 근데 좀 재미있는 걸 하고 싶어. 거기 계신 분들을 위해 파티를 여는 게 어떨까?
G: 좋은 생각이야. 우리가 파티에서 뭘 할 수 있지?
B1: 음식을 대접할 수 있지.
B2: 그리고 연주를 하는 게 어때? 나 피아노 칠 수 있어.
G: 나는 첼로를 켤 수 있어.
B1: 아주 좋은 계획 같아.

Do It Yourself A

G1: We have a class activity day next Friday. What do you want ________ ________ on that day?

B: Why ________ we do some ________ ________? We can help others and ________ our community better.

G1: That sounds great, but choosing a good place ________ not easy.

B: We need someone ________ ________ ________ a lot.

G1: I know Sumin ________ ________ a lot. Sumin, can you ________ ________ ________ some good places?

G2: Sure. I usually ________ ________ information on the internet. Why ________ ________ ________ the volunteering website for teens?

B: That's a good idea.

G1:우리 다음 주 금요일에 학급 활동이 있어. 그 날 어떤 것을 하고 싶니?
B: 우리 자원 봉사 활동들을 해 보는 게 어때? 우리가 다른 사람들을 도울 수 있고, 우리의 지역 사회를 더 좋게 만들 수 있어.
G1:그거 좋다, 하지만 좋은 장소를 고르는 건 쉽지 않아.
B: 우리는 봉사 활동을 많이 해본 사람이 필요해.
G1:나는 수민이가 봉사 활동을 많이 한 것을 알고 있어. 수민아, 우리가 좋은 장소들을 찾는 것을 도와주겠니?
G2:물론. 나는 주로 인터넷에서 정보를 찾아. 십대들을 위한 자원 봉사 웹사이트를 확인해 보는 게 어떠니?
B: 좋은 생각이다.

[01~02] 다음 중 의미하는 바가 다른 하나를 고르시오.

01 ① Why don't we go on a bike ride?
② Why don't you go on a bike ride?
③ How about going on a bike ride?
④ Let's go on a bike ride.
⑤ What about going on a bike ride?

02 ① Can you help me?
② Can you do me a favor?
③ Can you please help me?
④ Can I ask you a favor?
⑤ Can I give you a hand?

03 다음 대화의 빈칸에 들어갈 말로 적절하지 않은 것은?

> B: Mia, _______ you help me move these books?
> G: Sure. What are you going to do with them?
> B: I'm going to donate them to a children's library.

① can ② will ③ should ④ could ⑤ would

04 다음 대화의 빈칸에 적절한 것을 고르시오.

> G: What kinds of volunteer activities can we do?
> B: ______________________________
> G: All right! Let's do it.

① Why don't we do volunteer work?
② Why don't we clean up our town's streets?
③ How about helping others?
④ Can you help me move these books?
⑤ Is there anything I can do for you?

[01~02] 다음 대화를 읽고 물음에 답하시오.

B: Mia, can you help me (A)________ these books?
G: Sure. What are you going (B)_______ with (C)______?
B: I'm going to donate them to a children's library.

01 빈칸 (A)에 들어갈 말로 적절한 것을 모두 고르시오.

① move ② moving
③ to move ④ moved
⑤ having moved

중요
02 빈칸 (B)와 (C)에 들어갈 말로 알맞게 짝지어진 것은?

	(B)	(C)
①	do	it
②	to do	it
③	to do	them
④	doing	it
⑤	doing	them

[03~04] 다음 대화를 읽고 물음에 답하시오.

B: Hey, Minji! What's wrong with your leg?
G: I broke it last week. (①)
B: Really? What happened? (②)
G: I was in a hurry to catch a train. (③)
B: Oh, that's terrible! (④) Is there anything I can do for you?
G: Well, can you help me carry this bag? (⑤)
B: Sure.

03 위 대화의 ①~⑤ 중 주어진 문장이 들어갈 알맞은 곳은?

But I fell down in the street.

① ② ③ ④ ⑤

04 위 대화를 읽고 답할 수 없는 질문은?

① How will the boy help the girl?
② When did the girl hurt?
③ Why was the girl in a hurry?
④ Where will they go?
⑤ What did the girl break?

05 다음 짝지어진 대화가 어색한 것은?

① A: Why don't we join the Mozart Club?
B: That sounds fun. I love music.
② A: Can I give you a hand?
B: Oh, I'm sorry but I can't.
③ A: Jane, your books look so heavy. Can I help you?
B: Yes. Thank you.
④ A: Why don't we go to the movies today?
B: That's a good idea.
⑤ A: Let's go to the movies after school.
B: Why don't we watch TV at home?

서답형
06 밑줄 친 우리말과 일치하도록 영작하시오.

A: Excuse me. 기차표를 사는 거 도와줄 수 있니? (8 단어)
B: Sure.

➡ ________________________

[07~10] 다음 담화문을 읽고 물음에 답하시오.

G: Good morning, students! (A)_____ you know, there was a big fire in Mapletown. Why don't we raise money and help the people there? Come to our special event at the school grounds on May 3! 물품들을 가져와서 그것들을 기부해 주세요. We will sell your items. Then, we will (B)_____ all the money to Mapletown. Please (C)_____ a hand to people in need.

07 빈칸 (A)에 알맞은 말을 고르시오.

① When ② Although ③ As
④ Since ⑤ For

서답형
08 빈칸 (B)와 (C)에 공통으로 들어갈 말을 쓰시오.

➡ ____________________

서답형
09 밑줄 친 우리말에 맞게 주어진 단어를 이용해 빈칸을 채우시오.

➡ Please ____________________.
(your items)

10 위 글을 읽고 알 수 없는 것을 고르시오.

① the purpose of the special event
② where the special event will be held
③ when the special event will be held
④ what items can't be donated
⑤ where the raised money at the special event will be given

[11~13] 다음 대화를 읽고 물음에 답하시오.

B1: Next Wednesday is Volunteer Day. We cleaned up the park last time. What are we going to do this time?
G: Why don't we visit a nursing home and clean it up?
B2: That's not a bad idea. But I want to do something fun. (A)____________________
G: That's a good idea. What can we do at the party?
B1: We can serve some food.
B2: 그리고 연주를 하는 게 어때? I can play the piano.
G: And I can play the cello.
B1: It sounds like a good plan.

11 빈칸 (A)에 알맞은 말을 고르시오.

① Why don't we volunteer work at the animal care center?
② Why don't we play the piano?
③ Why don't we clean up the nursing home?
④ Why don't we hold a party for the people there?
⑤ Why don't we play tennis there?

서답형
12 밑줄 친 우리말을 주어진 단어를 이용해 영작하시오.

➡ ____________________
(music, how, some)

중요
13 위의 대화를 읽고 답할 수 없는 질문은?

① What musical instrument can the girl play?
② What food will they serve to people at a nursing home?
③ When is Volunteer Day?
④ Where are they going to go to do volunteer work?
⑤ What are they going to do at a nursing home?

[01~02] 주어진 문장 뒤에 이어질 대화의 순서를 바르게 배열하시오.

중요 01

Hey, Minji! What's wrong with your leg?

(A) I was in a hurry to catch a train. But I fell down in the street.
(B) Really? What happened?
(C) Oh, that's terrible!
(D) I broke it last week.

➡ ______________________

02

Next Wednesday is Volunteer Day. We cleaned up the park last time. What are we going to do this time?

(A) Why don't we visit a nursing home and clean it up?
(B) That's a good idea. What can we do at the party?
(C) That's not a bad idea. But I want to do something fun. Why don't we hold a party for the people there?
(D) We can serve some food.

➡ ______________________

[03~04] 다음 대화를 읽고 물음에 답하시오.

G1: We have a class activity day next Friday. What do you want to do on that day?
B: Why don't we ①do some volunteer activities? We can help others and ②make our community better.
G1: That sounds great, but ③choosing a good place is not easy.
B: We need someone ④which has volunteered a lot.
G1: I know Sumin ⑤has volunteered a lot. Sumin, 우리가 좋은 장소들을 찾는 것을 도와주겠니? (help, some, can, places, you, us, good, find, ?)
G2: Sure. I usually search for information on the internet. Why don't we check the volunteering website for teens?
B: That's a good idea.

고난이도 03 위 대화의 ①~⑤ 중 어색한 것을 골라 고치시오.

➡ ______________________
____

04 밑줄 친 우리말에 맞게 괄호 안에 주어진 단어를 알맞게 배열하시오

➡ ______________________

[05~06] 다음 대화를 읽고 물음에 답하시오.

A: Why don't we (A)_____ volunteer work at the animal care center?
B: Sounds good. What can we do there?
A: We can take care (B)______ the dogs and cats.

05 빈칸 (A)에 알맞은 말을 쓰시오.

➡ ______________________

중요 06 빈칸 (B)에 알맞은 전치사를 쓰시오.

➡ ______________________

교과서

Grammar

1 목적격 관계대명사

The little black dress **which** she wore in a movie is famous even today. 그녀가 영화에서 입었던 아담한 검은 드레스는 오늘날까지도 유명하다.

■ 관계대명사가 관계대명사절 내에서 목적어의 역할을 할 때 이것을 목적격 관계대명사라고 한다.

■ 목적격 관계대명사는 선행사가 사람이면 who나 whom, that을, 사물이나 동물은 which나 that을 쓴다. 일반적으로 목적격 관계대명사는 생략할 수 있다.

선행사	사람	사물, 동물	사람, 사물, 동물
목적격 관계대명사	who/whom	which	that

• He was the man (**who/whom/that**) I saw on TV. (그는 내가 TV에서 본 남자였다.)

• He showed me the photos (**which/that**) he had taken. (그는 그가 찍은 사진들을 내게 보여주었다.)

■ 목적격 관계대명사절에서는 앞에 있는 관계대명사가 동사의 목적어 역할을 하기 때문에 동사 뒤에 목적어가 없다는 것에 특히 주의해야 한다.

• These are the boys. I like them(=the boys) most in my class.
= These are the boys (**who/whom/that**) I like most in my class.

• This is the book. I have to read it(=the book).
= This is the book (**which/that**) I have to read.

■ 목적격 관계대명사가 전치사의 목적어인 경우 전치사는 관계대명사절의 끝에 오거나 관계대명사 앞에 올 수 있다. 전치사가 관계대명사절의 끝에 올 경우에는 관계대명사를 생략할 수 있지만 전치사가 관계대명사 앞에 올 경우에는 관계대명사를 생략하지 않으며 관계대명사 that을 쓸 수 없다.

• I need a chair (**which/that**) I can sit **on**. (나는 내가 앉을 수 있는 의자가 필요하다.)
= I need a chair **on which** I can sit.
= I need a chair on that I can sit. (X)

핵심 Check

1. 다음 괄호 안에서 알맞은 말을 고르시오.

(1) David is the boy with (whom / that) I often play soccer.

(2) Tom is reading the book (whom / which) I gave to him.

2 감정을 나타내는 과거분사

- She was **shocked** because their lives were very difficult. 그녀는 그들의 삶이 매우 어려웠기 때문에 충격을 받았다.

■ 현재분사는 '능동'의 의미를 갖고, 과거분사는 '수동'의 의미를 갖는다.

- Math is the most **interesting** subject to me. (능동: 수학이 흥미를 불러일으키는 과목이다.) (수학은 내게 가장 흥미로운 과목이다.)
- I'm **interested** in math. (수동: 내가 흥미를 느끼게 되는 것이다.) (나는 수학에 흥미가 있다.)

■ 감정을 나타내는 타동사의 과거분사는 '~한 감정을 느끼는'이라는 의미로, 주로 사람을 주어로 하여 형용사로 쓰일 때가 많다.

- I was very **disappointed** at my friends. (나는 내 친구들에게 무척 실망했다.)

■ 주로 사물을 주어로 하여 '~한 감정을 유발하는'의 의미를 나타내는 현재분사와 혼동하지 않도록 유의한다.

- It can be very **disappointing** to lose important matches. (중요한 경기에서 패하는 것은 매우 실망스러울 수 있다.)

■ 주어가 사람일 때도 현재분사를 쓸 수 있으므로, 의미에 따라 구분하여 쓴다.

- She was certainly not **boring**. (그녀는 분명히 따분하지 않다.)
- She was **bored** with hearing about the work. (그녀는 그 일에 관련된 이야기를 듣는 것이 따분했다.)

핵심 Check

2. 다음 괄호 안에서 알맞은 말을 고르시오.
(1) Look at the (sleeping / slept) dog.
(2) It was an (exciting / excited) game.
(3) He showed me a book (writing / written) in English.
(4) I'm (exciting / excited) to get married.

01 다음 빈칸에 들어갈 말로 알맞지 않은 것을 모두 고르시오.

The only food ________ they could find was grass.

① who ② whose ③ whom
④ that ⑤ which

02 다음 우리말을 영어로 옮길 때, 빈칸에 알맞은 말이 순서대로 짝지어진 것은?

• 그 게임은 재미있어 보였지만 나는 곧 내가 그 게임에 흥미가 없다는 것을 알아차렸다.
→ The game looked ________ but soon I noticed that I was not ________ in the game.

① interested – interesting
② interested – interested
③ interesting – interesting
④ interesting – interested
⑤ interest – interest

03 다음 문장에서 어법상 어색한 부분을 바르게 고쳐 쓰시오.

adopt: 입양하다
at the thought of: ~을 생각하면, ~생각에

(1) He likes the dog who he adopted last month.
________ ➡ ________

(2) Anna is the woman which I like most.
________ ➡ ________

(3) I'm exciting at the thought of going skiing tomorrow.
________ ➡ ________

04 다음 우리말에 맞게 괄호 안에 주어진 단어를 빈칸에 바르게 배열하시오. (필요하면 어형을 바꿀 것)

우리 엄마가 만든 치킨 샐러드는 정말 맛있다. (my mom, is, made, delicious, the chicken salad, very, which)

➡ ________________________________

01 다음 〈보기〉의 밑줄 친 부분과 용법이 다른 것은?

> 보기
> Lee Jieun is a singer that my partner likes.

① Breakfast is the meal that people eat in the morning.
② People that respect her will come to help her.
③ I want to have a date with a girl who I love.
④ Kate will read the book which her friend wrote.
⑤ This is the TV program that I really wanted to watch.

중요
02 다음 빈칸에 들어갈 수 있는 말이 다른 하나는?

① *The Old Man and the Sea* is the book ________ I have read several times.
② This is the wallet ________ you were looking for.
③ Select the album ________ cover you'd like to change.
④ Billy is my roommate ________ I have lived with for five years.
⑤ This is the cat ________ I like.

03 다음 빈칸에 알맞은 것은?

She was really __________ at the news.

① surprise ② surprises
③ surprised ④ surprising
⑤ to surprise

서답형
04 주어진 어휘를 이용하여 다음 우리말을 영어로 쓰시오.

Alex가 나에게 보낸 박스에 드레스가 있다. (there, a dress, sent)

➡ ______________________________
____

서답형
05 다음 괄호 안에서 알맞은 말을 고르시오.

(1) *Tom and Jerry* is a cartoon (who / that) I often watch.
(2) Mike needs someone (who / which) he can trust.
(3) Jane is the girl with (that / whom) I had dinner at the restaurant.
(4) I am not (interested / interesting) in that sort of thing.
(5) The children found the game (interesting / interested).

06 다음 중 어법상 바르지 않은 것은?

① Well, I'm excited.
② The movie was exciting.
③ Mr. Sing said he was pleased with the outcome.
④ The children were frightening at the way their mom yelled.
⑤ I feel scared when I walk home alone.

중요

07 다음 중 어법상 옳은 문장을 고르시오.

① This is the picture I took yesterday with my new camera.

② Seoul Grand Park is a park who my uncle often visits.

③ The book I read it yesterday was very interesting.

④ The student which I am very close with is Steve.

⑤ It is the building at that he has worked for over 5 years.

08 다음 밑줄 친 that의 성격이 나머지 넷과 다른 것은?

① Jiho is eating the fried rice that his sister made.

② The important thing is that we stay on schedule.

③ Ethan never eats food that is sold at a fast food store.

④ Audrey is the only woman that I love.

⑤ The movie that I watched last Sunday was *Alita*.

서답형

09 다음 〈보기〉에 주어진 단어를 변형하여 문맥에 맞게 빈칸에 쓰시오. (한 번씩만 쓸 것)

보기
embarrass scare shock

(1) Do not be ________ of bees.

(2) He put me in a very ________ situation.

(3) The members of his team were ________ at the results.

10 다음 두 문장을 한 문장으로 바르게 바꾸지 않은 것을 모두 고르시오.

• *Donald Duck* is a cartoon.
• My partner often watches *Donald Duck*.

① *Donald Duck* is a cartoon which my partner often watches.

② *Donald Duck* is a cartoon that my partner often watches.

③ *Donald Duck* is a cartoon who my partner often watches.

④ *Donald Duck* is a cartoon my partner often watches.

⑤ *Donald Duck* is a cartoon which my partner often watches it.

서답형

11 다음 문장에서 생략할 수 있는 것을 찾아 쓰시오.

(1) I met the woman who you ate dinner with last Sunday.

(2) I received an email that my friend in Chicago had sent to me.

(3) Seoul is a city which is full of energy.

➡ (1) ________ (2) ________ (3) ________

중요

12 다음 중 밑줄 친 부분의 쓰임이 잘못된 것은?

① Rina looked bored in the science class.

② Who was the girl that you met in front of the library?

③ The dog which I raise has a long tail.

④ Everyone feels depressing at some time or another.

⑤ Don't be disappointed about such a thing.

서답형

13 다음 두 문장을 관계대명사를 사용하여 한 문장으로 바꾸시오.

(1) • Audrey Hepburn is a person.
• My partner respects her a lot.
➡ ______________________________
____

(2) • This is the ID.
• The spy used the ID before.
➡ ______________________________

(3) • The letter made me happy.
• You sent the letter to me last week.
➡ ______________________________
____

(4) • Do you remember the girl?
• I met her at the party.
➡ ______________________________
____

(5) • I like the music.
• I often listen to the music.
➡ ______________________________
____

(6) • Do you know the girl?
• Anne is talking to the girl.
➡ ______________________________
____

중요

14 다음 빈칸에 들어갈 말로 알맞은 것은?

I don't like English. It is difficult and ______.

① exciting ② excited
③ boring ④ bored
⑤ annoyed

15 다음 밑줄 친 부분의 쓰임이 어색한 것은?

① The chicken salad which Lee Yeonbok made is very delicious.
② Winter is the season that comes after autumn.
③ Here are some of the people whom I helped.
④ That man over there is the dentist about that I told you.
⑤ I want to call the boy who I met at the party.

서답형

16 우리말에 맞게 괄호 안의 어휘를 바르게 배열하시오.

(1) 그녀는 그들의 삶이 매우 어려웠기 때문에 충격을 받았다. (she, lives, because, was, were, difficult, shocked, their, very)
➡ ______________________________

(2) 나는 사파리에서 보았던 호랑이를 잊을 수 없다. (I, I, the tiger, safari, saw, which, forget, can't, on)
➡ ______________________________

(3) 여행 가이드로서의 직업에 만족하십니까? (you, your, are, satisfied, job, tour guide, as, a, with)
➡ ______________________________

서답형

17 다음 빈칸에 amaze의 알맞은 형태를 쓰시오.

(1) People were ________ at the fire.
(2) It is ________ how the sea water looks different each season.

Grammar 서술형 시험대비

01 다음 그림을 보고 괄호 안에 주어진 어휘를 이용하여 문장을 완성하시오.

(play / excite)

________ a basketball game makes me ________.

02 중요 괄호 안에 주어진 말을 바르게 배열하여 문장을 완성하시오. (단어 하나를 문맥에 맞게 변형할 것.)

(1) (I, you, Latin dance, know, were, didn't, interest, in)

➡ ________________________

(2) (Emma, test score, her, disappoint, was, at)

➡ ________________________

(3) (I, highway signs, confuse, think, are, these, very)

➡ ________________________

(4) (I, a thing, one, no, that, knows, worry, such, am, about)

➡ ________________________

(5) (he, I, for me, was, was, not, not, bore, bore, so) (For me로 시작할 것)

➡ ________________________

03 다음 문장에서 어법상 틀린 부분을 찾아 바르게 고쳐 쓰시오.

This is the house in that he was born.

________ ➡ ________

고난이도

04 다음 두 문장을 관계대명사를 이용하여 한 문장으로 연결하여 쓰시오.

(1) • Jayu Park is a park.
• My grandfather often visits the park.

➡ ________________________

____

(2) • *Tom and Jerry* is a cartoon.
• My little sister often watches *Tom and Jerry*.

➡ ________________________

____

(3) • That is the girl.
• I saw the girl this morning.

➡ ________________________

(4) • The girl did not participate in the meeting.
• I wanted to meet the girl.

➡ ________________________

____

(5) • The woman is Ms. Larson.
• Mom is talking to Ms. Larson.

➡ ________________________

____

____

(6) • Mariel took pictures of Ben and his car.
• Ben and his car were on the crime scene.

➡ ________________________

____

05 잘못된 부분을 바르게 고쳐 문장을 다시 쓰시오.

(1) King Sejong is a person which my brother respects a lot.
➡ ______________________
____

(2) This is the bridge who they built about 20 years ago.
➡ ______________________
____

(3) The girl talked to a boy whom she met him at the party.
➡ ______________________

(4) I don't like the movie which I saw it yesterday.
➡ ______________________

(5) There are many subjects about that people feel little interest.
➡ ______________________
____
____

06 중요 괄호 안에 주어진 어휘를 이용하여 우리말에 맞게 영작하시오.

(1) 나는 어젯밤 잠을 잘 자지 못했기 때문에 하루 종일 매우 피곤했다. (tire, all day, feel, well, because) (I로 시작할 것)
➡ ______________________
____

(2) 나는 집에 홀로 남겨지는 것이 두려웠다. (home, to be, scare, leave, alone)
➡ ______________________

(3) 야구 경기를 보는 것은 나를 지루하게 한다. (watch, a baseball game, make, bore)
➡ ______________________

07 고난이도 두 문장을 관계대명사를 사용하여 한 문장으로 썼을 때, 빈칸에 해당하는 문장을 쓰시오.

(1) • ______________________
• My partner often watches *The Smurfs*.
→ *The Smurfs* is a cartoon that my partner often watches.

(2) • ______________________
• I traveled with my friend.
→ Let me introduce my friend with whom I traveled.

(3) • The key was under the sofa.
• ______________________
→ The key that Laura was looking for all day long was under the sofa.

(4) • There is a certain reason.
• ______________________
→ There is a certain reason for which I cannot speak about it.

08 다음 문장을 어법에 맞게 고쳐 쓰시오.

(1) He put me in a very embarrassed situation.
➡ ______________________

(2) My mom was surprising at the news.
➡ ______________________

(3) It was shocked that he lied to me.
➡ ______________________

(4) We were all exciting because my brother made a goal in the soccer game.
➡ ______________________
____

교과서

Reading

The Spirit of Audrey

During World War II, a little girl and her mother were hungry and sick. The only food that they could find was grass. The little girl felt scared all the time. Luckily, the girl survived, thanks to the help of others. One of the groups that helped her was UNICEF. Later, the girl became a worldwide movie star. Her name was Audrey Hepburn.

(During: during+특정 기간을 나타내는 명사 / that: 선행사 The only food를 수식하는 목적격 관계대명사 / scared: 주어인 The little girl의 감정을 나타내는 형용사 / thanks to: ~ 덕택에 / that: 선행사 the groups를 수식하는 주격 관계대명사 / Later: 후에)

spirit 마음, 정신
grass 풀, 잔디
all the time 늘, 내내
luckily 운이 좋게도, 다행스럽게도
survive 살아남다, 생존하다
thanks to ~ 덕택에, ~ 때문에
worldwide 세계적인

확인문제

- 다음 문장이 본문의 내용과 일치하면 T, 일치하지 않으면 F를 쓰시오.

1. During World War II, Hepburn and her mother were hungry and sick. ☐
2. Hepburn survived World War II for herself. ☐
3. One of the groups that helped Hepburn was UNESCO. ☐
4. Hepburn became a worldwide movie star. ☐

When she grew up, Hepburn became a symbol of beauty. She was very popular because of her hit movies, such as *My Fair Lady* and *Roman Holiday*. The little black dress which she wore in a movie is famous even today. Many people still love her style.

(When: 접속사(~할 때) / because of: ~ 때문에 / such as: ~와 같은 / which: 선행사 The little black dress를 수식하는 목적격 관계대명사 / is: 주어 The little black dress를 서술하는 동사)

The autumn of 1987 was a turning point in Hepburn's life. She went to an international music festival in Macau. Many people donated money at the festival, and the money went to UNICEF. Thanks to her fame, UNICEF collected more money than ever before. Hepburn realized that her fame could help others, so she became a UNICEF Goodwill Ambassador.

(a turning point: 전환점 / an international music festival: 국제 음악 축제 / the festival: an international music festival / Thanks to: ~ 덕택에 / more ... than: 비교급 than: ~보다 더 / that: 목적어에 해당하는 명사절을 이끄는 접속사)

beauty 아름다움, 미(美)
turning point 전환점
international 국제적인, 국제의
donate 기부하다
fame 명성
collect 모으다, 수집하다
realize 깨닫다
goodwill ambassador 친선 대사

확인문제

- 다음 문장이 본문의 내용과 일치하면 T, 일치하지 않으면 F를 쓰시오.

1 When she was young, Hepburn was a symbol of peace. ☐
2 The little black dress which she wore in a movie is famous even today. ☐
3 In spite of her fame, UNICEF collected less money than ever before. ☐
4 Hepburn became a UNICEF Goodwill Ambassador. ☐

First, Hepburn went to Ethiopia in 1988. There, she brought food to hungry children. She was shocked because their lives were very difficult. After that, she volunteered in other countries. In 1990, she visited Vietnam to hand out medicine and support clean drinking water programs. Her last trip was to Somalia in 1992, and she passed away the following year.

There: = In Ethiopia
shocked: shocking(×).
because: because+주어+동사
to hand out: to부정사의 부사적 용법(목적)
support: to에 연결하는 원형동사
passed away: = died
the following year: 이듬해

Many people praised her beauty and style, but Hepburn's real beauty was her heart. To honor her, UNICEF made a statue, *The Spirit of Audrey*. People who respect her keep her mission alive.

beauty: beautiful의 명사형
To honor: to부정사의 부사적 용법(목적)
who: 선행사 People을 수식하는 주격 관계대명사.
keep her mission alive: keep+목적어+형용사: …을 ~한 상태로 유지하다

Her favorite saying shows her mission.

As you get older, remember you have two hands. One is for helping yourself, and the other is for helping others.

As: (비례) ~함에 따라, ~할수록
the other: 둘 중 나머지 하나

hand out 나누어 주다
medicine 약
support 후원하다, 지원하다
pass away 죽다
following (그) 다음의
praise 칭찬하다
honor 예우하다, 존중하다
statue 상, 조각상
respect 존경하다
mission 임무, 사명
alive 살아 있는
saying 속담, 격언

확인문제

- 다음 문장이 본문의 내용과 일치하면 T, 일치하지 않으면 F를 쓰시오.

1 In Ethiopia Hepburn brought food to hungry children. ☐
2 Hepburn was pleased because the children's lives were very comfortable in Ethiopia. ☐
3 In 1990, Hepburn visited Somalia to hand out medicine. ☐
4 In Vietnam Hepburn supported clean drinking water programs. ☐
5 Hepburn passed away in 1993. ☐
6 Hepburn's real beauty was her style. ☐

- 우리말을 참고하여 빈칸에 알맞은 말을 쓰시오.

1 The _______ of Audrey

2 _______ World War II, a little girl and her mother _______ hungry and sick.

3 _______ _______ food _______ they could find _______ grass.

4 The little girl _______ _______ all the time.

5 _______, the girl survived, _______ _______ the help of others.

6 _______ _______ _______ _______ _______ helped her _______ UNICEF.

7 Later, the girl became _______ _______ _______ _______.

8 _______ _______ was Audrey Hepburn.

9 When she grew up, Hepburn became _______ _______ _______ _______.

10 She was very popular _______ _______ her hit movies, _______ _______ *My Fair Lady* and *Roman Holiday*.

11 The little black dress _______ _______ _______ in a movie is famous even today.

12 Many people _______ _______ her style.

13 The autumn of 1987 was _______ _______ _______ in Hepburn's life.

14 She went to _______ _______ _______ _______ in Macau.

15 Many people _______ _______ at the festival, and the money went to UNICEF.

1 오드리의 정신

2 제2차 세계 대전 동안, 한 어린 소녀와 그녀의 어머니는 굶주리고 아팠다.

3 그들이 찾을 수 있었던 유일한 음식은 풀뿐이었다.

4 어린 소녀는 내내 겁에 질려 있었다.

5 다행히도, 소녀는 다른 사람들의 도움 덕분에 살아남았다.

6 그녀를 도왔던 단체 중 하나는 유니세프(국제 연합 아동 기금)였다.

7 후에, 소녀는 세계적인 영화배우가 되었다.

8 그녀의 이름은 오드리 헵번이었다.

9 그녀가 자랐을 때, 헵번은 아름다움의 상징이 되었다.

10 그녀는 〈마이 페어 레이디〉와 〈로마의 휴일〉과 같은 흥행 영화들로 인해 매우 인기가 있었다.

11 그녀가 영화에서 입었던 아담한 검은 드레스는 심지어 오늘날까지도 유명하다.

12 많은 사람이 여전히 그녀의 스타일을 사랑한다.

13 1987년 가을은 헵번의 인생 전환점이었다.

14 그녀는 마카오의 한 국제 음악 축제에 갔다.

15 많은 사람이 축제에서 돈을 기부했고, 그 돈은 유니세프로 보내졌다.

16 _______ _______ her fame, UNICEF collected _______ money _______ ever before.

17 Hepburn _______ _______ her fame could help others, so she became _______ _______ _______ _______.

18 First, Hepburn _______ _______ Ethiopia in 1988.

19 There, she _______ food _______ hungry children.

20 She was _______ because their _______ were very difficult.

21 After that, she _______ in other countries.

22 In 1990, she visited Vietnam _______ _______ _______ medicine and _______ clean drinking water programs.

23 Her last trip was _______ Somalia in 1992, and she _______ _______ the _______ year.

24 Many people _______ her beauty and style, but Hepburn's _______ _______ was her heart.

25 _______ _______ her, UNICEF made a statue, *The Spirit of Audrey.*

26 People _______ respect her _______ her mission _______.

27 Her _______ _______ shows her mission.

28 _______ *you* _______ *older, remember you have two hands.*

29 _______ *is for helping* _______, *and* _______ _______ *is for helping* _______.

16 그녀의 명성 덕분에, 유니세프는 어느 때보다도 더 많은 돈을 모았다.

17 헵번은 자신의 명성이 다른 사람들을 도울 수 있다는 것을 깨닫고, 유니세프 친선 대사가 되었다.

18 먼저, 헵번은 1988년에 에티오피아로 갔다.

19 그곳에서, 그녀는 굶주린 아이들에게 음식을 가져다주었다.

20 그녀는 그들의 삶이 매우 어려웠기 때문에 충격을 받았다.

21 그 후, 그녀는 다른 나라들에서도 봉사하였다.

22 1990년, 그녀는 의약품을 나눠 주고 깨끗한 식수 프로그램을 지원하기 위하여 베트남을 방문하였다.

23 그녀의 마지막 여행은 1992년 소말리아에 간 것이었으며, 이듬해 그녀는 사망하였다.

24 많은 사람이 그녀의 아름다움과 스타일을 칭송했지만, 헵번의 진정한 아름다움은 그녀의 마음이었다.

25 그녀를 기리기 위해, 유니세프는 '오드리의 정신'이라는 동상을 만들었다.

26 그녀를 존경하는 사람들이 그녀의 사명을 이어 나가고 있다.

27 그녀가 가장 좋아했던 구절은 그녀의 사명을 보여 준다.

28 나이가 들어갈수록, 당신에게 손이 두 개가 있다는 것을 기억하라.

29 한 손은 자신을 돕기 위한 것이고, 다른 한 손은 타인을 돕기 위한 것이다.

Reading 교과서 확인학습 B

• 우리말을 참고하여 본문을 영작하시오.

1 오드리의 정신
➡ ______

2 제2차 세계 대전 동안, 한 어린 소녀와 그녀의 어머니는 굶주리고 아팠다.
➡ ______

3 그들이 찾을 수 있었던 유일한 음식은 풀뿐이었다.
➡ ______

4 어린 소녀는 내내 겁에 질려 있었다.
➡ ______

5 다행히도, 소녀는 다른 사람들의 도움 덕분에 살아남았다.
➡ ______

6 그녀를 도왔던 단체 중 하나는 유니세프(국제 연합 아동 기금)였다.
➡ ______

7 후에, 소녀는 세계적인 영화배우가 되었다.
➡ ______

8 그녀의 이름은 오드리 헵번이었다.
➡ ______

9 그녀가 자랐을 때, 헵번은 아름다움의 상징이 되었다.
➡ ______

10 그녀는 〈마이 페어 레이디〉와 〈로마의 휴일〉과 같은 흥행 영화들로 인해 매우 인기가 있었다.
➡ ______

11 그녀가 영화에서 입었던 아담한 검은 드레스는 심지어 오늘날까지도 유명하다.
➡ ______

12 많은 사람이 여전히 그녀의 스타일을 사랑한다.
➡ ______

13 1987년 가을은 헵번의 인생 전환점이었다.
➡ ______

14 그녀는 마카오의 한 국제 음악 축제에 갔다.
➡ ______

15 많은 사람이 축제에서 돈을 기부했고, 그 돈은 유니세프로 보내졌다.
➡ ______

16 그녀의 명성 덕분에, 유니세프는 어느 때보다도 더 많은 돈을 모았다.
➡ ______

17 헵번은 자신의 명성이 다른 사람들을 도울 수 있다는 것을 깨닫고, 유니세프 친선 대사가 되었다.

➡ ______________________________

18 먼저, 헵번은 1988년에 에티오피아로 갔다.

➡ ______________________________

19 그곳에서, 그녀는 굶주린 아이들에게 음식을 가져다주었다.

➡ ______________________________

20 그녀는 그들의 삶이 매우 어려웠기 때문에 충격을 받았다.

➡ ______________________________

21 그 후, 그녀는 다른 나라들에서도 봉사하였다.

➡ ______________________________

22 1990년, 그녀는 의약품을 나눠 주고 깨끗한 식수 프로그램을 지원하기 위하여 베트남을 방문하였다.

➡ ______________________________

23 그녀의 마지막 여행은 1992년 소말리아에 간 것이었으며, 이듬해 그녀는 사망하였다.

➡ ______________________________

24 많은 사람이 그녀의 아름다움과 스타일을 칭송했지만, 헵번의 진정한 아름다움은 그녀의 마음이었다.

➡ ______________________________

25 그녀를 기리기 위해, 유니세프는 '오드리의 정신'이라는 동상을 만들었다.

➡ ______________________________

26 그녀를 존경하는 사람들이 그녀의 사명을 이어 나가고 있다.

➡ ______________________________

27 그녀가 가장 좋아했던 구절은 그녀의 사명을 보여 준다.

➡ ______________________________

28 나이가 들어갈수록, 당신에게 손이 두 개가 있다는 것을 기억하라.

➡ ______________________________

29 한 손은 자신을 돕기 위한 것이고, 다른 한 손은 타인을 돕기 위한 것이다.

➡ ______________________________

Reading 시험대비 실력평가

[01~04] 다음 글을 읽고 물음에 답하시오.

(A)[During / While] World War II, a little girl and her mother were hungry and sick. The only food that ⓐthey could find (B)[being / was] grass. The little girl felt scared all the time. Luckily, the girl survived, ⓑthanks to the help of others. One of the groups that helped her (C)[was / were] UNICEF. ⓒLate, the girl became a worldwide movie star. Her name was Audrey Hepburn.

서답형

01 위 글의 괄호 (A)~(C)에서 어법상 알맞은 낱말을 골라 쓰시오.

➡ (A)________ (B)________ (C)________

서답형

02 위 글의 밑줄 친 ⓐthey가 가리키는 것을 본문에서 찾아 쓰시오.

➡ ________________________________

03 위 글의 밑줄 친 ⓑthanks to와 뜻이 다른 말을 고르시오.

① due to
② because of
③ instead of
④ owing to
⑤ on account of

중요

04 위 글의 밑줄 친 ⓒ를 알맞은 어형으로 고치시오.

➡ ____________________

[05~08] 다음 글을 읽고 물음에 답하시오.

When she grew up, Hepburn became a symbol of beauty. She was very popular because of her hit movies, ⓐsuch as *My Fair Lady* and *Roman Holiday*. The little black dress which she wore in a movie is famous even today. Many people still love her style.

The autumn of 1987 was a turning point in Hepburn's life. She went to an international music festival in Macau. Many people donated money at the festival, and the money went to UNICEF. Thanks to her ___ⓑ___, UNICEF collected more money than ever before. Hepburn realized ⓒthat her ___ⓓ___ could help others, so she became a UNICEF Goodwill Ambassador.

서답형

05 위 글의 밑줄 친 ⓐsuch as와 바꿔 쓸 수 있는 단어를 쓰시오.

➡ ____________________

서답형

06 본문의 한 단어를 변형하여 위 글의 빈칸 ⓑ와 ⓓ에 공통으로 들어갈 알맞은 단어를 쓰시오.

➡ ____________________

07 위 글의 밑줄 친 ⓒthat과 문법적 쓰임이 같은 것을 모두 고르시오.

① Kate knows that you like Mike.
② She is the girl that he loves.
③ Give me the pen that is on the desk.
④ He is the man that I met yesterday.
⑤ The point is that he is still careless.

08 위 글의 Hepburn에 관한 내용으로 적절하지 않은 것은?

① 그녀는 자랐을 때, 아름다움의 상징이 되었다.
② 그녀가 영화에서 입었던 아담한 검은 드레스는 오늘날까지도 유명하다.
③ 1987년 가을에 그녀는 배우로서 쇠퇴기에 들어섰다.
④ 1987년 가을에 그녀는 마카오의 한 국제 음악 축제에 갔다.
⑤ 자신의 명성이 다른 사람들을 도울 수 있다는 것을 깨닫고, 그녀는 유니세프 친선 대사가 되었다.

[09~12] 다음 글을 읽고 물음에 답하시오.

First, Hepburn went to Ethiopia in 1988. (①) There, she brought food to hungry children. (②) She was shocked because their lives were very difficult. (③) In 1990, she visited Vietnam to hand out medicine and support clean drinking water programs. (④) Her last trip was to Somalia in 1992, and she passed away the following year. (⑤)

Many people praised her beauty and style, but Hepburn's real beauty was her heart. To honor her, UNICEF made a statue, *The Spirit of Audrey*. People who respect her keep her mission alive. Her favorite saying shows her mission.

As you get older, remember you have two hands. One is for ⓐhelping yourself, and the other is for helping others.

09 위 글의 흐름으로 보아, 주어진 문장이 들어가기에 가장 적절한 곳은?

After that, she volunteered in other countries.

① ② ③ ④ ⑤

10 아래 <보기>에서 위 글의 밑줄 친 ⓐhelping과 문법적 쓰임이 다른 것의 개수를 고르시오.

보기
① I remember posting his letter.
② Would you mind calling back later?
③ He was watching TV in the room.
④ Thank you for visiting my website.
⑤ She smelled something burning.

① 1개 ② 2개 ③ 3개 ④ 4개 ⑤ 5개

11 위 글의 종류로 알맞은 것을 고르시오.

① article ② diary ③ book report
④ essay ⑤ biography

12 위 글의 내용과 일치하지 않는 것은?

① 헵번은 1988년에 에티오피아로 갔다.
② 헵번은 에티오피아에서 의약품을 나눠 주었다.
③ 1990년, 헵번은 베트남을 방문하였다.
④ 헵번의 마지막 여행은 1992년 소말리아에 간 것이었다.
⑤ 헵번은 1993년에 사망하였다.

[13~15] 다음 인터뷰를 읽고 물음에 답하시오.

Reporter: ___ⓐ___ was your life during World War II? Can you tell me about it?
Audrey: It was terrible. ⓑMy family and I was hungry and sick. We survived thanks to the help of others.
Reporter: ___ⓒ___ did you begin to work for UNICEF?
Audrey: In 1987, a musical festival in Macau changed my life. I learned that my fame could help other people.
Reporter: After that, what did you do?
Audrey: I visited some countries in Africa and Asia and volunteered there.

13 위 인터뷰의 빈칸 ⓐ와 ⓒ에 공통으로 들어갈 알맞은 말을 고르시오.

① How ② What ③ When
④ Why ⑤ Where

서답형

14 위 인터뷰의 밑줄 친 ⓑ에서 어법상 틀린 부분을 찾아 고치시오.

➡ ____________________

서답형

15 다음 문장에서 위 인터뷰의 내용과 다른 부분을 찾아서 고치시오.

Audrey visited some countries in Africa and Asia and volunteered there before 1987.

➡ ____________________

[16~19] 다음 글을 읽고 물음에 답하시오.

First, Hepburn went to Ethiopia in 1988. There, she brought food __ⓐ__ hungry children. She was shocked because their lives were very difficult. After that, she volunteered in other countries. In 1990, she visited Vietnam ⓑto hand out medicine and support clean drinking water programs. Her last trip was __ⓐ__ Somalia in 1992, and she passed away the following year.

Many people praised her beauty and style, but Hepburn's real beauty was her heart. To honor her, UNICEF made a statue, *The Spirit of Audrey*. People who respect her keep her mission alive. Her favorite saying shows her mission.

As you get older, remember you have two hands. One is __ⓒ__ helping yourself, and the other is __ⓒ__ helping others.

중요

16 위 글의 빈칸 ⓐ와 ⓒ에 들어갈 전치사가 바르게 짝지어진 것은?

① for – by ② to – by
③ to – for ④ for – to
⑤ at – for

17 위 글의 밑줄 친 ⓑto hand와 to부정사의 용법이 다른 것을 고르시오. (2개)

① He grew up to be a scientist.
② Do you know how to make it?
③ She was happy to solve the problem.
④ It's time to go to bed.
⑤ They ran fast to win the race.

중요

18 위 글의 내용으로 보아 알 수 없는 것은?

① 헵번은 여러 나라들에서 봉사하였다.
② 많은 사람이 헵번의 아름다움과 스타일을 칭송했다.
③ 헵번은 배우로서는 성공하지 못했다.
④ 헵번을 기리기 위해, 유니세프는 '오드리의 정신'이라는 동상을 만들었다.
⑤ 헵번을 존경하는 사람들이 그녀의 사명을 이어나가고 있다.

19 위 글을 읽고 대답할 수 없는 질문은?

① When did Hepburn go to Ethiopia?
② In Ethiopia, what did Hepburn bring to hungry children?
③ Why did Hepburn visit Vietnam?
④ When was Hepburn's last trip?
⑤ Where did UNICEF make a statue, *The Spirit of Audrey*?

[20~22] 다음 글을 읽고 물음에 답하시오.

My little big hero is my mom. She was born in 1972. She lives in Seoul.
She smiles a lot and tries to see the good in everything.
My mom had a serious car accident. She was in the hospital for six months. But she was very strong and ⓐfinally got better.
She always helps people in need. She donates money and does volunteer work. She is my big hero!

20 위 글의 밑줄 친 ⓐfinally와 뜻이 다른 것을 모두 고르시오.

① at last ② actually
③ in the end ④ at least
⑤ in the long run

중요
21 글쓴이의 엄마의 성격으로 알맞지 않은 것을 고르시오.

① strong-willed ② selfish
③ friendly ④ charitable
⑤ generous

22 위 글을 읽고 답할 수 없는 질문은?

① Who is the writer's hero?
② What is the writer's mom like?
③ When does the writer's mom feel happy?
④ What was one of the most important moments in the writer's mom's life?
⑤ Why does the writer think that his or her mom is a hero?

[23~25] 다음 글을 읽고 물음에 답하시오.

First, Hepburn went to Ethiopia in 1988. There, she brought food to hungry children. She was shocked because their lives were very difficult. After that, she volunteered in other countries. In 1990, she visited Vietnam to hand out medicine and support clean ⓐ drinking water programs. Her last trip was to Somalia in 1992, and she passed away the following year.
Many people praised her beauty and style, but Hepburn's real beauty was her heart. To honor her, UNICEF made a statue, *The Spirit of Audrey*. People who respect her keep her mission alive. Her favorite saying shows her mission.
As you get older, remember you have two hands. One is for helping yourself, and the other is for helping others.

중요
23 위 글의 제목으로 알맞은 것을 고르시오.

① Hepburn Visited Ethiopia!
② Hepburn's Real Beauty Was Her Heart!
③ Why Was Hepburn Shocked?
④ People Praised Hepburn's Beauty!
⑤ Hepburn's Favorite Saying

24 위 글의 밑줄 친 ⓐdrinking과 문법적 쓰임이 같은 것을 모두 고르시오.

① I know the girl drinking water there.
② Who was drinking water in the room?
③ I saw a man drinking water in a bus.
④ She enjoys drinking water in summer.
⑤ He is fond of drinking water when he's tired.

서답형
25 다음 질문에 대한 알맞은 대답을 영어로 쓰시오.

Q: What did UNICEF do to honor Hepburn?

➡ ______________________

[01~03] 다음 글을 읽고 물음에 답하시오.

During ⓐWorld War II, a little girl and her mother were hungry and sick. The only food ___ⓑ___ they could find was grass. The little girl felt scared all the time. Luckily, the girl survived, thanks to the help of others. One of the groups that helped her was UNICEF. Later, the girl became a worldwide movie star. Her name was Audrey Hepburn.

01 위 글의 밑줄 친 ⓐWorld War II를 영어로 읽는 법을 쓰시오.

➡ ______________________________

중요
02 위 글의 빈칸 ⓑ에 들어갈 알맞은 말을 쓰시오.

➡ ____________________

03 다음 빈칸 (A)와 (B)에 알맞은 단어를 넣어 Audrey Hepburn에 대한 소개를 완성하시오.

> Audrey Hepburn survived World War II thanks to (A)_______ _______ of others and later became a worldwide (B)_______ _______.

[04~07] 다음 글을 읽고 물음에 답하시오.

When she grew up, Hepburn became a symbol of beauty. She was very popular because of her hit movies, such as *My Fair Lady* and *Roman Holiday*. The little black dress which she wore in a movie is famous even today. Many people still love her style.

The autumn of 1987 was ⓐa turning point in Hepburn's life. She went to an international music festival in Macau. Many people ___ⓑ___ money at the festival, and the money went to UNICEF. (A)[In spite of / Thanks to] her fame, UNICEF (B)[collected / corrected] more money (C)[than / then] ever before. ⓒHepburn realized that her fame could help others, so she became a UNICEF Goodwill Ambassador.

04 다음 빈칸 (A)와 (B)에 알맞은 단어를 넣어 ⓐa turning point에 대한 서술을 완성하시오.

> Hepburn who was a very popular actress went to an international (A)_______ _______ in Macau in the autumn of 1987. Then she realized that her fame could help others, so she became a (B)_______ _______ _______.

05 주어진 영영풀이를 참고하여 빈칸 ⓑ에 철자 d로 시작하는 단어를 시제에 맞춰 쓰시오.

> give to a charity or good cause

➡ ____________________

중요
06 위 글의 괄호 (A)~(C)에서 문맥이나 어법상 알맞은 것을 골라 쓰시오.

➡ (A)_______ (B)_______ (C)_______

07 위 글의 밑줄 친 ⓒ를 다음과 같이 바꿔 쓸 때 빈칸에 들어갈 알맞은 말을 쓰시오.

➡ ________ Hepburn realized that her fame could help others, she became a UNICEF Goodwill Ambassador.

[08~10] 다음 글을 읽고 물음에 답하시오.

First, Hepburn went to Ethiopia in 1988. There, she brought food to hungry children. She was (A)[shocking / shocked] because their lives were very difficult. After that, she volunteered in other countries. In 1990, she visited Vietnam to hand out medicine and support clean drinking water programs. Her last trip was to Somalia in 1992, and she ⓐpassed away the following year.

Many people praised her beauty and style, but Hepburn's real beauty was her heart. To honor her, UNICEF made a statue, T*he Spirit of Audrey*. People who respect her (B)[keep / keeps] her mission alive. Her favorite saying shows her mission.

As you ⓑget older, remember you have two hands. One is for helping yourself, and (C) *[another / the other] is for helping others.*

08 중요 위 글의 괄호 (A)~(C)에서 어법상 알맞은 낱말을 골라 쓰시오.

➡ (A)________ (B)________ (C)________

09 위 글의 내용과 일치하도록 다음 빈칸 (A)와 (B)에 알맞은 단어를 본문에서 찾아 쓰시오.

Judging from the fact that Hepburn visited many countries and (A)________ there, Hepburn's real beauty was (B)________ ________.

10 위 글의 밑줄 친 ⓐpassed away, ⓑget과 바꿔 쓸 수 있는 단어를 각각 쓰시오.

➡ ⓐ ________________ ⓑ ________________

[11~13] 다음 인터뷰를 읽고 물음에 답하시오.

Reporter: How was your life during World War II? Can you tell me about ⓐit?

Audrey: It was terrible. My family and I were hungry and sick. We survived thanks to the help of others.

Reporter: How did you begin to work for UNICEF?

Audrey: In 1987, a musical festival in Macau changed my life. I learned that my fame could help ⓑother people.

Reporter: After that, what did you do?

Audrey: I visited some countries in Africa and Asia and volunteered there.

11 위 인터뷰의 밑줄 친 ⓐit가 가리키는 것을 본문에서 찾아 쓰시오.

➡ ________________________________

12 위 인터뷰의 밑줄 친 ⓑother people과 바꿔 쓸 수 있는 단어를 본문에서 찾아 쓰시오.

➡ ________________________

13 다음 빈칸 (A)와 (B)에 공통으로 들어갈 알맞은 단어를 넣어, Audrey가 UNICEF를 위해 일하게 된 이유를 그녀의 어린 시절과 연결하여 완성하시오.

During World War II, Audrey's family and Audrey were hungry and sick. They survived thanks to the (A)________ of others. In 1987, after a musical festival in Macau, Audrey learned that her fame could (B)________ other people, so she began to work for UNICEF.

교과서

구석구석

Presentation Time

Lee Taeseok was a great person. He was a priest(성직자) and also a doctor. He built(build(짓다)의 과거형) hospitals and schools for the people of Tonj. He took care of(돌보았다) them and taught classes(수업을 했다). From this person, I learned that(learned의 목적어로 that절이 사용되었다.) I should help people in need(어려움에 처한).

해석

이태석은 위대한 사람이었다. 그는 성직자이고 또한 의사였다. 그는 톤즈의 사람들을 위해 병원과 학교를 세웠다. 그는 그들을 돌보고 수업을 했다. 이 사람으로부터, 나는 어려움에 처한 사람들을 도와야 한다고 배웠다.

After You Read B

Reporter: How was your life during(during+특정 기간을 나타내는 명사) World War II? Can you tell me about it(your life during World War II)?

Audrey: It(My life during World War II) was terrible. My family and I were hungry and sick.
We survived thanks to(~ 덕택에, ~ 때문에) the help of others.

Reporter: How did you begin to work(= working) for UNICEF?

Audrey: In 1987, a musical festival in Macau changed my life. I learned that(목적어에 해당하는 명사절을 이끄는 접속사) my fame could help other people.

Reporter: After that(앞에 나온 문장을 받는 지시대명사), what did you do?

Audrey: I visited some countries in Africa and Asia and volunteered there(some countries in Africa and Asia를 가리킨다.).

구문해설 • during: ~ 동안, ~ 중에 • terrible: 끔찍한 • survive 살아남다, 생존하다
• thanks to ~ 덕택에, ~ 때문에 • volunteer: 자원 봉사를 하다

리포터: 제2차 세계 대전 동안 당신의 삶은 어땠습니까? 그것에 대해 말해주실 수 있나요?
오드리: 끔찍했어요. 제 가족과 저는 굶주리고 아팠어요. 우리는 다른 사람들의 도움 덕분에 살아남았어요.
리포터: 당신은 어떻게 유니세프를 위해 일하게 되었나요?
오드리: 1987년에, 마카오의 한 음악 축제가 제 삶을 바꿨어요. 저는 제 명성이 다른 사람들을 도울 수 있다는 것을 알게 되었어요.
리포터: 그 다음에, 무엇을 했나요?
오드리: 아프리카와 아시아의 몇몇 나라들을 방문해서 그곳에서 자원 봉사를 했어요.

Culture Link

Talking Books Program

This is a program that(주격 관계대명사) makes audiobooks for blind people. It was started(수동태) in 1931 in(년도와 넓은 장소 앞에 쓴 전치사 in) the United States. You just read books and record your voice. These audiobooks are given to(give는 'to+간접목적어'의 형태를 쓴다.) blind people for free(무료로).

구문해설 • blind: 눈이 먼, 맹인인 • audiobook: 오디오북 (책의 내용을 녹음한 것)

말하는 책 프로그램

이것은 시각장애인을 위한 오디오북을 만드는 프로그램이다. 이것은 1931년 미국에서 시작되었다. 당신은 책을 읽고 당신의 목소리를 녹음하기만 하면 된다. 이러한 오디오북들은 시각장애인들에게 무료로 주어진다.

영역별 핵심문제

Words & Expressions

01 다음 제시된 단어를 사용하여 자연스러운 문장을 만들 수 없는 것은? (형태 변화 가능)

> 보기
> elderly following homeless international

① There are many _________ people at the subway station.
② Many younger Koreans offer their seats to _________ people.
③ It's a _________ movement to build houses for the homeless.
④ The _________ police finally caught him.
⑤ I left Madrid last Sunday and arrived in Seoul the _________ day.

02 우리말에 맞게 주어진 철자로 시작하여 빈칸을 완성하시오.

(1) 우리는 그 여행의 모든 순간을 즐겼다.
➡ We enjoyed every m_________ of the trip.
(2) 우리는 그녀의 요리를 칭찬했다.
➡ We p_________ her cooking.
(3) 나는 건강의 소중함을 깨달았다.
➡ I r_________ the value of health.
(4) 내 취미는 우표를 수집하는 것이다.
➡ My hobby is c_________ stamps.

03 다음 영영풀이에 해당하는 단어를 고르시오.

> the state of being famous

① wealth ② favor
③ difficulty ④ fame
⑤ population

04 빈칸에 들어갈 알맞은 말을 〈보기〉에서 골라 쓰시오. (형태 변화 가능)

> 보기
> clean fall hold raise

(1) When are you going to _________ a party?
(2) I lost my balance and _________ down.
(3) You should _________ up your room.
(4) He will also _________ money for the World Food Program.

Conversation

[05~07] 다음 대화를 읽고 물음에 답하시오.

> **B1:** Wow! These dogs are so dirty. Jay, 그 개들을 씻기는 거 도와줄 수 있니?(them, you, help, wash, can, me, ?)
> **B2:** Allen, I'm sorry, but I can't. I have to feed the cats now. (A)_____ don't you ask Nicky?
> **B1:** Okay! Nicky, can I ask you a favor?
> **G:** Sure, Allen. (B)_____ is it?
> **B1:** Can you help me wash these dogs?
> **G:** Sure. But I have to walk these dogs first. After that, I will help you.
> **B1:** All right! Thank you.

05 밑줄 친 우리말에 맞게 괄호 안의 단어를 바르게 배열하시오.

➡ _______________________________

06 빈칸 (A)와 (B)에 알맞은 의문사를 쓰시오.

➡ (A) ___________, (B) ___________

07 대화가 끝난 후 여자아이가 할 일로 가장 알맞은 것을 고르시오.

① 고양이 먹이 주기
② 동물 병원 들르기
③ 개 산책시키기
④ 개 목욕시키기
⑤ 개 집 청소하기

[08~09] 다음 글을 읽고 물음에 답하시오.

> G: Good morning, students! As you know, there was a big fire in Mapletown. Why don't we raise money and help the people there? Come to our special event at the school grounds on May 3! Please bring your items and donate them. We will sell your items. Then, we will give all the money to Mapletown. Please give a hand to people in need.

08 밑줄 친 부분과 같은 뜻이 되도록 주어진 단어를 이용해 문장을 완성하시오.

➡ (shall) ______________________

____

(let's) ______________________

09 위 글을 읽고 답할 수 없는 질문은?

① How can they raise money for the people in need?
② Where will the special event be held?
③ When will the special event be held?
④ Where was a big fire?
⑤ When was a big fire in Mapletown?

[10~11] 다음 대화를 읽고 물음에 답하시오.

> B: Mia, 이 책들 옮기는 거 도와줄 수 있어?
> G: Sure. What are you going to do with them?
> B: I'm going to donate them to a children's library.

10 주어진 단어를 이용해 밑줄 친 우리말을 영작하시오.

➡ ______________________

(these, move, help)

11 다음 영영풀이에 해당하는 단어를 대화에서 찾아 쓰시오.

to give something to help people

➡ ______________________

12 다음 대화의 빈칸에 알맞은 것은?

> A: What do you want to do this afternoon?
> B: ______________________
> A: That sounds like fun. Let's go.

① Where do you usually play tennis?
② Why don't we play tennis together?
③ Do you know how to play tennis?
④ Can you tell me how to play tennis?
⑤ Why didn't you play tennis this morning?

Grammar

13 다음 우리말을 주어진 어휘를 이용하여 영어로 옮기시오.

> 요가를 하는 것은 나를 느긋하게 해준다.
> (do, yoga, make relax)

➡ ______________________

14 다음 대화의 빈칸에 알맞은 말이 순서대로 바르게 짝지어진 것을 고르시오.

> A: Juliet was __________ when she knew that Romeo had left her.
> B: Yes. It was really ________.

① interesting – surprised
② shocking – shocking
③ shocked – surprising
④ interested – surprised
⑤ shocked – shocked

15 다음 중 두 문장을 한 문장으로 만들 때 의미가 다른 하나는?

① The little black dress is famous even today. She wore it in a movie.
→ The little black dress which she wore in a movie is famous even today.
② He is the boy. Mary talked about him yesterday.
→ He is the boy about whom Mary talked yesterday.
③ Do you remember the watch? Herold was wearing it.
→ Do you remember the watch that Herold was wearing?
④ Susan is the woman. I helped her on the street.
→ Susan is the woman who helped me on the street.
⑤ The man comes from Finland. Eveline is going to marry him.
→ The man who Eveline is going to marry comes from Finland.

16 다음 중 어법상 옳은 문장을 모두 고르시오.

① The little girl felt scaring all the time.
② I feel relaxed when I listen to classical music.
③ I am bored with the computer game.
④ Riding a roller coaster makes me exciting.
⑤ It was very excited, and I became interested in hockey!

17 〈보기〉의 밑줄 친 which와 용법이 다른 것은? (2개)

> 보기
> He bought his daughter the bag which she always wanted.

① I will never forget the people that I met in Korea.
② This is the house which Gibson lived in when he was young.
③ I know the boy who helped the old lady cross the road.
④ I ran into the man with whom I had worked for about a year.
⑤ We went to the restaurant which sold delicious Canadian food.

18 주어진 어휘를 이용하여 우리말의 의미에 맞도록 빈칸에 알맞게 쓰시오.

(1) 그녀의 직업은 전혀 재미있지 않았다. 그녀는 매우 지루했다.
→ Her job was not __________ at all. She was so __________. (interest, bore)
(2) 나는 하루 종일 매우 피곤함을 느꼈다.
→ I felt very __________ all day long. (tire)

19 다음 괄호 안에 주어진 어휘를 사용해 다음을 영작하시오. (that 사용 금지)

(1) 내가 카페에서 본 남자는 Park Jisung이었다. (the man, the café)

➡ ______________________

(2) 나는 나의 할머니가 입양한 개를 사랑한다. (my grandmother, adopt)

➡ ______________________

(3) Jason은 그 파티에 대해서 몰랐으므로 정말로 놀랐다. (about, so, really, surprise)

➡ ______________________

____

(4) 우리는 사고에 대해 들었을 때 너무 충격 받았다. (so, shock, about, when, the accident)

➡ ______________________

____

Reading

[20~21] 다음 글을 읽고 물음에 답하시오.

When she grew up, Hepburn became a symbol of beauty. She was very popular because of her hit movies, such as *My Fair Lady* and *Roman Holiday*. ⓐThe little black dress which she wore in a movie is famous even today. Many people still love her style.

The autumn of 1987 was a turning point in Hepburn's life. She went to an international music festival in Macau. Many people donated money at the festival, and the money went to UNICEF. Thanks to her fame, UNICEF collected more money than ever before. Hepburn realized that her fame could help others, so she became a UNICEF Goodwill Ambassador.

20 위 글의 밑줄 친 ⓐ에서 어법상 생략할 수 있는 단어를 찾아 쓰시오.

➡ ______________________

21 위 글의 내용과 일치하지 않는 것은?

① 헵번은 <마이 페어 레이디>와 <로마의 휴일>과 같은 흥행 영화들로 인해 매우 인기가 있었다.
② 많은 사람들은 헵번의 스타일이 요즘은 구식이라고 생각한다.
③ 1987년 가을 마카오의 한 국제 음악 축제에서 헵번의 명성 덕분에, 유니세프는 어느 때보다도 더 많은 돈을 모았다.
④ 헵번은 자신의 명성이 다른 사람들을 도울 수 있다는 것을 깨달았다.
⑤ 헵번은 유니세프 친선 대사가 되었다.

[22~24] 다음 글을 읽고 물음에 답하시오.

First, Hepburn went to Ethiopia in 1988. There, she brought food to hungry children. She was shocked because their lives were very difficult. After that, she volunteered in other countries. In 1990, she visited Vietnam to hand out medicine and support clean drinking water programs. Her last trip was to Somalia in 1992, and she passed away the following year.

Many people praised her beauty and style, but Hepburn's real beauty was her heart. To honor her, UNICEF made a statue, *The Spirit of Audrey*. ⓐ그녀를 존경하는 사람들이 그녀의 사명을 이어 나가고 있다. Her favorite saying shows her mission.

ⓑ*As you get older, remember you have two hands. One is for helping yourself, and the other is for helping others.*

22 위 글의 밑줄 친 ⓐ의 우리말에 맞게 한 단어를 보충하여, 주어진 어휘를 배열하시오.

her / respect / alive / mission / keep / people / her

➡ ______________________

23 위 글의 밑줄 친 ⓑAs와 같은 의미로 쓰인 것을 고르시오

① She works as hard as her mother.
② Do as you would be done by.
③ He came up as I was speaking.
④ As he is honest, everyone likes him.
⑤ Her anger grew as she talked.

24 위 글을 읽고 Hepburn이 방문한 나라와 방문 연도를 순서대로 쓰시오. (나라 이름은 우리말로 쓰시오)

➡ (1) ____________, (2) ____________,
(3) ____________

[25~27] 다음 인터뷰를 읽고 물음에 답하시오.

Reporter: How was your life during World War II? Can you tell me about it?
Audrey: It was (A)[terrible / terrific]. My family and I were hungry and sick. We survived thanks to the help of others.
Reporter: ⓐHow did you begin to work for UNICEF?
Audrey: In 1987, a musical festival in Macau (B)[changed / exchanged] my life. I learned that my fame could help other people.
Reporter: After that, (C)[how / what] did you do?
Audrey: I visited some countries in Africa and Asia and volunteered there.

25 위 인터뷰의 괄호 (A)~(C)에서 문맥이나 어법상 알맞은 낱말을 골라 쓰시오.

➡ (A)________ (B)________ (C)________

26 위 인터뷰의 밑줄 친 ⓐ를 다음과 같이 바꿔 쓸 때 빈칸에 들어갈 알맞은 말을 쓰시오.

➡ How did you begin __________ for UNICEF?

27 위 인터뷰를 읽고 답할 수 없는 질문은?

① How was Audrey's life during World War II?
② How did Audrey survive World War II?
③ How did Audrey begin to work for UNICEF?
④ Why did Audrey participate in a musical festival in Macau?
⑤ What countries did Audrey visit after working for UNICEF?

[28~29] 다음 글을 읽고 물음에 답하시오.

For my volunteer work, I helped young students with math homework. I ⓐdid this at my community library. ⓑFrom this volunteer work, I learned that helping others are a great experience.

28 위 글의 밑줄 친 ⓐdid this가 가리키는 것을 본문에서 찾아 쓰시오.

➡ ______________________________

29 위 글의 밑줄 친 ⓑ에서 어법상 틀린 부분을 찾아 고치시오.

➡ ____________________

단원별 예상문제

출제율 90%

01 다음 짝지어진 두 단어의 관계가 같도록 빈칸에 알맞은 단어를 쓰시오.

beauty : beautiful – ________ : favorable

출제율 95%

02 다음 〈보기〉에서 사람의 성격을 묘사할 때 쓸 수 있는 단어의 개수는?

보기
- beautiful
- friendly
- gentle
- curious
- polite
- careful
- outgoing
- patient

① 4개 ② 5개 ③ 6개 ④ 7개 ⑤ 8개

출제율 100%

03 다음 빈칸에 공통으로 들어갈 말을 쓰시오.

- ________ kinds of movies do you want to see this evening?
- ________ about enjoying art at home without going outside?

출제율 90%

04 다음 밑줄 친 단어와 뜻이 같은 단어를 모두 고르시오.

Thanks to you, I won the dancing contest.

① For ② Because of
③ Without ④ Despite
⑤ Due to

[05~06] 다음 대화의 순서를 바르게 배열한 것을 고르시오.

출제율 90%

05

(A) I'm going to donate them to a children's library.
(B) Mia, can you help me move these books?
(C) Sure. What are you going to do with them?

① (A) – (C) – (B) ② (B) – (A) – (C)
③ (B) – (C) – (A) ④ (C) – (A) – (B)
⑤ (C) – (B) – (A)

출제율 90%

06

(A) We can play music for the sick children
(B) Sounds good. What can we do there?
(C) Why don't we do volunteer work at the children's hospital?

① (A) – (C) – (B) ② (B) – (A) – (C)
③ (B) – (C) – (A) ④ (C) – (A) – (B)
⑤ (C) – (B) – (A)

[07~09] 다음 대화를 읽고 물음에 답하시오.

B1: Next Wednesday is Volunteer Day. We cleaned up the park last time. (①)
G: Why don't we ⓐvisiting a nursing home and ⓑclean up it? (②)
B2: That's not a bad idea. But I want ⓒdoing ⓓfun something. (③) Why don't we ⓔheld a party for the people there?
G: That's a good idea. (④) What can we do at the party?
B1: We can serve some food.
B2: And how about playing some music? I can play the piano. (⑤)
G: And I can play the cello.
B1: It sounds like a good plan.

출제율 85%

07 위 대화의 ①~⑤ 중 주어진 문장이 들어갈 알맞은 곳은?

> What are we going to do this time?

① ② ③ ④ ⑤

출제율 95%

08 ⓐ~ⓔ 중 어법상 어색한 것의 개수를 고르시오.

① 1개 ② 2개 ③ 3개 ④ 4개 ⑤ 5개

출제율 90%

09 다음 영영풀이에 해당하는 단어를 위 대화에서 찾아 쓰시오.

> a place where people who are too old or sick to take care of themselves live

➡ ______________________

[10~12] 다음 대화를 읽고 물음에 답하시오.

G1: We have a class activity day next Friday. What do you want to do on that day? (①)
B: Why don't we (A)______ some volunteer activities? (②)
G1: That sounds great, but choosing a good place is not easy.
B: We need someone who has volunteered a lot. (③)
G1: I know Sumin has volunteered a lot. Sumin, can you help us find some good places?
G2: Sure. (④) I usually search for information on the internet. (B)<u>십대들을 위한 자원 봉사 웹사이트를 확인해 보는 게 어떠니?</u>
B: That's a good idea. (⑤)

출제율 85%

10 위 대화의 ①~⑤ 중 주어진 문장이 들어갈 알맞은 곳은?

> We can help others and make our community better.

① ② ③ ④ ⑤

출제율 100%

11 빈칸 (A)에 적절한 것을 고르시오.

① prepare ② join ③ do
④ keep ⑤ have

출제율 95%

12 밑줄 친 (B) 우리말을 주어진 어구를 이용해 영작하시오.

➡ ______________________
(check, for, why, teens, the volunteering website)

출제율 90%

13 어법상 어색한 것을 바르게 고쳐 문장을 다시 쓰시오.

(1) This is the cell phone who I broke yesterday.
➡ ______________________

(2) The speed at that everything moved felt strange.
➡ ______________________

(3) The girl who I met her the other day was very pretty.
➡ ______________________

(4) I was very worring about his health.
➡ ______________________

출제율 90%

14 다음 두 문장의 의미가 같도록 빈칸에 알맞은 말을 쓰시오.

(1) The game was exciting to me.
= I was ___________ about the game.

(2) Jack thinks baseball is boring.
= Jack isn't ___________ in baseball.

[15~16] 다음 글을 읽고 물음에 답하시오.

During World War II, a little girl and her mother were hungry and sick. ①The only food ⓐthat they could find was grass. The little girl felt ②excited all the time. ③Luckily, the girl survived, ④thanks to the help of others. One of the groups that helped her was UNICEF. Later, the girl became a ⑤worldwide movie star. Her name was Audrey Hepburn.

출제율 90%

15 위 글의 밑줄 친 ①~⑤에서 흐름상 어색한 부분을 찾아 고치시오.

➡ ______________________________

출제율 95%

16 위 글의 밑줄 친 ⓐthat과 문법적 쓰임이 다른 것을 모두 고르시오.

① There's a man that wants to see you.
② Is this the farm that they talked about?
③ He said that the story was true.
④ These are the books that you lent me.
⑤ I was afraid that she might be late.

[17~19] 다음 글을 읽고 물음에 답하시오.

When she grew up, Hepburn became a symbol of beauty. She was very popular (A) [because / because of] her hit movies, such as *My Fair Lady* and *Roman Holiday*. The little black dress which she wore in a movie (B)[is / to be] famous even today. Many people still love her style.

(①) The autumn of 1987 was a (C)[turning / turned] point in Hepburn's life. (②) She went to an international music festival in Macau. (③) Many people donated money at the festival, and the money went to UNICEF. (④) Hepburn realized that her fame could help others, so she became a UNICEF Goodwill Ambassador. (⑤)

출제율 100%

17 위 글의 괄호 (A)~(C)에서 어법상 알맞은 낱말을 골라 쓰시오.

➡ (A)________ (B)________ (C)________

출제율 95%

18 위 글의 흐름으로 보아, 주어진 문장이 들어가기에 가장 적절한 곳은?

Thanks to her fame, UNICEF collected more money than ever before.

① ② ③ ④ ⑤

출제율 85%

19 다음 질문에 대한 알맞은 대답을 주어진 단어로 시작하여 쓰시오. (7~8 단어)

Q: Why did Hepburn become a UNICEF Goodwill Ambassador?
A: Because ______________________.

[20~22] 다음 글을 읽고 물음에 답하시오.

First, Hepburn went to Ethiopia in 1988. There, she brought food to hungry children. She was shocked because their lives were very difficult. After that, she ___ⓐ___ in other countries. In 1990, she visited Vietnam to hand out medicine and support clean drinking water programs. Her last trip was to Somalia in 1992, and she passed away the following year.

Many people praised her beauty and style, but Hepburn's real beauty was her heart. To honor her, UNICEF made a statue, *The Spirit of Audrey*. People who respect her keep her mission alive. Her favorite saying shows ⓑher mission.

As you get older, remember you have two hands. ⓒOne is for helping you, and the other is for helping others.

출제율 90%

20 주어진 영영풀이를 참고하여 빈칸 ⓐ에 철자 v로 시작하는 단어를 시제에 맞춰 쓰시오.

to offer to do something without being forced to do it

➡ ______________________

출제율 100%

21 위 글의 밑줄 친 ⓑher mission이 가리키는 것을 본문에서 찾아 쓰시오.

➡ ______________________

출제율 90%

22 위 글의 밑줄 친 ⓒ에서 어법상 틀린 부분을 찾아 고치시오.

➡ ______________________

[23~25] 다음 인터뷰를 읽고 물음에 답하시오.

Reporter: How was your life during World War II? Can you tell me about it?

Audrey: It was terrible. My family and I were hungry and sick. ⓐ우리는 다른 사람들의 도움 덕분에 살아남았다.

Reporter: How did you begin to work for UNICEF?

Audrey: In 1987, a musical festival in Macau changed my life. I learned that my fame could help other people.

Reporter: After that, what did you do?

Audrey: I visited some countries in Africa and Asia and volunteered ⓑthere.

출제율 100%

23 위 인터뷰의 밑줄 친 ⓐ의 우리말에 맞게 주어진 어휘를 이용하여 8 단어로 영작하시오.

thanks to

➡ ______________________

출제율 95%

24 위 인터뷰의 밑줄 친 ⓑthere가 가리키는 것을 본문에서 찾아 쓰시오.

➡ ______________________

출제율 90%

25 위 인터뷰의 내용과 일치하지 않는 것은?

① 제2차 세계 대전 동안 Audrey의 삶은 끔찍했다.
② 제2차 세계 대전 동안 Audrey의 가족과 Audrey는 굶주리고 아팠다.
③ Audrey가 유니세프를 위해 일하게 된 계기는 1987년 마카오의 한 음악 축제였다.
④ Audrey는 유니세프를 위해 일하면서 아프리카와 아시아의 몇몇 나라들을 방문했다.
⑤ Audrey는 아프리카와 아시아의 몇몇 나라들에서 영화배우로 일했다.

서술형 실전문제

[01~02] 다음 대화를 읽고 물음에 답하시오.

B: Hey, Minji! What's wrong ⓐ_____ your leg?
G: I broke it last week.
B: Really? What happened?
G: I was ⓑ______ a hurry ⓒ______ catch a train. But I fell ⓓ_____ in the street.
B: Oh, that's terrible! 내가 너를 위해 해줄 게 있니?
G: Well, can you help me carry this bag?

01 빈칸 ⓐ~ⓓ에 들어갈 단어를 <보기>에서 찾아 쓰시오.

보기
to down of in for with

➡ ______________________________

02 (중요) 밑줄 친 우리말을 주어진 단어를 이용하여 영어로 옮기시오.

➡ ______________________________
(there, anything)

03 우리말에 맞게 주어진 단어를 이용해 영어로 옮기시오.

G: Good morning, students! As you know, there was a big fire in Mapletown. (A) 우리가 돈을 모금해서 그곳 사람들을 도와주는 게 어떨까요? Come to our special event at the school grounds on May 3! Please bring your items and donate them. We will sell your items. Then, we will give all the money to Mapletown. (B)어려운 사람들에게 도움을 주십시오.

➡ (A) ______________________________
(raise, help, why, there)
(B) ______________________________
(in, please, give, people)

04 (중요) 두 문장을 관계대명사를 사용하여 한 문장으로 썼을 때 빈칸에 알맞은 문장을 쓰시오.

(1) • This is my aint.
• ______________________________
➡ This is my aunt about whom I told you.

(2) • This is the cake.
• ______________________________
➡ This is the cake which I made for my family.

(3) • ______________________________
• It was served at the restaurant.
➡ The food that was served at the restaurant was delicious.

(4) • I met the woman.
• ______________________________
➡ I met the woman you ate dinner with last Sunday.

05 다음 두 문장의 의미가 같도록 빈칸에 알맞은 말을 쓰시오.

(1) Nick thinks the result was disappointing.
= Nick was ____________ with the result.
(2) Richard thinks *Alita* is exciting.
= Richard is ____________ about *Alita*.

[06~08] 다음 글을 읽고 물음에 답하시오.

When she grew up, Hepburn became a symbol of beauty. She was very popular because of her hit movies, such as *My Fair Lady* and *Roman Holiday*. ⓐ그녀가 영화에서 입었던 아담한 검은 드레스는 심지어 오늘날까지도 유명하다. Many people still love her style.

The autumn of 1987 was a turning point in Hepburn's life. She went to an international music festival in Macau. Many people donated money at the festival, and the money went to UNICEF. Thanks to her fame, UNICEF collected more money than ever before. Hepburn realized that her fame could help others, so she became a UNICEF Goodwill Ambassador.

06 다음 문장에서 위 글의 내용과 다른 부분을 찾아서 고치시오.

Hepburn was very popular because she was a UNICEF Goodwill Ambassador.

➡ ______________________________
____
____

07 중요 위 글의 밑줄 친 ⓐ의 우리말에 맞게 한 단어를 보충하여, 주어진 어휘를 배열하시오.

is / she / the little black dress / today / which / wore / famous / in a movie

➡ ______________________________
____

08 위 글의 내용과 일치하도록 다음 빈칸에 알맞은 단어를 쓰시오.

The event which became ________ ________ ________ in Hepburn's life was an international music festival in Macau in the autumn of 1987.

[09~11] 다음 글을 읽고 물음에 답하시오.

First, Hepburn went to Ethiopia in 1988. There, she brought food to hungry children. She was (A)[pleased / shocked] because their lives were very ①difficult. After that, she volunteered in other countries. In 1990, she visited Vietnam to hand out medicine and support clean drinking water programs. Her (B)[last / latest] trip was ②from Somalia in 1992, and she passed away the ③following year.

Many people praised her beauty and style, but Hepburn's ④real beauty was her heart. To honor her, UNICEF made a statue, *The Spirit of Audrey*. People who respect her keep her mission (C)[alive / live]. Her ⑤favorite saying shows her mission.

As you get older, remember you have two hands. One is for helping yourself, and the other is for helping others.

09 중요 위 글의 괄호 (A)~(C)에서 문맥상 알맞은 낱말을 골라 쓰시오.

➡ (A)________ (B)________ (C)________

10 위 글의 밑줄 친 ①~⑤에서 흐름상 어색한 부분을 찾아 고치시오.

➡ ______________________________

11 다음 질문에 대한 알맞은 대답을 영어로 쓰시오. (5 단어)

Q: In what year did Hepburn pass away?

➡ ______________________________

창의사고력 서술형 문제

01 다음 대화의 흐름에 맞게 빈칸을 완성하시오. (제안하기의 표현을 사용할 것)

> **A:** Are you interested in recycled art?
> **B:** Yes, I am.
> **A:** There is a recycled art festival in City Park. ______________ go and see some works of recycled art?
> **B:** That's good. __________________ (1, how, meet)
> **A:** __________________ (afraid) __________________ at 2? (meet, what)
> **B:** OK. _________ meet in front of the front gate of City Park.

02 다음 정보를 바탕으로 자신의 영웅에 대한 이야기 카드를 만드시오.

> **Personal Information**
> • Who is your hero?: my mom
> • When was he/she born?: in 1972
> • Where does he/she live?: in Seoul
> **Personality**
> What is he/she like?
> She smiles a lot and tries to see the good in everything.
> **Important Moments**
> What are some of the most important moments in his/her life?
> She had a serious car accident.
> **Reason**
> Why is he/she your hero?
> She always helps people in need.

> My little big hero is (A)______________. She was born in 1972. She lives in Seoul. She smiles a lot and tries to see (B)______________ in everything. My mom had a serious (C)______________. She was in the hospital for six months. But she was very strong and finally got better. She always helps people (D)______________. She donates money and does volunteer work. She is my (E)______________!

단원별 모의고사

[01~02] 다음 빈칸에 알맞은 단어를 고르시오.

01

She ________ music records as a hobby.

① breaks ② carries
③ honors ④ serves
⑤ collects

02

They decided to ______ an essay contest.

① take ② do ③ hold
④ get ⑤ bring

03 다음 우리말과 일치하도록 빈칸을 채우시오. (주어진 철자가 있을 경우 그 철자로 시작할 것)

(1) 많은 사람들이 여왕에게 존경을 표하기 위해 왔다.
➡ Many people came to h________ the queen.

(2) 나는 그 자동차 사고로 다리가 부러졌다.
➡ I ________ my leg in the car ________.

(3) 그들은 임무를 성공적으로 완수했다.
➡ They finished their ________ successfully.

(4) 광장에는 그 왕의 조각상이 서 있다.
➡ The ________ of the king stands in the square.

(5) 그 추락 사고에서 다섯 명만이 살아남았다.
➡ Only five people ________ the crash.

04 다음 주어진 문장과 같은 의미가 되도록 빈칸을 채우시오. (3 단어)

My sister always listens to music.
➡ My sister listens to music ____________.

[05~06] 다음 대화를 읽고 물음에 답하시오.

B: Hey, Minji! ⓐWhat's wrong with your leg?
G: ⓑI broke it last week.
B: Really? What happened?
G: ⓒI am in a hurry to catch a train. ⓓBut I fell down in the street.
B: ⓔOh, that's terrific! Is there anything I can do for you?
G: Well, 이 가방을 드는 걸 도와줄 수 있니?
B: Sure.

05 ⓐ~ⓔ 중 문법상 또는 흐름상 어색한 부분을 찾아 고치시오. (2개)

➡ ________________________________

06 밑줄 친 우리말을 영작하시오.

➡ ________________________________

07 다음 대화의 빈칸 ⓐ~ⓔ에 들어갈 수 없는 표현을 고르시오.

B: Mia, ⓐ______ me ⓑ______?
G: ⓒ______. ⓓ______ to do with them?
B: ⓔ______ donate them to a children's library.

① What are you going
② move these books
③ Of course not
④ can you help
⑤ I'm going to

08 다음 대화의 밑줄 친 우리말을 영작하시오.

A: 수학 문제 푸는 걸 도와줄 수 있니?
B: I'm sorry, but I can't.

➡ ________________________________

[09~12] 다음 대화를 읽고 물음에 답하시오.

G1: ⓐWe have a class activity day next Friday. ⓑWhat do you want to do on that day?
B: ⓒWhy don't we do some volunteer activities? ⓓWe can help others and make our community better.
G1: That sounds great, ⓔbut choosing a good place are not easy.
B: (need, we, who, a, someone, volunteered, lot, has)
G1: I know Sumin has volunteered a lot. Sumin, can you help us find some good places?
G2: Sure. I usually search (A)____ information on the internet. Why don't we check the volunteering website (B)_____ teens?
B: That's a good idea.

09 위 대화의 ⓐ~ⓔ 중에서 어법상 어색한 것을 고르시오.

① ⓐ ② ⓑ ③ ⓒ ④ ⓓ ⑤ ⓔ

10 괄호 안의 단어를 알맞게 배열하여 영작하시오.

➡ ________________________________

11 빈칸 (A)와 (B)에 공통으로 들어갈 단어를 쓰시오.

➡ ______________________

12 위 대화의 내용과 일치하지 않는 것은?

① 봉사 활동을 많이 해 본 사람이 필요하다.
② 수민이는 봉사 활동을 위한 좋은 장소를 고르는 것이 쉽지 않다고 생각한다.
③ 남자아이는 봉사활동이 다른 사람들을 돕고 지역 사회를 더 좋게 만들 수 있다고 생각한다.
④ 다음 주 금요일에 학급 활동이 있다.
⑤ 그들은 대화 후에 십대들을 위한 자원 봉사 웹사이트를 확인할 것이다.

13 다음 중 어법상 바르지 않은 것은?

① The man is going to meet the students who he taught a long time ago.
② Everyone was surprised at the fact.
③ Andy bought the same bike that I wanted.
④ This is the backpack which I bought it yesterday.
⑤ I'm really interested in this book. I want to read it.

14 다음 〈보기〉에 주어진 단어를 변형하여 문맥에 맞게 문장을 완성하시오.

보기: relax interest

(1) Watching movies makes me ________.
(2) They found the game ________.

15 다음 빈칸에 들어갈 알맞은 말을 모두 고르시오.

The man _______ you met yesterday is a spy.

① who ② whose
③ whom ④ that
⑤ which

16 괄호 안에 주어진 어휘를 이용하여 우리말을 영작하시오.

(1) 그녀가 읽고 있었던 책이 없어졌다. (missing)

➡ ____________________

(2) 내가 함께 점심을 먹고 있던 남자는 Yoojin이었다. (the man, have)

➡ ____________________

____

____

(3) 우리는 그 아름다운 풍경에 놀랐다. (amaze, at, scenery)

➡ ____________________

(4) Dan은 재미있는 남자는 아니지만, 그와 있을 때 나는 지루하지 않다. (a funny guy, bore)

➡ ____________________

____

17 다음 중 어법상 바르지 않은 것은?

① I am going to go on a trip tomorrow. I'm so excited.

② I'll give you the butterflies which I caught yesterday.

③ I met the girl in whom you are interested.

④ The child was very scared of the crocodile and began to cry.

⑤ Someone was following me, and I felt scaring.

[18~19] 다음 글을 읽고 물음에 답하시오.

When she grew up, Hepburn became a symbol of beauty. She was very popular because of her hit movies, such as *My Fair Lady* and *Roman Holiday*. The little black dress which she wore in a movie is famous even today. Many people still love her style.

The autumn of 1987 was a turning point in Hepburn's life. She went to an international music festival in Macau. Many people donated money at the festival, and the money went to UNICEF. Thanks to her fame, UNICEF collected more money than ever before. Hepburn realized that her fame could help others, so she became a UNICEF Goodwill Ambassador.

18 다음 질문에 대한 알맞은 대답을 빈칸에 쓰시오.

Q: For what reason could UNICEF collect more money than ever before in an international music festival in Macau in the autumn of 1987?

A: It could do so ________ ________ ________ ________.

19 위 글의 주제로 알맞은 것을 고르시오.

① Hepburn's life as a symbol of beauty

② Hepburn's hit movies, such as *My Fair Lady* and *Roman Holiday*

③ Hepburn's fame and a turning point in her life

④ an international music festival in Macau

⑤ Hepburn's life as a UNICEF Goodwill Ambassador

[20~22] 다음 글을 읽고 물음에 답하시오.

First, Hepburn went to Ethiopia in 1988. There, she brought food to hungry children. She was shocked because ⓐtheir lives were very difficult. After that, she volunteered in other countries. In 1990, she visited Vietnam to hand out medicine and support clean drinking water programs. Her last trip was to Somalia in 1992, and she passed away the following year.

Many people praised her beauty and style, but Hepburn's real beauty was her heart. To honor her, UNICEF made a statue, *The Spirit of Audrey*. People ⓑwho respect her keep her mission alive. Her favorite saying shows her mission.

As you get older, remember you have two hands. One is for helping yourself, and the other is for helping ___ⓒ___.

20 다음 빈칸에 알맞은 단어를 넣어 밑줄 친 ⓐtheir lives가 가리키는 것을 설명하시오.

the lives of ________ ________ in Ethiopia

21 위 글의 밑줄 친 ⓑwho와 문법적 쓰임이 같은 것을 고르시오.

① Who is that woman?
② Who can jump farther, Tom or Bill?
③ Nobody knew who he was.
④ Who do you mean?
⑤ Anyone who wants to come is welcome.

22 위 글의 빈칸 ⓒ에 들어갈 알맞은 말을 고르시오.

① the other
② others
③ one
④ your family
⑤ another

[23~25] 다음 글을 읽고 물음에 답하시오.

My little big hero is my mom. She was born in 1972. She lives in Seoul.
She smiles a lot and tries to see the good in everything.
My mom had a serious car accident. She was in the hospital for six months. But she was very strong and finally got better.
She always helps people in need. She donates money and does volunteer work. She is my big hero!

23 위 글의 제목으로 알맞은 것을 고르시오.

① Mom Was Born in 1972!
② Try to See the Good in Everything
③ Mom Had a Serious Car Accident
④ My Little Big Hero
⑤ My Friendly Mom and Me

24 다음 질문에 대한 알맞은 대답을 완전한 문장으로 쓰시오.

Q: How long was the writer's mom in the hospital?

➡ ______________________________

25 위 글의 글쓴이의 엄마에 관한 내용으로 적절하지 않은 것은?

① 서울에 산다.
② 많이 웃는다.
③ 자동차 사고로 몸이 불편하다.
④ 어려움에 처한 사람들을 항상 돕는다.
⑤ 자원 봉사를 한다.

The Best Trip of Your Life

의사소통 기능

- 계획 묻고 답하기
  A: What are you planning to do on your trip?
  B: I'm planning to go hiking.
- 소요 시간 묻고 답하기
  A: How long does it take to get to school?
  B: It takes 20 minutes.

언어 형식

- 가주어 It
  It was nice **to relax in a café and read them.**
- 간접의문문
  Do you know **where the first train station in Korea is?**

교과서

Words & Expressions

Key Words

- □ **amazing** [əméiziŋ] 형 놀라운, 멋진
- □ **amusement park** 놀이공원
- □ **art museum** 미술관
- □ **art show** 미술 전시회
- □ **autumn** [ɔ́:təm] 명 가을
- □ **awesome** [ɔ́:səm] 형 매우 멋진
- □ **block** [blɑk] 명 블록, 구역
- □ **cafe** [kæféi] 명 카페, 커피숍
- □ **comic book** 만화책
- □ **condition** [kəndíʃən] 명 상태, 상황
- □ **field trip** 견학 여행, 현장 학습
- □ **foreign** [fɔ́:rən] 형 외국의
- □ **get** [get] 동 (장소 · 위치에) 도착하다, 얻다
- □ **goods** [gudz] 명 상품, 물건
- □ **hike** [haik] 동 하이킹하다, 도보 여행하다
- □ **historical** [histɔ́:rikəl] 형 역사적인, 역사상의
- □ **history** [hístəri] 명 역사
- □ **holiday** [hɑ́lədèi] 명 휴가, 공휴일, 휴일
- □ **international** [ìntərnǽʃənəl] 형 국제적인
- □ **museum** [mju:zíəm] 명 박물관, 미술관
- □ **natural** [nǽtʃərəl] 형 자연의
- □ **painting** [péintiŋ] 명 그림
- □ **picture** [píktʃər] 명 사진, 그림
- □ **plan** [plæn] 동 계획하다 명 계획
- □ **presentation** [prèzəntéiʃən] 명 발표
- □ **purpose** [pə́:rpəs] 명 목적, 목표
- □ **rafting** [rǽftiŋ] 명 래프팅, 급류 타기
- □ **relax** [rilǽks] 동 휴식을 취하다, 느긋이 쉬다
- □ **roller coaster** 롤러코스터
- □ **rough** [rʌf] 형 거친, 파도가 심한
- □ **scenery** [sí:nəri] 명 풍경, 경치
- □ **site** [sait] 명 장소
- □ **stadium** [stéidiəm] 명 경기장, 스타디움
- □ **stop** [stɑp] 명 멈춤, 정거장, (여행 중) 머무른 곳
- □ **straight** [streit] 부 똑바로, 일직선으로
- □ **street food** 길거리 음식
- □ **take** [teik] 동 (얼마의 시간이) 걸리다, (사진을) 찍다
- □ **turn** [tə:rn] 동 (가는 방향을 바꾸어) 돌다, 돌리다
- □ **university** [jù:nəvə́:rsəti] 명 대학교
- □ **view** [vju:] 명 전망
- □ **village** [vílidʒ] 명 마을
- □ **visit** [vízit] 동 방문하다, 찾아가다
- □ **Western-style** [wéstərn-stail] 형 서양풍의, 서양식의

Key Expressions

- □ **a variety of**: 여러 가지의, 다양한
- □ **at the same time**: 동시에, 한꺼번에
- □ **be able to** 동사원형: ~할 수 있다
- □ **be going to** 동사원형: ~할 예정이다
- □ **be planning to** 동사원형: ~할 계획이다
- □ **by bus**: 버스로
- □ **Can you tell me how to get** ~?: ~에 어떻게 가는지 말해 줄 수 있나요?
- □ **focus on**: (~에) 집중하다, 초점을 맞추다
- □ **get off**: 내리다, 하차하다
- □ **get on**: 타다, 승차하다
- □ **get to** 장소: ~에 도착하다
- □ **Have a good trip**.: 좋은 여행하길 바라.
- □ **How can/do I get to** 장소?: ~에 어떻게 갈 수 있어?
- □ **How long does it take to go** ~?: ~까지 가는 데 얼마나 걸리나요?
- □ **in front of**: ~ 앞에서
- □ **It takes** (**about**) 시간: ~ (정도) 걸려.
- □ **lots of**: 많은
- □ **on foot** 걸어서, 도보로
- □ **turn off**: (등, 전화기 등을) 끄다
- □ **What are you going to** 동사원형 ~?: 너는 무엇을 할 거니?
- □ **What are you planning to** 동사원형 ~?: 너는 무엇을 할 계획이니?
- □ **no longer**: 더 이상 ~하지 않는

Word Power

※ 어원은 같지만 뜻이 다른 어휘들

- □ **awesome**(매우 멋진) – **awful**(형편없는)
- □ **fun**(재미있는, 즐거운) – **funny**(웃기는, 우스운, 기이한)
- □ **terrible**(끔찍한) – **terrific**(아주 좋은)

※ 서로 비슷한 뜻을 가진 어휘

- □ **amazing**(놀라운, 멋진) : **incredible**(믿을 수 없는)
- □ **goods**(상품, 물건) : **item**(물품)
- □ **site**(장소) : **place**(장소, 곳)
- □ **condition**(상태, 상황) : **state**(상태)
- □ **holiday**(휴가) : **vacation**(휴가)

※ '여행'을 의미하는 다양한 영어 어휘

- □ **trip**: 가장 일반적으로 쓰이는 말로, 비교적 짧은 기간의 단거리 여행을 말할 때 주로 쓴다.
- □ **travel**: 상대적으로 장기간에 걸친 여행을 말할 때 쓰는 경우가 많다.
- □ **journey**: 보다 격식을 갖춘 단어이다.
- □ **voyage**: 배를 이용한 장기간의 여행을 의미한다.
- □ **expedition**: '탐험, 원정'이라는 말로 어떤 단체나 조직이 구체적인 목적을 가지고 떠나는 여행을 가리킨다.

English Dictionary

□ **amusement park**: 놀이공원
→ a place that has many games and rides
많은 게임이나 탈것들이 있는 장소

□ **autumn**: 가을
→ the season after summer and before winter
여름 후와 겨울 전의 계절

□ **awesome**: 매우 멋진
→ wonderful or impressive
멋지거나 인상적인

□ **condition**: 상태, 상황
→ the state of something
어떤 것의 상태

□ **field trip**: 견학 여행, 현장 학습
→ a visit made by students and teachers to learn about something
학생들과 선생님들이 무엇인가를 배우기 위해 방문하는 것

□ **foreign**: 외국의
→ from another country
다른 나라에서 온

□ **goods**: 상품, 물건
→ products for sale
판매를 위한 물품

□ **history**: 역사
→ events that have happened in the past
과거에 발생한 사건들

□ **museum**: 박물관, 미술관
→ a building where historical or artistic objects are displayed
역사적이거나 예술적인 물건들이 전시되어 있는 건물

□ **natural**: 자연의
→ produced by nature
자연에 의해 만들어진

□ **purpose**: 목적, 목표
→ the reason why something is used or done
어떤 것이 사용되거나 행해지는 이유

□ **relax**: 휴식을 취하다, 느긋이 쉬다
→ not to do anything
아무것도 하지 않다

□ **rough**: 거친
→ having a bumpy surface
울퉁불퉁한 표면을 가진

□ **scenery**: 풍경, 경치
→ a beautiful view of nature
자연의 아름다운 경치

□ **site**: 장소
→ a place 장소

□ **stadium**: 경기장, 스타디움
→ a large sports field
규모가 큰 운동 경기장

□ **stop**: (여행 중) 머무른 곳
→ a place where one stops during a trip
여행 중에 멈춘 장소

□ **Western-style**: 서양풍의, 서양식의
→ a particular way or form relating to Western countries
서양 국가들과 관련된 특별한 방식이나 형식

[01~02] 다음 밑줄 친 단어와 바꿔 쓸 수 있는 것을 고르시오.

01

I bought these items at a low price because they are used ones.

① sites ② stops
③ goods ④ markets
⑤ views

02

Somi has many different kinds of chocolate.

① a sort of ② a lot of
③ a variety of ④ a few
⑤ the number of

서답형

03 다음 빈칸에 알맞은 것을 <보기>에서 찾아 쓰시오.

보기
amusement park / autumn / condition / scenery / stop

(1) I recommend this beach. It has the most beautiful ________.
(2) The car is in good ________.
(3) The leaves turn red in ________.
(4) They are having fun in the ________.

[04~05] 다음 영영풀이에 해당하는 단어를 주어진 철자로 시작하여 쓰시오.

서답형

04

a________: wonderful or impressive

05

p________: the reason why something is used or done

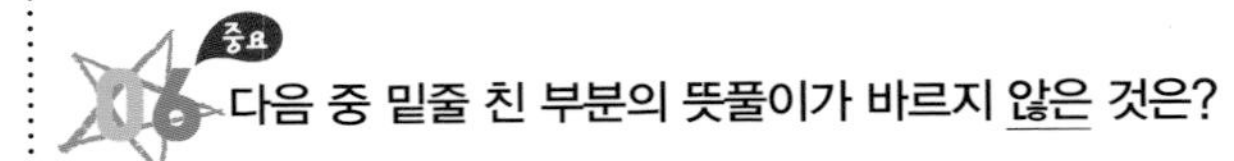

중요

06 다음 중 밑줄 친 부분의 뜻풀이가 바르지 않은 것은?

① I visit my uncle in Cheongju every year. (방문하다)
② Why don't you relax for a moment? (휴식을 취하다)
③ We will go on a field trip to Olympic Park. (현장 학습)
④ It takes about two hours by train from Seoul to Daegu. (가져가다)
⑤ We should get off at the next stop. (정거장)

[07~08] 다음 빈칸에 들어갈 말로 가장 적절한 것을 고르시오.

07

We're going to ________ to the airport very soon.

① do ② have ③ get
④ make ⑤ take

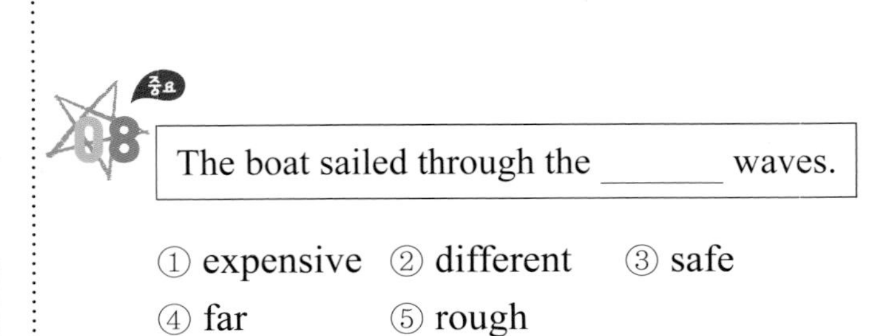

중요

08

The boat sailed through the ________ waves.

① expensive ② different ③ safe
④ far ⑤ rough

01 중요 다음 주어진 영영풀이의 어휘를 빈칸에 써 넣으시오. (5글자)

products for sale

They imported expensive ________ from England.

02 다음 밑줄 친 부분과 의미가 가장 가까운 것을 주어진 철자로 시작하여 쓰시오.

The city has a lot of important historical sites.

➡ p____________________

03 고난이도 다음 우리말에 맞게 주어진 어구를 바르게 배열하시오.

(1) 유진의 바이올린은 낡긴 했지만, 여전히 좋은 상태이다.
(Eugene's, good, is, still, violin, condition, old, in, but)
➡ ________________________________

(2) 그 식당은 다양한 후식이 특징이다.
(variety, desserts, the restaurant, of, a, features)
➡ ________________________________

(3) 너는 공부에 집중해야 한다.
(focus, studies, you, to, on, have, your)
➡ ________________________________

(4) 나는 지난달에 외국을 방문했다.
(last, I, month, a, country, visited, foreign)
➡ ________________________________

04 중요 주어진 단어를 이용해 우리말 해석에 맞게 빈칸을 완성하시오.

(1) 무대를 위한 그의 디자인은 아주 놀라웠다.
(amaze)
→ His design for the stage is very ________.

(2) 그들은 자연식품의 신선한 맛을 즐겼다.
(nature)
→ They enjoyed the fresh taste of ________ foods.

[05~06] 다음 빈칸에 공통으로 들어갈 말을 쓰시오.

05

• You need to ________ off at the next stop. • He waited for the lady to ________ on the bus.

06 중요

• Can you tell me ________ to get to the art museum? • ________ long does it take to go to Busan in a bus?

07 다음 빈칸에 알맞은 단어를 <보기>에서 골라 쓰시오. (형태 변화 가능)

보기
block cafe comic book plan

(1) Those ________ are very popular among teenagers.
(2) I don't have any ________ for today.
(3) City Hall is on the next ________.
(4) Many people are sitting at an outdoor ________.

교과서

Conversation

1 계획 묻고 답하기

A What are you planning to do on your trip? 여행에서 뭐 할 계획이니?
B I'm planning to go hiking. 하이킹을 할 계획이야.

- 계획을 물을 때는 동사 plan을 써서 'What are you planning to 동사원형 ~?'으로 물을 수 있다. to부정사 뒤에는 구체적인 활동이나 계획을 나타낸다. 답을 할 때는 마찬가지로 'I'm planning to 동사원형 ~.'을 사용하여 세부 내용을 나타낸다.
- 계획을 물을 때 의문사 What을 쓰지 않고 구체적인 내용으로 물어볼 수도 있다.

계획을 물을 때

- What are you going to 동사원형 ~? (너는 무엇을 할 거니?/너는 무엇을 할 예정이니?)
- What are you planning to 동사원형 ~? (너는 무엇을 할 계획이니?)
- What are your plans for ~? (~에 대한 너의 계획은 무엇이니?)

계획을 대답할 때

- I'm going to 동사원형 ~. (~하려고 해.)
- I'm thinking of (동)명사 ~. (~할 생각이야.)
- I'm planning to 동사원형 ~. (~할 계획이야.)

핵심 Check

1. 다음 우리말과 같도록 대화의 빈칸을 채우시오.

A: ______________ planning ________ after school? (너는 방과 후에 무엇을 할 계획이니?)
B: ______________________ my history homework. (나는 역사 숙제를 할 계획이야.)
A: ______________ going to do tomorrow? (너는 내일 무엇을 할 거니?)
B: I'm ______________________. (나는 영화를 볼 거야.)

2. 괄호 안의 단어들을 바르게 배열하여 대화를 완성하시오.

A: ____________________________________ (weekend, planning, what, this, do, are, to, you, ?)
B: ____________________________________ (in, to, I'm, Seoul, planning, visit, my, grandparents)

2 소요 시간 묻고 답하기

A How long does it take to get to school? 학교에 가는 데 얼마나 걸려?
B It takes 20 minutes. 20분 걸려.

- 어떤 일을 하는 데 소요되는 시간을 물을 때는 'How long does it take?'를 사용한다. 이때 'How long does it take to get to the airport?'에서처럼 to부정사를 이용하여 구체적인 내용을 밝힐 수 있다.
- 답으로는 'It takes ~.'에 시간 표현을 넣어 말한다. 여기서 take는 '(시간이) 걸리다'라는 의미로 사용되었다. 소요 시간을 말할 때 대략적인 시간을 말할 경우에는 시간 앞에 about을 붙여 쓴다. about은 '약, ~쯤'의 의미이다.

  ex) It takes about an hour to get home. (집에 도착하는 데 1시간쯤 걸려.)

소요 시간 묻기

- How long does it take to go to ~? (~에 가는 데 얼마나 걸려?)

소요 시간 대답하기

- It takes (about) 시간. (~ (정도) 걸려.)

핵심 Check

3. 대화가 자연스럽게 이어지도록 배열하시오.

(1) (A) I usually ride a bike.
(B) How long does it take?
(C) How do you go to school?
(D) It takes about 20 minutes.
➡ ______________________

(2) (A) It takes about 30 minutes by bus.
(B) Yes, there's one in Big Mall.
(C) How long does it take to get there?
(D) Is there a movie theater around here?
(E) OK. Thanks.
➡ ______________________

4. 괄호 안의 단어들을 바르게 배열하여 대화를 완성하시오.

A: ______________________ (how, does, take, it, long, ?)
B: ______________________ (bus, takes, 30, it, by, minutes)

Conversation 교과서 대화문 익히기

Listen & Talk 1 B

B: We have a long ❶holiday this month. ❷Do you have any plans?
G: ❸I'm going to visit my grandparents in Jeonju.
B: Oh, really? That's nice. ❹What are you planning to do with them?
G: ❺I'm planning to go to Hanok Village with them. How about you? ❻What are your plans for the holiday?
B: ❼I'm going to stay home and relax.
G: That's also a good idea!

남: 우리 이번 달에 긴 휴가가 있어. 무슨 계획이라도 있니?
여: 나는 전주에 있는 나의 조부모님을 방문할 예정이야.
남: 아, 그래? 좋구나. 그분들과 어떤 것을 할 계획이야?
여: 그분들과 한옥 마을에 갈 계획이야. 너는 어때? 휴가 때 무슨 계획 있어?
남: 나는 집에 머물면서 쉴 거야.
여: 그것도 좋은 아이디어다!

❶ holiday: 휴가, 공휴일, 휴일
❷ 'Do you have any plans (for ~)?'는 계획이나 계획 여부를 물어보는 표현이다. 뒤에 for the long holiday가 생략되어 있다. 'What are you planning to do for the long holiday?', 'What are you going to do for the long holiday?'로 바꾸어 쓸 수 있다.
❸ 계획을 묻는 표현에 'be going to 동사원형(~할 예정이다.)'을 이용해 대답할 수 있다.
❹ them은 your grandparents를 받고 있다. 계획을 물을 때는 동사 plan을 써서 'What are you planning to 동사원형 ~?'으로 물을 수 있다. What are you planning to do with them? = What are you going to do with them?
❺ be planning to 동사원형: ~할 계획이다
❻ 'What are your plans for ~'는 '~에 무슨 계획이 있어?'라는 뜻으로 계획을 묻는 표현이다.
❼ be going to 동사원형: ~할 예정이다 stay(머무르다)와 relax(휴식을 취하다, 느긋이 쉬다)는 접속사 and로 연결되어 있다.

Check(√) True or False

(1) They boy will stay home during the holiday. T ☐ F ☐
(2) The girl visited her grandparents in Jeonju. T ☐ F ☐

Listen & Talk 2 A

G: ❶How do you get to school?
B: I go to school ❷by bus.
G: ❸How long does it take to get there?
B: ❹It takes 15 minutes.

여: 너 학교에 어떻게 가니?
남: 버스 타고 가.
여: 거기까지 가는 데 얼마나 걸려?
남: 15분 걸려.

❶ get to 장소: ~에 도착하다
❷ by 교통수단: 교통수단으로 → by bus: 버스로
❸ 특정 장소까지의 소요 시간을 물을 때는 'How long does it take to get ~?'라고 묻는다.
❹ 소요 시간을 묻는 질문의 대답은 'It takes 시간.'으로 대답한다. take: (얼마의 시간이) 걸리다

Check(√) True or False

(3) The boy goes to school by subway. T ☐ F ☐
(4) The girl asks the boy how he goes to school. T ☐ F ☐

Listen & Talk 1 A

B: ❶What are you going to do this weekend?
G: ❷I'm going to go to Jeju-do.
B: ❸What are you planning to do there?
G: ❹I'm planning to go hiking on Hallasan.

❶ 'What are you going to 동사원형 ~?'은 '너는 무엇을 할 거니?, 너는 무엇을 할 예정이니?'라는 뜻으로 계획에 대해 물을 때 사용하는 표현이다. (= What will you do this weekend? = What are you planning to do this weekend? = What are you thinking of doing this weekend?) this weekend: 이번 주말
❷ be going to 동사원형: ~할 예정이다
❸ What are you planning to 동사원형 ~?: 뭐 할 계획이야? there는 앞에 나온 Jeju-do를 받는다.
❹ be planning to 동사원형: ~할 계획이다

Listen & Talk 1 C

B: Hi, Nuri. Where is your class going for the ❶ field trip tomorrow?
G: Hello, Mike. ❷We are going to the art museum.
B: ❸Sounds interesting. ❹What are you planning to see there?
G: ❺There are three art shows right now. ❻I'm planning to see Vincent van Gogh's paintings. Where is your class going?
B: ❼We are going to the amusement park. ❽I'm excited to ride a roller coaster!
G: That sounds fun. ❾Have a good trip!

❶ field trip: 견학 여행, 현장 학습
❷ be going to 동사원형: ~할 예정이다 art museum: 미술관
❸ 상대방이 한 말에 대하여 '재미있겠다'라는 표현으로 'Sounds interesting.'이나 'How interesting!' 등의 표현을 사용할 수 있다.
❹ What are you planning to 동사원형 ~?: 뭐 할 계획이야? there는 앞에서 나온 the art museum을 의미한다.
❺ there are+복수명사: ~가 있다 art show: 미술 전시회
❻ be planning to 동사원형: ~할 계획이다
❼ amusement park: 놀이공원
❽ 감정을 나타내는 동사의 경우 과거분사는 '~하게 된'의 뜻으로 감정을 느끼는 대상에 쓰인다. 그러므로 excited는 '신이 난'의 의미로 해석한다. to ride a roller coaster는 to부정사의 부사적 용법 중 감정의 원인으로 사용되었다.
❾ Have a good trip!: 좋은 여행하길 바라!

Listen & Talk 2 B

B: Wow, these ❶pictures are so beautiful. Where did you ❷take them?
G: At Riverside Park. There were ❸lots of flowers. ❹You should go there!
B: ❺I want to. ❻How do I get there from our school?
G: ❼Get on bus number 135 and get off at the Riverside Stadium stop. You can see the park ❽in front of the bus stop.
B: ❾How long does it take to get there?
G: It takes 30 minutes.
B: Thanks. I'll go there next weekend.

❶ picture: 사진
❷ take: (사진을) 찍다 them은 pictures를 받는 대명사이다.
❸ lots of: 많은 (= a lot of = many)
❹ 충고하는 표현으로 'You'd better go there!'로 바꾸어 쓸 수 있다.
❺ 'I want to.'뒤에 'go there'가 생략되어 있다.
❻ 찾아가려고 하는 장소를 물을 때 'How do I get 장소부사(to+장소)?'의 표현을 쓸 수 있다.
❼ get on: 타다, 승차하다 get off: 내리다, 하차하다 stop: 정거장
❽ in front of: ~ 앞에서
❾ 특정 장소까지의 소요 시간을 물을 때는 'How long does it take to get ~?'라고 묻는다.

Listen & Talk 2 C

B: Excuse me. How do I get to Hanguk University from here?
W: ❶You can go there by bus or on foot.
B: How long does it take to get there?
W: It takes five minutes by bus and 20 minutes on foot.
B: Oh, then I will walk there. ❷Can you tell me how to get there?
W: Go straight for two blocks, and then ❸turn left. You will see Hanguk University on your right.
B: Go straight for two blocks and turn left. Thank you!

❶ there는 Hanguk University를 의미한다. by bus: 버스로 on foot 걸어서, 도보로
❷ 'Can you tell me how to get ~?'은 길을 물어보는 표현이다. 'How can/do I get ~?'으로 바꾸어 쓸 수 있다.
❸ turn left: 좌회전하다 on your right: 당신의 오른편에

Conversation 교과서 확인학습

● 다음 우리말과 일치하도록 빈칸에 알맞은 말을 쓰시오. (주어진 철자가 있으면 그 철자로 시작할 것)

Listen & Talk 1 A

B: ________ ________ ________ going to do ________ weekend?

G: I'm ________ to ________ to Jeju-do.

B: ________ are ________ planning to ________ there?

G: ________ ________ ________ go hiking on Hallasan.

해석

남: 너 이번 주말에 뭐 할 거야?
여: 제주도에 갈 거야.
남: 거기서 뭐 할 계획이야?
여: 한라산에 올라갈 계획이야.

Listen & Talk 1 B

B: We ________ a long holiday ________ month. Do you ________ ________ plans?

G: I'm g________ to visit my grandparents in Jeonju.

B: Oh, really? That's nice. ________ are you p________ ________ do ________ them?

G: ________ p________ to go to Hanok Village ________ ________. How ________ you? What are your ________ ________ the holiday?

B: I'm g________ to ________ home and ________.

G: That's also a good idea!

남: 우리 이번 달에 긴 휴가가 있어. 무슨 계획이라도 있니?
여: 나는 전주에 있는 나의 조부모님을 방문할 예정이야.
남: 아, 그래? 좋다. 그분들과 어떤 것을 할 계획이야?
여: 그분들과 한옥 마을에 갈 계획이야. 너는 어때? 휴가 때 무슨 계획 있어?
남: 나는 집에 머물면서 쉴 거야.
여: 그것도 좋은 아이디어다!

Listen & Talk 1 C

B: Hi, Nuri. ________ is your class going for the ________ ________ tomorrow?

G: Hello, Mike. ________ ________ ________ ________ the art museum.

B: Sounds i________. What are you p________ ________ ________ there?

G: There ________ three art shows right now. ________ p________ ________ ________ Vincent van Gogh's paintings. ________ is your class going?

B: ________ ________ ________ ________ the ________ park. I'm ________ to ride a roller coaster!

G: That sounds fun. Have a good trip!

남: 안녕, 누리야. 너희 반은 내일 현장 학습으로 어디 가니?
여: 안녕, 마이크. 우리는 미술관에 갈 거야.
남: 재미있겠다. 너 거기서 뭐 볼 계획이니?
여: 지금 3개의 전시회가 있어. 나는 빈센트 반 고흐의 그림을 볼 거야. 너희 반은 어디로 가니?
남: 우리는 놀이동산에 갈 거야. 롤러코스터를 타게 되어 신나!
여: 재미있겠다. 좋은 여행하길 바라!

Listen & Talk 2 A

G: ________ do you ________ to school?

B: I go to school ________ bus.

G: ________ ________ does it ________ to ________ there?

B: ________ ________ 15 minutes.

여: 너 학교에 어떻게 가니?
남: 버스 타고 가.
여: 거기까지 가는 데 얼마나 걸려?
남: 15분 걸려.

Listen & Talk 2 B

B: Wow, these ________ are so ________. ________ did you ________ them?

G: At Riverside Park. There ________ lots ________ flowers. You ________ go there!

B: I want ________. ________ do I ________ there ________ our school?

G: ________ ________ bus number 135 and get ________ at the Riverside Stadium stop. You can ________ the park in ________ of the bus stop.

B: How ________ does it ________ to get there?

G: It ________ 30 minutes.

B: Thanks. I'll go there ________ ________.

해석

남: 와, 이 사진들 너무 예쁘다. 어디서 찍었어?
여: Riverside Park에서. 꽃이 많았어. 넌 거기 꼭 가 봐야 해!
남: 나도 가고 싶어. 학교에서 거기까지 어떻게 가니?
여: 135번 버스를 타고 Riverside Stadium 정류장에서 내리면 돼. 버스 정류장 앞에 공원이 보일 거야.
남: 거기까지 가는 데 얼마나 걸려?
여: 30분 걸려.
남: 고마워. 다음 주말에 그곳에 가야겠다.

Listen & Talk 2 C

B: Excuse me. ________ ________ ________ ________ ________ Hanguk University from here?

W: You can ________ ________ ________ ________ ________ ________ ________.

B: ________ ________ does it ________ to get there?

W: It takes five minutes ________ bus and 20 minutes ________ ________.

B: Oh, then I will walk there. ________ ________ ________ me ________ ________ ________ there?

W: ________ straight for two blocks, and then ________ left. You will see Hanguk University ________ your right.

B: ________ straight ________ two blocks and ________ ________. Thank you!

남: 실례합니다. 여기서 한국 대학교까지 어떻게 가나요?
여: 버스 타고 가거나 걸어서 갈 수 있어요.
남: 거기까지 가는 데 얼마나 걸리나요?
여: 버스 타면 5분 걸리고, 걸어서는 20분 걸려요.
남: 아, 그러면 걸어서 갈래요. 어떻게 가는지 말해 줄 수 있나요?
여: 2블록 직진한 다음에 좌회전하세요. 그러면 오른쪽에 한국 대학교가 보일 거예요.
남: 2블록 직진해서 좌회전이요. 감사합니다!

Do It Yourself A

G: ________ are you p________ ________ ________ ________ weekend?

B: I'm planning ________ ________ ________ a baseball game in Daegu.

G: ________ ________ going ________ ________ the All-Star Game?

B: Yes. It ________ be fun. Also, ________ planning ________ ________ my friend there.

G: Nice. ________ ________ does it take to get there?

B: It takes ________ ________ ________ ________ ________ ________ express train.

G: Wow, it's ________ faster ________ I thought. I hope you ________ a good trip!

B: Thank you.

여: 이번 주말에 너는 무엇을 할 계획이니?
남: 나는 대구에 야구 경기를 보러 갈 계획이야.
여: 올 스타 경기를 보러 갈 예정이야?
남: 응. 재미있을 거야. 또한, 그곳에서 내 친구를 만날 계획이야.
여: 좋다. 거기까지 가는 데 얼마나 걸리니?
남: 급행열차로 1시간 40분이 걸려.
여: 와, 내가 생각한 것보다 훨씬 더 빠르다. 즐거운 여행이 되길 바랄게.
남: 고마워.

Conversation 시험대비 기본평가

Step4

01 대화의 빈칸에 들어갈 말로 적절한 것을 모두 고르시오.

> B: ______________________
> G: I'm going to go to Jeju-do.

① What did you do last weekend?
② What are you going to do this weekend?
③ Where are you going now?
④ How was your trip to Jeju-do?
⑤ What are you planning to do this weekend?

02 대화의 빈칸에 들어갈 말로 적절한 것을 고르시오.

> G: How do you get to school?
> B: I go to school by bus.
> G: How long does it take to get there?
> B: ______________________

① I usually take the bus.
② It arrives at 8.
③ I'd like to go to school by bus.
④ It takes 15 minutes.
⑤ I'm going to school.

03 대화의 빈칸에 들어갈 말로 적절하지 않은 것은?

> G: What are you planning to do this weekend?
> B: I ____________ to a baseball game in Daegu.

① am planning to go
② am going to go
③ am able to go
④ am thinking of going
⑤ will go

04 다음 중 의미가 다른 하나를 고르시오.

① What are your plans for the holiday?
② What are you going to do for the holiday?
③ What are you doing for the holiday?
④ What are you planning to do for the holiday?
⑤ What are you thinking of doing for the holiday?

[01~03] 다음 대화를 읽고 물음에 답하시오.

B: Wow, these pictures are so beautiful. (①)
G: At Riverside Park. There were lots of flowers. (②) You should go there!
B: (A)I want to. (③) How do I get there from our school?
G: Get on bus number 135 and get off at the Riverside Stadium stop. (④) You can see the park in front of the bus stop.
B: How long does it take to get there? (⑤)
G: It takes 30 minutes.
B: Thanks. I'll go there next weekend.

01 위 대화의 ①~⑤ 중 주어진 문장이 들어갈 알맞은 곳은?

Where did you take them?

① ② ③ ④ ⑤

서답형

02 밑줄 친 문장 (A)에서 뒤에 생략된 것을 대화에서 찾아 쓰시오.

➡ ______________________

03 위 대화의 내용과 일치하지 않는 것을 고르시오.

① To get to Riverside Park from school, the boy has to take bus number 135.
② The girl took pictures at Riverside Park.
③ It takes 30 minutes to go from school to Riverside Park by bus.
④ The boy is going to Riverside Park this weekend.
⑤ There are a lot of flowers at Riverside Park.

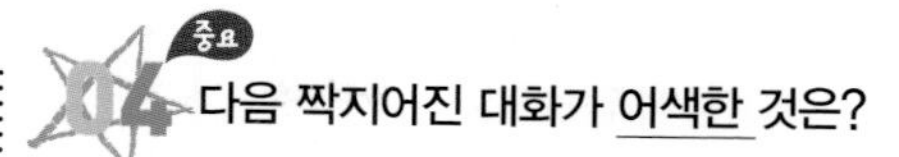

04 중요 다음 짝지어진 대화가 어색한 것은?

① A: What are you going to do this weekend?
B: I'm going to take a trip with my family.
② A: Are you going to take a taxi?
B: Yes, I am.
③ A: Where are you going to go this weekend?
B: I'm planning to go to the library to borrow some books.
④ A: How long does it take to get there?
B: It is about 5 km.
⑤ A: How do you get to school?
B: I go to school on foot.

05 대화의 순서가 올바르게 배열된 것을 고르시오.

(A) How long does it take to get there? (B) I go to school by bus. (C) How do you get to school? (D) It takes 15 minutes.

① (A) – (C) – (D) – (B)
② (A) – (D) – (B) – (C)
③ (C) – (A) – (D) – (B)
④ (C) – (B) – (A) – (D)
⑤ (C) – (D) – (B) – (A)

[06~08] 다음 대화를 읽고 물음에 답하시오.

B: Excuse me. (A)_____ do I get to Hanguk University from here? (①)
W: You can go there by bus or on foot.
B: (B)_____ does it take to get there? (②)
W: It (C)<u>takes</u> five minutes by bus and 20 minutes on foot. (③)
B: Oh, then I will walk there. (④)
W: Go straight for two blocks, and then turn left. You will see Hanguk University on your right. (⑤)
B: Go straight for two blocks and turn left. Thank you!

06 위 대화의 ①~⑤ 중 주어진 문장이 들어갈 알맞은 곳은?

Can you tell me how to get there?

① ② ③ ④ ⑤

중요
07 빈칸 (A)와 (B)에 들어갈 말이 알맞게 짝지어진 것을 고르시오.

	(A)	(B)
①	How	How long
②	How	How
③	How long	How long
④	How long	How
⑤	How	How far

08 밑줄 친 (C)<u>takes</u>와 같은 의미로 쓰인 것을 <u>모두</u> 고르시오.

① I want to <u>take</u> some pictures.
② It doesn't <u>take</u> much time.
③ Did you <u>take</u> an umbrella in the morning?
④ When I go to school, I <u>take</u> a bus.
⑤ It will <u>take</u> a lot of time to prepare it.

[09~12] 다음 대화를 읽고 물음에 답하시오.

B: We (A)_____ a long holiday this month. Do you (B)_____ any plans?
G: (C)____________________ (①)
B: Oh, really? (②) That's nice. What are you planning to do with them? (③)
G: I'm planning to go to Hanok Village with them. How about you? (④)
B: <u>나는 집에 머물면서 쉴 거야.</u> (⑤)
G: That's also a good idea!

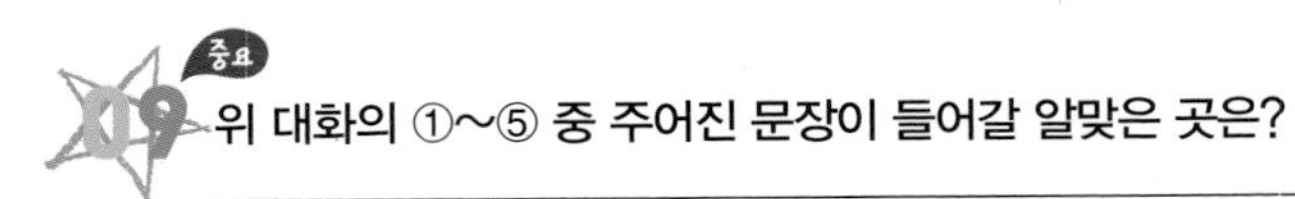

중요
09 위 대화의 ①~⑤ 중 주어진 문장이 들어갈 알맞은 곳은?

What are your plans for the holiday?

① ② ③ ④ ⑤

서답형
10 빈칸 (A)와 (B)에 공통으로 들어갈 말을 쓰시오.

➡ ____________________

11 빈칸 (C)에 알맞은 말을 고르시오.

① I'm going to go to Jeonju.
② I'm planning to go hiking.
③ I'm going to go to Jeju-do.
④ I'm planning to eat local dishes in Jeonju.
⑤ I'm going to visit my grandparents in Jeonju.

서답형
12 밑줄 친 우리말에 맞게 주어진 단어를 이용해 빈칸을 채우시오.

➡ ____________________
(stay, going, relax)

[01~02] 다음 대화를 읽고 물음에 답하시오.

B: What are you going (A)________ this weekend?
G: I'm going to go to Jeju-do.
B: What are you planning (B)________ there?
G: I'm planning to go hiking on Hallasan.

01 빈칸 (A)와 (B)에 공통으로 들어갈 말을 쓰시오.

➡ ____________________

고난이도

02 대화의 내용과 일치하도록 빈칸을 채우시오.

The boy is asking the girl what ________ ________________. She ________ ________ Jeju-do and she ________ ________ on Hallasan.

[03~04] 다음 대화를 읽고 물음에 답하시오.

A: Where will you go?
B: ____________________
A: ____________________
B: ____________________
A: ____________________
B: ⓐI'm planning to watch a soccer game.

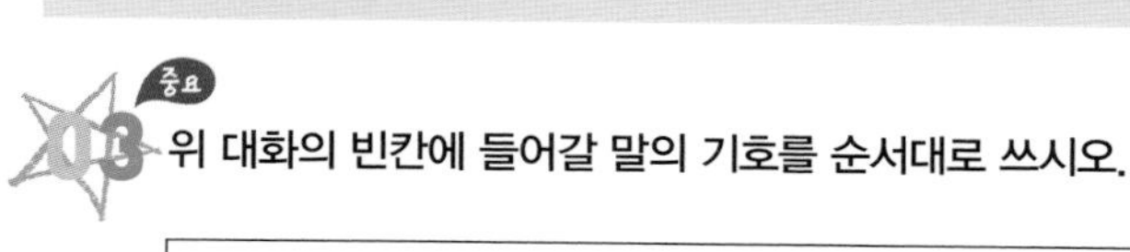

중요 **03** 위 대화의 빈칸에 들어갈 말의 기호를 순서대로 쓰시오.

(A) It takes 14 hours by plane.
(B) How long does it take to get there?
(C) What are you planning to do there?
(D) I will go to Barcelona.

➡ ____________________

04 밑줄 친 ⓐ와 같은 뜻이 되도록 주어진 단어를 이용해 영작하시오.

(1) ____________________ (will)
(2) ____________________ (go)
(3) ____________________ (think)

[05~06] 다음 대화를 읽고 물음에 답하시오.

B: Hi, Nuri. Where is your class going for the field trip tomorrow?
G: Hello, Mike. We are going to the art museum.
B: Sounds (A)________(interest). <u>너 거기서 뭐 볼 계획이니?</u>
G: There are three art shows right now. I'm planning to see Vincent van Gogh's paintings. Where is your class going?
B: We are going to the amusement park. I'm (B)________(excite) to ride a roller coaster!
G: That sounds fun. Have a good trip!

중요 **05** 빈칸 (A)와 (B)를 주어진 단어를 이용하여 채우시오.

➡ (A) ____________ (B) ____________

06 밑줄 친 우리말에 맞게 영작하시오. (7 단어)

➡ ____________________

교과서

Grammar

1 가주어 it

- **It** was interesting **to see** all the international goods there. 그곳에서 세계 곳곳의 상품들을 모두 볼 수 있어서 흥미로웠다.
- **It** is good **to have** friends but bad **to need** them. 친구가 있는 것은 좋다. 그러나 그들이 필요하게 되면 좋지 않다. (서양 속담)

■ 문장의 주어로 쓰인 to부정사가 수식어로 인해 길어진 경우, 보통 to부정사를 뒤로 보내고 대신 주어 자리에 가주어 it을 둔다. 이때 쓰인 it은 가주어이므로 구체적인 뜻이 없으며, '…하는 것은 ~하다'로 해석한다.

- **It** is easy **to use** a fire alarm box. 화재 경보 박스를 이용하는 것은 쉽다.
  = **To use** a fire alarm box is easy.
- **It** is interesting **to learn** a new language. 새로운 언어를 배우는 것은 흥미로운 일이다.
  = **To learn** a new language is interesting.
- **It** is so exciting **to watch** the soccer game with my friends. 나의 친구들과 함께 축구 경기를 관람하는 것은 정말 흥미진진하다.
  = **To watch** the soccer game with my friends is so exciting.

■ to부정사의 의미상 주어가 필요한 경우에는 'for+명사[목적격 대명사]'를 to부정사 앞에 쓴다. 또한 to부정사의 부정은 to부정사 앞에 not[never]을 써서 'not[never]+to V'로 나타내며 '…하지 않는 것은 ~하다'로 해석한다.

- **It** is good for children **to drink** milk often. 어린이들이 우유를 자주 마시는 것은 좋다.
- **It** is important **not to use** your phone while walking. 걸어가면서 전화기를 사용하지 않는 것은 중요하다.
- I had to try hard **not to cry**. 나는 울지 않으려고 무척 노력해야 했어요.

핵심 Check

1. 다음 우리말과 일치하도록 빈칸에 알맞은 말을 쓰시오.
   (1) 이 시간에 길에 주차하는 것이 안전한가요?
   ➡ Is ________ ________ ________ park on the street at this time?
   (2) 최저 임금으로 가정을 부양하기란 힘들다.
   ➡ ________ is difficult ________ support a family on the minimum wage.
   (3) 붐비는 시간에는 차를 안 가지고 나가는 게 중요하다.
   ➡ It is ________ ________ ________ take the car out during rush hours.

2 간접의문문

- Do you know **where the first train station in Korea is?** 한국 최초의 기차역이 어디인지 아세요?
- Tell me **whether he is at home.** 그가 집에 있는지 말해 줘.

■ 간접의문문이란 의문문이 '의문사+주어+동사' 형태로 다른 문장 안에서 주어, 목적어, 보어 역할을 하는 것을 말한다. 명사처럼 쓰이므로 주로 '…가 ~하는지'로 해석한다.

- **How he solved it** is unknown. <주어 역할> 그가 그것을 어떻게 해결했는지는 알려지지 않았다.
- Rob didn't remember **what her name was.** <목적어 역할> Rob는 그녀의 이름이 무엇이었는지 기억하지 못했다.
- This is **how she solved the problem.** <보어 역할> 이런 식으로 그녀는 그 문제를 처리했다.

■ 의문사가 주어인 경우에는 의문사가 주어 역할을 하므로 직접의문문처럼 '의문사+동사'의 어순임에 유의한다.

- Do you know **who wrote this book**? 누가 이 책을 썼는지 아니?

■ 간접의문문으로 바꾸어 쓸 때에는 조동사 do를 삭제한다. 이때, 의문문에 쓰인 조동사의 시제를 간접의문문의 동사에 반영해야 한다는 점에 유의해야 한다.

- Please tell me. + What did you do last night?
  → Please tell me **what you did last night.**

■ 의문사가 없는 경우에는 의문사 대신에 if나 whether를 쓴다.

- Will you tell me? + Are you hungry?
  → Will you tell me **if[whether] you are hungry**? 배가 고픈지 내게 말해 줄래?

■ believe, imagine, suppose, consider, expect, think, guess 등과 같은 동사가 주절에 있을 경우 간접의문문의 의문사를 문장 맨 앞에 놓는다.

- Do you think? + Who is he?
  → Do you think who he is? (×)
  → **Who** do you think **he is**? (○) 너는 그가 누구라고 생각하니?

핵심 Check

2. 다음 우리말과 일치하도록 빈칸에 알맞은 말을 쓰시오.

(1) 네가 무엇을 샀는지 말해 줄 수 있니?
➡ Can you tell me ________ ________ ________?

(2) 나는 네가 그것을 좋아하는지 궁금해.
➡ I wonder ________ ________ ________ it.

(3) 너는 누가 그 경기에서 이길 거라고 생각하니?
➡ ________ ________ ________ ________ ________ win the game?

Grammar 시험대비 기본평가

01 다음 두 문장을 한 문장으로 연결할 때 올바른 것은?

• Do you know? • What is it famous for?

① Do you know what is it famous for?
② Do you know what it is famous for?
③ Do you know it is famous for what?
④ What do you know it is famous for?
⑤ What do you know is it famous for?

02 다음 밑줄 친 부분의 쓰임이 나머지와 다른 하나는?

① For me, it is possible to do ten push-ups.
② It is exciting to fly a model airplane.
③ It's about two miles from here to the beach.
④ It is very difficult to be good at English.
⑤ It's not easy to have meals in space.

03 다음 빈칸에 알맞은 것을 고르시오.

A: Do you know ____________________? B: It's on the desk.

① where does the book
② where the books are
③ where are the books
④ where is the book
⑤ where the book is

04 주어진 어구를 바르게 배열하여 다음 우리말을 영어로 쓰시오.

(1) 카페에서 휴식을 취하며 그 책들을 읽는 것이 좋았다. (in a café, nice, relax, read, was, the books, it, and, to)
➡ ____

(2) 한국 최초의 기차역이 어디인지 아세요? (the first train station, Korea, where, you, know, is, do, in, ?)
➡ ____

Grammar 시험대비 실력평가

01 다음 중 어법상 바르지 않은 것은?

① It is difficult to study English hard every day.
② That's so kind of you to say so.
③ It is not good to watch too much TV.
④ It's important to decide a topic for the presentation.
⑤ Homer wonders why he feels so hungry today.

02 다음 빈칸에 들어갈 말로 가장 적절한 것은?

Do you know ____________________?

① Hammington is from where
② where is Hammington from
③ where Hammington is from
④ is where Hammington from
⑤ from Hammington is where

서답형

03 다음 괄호 안에서 알맞은 말을 고르시오.

(1) (It / That) is difficult to say how many people use it.
(2) It is great (to win / win) a race.
(3) For me, it is possible to (stand / standing) on one leg for a minute.
(4) We have no idea when (she left / did she leave) the village.
(5) She knows who (is he / he is).
(6) I don't know (that / if) he will come.

중요

04 다음 중 밑줄 친 부분의 쓰임이 다른 하나는?

① It is difficult to live without a smartphone.
② It is good to change the water filter every month.
③ It's common practice to tip 15 percent of the total bill.
④ It was found behind the sofa in the living room.
⑤ It is dangerous for her to climb the mountain.

05 다음 우리말을 영어로 바르게 옮긴 것은?

너는 그의 생일이 언제인지 기억하니?

① When do you remember his birthday is?
② When do you remember is his birthday?
③ Do you remember when is his birthday?
④ Do you remember his birthday is when?
⑤ Do you remember when his birthday is?

서답형

06 주어진 단어를 활용하여 다음 우리말을 영어로 쓰시오.

한국에서 인터넷을 사용하는 것은 어렵지 않다. (it, difficult, the Internet)

➡ ________________________________

07 중요 다음 중 밑줄 친 부분의 어순이 올바르지 않은 것은?

① Do you know when World War II ended?
② Why he has bad breath is unknown.
③ I wondered if she would come to the party or not.
④ Tell me if or not you like Jenny.
⑤ I'm not sure whether it is enough or not.

08 다음 중 빈칸에 들어갈 말이 바르게 짝지어진 것은?

• ________ is no use ________ over spilt milk.

① This – crying
② That – cry
③ That – crying
④ It – cry
⑤ It – crying

09 다음 중 어법상 바르지 않은 것은?

①It ②is ③good ④to exercising ⑤every day.

① ② ③ ④ ⑤

10 중요 다음 중 어법상 바르지 않은 문장의 개수는?

ⓐ It's nice of you help the elderly.
ⓑ Do you know how dogs swim?
ⓒ I wonder will he come today.
ⓓ It was difficult for me understanding the story.
ⓔ It was wonderful to share the moment with you.

① 1개 ② 2개 ③ 3개 ④ 4개 ⑤ 5개

11 우리말과 의미가 같도록 빈칸에 들어갈 말로 알맞은 것을 고르시오.

• 나는 그가 내일 집으로 돌아올지 알 필요가 있어.
→ I need to know ________ back home tomorrow.

① if he will come
② he will come
③ will he come
④ whether he comes
⑤ that he comes

12 중요 다음 중 빈칸에 들어갈 말이 다른 하나는?

① ______ is brave of you to share such personal things about yourself.
② ______ English in a short period is not easy.
③ ______ was careless of you to say such a thing.
④ ______ is great to find cute animals.
⑤ ______ is necessary for you to go there right now.

13 다음 두 문장을 간접의문문으로 바르게 바꾼 것은?

• Do you know?
• Who is Leonardo da Vinci?

① Who is Leonardo da Vinci do you know?
② Who do you know is Leonardo da Vinci?
③ Who do you know Leonardo da Vinci is?
④ Do you know who is Leonardo da Vinci?
⑤ Do you know who Leonardo da Vinci is?

14 다음 중 어법상 바르지 않은 것은?

① It is interesting to ride a skateboard.
② It was foolish of her think so.
③ It's important for children to be taught grammar.
④ It is difficult to learn Greek.
⑤ It is fun to learn a foreign language.

서답형
15 다음 문장에서 어법상 어색한 것을 바르게 고쳐 다시 쓰시오.

(1) Ride a motorcycle without a helmet is dangerous.
➡ ______________________
____

(2) It is great make good friends in your life.
➡ ______________________

(3) This is not easy to keep a diary in English every day.
➡ ______________________

(4) It is important for learn the history of your country.
➡ ______________________
____

(5) The girl is asking where is the nearest bus stop.
➡ ______________________

(6) Do you know will the leaves turn yellow in autumn?
➡ ______________________
____

(7) Will you tell me when did you meet her?
➡ ______________________

중요
16 다음 빈칸에 들어갈 말로 알맞은 것은?

I'd like to ask you ________ you're free tonight.

① because ② that ③ as
④ if ⑤ what

17 다음 두 문장이 같도록 할 때 빈칸에 알맞은 것은?

To understand others fully is not easy.
→ It is not easy ________ others fully.

① understand ② understands
③ to understanding ④ to understands
⑤ to understand

중요
18 다음 중 밑줄 친 부분의 쓰임이 다른 하나는?

① It is fun to play volleyball on the beach.
② I was so glad to hear from you again.
③ Mike must be a fool to do such a stupid thing.
④ Carol went to her home country never to return.
⑤ Her grandmother lived to be 110 years old.

서답형
19 그림을 참고하여 다음 빈칸에 알맞은 말을 쓰시오.

A: Let me know ________ ________ ________ study last night.
B: I couldn't because of the loud music.

01 다음 두 문장을 하나의 문장으로 바꿔 쓰시오.

(1) Tell me. + What do you want for Christmas?

➡ ______________________________

(2) She asked me. + How much sugar is there in the coke?

➡ ______________________________

(3) Do you know? + Where is Greece on the map?

➡ ______________________________

(4) I wonder. + Is he a singer?

➡ ______________________________

(5) I have no idea. + Will he join us soon?

➡ ______________________________

(6) Do you think? + Where does your soul go after you die?

➡ ______________________________

중요

02 to부정사를 진주어로 하여 주어진 문장과 같은 의미가 되도록 쓰시오.

(1) That high mountain is dangerous to climb.

➡ ______________________________

(2) This road is not safe to walk on as it is very slippery.

➡ ______________________________

(3) He is very smart to teach himself.

➡ ______________________________

03 다음 사진을 참고하여 주어진 대화의 빈칸을 완성하시오.

A: Look at this picture. Do you know (1)______________?

B: Yeah, it's Moai.

A: Could you tell me (2)______________?

B: It is in Easter island in Chile.

고난이도

04 다음 문장을 가주어 · 진주어 구문으로 바꿔 쓰시오.

(1) To ride on the rough water and enjoy the view at the same time was exciting.

➡ ______________________________

____

(2) Trying to excuse yourself is no good.

➡ ______________________________

(3) Not to take the car out during rush hours is wise.

➡ ______________________________

(4) Continuing the search is no use.

➡ ______________________________

(5) For Laura to marry such a man is highly regrettable.

➡ ______________________________

고난이도

05 두 문장을 한 문장으로 만들었을 때, 나머지 한 문장을 쓰시오.

(1) • He is asking.
+ • ______________________________
→ He is asking how long it takes to reach the top.

(2) • The woman was not sure.
+ • ______________________________
→ The woman was not sure if the thief was a man or a woman.

(3) • Do you believe?
+ • ______________________________
→ What do you believe the secret of his success is?

06 다음 문장을 It으로 시작하여 다시 쓰시오.

(1) To read your handwriting is hard.
➡ ______________________________

(2) To swim in this river is very dangerous.
➡ ______________________________

(3) To read and write Hangeul is very easy.
➡ ______________________________

(4) For me to run 1,000 meters in three minutes is impossible.
➡ ______________________________
____

(5) That she passed the exam is unbelievable.
➡ ______________________________

중요

07 다음 문장을 어법에 맞게 고쳐 쓰시오.

(1) This is dangerous to cross this street at night.
➡ ______________________________

(2) It is important to not give up.
➡ ______________________________

(3) That was believed that Mike told a lie to his friends.
➡ ______________________________

(4) The doctor will ask you what did you eat for breakfast.
➡ ______________________________

(5) Please let us know are you able to attend.
➡ ______________________________
____

(6) Do you suppose what they are thinking?
➡ ______________________________

08 괄호 안에 주어진 어휘를 이용하여 다음 우리말을 영작하시오.

(1) 그곳의 자연의 아름다움을 보는 것은 매우 놀라웠다. (amazing, so, it, to)
➡ ______________________________

(2) 작은 모험을 하는 것이 필요했다. (necessary, take, risks, it, to)
➡ ______________________________

(3) Daniel은 그가 어떻게 가수가 되었는지 우리에게 말해 주었다. (become, a singer)
➡ ______________________________

(4) 그가 올지 안 올지 의심스럽다. (doubtful, whether, come, or)
➡ ______________________________

교과서

Reading

The Best Moment of the Field Trip

Teacher: Good morning, everyone! How were your field trips last week? Please tell us about them!
지난주에 / =your field trips last week

Busan, Market Heaven

Do you like traditional markets? Then go to Gukje Market in Busan. It is one of the most famous markets in Busan. Do you know what it is famous for? It is famous for selling a variety of goods from different countries. It was interesting to see all the international goods there. We also ate many kinds of street food, such as *Gimbap*, fish cake, and *Hotteok*. Then we walked to Bosu-dong Book Street. Many bookstores there sell used books.

We were really excited because we found some old comic books!

It was nice to relax in a café and read them.

- Then: =If you like traditional markets.
- one of the most famous markets: one of the +최상급+복수 명사: ~ 중의 하나
- what it is famous for: '의문사+주어+동사'의 어순으로 쓰인 간접의문문으로, 동사 know의 목적어
- It: 가주어 / to see all the international goods there: to see 이하는 진주어
- such as: = like: ~와 같은
- there: 그곳에 있는 / used books: 중고 책
- because: ~이기 때문에(접속사)
- It: 가주어 / to relax in a café and read them: to relax 이하는 진주어

be famous for ~으로 유명하다
moment 순간
field trip 견학 여행, 현장 학습
traditional 전통적인
a variety of 여러 가지의, 다양한
goods 상품, 제품
bookstore 책방, 서점
comic book 만화책
relax 휴식을 취하다, 느긋이 쉬다

확인문제

- 다음 문장이 본문의 내용과 일치하면 T, 일치하지 않으면 F를 쓰시오.

1 Gukje Market is one of the most famous markets in Busan. ☐
2 Gukje Market is famous for selling a variety of goods made in Korea. ☐
3 Many bookstores on Bosu-dong Book Street sell new books. ☐
4 It was nice to relax in a café and read some old comic books. ☐

Gangwon-do, Full of Natural Beauty

There is no place like (~와 같은(전치사)) Gangwon-do for beautiful nature. First, we went to Baengnyong Cave. This 1.8-kilometer-long (형용사로 뒤에 나오는 명사를 꾸며주는 역할을 할 때는 단수로 써야 한다.) cave is still in good condition. It (가주어) was so amazing to see its natural beauty (to see 이하가 진주어). Near the end of our cave tour, the guide turned off (~을 껐다) the lights in the cave for a minute. Everything became very dark, so (그래서(접속사)) we were able to focus on the sounds there. It (앞 문장의 내용을 받음.) was the most amazing experience of the tour! Our next stop was Donggang. We went rafting! It (가주어) was exciting to ride on the rough water and enjoy the view at the same time (to ride 이하가 진주어).

Incheon, A City of Firsts

Do you know where the first train station in Korea is ('의문사+주어+동사'의 어순으로 쓰인 간접의문문으로, 동사 know의 목적어)? How about (~은 어떤가) the first *Jajangmyeon*? The answer is Incheon! This place has many (대명사) of Korea's firsts. To get (목적을 나타내는 부사적 용법의 to부정사) there, we went to Incheon Station.
The Jajangmyeon Museum is next to (~ 옆에) the station. We learned about the history of *Jajangmyeon* there. Later, we walked around Jayu Park, the first Western-style park in Korea (쉼표(,)와 함께 쓰인 Jayu Park와 the first Western-style park in Korea는 동격 관계). The view from the park was awesome! It (가주어) was great to see the historical sites of this city from the park (to see 이하가 진주어).
Teacher: Wow, these places sound great (감각동사+형용사 보어)! You all (=All of you) have done a wonderful job on your presentations!

condition 상태
focus on ~에 초점을 맞추다
stop 멈춤, (잠시) 머묾
rough 파도가 심한, 거친
at the same time 동시에, 한꺼번에
Western-style 서양풍의, 서양식의
site 장소
presentation 발표, 제출

확인문제

• 다음 문장이 본문의 내용과 일치하면 T, 일치하지 않으면 F를 쓰시오.

1 Baengnyong Cave is still in good condition. ☐
2 Near the end of the cave tour, the guide turned on the lights in the cave for a minute. ☐
3 Everything became very dark, so the students couldn't focus on the sounds in the cave. ☐
4 The first train station in Korea is in Incheon. ☐
5 The Jajangmyeon Museum is next to Incheon Station. ☐
6 Jayu Park is the first Eastern-style park in Korea. ☐

Reading 교과서 확인학습 A

• 우리말을 참고하여 빈칸에 알맞은 말을 쓰시오.

1 _______ _______ _______ of the Field Trip

2 Teacher: Good morning, everyone! _______ _______ your field trips last week? _______ _______ _______ about them!

3 Busan, _______ _______

4 Do you like _______ _______?

5 _______ go to Gukje Market in Busan.

6 It is _______ _______ _______ _______ _______ _______ in Busan.

7 Do you know _______ _______ _______ _______ _______?

8 It is famous for selling _______ _______ _______ goods from different countries.

9 It was interesting to see _______ _______ _______ _______ there.

10 We also ate _______ _______ _______ street food, _______ _______ *Gimbap*, fish cake, and *Hotteok*.

11 _______ we walked to Bosu-dong Book Street.

12 Many bookstores there sell _______ _______.

13 We were _______ _______ because we found some old comic books!

14 It was nice _______ _______ in a café and read them.

15 Gangwon-do, _______ _______ _______ _______

16 There is _______ _______ _______ Gangwon-do for beautiful nature.

17 _______, we went to Baengnyong Cave.

18 This 1.8-kilometer-long cave is still _______ _______ _______.

19 It was _______ _______ to see its natural beauty.

1 수학여행에서의 가장 좋았던 순간
2 교사: 안녕하세요, 여러분! 지난 주 수학여행은 어땠나요? 얘기해 봅시다!
3 부산, 시장 천국
4 전통 시장을 좋아하세요?
5 그렇다면 부산에 있는 국제시장으로 가세요.
6 그곳은 부산에서 가장 유명한 시장 중 하나입니다.
7 그곳이 무엇으로 유명한지 아세요?
8 그 시장은 여러 나라에서 온 다양한 제품들을 파는 것으로 유명합니다.
9 그곳에서 세계 곳곳의 제품들을 모두 볼 수 있어서 흥미로웠습니다.
10 우리는 또한 김밥, 어묵 그리고 호떡과 같은 여러 종류의 길거리 음식을 먹었습니다.
11 그러고 나서 우리는 보수동 책방 거리로 걸어갔습니다.
12 그곳의 많은 서점에서는 중고 책을 팝니다.
13 우리는 몇 권의 오래된 만화책을 발견해서 정말 신이 났습니다!
14 카페에서 휴식을 취하며 그 책들을 읽는 것이 좋았습니다.
15 강원도, 자연의 아름다움으로 가득한 곳
16 아름다운 자연에 관한 한 강원도만 한 곳이 없습니다.
17 우선, 우리는 백룡동굴로 갔습니다.
18 이 1.8킬로미터 길이의 동굴은 여전히 잘 보존된 상태입니다.
19 그곳의 자연의 아름다움을 보는 것은 매우 놀라웠습니다.

20 Near the end of our cave tour, the guide ________ ________ the lights in the cave ________ ________ ________.

21 Everything became very dark, so we were able to ________ ________ the sounds there.

22 It was ________ ________ ________ ________ of the tour!

23 ________ ________ ________ was Donggang.

24 We ________ ________!

25 It was exciting to ride on the rough water and enjoy the view ________ ________ ________ ________.

26 Incheon, A City of ________

27 Do you know ________ the first train station in Korea ________ ?

28 ________ ________ the first *Jajangmyeon*?

29 ________ ________ is Incheon!

30 This place has many of ________ ________.

31 ________ ________ ________, we went to Incheon Station.

32 The Jajangmyeon Museum is ________ ________ the station.

33 We learned about ________ ________ ________ ________ there.

34 Later, we walked around Jayu Park, ________ ________ ________ ________ in Korea.

35 The view ________ the park was ________!

36 It was great to see ________ ________ ________ of this city from the park.

37 Teacher: Wow, these places ________ ________!

38 You all have done a wonderful job ________ ________ ________!

20 동굴 관광의 끝 무렵, 안내인이 동굴 안의 불을 잠시 껐습니다.

21 모든 것이 매우 어두워져서, 우리는 그곳의 소리에 집중할 수 있었습니다.

22 그것은 여행에서 가장 경이로운 경험이었습니다!

23 우리의 다음 여행지는 동강이었습니다.

24 우리는 래프팅을 하러 갔습니다!

25 급류를 타면서 동시에 경치를 즐기는 것은 흥미진진했습니다.

26 인천, '최초의 것'들의 도시

27 한국 최초의 기차역이 어디인지 아세요?

28 첫 번째 자장면은요?

29 그 답은 인천입니다!

30 이곳에는 한국의 최초의 것들이 많이 있습니다.

31 그곳으로 가기 위하여, 우리는 인천역으로 갔습니다.

32 자장면 박물관은 역 옆에 있습니다.

33 우리는 그곳에서 자장면의 역사에 대하여 배웠습니다.

34 다음에는, 한국 최초의 서구식 공원인 자유 공원을 거닐었습니다.

35 공원에서 바라본 경치는 정말 멋있었습니다!

36 공원에서 이 도시의 역사적인 장소들을 바라보는 것은 아주 좋았습니다.

37 교사: 와, 이 장소들은 멋지게 들리네요!

38 여러분 모두 발표를 훌륭하게 잘했어요!

Reading 교과서 확인학습 B

• 우리말을 참고하여 본문을 영작하시오.

1 수학여행에서의 가장 좋았던 순간
➡ ______________________________

2 교사: 안녕하세요, 여러분! 지난주 수학여행은 어땠나요? 얘기해 봅시다!
➡ ______________________________

3 부산, 시장 천국
➡ ______________________________

4 전통 시장을 좋아하세요?
➡ ______________________________

5 그렇다면 부산에 있는 국제시장으로 가세요.
➡ ______________________________

6 그곳은 부산에서 가장 유명한 시장 중 하나입니다.
➡ ______________________________

7 그곳이 무엇으로 유명한지 아세요?
➡ ______________________________

8 그 시장은 여러 나라에서 온 다양한 제품들을 파는 것으로 유명합니다.
➡ ______________________________

9 그곳에서 세계 곳곳의 제품들을 모두 볼 수 있어서 흥미로웠습니다.
➡ ______________________________

10 우리는 또한 김밥, 어묵 그리고 호떡과 같은 여러 종류의 길거리 음식을 먹었습니다
➡ ______________________________

11 그러고 나서 우리는 보수동 책방 거리로 걸어갔습니다.
➡ ______________________________

12 그곳의 많은 서점에서는 중고 책을 팝니다.
➡ ______________________________

13 우리는 몇 권의 오래된 만화책을 발견해서 정말 신이 났습니다!
➡ ______________________________

14 카페에서 휴식을 취하며 그 책들을 읽는 것이 좋았습니다.
➡ ______________________________

15 강원도, 자연의 아름다움으로 가득한 곳
➡ ______________________________

16 아름다운 자연에 관한 한 강원도만 한 곳이 없습니다.
➡ ______________________________

17 우선, 우리는 백룡동굴로 갔습니다.
➡ ______________________________

18 이 1.8킬로미터 길이의 동굴은 여전히 잘 보존된 상태입니다.
➡ ______________________________

19 그곳의 자연의 아름다움을 보는 것은 매우 놀라웠습니다.
➡ ___

20 동굴 관광의 끝 무렵, 안내인이 동굴 안의 불을 잠시 껐습니다.
➡ ___

21 모든 것이 매우 어두워져서, 우리는 그곳의 소리에 집중할 수 있었습니다.
➡ ___

22 그것은 여행에서 가장 경이로운 경험이었습니다!
➡ ___

23 우리의 다음 여행지는 동강이었습니다.
➡ ___

24 우리는 래프팅을 하러 갔습니다!
➡ ___

25 급류를 타면서 동시에 경치를 즐기는 것은 흥미진진했습니다.
➡ ___

26 인천, '최초의 것'들의 도시
➡ ___

27 한국 최초의 기차역이 어디인지 아세요?
➡ ___

28 첫 번째 자장면은요?
➡ ___

29 그 답은 인천입니다!
➡ ___

30 이곳에는 한국의 최초의 것들이 많이 있습니다.
➡ ___

31 그곳으로 가기 위하여, 우리는 인천역으로 갔습니다.
➡ ___

32 자장면 박물관은 역 옆에 있습니다.
➡ ___

33 우리는 그곳에서 자장면의 역사에 대하여 배웠습니다.
➡ ___

34 다음에는, 한국 최초의 서구식 공원인 자유 공원을 거닐었습니다.
➡ ___

35 공원에서 바라본 경치는 정말 멋있었습니다!
➡ ___

36 공원에서 이 도시의 역사적인 장소들을 바라보는 것은 아주 좋았습니다.
➡ ___

37 교사: 와, 이곳들은 멋지게 들리네요!
➡ ___

38 여러분 모두 발표를 훌륭하게 잘했어요!
➡ ___

Reading 시험대비 실력평가

[01~03] 다음 글을 읽고 물음에 답하시오.

ⓐ ________________

Do you like traditional markets? (①) It is one of the most famous markets in Busan. (②) Do you know what it is famous for? (③) It is famous for selling a variety of goods from different countries. (④) ⓑIt was interesting to see all the international goods there. (⑤) We also ate many kinds of street food, such as *Gimbap*, fish cake, and *Hotteok*. Then we walked to Bosu-dong Book Street. Many bookstores there sell used books. We were really excited because we found some old comic books! It was nice to relax in a café and read them.

01 중요 위 글의 빈칸 ⓐ에 들어갈 제목으로 알맞은 것을 고르시오.

① Busan, a Cultural City
② Busan, Market Heaven
③ How to Enjoy Street Food
④ Selling Goods at Gukje Market
⑤ Wow! Look at These Comic Books

02 중요 위 글의 흐름으로 보아, 주어진 문장이 들어가기에 가장 적절한 곳은?

Then go to Gukje Market in Busan.

① ② ③ ④ ⑤

03 위 글의 밑줄 친 ⓑIt과 문법적 쓰임이 같은 것을 모두 고르시오.

① It is time to start for the airport.
② I think it wrong to tell a lie.
③ Is it possible to solve the problem?
④ It is important to exercise every day.
⑤ It is raining too heavily to go out.

[04~07] 다음 글을 읽고 물음에 답하시오.

Incheon, A City of Firsts

Do you know where the first train station in Korea is? ⓐHow about the first *Jajangmyeon*? The answer is Incheon! ⓑ이곳에는 한국의 최초의 것들이 많이 있습니다. To get there, we went to Incheon Station. The Jajangmyeon Museum is next to the station. We learned about the history of *Jajangmyeon* ⓒthere. Later, we walked around Jayu Park, the first Western-style park in Korea. The view from the park was awesome! It was great ⓓto see the historical sites of this city from the park.

04 서답형 위 글의 밑줄 친 ⓐHow about과 바꿔 쓸 수 있는 말을 쓰시오.

➡ ________________

05 서답형 위 글의 밑줄 친 ⓑ의 우리말에 맞게 주어진 어휘를 이용하여 7 단어로 영작하시오.

has, of, firsts

➡ ________________

06 서답형 위 글의 밑줄 친 ⓒthere가 가리키는 것을 영어로 쓰시오. (4 단어)

➡ ________________

07 위 글의 밑줄 친 ⓓto see와 to부정사의 용법이 같은 것을 고르시오. (2개)

① I am sorry to hear the news.
② To get up early is good for your health.
③ She has many friends to play with.
④ I found it easy to do so.
⑤ I go to school to learn many things.

[08~10] 다음 글을 읽고 물음에 답하시오.

Busan, Market Heaven

Do you like ①traditional markets? Then go to Gukje Market in Busan. It is one of the most famous markets in Busan. Do you know what it is famous for? It is famous for ⓐselling a variety of ②good from different countries. It was interesting to see all the ③international goods ⓑthere. We also ate many ④kinds of street food, ⑤such as *Gimbap*, fish cake, and *Hotteok*. Then we walked to Bosu-dong Book Street. Many bookstores ⓒthere sell used books. We were really excited because we found some old comic books! It was nice to relax in a café and read them.

서답형

08 위 글의 밑줄 친 ①~⑤에서 문맥상 낱말의 쓰임이 적절하지 않은 것을 찾아 알맞게 고치시오.

➡ ______________________

09 위 글의 밑줄 친 ⓐselling과 문법적 쓰임이 다른 것을 모두 고르시오.

① Do you know the woman selling *Hotteok* on the street?

② She gave up selling her used books on Bosu-dong Book Street.

③ He is proud of selling his products to different countries.

④ She is selling the popular street food at Gukje Market.

⑤ I want to visit Gukje Market selling various imported things.

서답형

10 다음 빈칸에 위 글의 밑줄 친 ⓑ와 ⓒ의 there가 가리키는 것을 각각 쓰시오.

➡ ⓑ at __________ ⓒ on __________

[11~13] 다음 글을 읽고 물음에 답하시오.

Gangwon-do, Full of Natural Beauty

There is no place like Gangwon-do for ⓐ_____. First, we went to Baengnyong Cave. This 1.8-kilometer-long cave is still in good condition. It was so amazing to see its natural beauty. Near the end of our cave tour, the guide turned off the lights in the cave for a minute. Everything became very dark, so we were able to focus on the sounds there. It was the most amazing experience of the tour! Our next stop was Donggang. We went rafting! It was exciting to ride on the rough water and enjoy the view at the same time.

11 위 글의 빈칸 ⓐ에 들어갈 알맞은 말을 고르시오.

① delicious food

② various historic sites

③ beautiful nature

④ artificial structures

⑤ traditional performances

서답형

12 주어진 영영풀이에 해당하는 단어를 본문에서 찾아 쓰시오.

a brief stay in the course of a journey

➡ ______________

중요

13 위 글을 읽고 대답할 수 없는 질문은?

① Where did the students go first in Gangwon-do?

② How long is the Baengnyong Cave?

③ What did the guide do near the end of the cave tour?

④ Where did the students go after they went to Baengnyong Cave?

⑤ How far is it from Baengnyong Cave to Donggang?

[14~17] 다음 글을 읽고 물음에 답하시오.

Gangwon-do, Full of (A)[Artificial / Natural] Beauty

There is no place like Gangwon-do for beautiful nature. First, we went to Baengnyong Cave. This 1.8-kilometer-long cave is still in good condition. ⓐIt was so amazing to see its natural beauty. Near the end of our cave tour, the guide turned (B)[on / off] the lights in the cave for a minute. Everything became very dark, so we were able to focus on the sounds there. ⓑIt was the most amazing experience of the tour! Our next stop was Donggang. We went rafting! It was exciting to ride on the (C)[rough / tough] water and enjoy the view at the same time.

서답형

14 위 글의 괄호 (A)~(C)에서 문맥상 알맞은 낱말을 골라 쓰시오.

➡ (A)________ (B)________ (C)________

15 위 글의 밑줄 친 ⓐ 대신 쓸 수 있는 문장을 모두 고르시오.

① It was not too amazing to see its natural beauty.
② To see its natural beauty was so amazing.
③ That was amazing enough to see its natural beauty.
④ Seeing its natural beauty was so amazing.
⑤ That was so amazing to see its natural beauty.

중요

16 위 글의 마지막 부분에서 알 수 있는 학생들의 심경으로 가장 알맞은 것을 고르시오.

① satisfied
② surprised
③ bored
④ disappointed
⑤ upset

서답형

17 위 글의 밑줄 친 ⓑ가 가리키는 것을 본문에서 찾아 쓰시오.

➡ ____________________
____
____
____

[18~20] 다음 글을 읽고 물음에 답하시오.

Incheon, A City of Firsts

Do you know where the first train station in Korea is? How about the first *Jajangmyeon*? The answer is Incheon! This place has many of Korea's ___ⓐ___. To get there, we went to Incheon Station. The Jajangmyeon Museum is next to the station. We learned about the history of *Jajangmyeon* there. Later, we walked around Jayu Park, the first Western-style park in Korea. The view from the park was awesome! It was great ⓑto see the historical sites of this city from the park.

중요

18 위 글의 빈칸 ⓐ에 들어갈 알맞은 말을 고르시오.

① surprises
② firsts
③ resources
④ inventions
⑤ traditions

서답형
19 What did the students learn from the Jajangmyeon Museum? Answer in English in a full sentence.

➡ ______________________________

서답형
20 본문의 내용과 일치하도록 다음 빈칸 (A)~(C)에 알맞은 단어를 쓰시오.

> The students went to places which are related to Korea's firsts such as (A)________ ________, (B)________ ________ ________, and (C)________ ________.

[21~23] 다음 글을 읽고 물음에 답하시오.

> Teacher: Good morning, everyone! How were your field trips last week? Please tell us about ⓐthem!
>
> **Busan, Market Heaven**
>
> Do you like traditional markets? Then go to Gukje Market in Busan. It is one of the most famous markets in Busan. Do you know what it is famous for? It is famous for selling a variety of goods from different countries. It was interesting to see all the international goods there. We also ate many kinds of street food, ⓑsuch as *Gimbap*, fish cake, and *Hotteok*. Then we walked to Bosu-dong Book Street. Many bookstores there sell used books. We were really excited because we found some old comic books! It was nice to relax in a café and read ⓒthem.

서답형
21 위 글의 밑줄 친 ⓐ와 ⓒ의 them이 가리키는 것을 본문에서 찾아 각각 쓰시오.

➡ ⓐ ______________________________

ⓒ ______________________________

서답형
22 위 글의 밑줄 친 ⓑsuch as와 바꿔 쓸 수 있는 한 단어를 쓰시오.

➡ ______________________

중요
23 위 글의 국제시장에 대한 내용과 일치하지 않는 것은?

① 부산에 있는 전통 시장이다.
② 부산에서 가장 유명한 시장 중 하나이다.
③ 여러 나라에서 온 다양한 제품들을 파는 것으로 유명하다.
④ 그곳에서 세계 곳곳의 상품들을 모두 볼 수 있다.
⑤ 그곳의 많은 서점에서는 중고 책을 판다.

[24~26] 다음 글을 읽고 물음에 답하시오.

> I live in Hang-dong, Seoul. There is an old railway. ⓐIt is no longer used. You can walk there and ___ⓑ___ pictures of beautiful scenery.

서답형
24 위 글의 밑줄 친 ⓐ를 능동태로 고치시오.

➡ ______________________________

25 위 글의 밑줄 친 ⓐ와 바꿔 쓸 수 없는 문장을 모두 고르시오.

① It is no more used.
② It is not used any longer.
③ It is not used no longer.
④ It is not used any more.
⑤ It is not used no more.

중요
26 위 글의 빈칸 ⓑ에 알맞은 것은?

① get
② take
③ let
④ bring
⑤ carry

[01~03] 다음 글을 읽고 물음에 답하시오.

Busan, Market Heaven

Do you like traditional markets? ⓐThen go to Gukje Market in Busan. ⓑ그곳은 부산에서 가장 유명한 시장 중 하나입니다. Do you know what it is famous for? It is famous for selling a variety of goods from different countries. It was (A)[interesting / interested] to see all the international goods there. We also ate many kinds of street food, such as *Gimbap*, fish cake, and *Hotteok*. Then we walked to Bosu-dong Book Street. Many bookstores there sell (B)[using / used] books. We were really (C)[exciting / excited] because we found some old comic books! It was nice to relax in a café and read them.

중요
01 위 글의 밑줄 친 ⓐThen을 If를 사용하여 고치시오.

➡ ________________

02 위 글의 밑줄 친 ⓑ의 우리말에 맞게 주어진 어휘를 이용하여 10 단어로 영작하시오.

famous, in Busan

➡ ________________

중요
03 위 글의 괄호 (A)~(C)에서 어법상 알맞은 낱말을 골라 쓰시오.

➡ (A) ________ (B) ________ (C) ________

[04~07] 다음 글을 읽고 물음에 답하시오.

Incheon, A City of Firsts

Do you know where the first train station in Korea is? ⓐHow about the first *Jajangmyeon*? The answer is Incheon! ⓑThis place has many of Korea's firsts. To get there, we went to Incheon Station. The Jajangmyeon Museum is next to the station. We learned about the history of *Jajangmyeon* there. Later, we walked around Jayu Park, the first Western-style park in Korea. The view from the park was awesome! It was great to see the historical sites of this city from the park.

04 위 글의 밑줄 친 ⓐ를 다음과 같이 바꿔 쓸 때 빈칸에 들어갈 알맞은 말을 쓰시오.

➡ Do you know ________ the first *Jajangmyeon* in Korea was introduced?

중요
05 위 글의 밑줄 친 ⓑ를 There로 시작하여 고치시오.

➡ ________________

06 위 글의 밑줄 친 문장 ⓑ의 many of Korea's firsts의 예를 본문에서 찾아 우리말로 쓰시오. (세 가지)

➡ (1) ________________
(2) ________________
(3) ________________

고난이도
07 What can you see from Jayu Park? Answer in English in a full sentence.

➡ ________________
____

[08~10] 다음 글을 읽고 물음에 답하시오.

Busan, Market Heaven

Do you like traditional markets? Then go to Gukje Market in Busan. It is one of the most famous markets in Busan. Do you know what it is famous for? It is famous for selling a variety of goods from different countries. It was interesting to see all the international goods there. We also ate many kinds of street food, such as *Gimbap*, fish cake, and *Hotteok*. Then we walked to Bosu-dong Book Street. Many bookstores there sell used books. We were really excited because we found some old comic books! It was nice to relax in a café and read them.

08 다음 문장에서 위 글의 내용과 다른 부분을 찾아서 고치시오.

• Gukje Market is the most famous market in Busan.

➡ ____________________

09 중요 위 글을 읽고 학생들이 국제시장에서 한 일을 우리말로 쓰시오. (두 가지)

➡ (1) ____________________

(2) ____________________

10 다음 빈칸에 알맞은 단어를 넣어 보수동 책방에 대한 소개를 완성하시오.

Many bookstores on Bosu-dong Book Street are famous for selling ________ ________.

[11~14] 다음 글을 읽고 물음에 답하시오.

Gangwon-do, Full of Natural Beauty

ⓐThere is no place like Gangwon-do for beautiful nature. First, we went to Baengnyong Cave. This 1.8-kilometer-long cave is still in good condition. It was so amazing to see its natural beauty. Near the end of our cave tour, the guide turned off the lights in the cave for a minute. Everything became very dark, so we were able to focus on the sounds there. It was the most amazing experience of the tour! Our next stop was Donggang. We went __ⓑ__ ! ⓒ급류를 타면서 동시에 경치를 즐기는 것은 흥미진진했습니다.

11 위 글의 밑줄 친 ⓐ를 다음과 같이 바꿔 쓸 때 빈칸에 들어갈 알맞은 말을 쓰시오.

➡ Gangwon-do is the ________ place for beautiful nature.

12 위 글의 빈칸 ⓑ에 raft를 알맞은 형태로 쓰시오.

➡ ____________________

13 고난이도 위 글의 밑줄 친 ⓒ의 우리말에 맞게 한 단어를 보충하여, 주어진 어휘를 알맞게 배열하시오.

the view / to ride / at the same time / it / and / was / enjoy / exciting / the rough water

➡ ____________________

14 중요 본문의 내용과 일치하도록 다음 빈칸 (A)와 (B)에 들어갈 알맞은 단어를 본문에서 찾아 쓰시오.

When the guide turned off the lights, everything became so dark that the students couldn't (A)________ the natural beauty of the cave, and it was possible for them to focus only on (B)________ ________ there.

교과서

구석구석

After You Read D

I live in Hang-dong, Seoul. There is an old railway. It is no longer used. You can walk there and take pictures of beautiful scenery.

live in: ~에서 살다 / There is 단수명사: ~가 있다 / no longer: 더 이상 ~하지 않는 / take pictures: 사진을 찍다

구문해설 • scenery: 풍경, 경치

해석

나는 서울의 항동에 산다. 거기에는 오래된 철도가 있다. 이것은 더 이상 사용되지 않는다. 너는 그 철길을 걸을 수 있고 예쁜 풍경 사진을 찍을 수도 있다.

Think & Write Step 3

Autumn Walk in Naejangsan

Last autumn, I went to Naejangsan with my family. I rode a cable car to the middle of the mountain. Then, I hiked to the top. At the top, I saw beautiful autumn scenery. I took many pictures. It was amazing and exciting to see beautiful autumn leaves.

Last: 지난 / rode: ride의 과거 / Then: 그러고 나서 / to the top: 정상까지 / scenery: 경치 / It: 가주어 / to see beautiful autumn leaves: 진주어(명사적 용법)

구문해설 • cable car: 케이블 카 • hike: 하이킹[도보 여행]을 가다 • amazing: 놀라운
• exciting: 흥미진진한

내장산에서의 가을 산행
지난 가을, 나는 가족과 함께 내장산에 갔다. 나는 산의 중간까지 케이블 카를 타고 갔다. 그러고 나서, 나는 정상까지 하이킹을 갔다. 정상에서, 나는 아름다운 가을 경치를 보았다. 나는 많은 사진을 찍었다. 아름다운 가을 나뭇잎을 보는 것은 놀랍고 흥미진진했다.

Culture Link

Eco Trip
Some people take trips in nature without hurting the environment. They think it is important to protect nature.

hurting: 전치사의 목적어로 동명사 / it: 가주어 / to protect: 진주어

Volunteer Trip
Some people go on trips for special purposes. They travel to do volunteer work. They help local communities or wild animals during their trips.

to do: 부정사의 부사적 용법(목적) / during: 전치사: 뒤에 명사구가 나옴

History Trip
On this trip, people visit historical sites and learn about history.

During this trip, people can understand the lives of people in the past.

lives: 생활, 삶(명사) / in the past: 과거의(형용사구)

구문해설 • take trips: 여행 가다 • go on trips: 여행 가다 • purpose: 목적 • community: 지역[공동] 사회
• historical: 역사(상)의, 역사적인 cf. historic: 역사적으로 유명한 • site: 유적

생태 여행
몇몇 사람들은 자연 속에서 환경을 해치지 않고 여행을 합니다. 그들은 자연을 보호하는 것이 중요하다고 생각합니다.

자원봉사 여행
몇몇 사람들은 특별한 목적을 위해 여행을 갑니다. 그들은 자원봉사를 하기 위해 여행합니다. 그들은 그들의 여행 중에 지역 사회와 야생 동물들을 돕습니다.

역사 여행
이 여행에서 사람들은 역사적인 유적들을 방문하고 역사에 대해 배웁니다. 이 여행 동안 사람들은 과거의 사람들의 삶을 이해할 수 있습니다.

영역별 핵심문제

Words & Expressions

01 다음 밑줄 친 단어 중 뜻이 다른 하나를 고르시오.

① You have to get there as soon as possible.
② I will write to you as soon as I get to Canada.
③ You can get the information from the library.
④ If you take a taxi, you can get there in 10 minutes.
⑤ We're never going to get to school on time.

02 다음 빈칸에 알맞은 말을 고르시오.

> Before the presentation, Jobs felt nervous but, __________, excited.

① at one time　② all at once
③ at once　④ at the same time
⑤ at a time

03 다음 빈칸에 공통으로 들어갈 말을 쓰시오.

> • Do you ______ any plans?
> • Nancy, ______ a good trip!

➡ ____________________

04 다음 〈보기〉의 단어를 사용하여 자연스러운 문장을 만들 수 없는 것은? (형태 변화 가능)

보기

> awesome / natural / rough / Western-style

① The mountain road was ________.
② The food chain is a ________ system.
③ Bread is a key element in a ________ breakfast.
④ How many ________ languages can you speak?
⑤ This school is ________ and I like my classmates, too.

Conversation

[05~06] 다음 대화의 빈칸에 알맞은 말을 고르시오.

05

> A: How do you get to school?
> B: I go to school by bus.
> A: ____________________
> B: It takes 15 minutes.

① What do you take to your school?
② When does your school end?
③ What time do you go to school?
④ How long does it take to get there?
⑤ What do you do after school?

06

> A: What are you planning to do this weekend?
> B: ____________________

① I had a wonderful time at the beach.
② I'm going to stay at home and get some rest.
③ It wasn't my plan to meet Peter.
④ I'm going to the library to read books now.
⑤ I have been to Jeju-do three times.

[07~10] 다음 대화를 읽고 물음에 답하시오.

G: What are you (A)planning to do this weekend?
B: (①) I'm (B)planning to go to a baseball game in Daegu.
G: Are you going to see the All-Star Game?
B: Yes. (②) It will be fun. Also, I'm planning to visit my friend there. (③)
G: Nice. How long does it take to get there?
B: 고속 열차로 1시간 40분이 걸려. (④)
G: (⑤) I hope you have a good trip!
B: Thank you.

07 위 대화의 ①~⑤ 중 주어진 문장이 들어갈 알맞은 곳은?

Wow, it's much faster than I thought.

① ② ③ ④ ⑤

08 (A)와 (B)의 밑줄 친 planning을 대신하여 바꿔 쓸 수 있는 말을 쓰시오.

➡ ______________________

09 주어진 단어를 이용하여 밑줄 친 우리말을 영작하시오.

➡ __________________________________
(express train)

10 다음 중 위 대화의 내용과 일치하지 않는 것을 고르시오.

① The boy's friend is in Daegu.
② The boy is going to visit his friend this weekend.
③ The All-Star Game is a baseball game.
④ Thy boy is planning to go to Daegu.
⑤ Thy boy is planning to see the All-Star Game with his friend.

[11~12] 다음 대화를 읽고 물음에 답하시오.

B: We have a long holiday this month. Do you have any plans?
G: I'm going to visit my grandparents in Jeonju.
B: Oh, really? That's nice. What are you planning to do with them?
G: I'm planning to go to Hanok Village with them. How about you? What are your plans for the holiday?
B: I'm going to stay home and relax.
G: That's also a good idea!

11 다음 영영풀이에 해당하는 단어를 위 대화에서 찾아 쓰시오.

not to do anything

➡ ______________________

12 다음 중 위 대화를 읽고 답할 수 없는 질문을 고르시오.

① What are they talking about?
② Where do the girl's grandparents live?
③ How long is the holiday?
④ Where is the girl planning to go with her grandparents?
⑤ What is the boy's plan for the holiday?

Grammar

13 다음 문장을 주어진 말로 시작하여 다시 쓰시오.

You should pay attention to your teacher in class.

➡ It is necessary ______________________
______________________.

14 다음 중 어법상 바르지 <u>않은</u> 것은?

① It is safe to say that Anna has always loved designing.
② It was exciting to sing in front of many people.
③ She wants to know who the winner is.
④ The woman is asking him where the best restaurant is around here.
⑤ I don't konw if or not Ann's Korean is perfect.

15 다음 밑줄 친 It[it]의 쓰임이 나머지와 <u>다른</u> 하나를 고르시오.

① <u>It</u> is true that the pen is mightier than the sword.
② <u>It</u> is interesting for me to study the habits of birds.
③ <u>It</u> is lucky to have a good friend like Amy.
④ <u>It</u> was Harry Potter that defeated Voltmore.
⑤ <u>It</u> is not good to stay in the house for a long time.

16 다음 우리말을 영어로 바르게 옮긴 것은?

내게 길을 안내해 주다니 Amanda는 참 착했다.

① It was kind to show me the way for Amanda.
② It was kind Amanda to show me the way.
③ It was kind to show me the way of Amanda.
④ It was kind for Amanda to show me the way.
⑤ It was kind of Amanda to show me the way.

17 다음 문장을 두 문장으로 나누어 쓰시오.

(1) Nobody knows why Lauren left the office early.
➡ ______________________________

(2) It is difficult to understand what the teacher says.
➡ ______________________________

(3) Steve didn't tell me when the movie began.
➡ ______________________________

(4) What do you think the most typical Korean dish is?
➡ ______________________________

(5) Mariel wants to know whether Kate is going to meet Asako.
➡ ______________________________

(6) They wonder if they can borrow a few books today.
➡ ______________________________

18 다음을 간접의문문을 이용하여 한 문장으로 쓰시오.

(1) • I'll tell you.
• Where has he been since last Monday?
➡ ______________________________

(2) • I'd like to know.
• Did you meet her?
➡ ______________________________

(3) • Do you think?
• Where can I find some fruit?
➡ ______________________________

19 괄호 안에 주어진 어휘를 이용하여 다음 우리말을 영작하시오.

(1) 심장이 오른쪽에 있는 것은 비정상적이다. (the heart, abnormal, have, it, to, on)

➡ ______________________

(2) 물고기를 맨손으로 잡는 것은 어렵다. (with your bare hands, grab, hard, it, to)

➡ ______________________

(3) 나는 그 소녀가 어디에 사는지 모른다. (the girl, live)

➡ ______________________

(4) 다음 기차가 언제 오는지 말해 줄 수 있습니까? (could, the next train)

➡ ______________________

Reading

[20~21] 다음 글을 읽고 물음에 답하시오.

Busan, Market Heaven

Do you like traditional markets? Then go to Gukje Market in Busan. ⓐIt is one of the most famous markets in Busan. Do you know what ⓑit is famous for? ⓒIt is famous for selling a variety of goods from different countries. ⓓIt was interesting to see all the international goods there. We also ate many kinds of street food, such as *Gimbap*, fish cake, and *Hotteok*. ⒶThen we walked to Bosu-dong Book Street. Many bookstores there sell used books. We were really excited because we found some old comic books! ⓔIt was nice to relax in a café and read them.

20 위 글의 밑줄 친 ⓐ~ⓔ 중 가리키는 대상이 같은 것끼리 짝지어진 것은?

① ⓐ – ⓑ
② ⓑ – ⓓ
③ ⓒ – ⓓ
④ ⓒ – ⓔ
⑤ ⓓ – ⓔ

21 위 글의 밑줄 친 ⒶThen을 After를 사용하여 고치시오.

➡ ______________________

____

[22~24] 다음 글을 읽고 물음에 답하시오.

Gangwon-do, Full of Natural Beauty

There is no place like Gangwon-do ___ⓐ___ beautiful nature. First, we went to Baengnyong Cave. (①) This 1.8-kilometer-long cave is still ___ⓑ___ good condition. (②) It was so amazing to see its natural beauty. (③) Near the end of our cave tour, the guide turned off the lights in the cave for a minute. (④) It was the most amazing experience of the tour! (⑤) Our next stop was Donggang. We went rafting! It was exciting to ride on the rough water and enjoy the view at the same time.

22 위 글의 흐름으로 보아, 주어진 문장이 들어가기에 가장 적절한 곳은?

> Everything became very dark, so we were able to focus on the sounds there.

① ② ③ ④ ⑤

23 위 글의 빈칸 ⓐ와 ⓑ에 들어갈 전치사가 바르게 짝지어진 것은?

① on – at
② for – in
③ to – in
④ for – at
⑤ on – to

24 위 글의 내용과 일치하지 않는 것은?

① 먼저, 학생들은 백룡동굴로 갔다.
② 백룡동굴의 길이는 1.8킬로미터이다.
③ 백룡동굴 안은 많이 훼손되어 있었다.
④ 학생들은 동강에 래프팅을 하러 갔다.
⑤ 급류를 타면서 동시에 경치를 즐기는 것은 흥미진진했다.

[25~27] 다음 글을 읽고 물음에 답하시오.

Incheon, A City of Firsts

Do you know where the first train station in Korea is? How about the first *Jajangmyeon*? The answer is Incheon! This place has many of Korea's firsts. ⓐTo get there, we went to Incheon Station. The Jajangmyeon Museum is next to the station. We learned about the history of *Jajangmyeon* there. (A)[Later / Latter], we walked around Jayu Park, the first Western-style park in Korea. The view from the park was (B)[awful / awesome]! It was great to see the historical sites of this city from the park.

Teacher: Wow, these places sound great! You all have done a wonderful job on your (C) [preparations / presentations]!

25 위 글의 괄호 (A)~(C)에서 문맥상 알맞은 낱말을 골라 쓰시오.

➡ (A)________ (B)________ (C)________

26 위 글의 밑줄 친 ⓐ와 바꿔 쓸 수 없는 문장을 고르시오.

① We went to Incheon Station in order to get there.
② We went to Incheon Station so that we could get there.
③ We went to Incheon Station in order that we might get there.
④ We went to Incheon Station so as that we might get there.
⑤ We went to Incheon Station so as to get there.

27 위 글을 읽고 대답할 수 없는 질문은?

① Where is the first train station in Korea?
② Who made the first *Jajangmyeon* in Korea?
③ Where did the students learn about the history of *Jajangmyeon*?
④ What is the first Western-style park in Korea?
⑤ How was the view from the park?

[28~29] 다음 글을 읽고 물음에 답하시오.

Autumn Walk in Naejangsan

Last autumn, I went to Naejangsan with my family. I rode a cable car to the middle of the mountain. Then, I hiked to the top. At the top, I saw beautiful autumn scenery. I took many pictures. ⓐIt was amazing and exciting to see beautiful autumn leaves.

28 글쓴이가 내장산의 정상에 도달한 방법을 우리말로 쓰시오.

➡ ________________________________

29 위 글의 밑줄 친 ⓐ를 다음과 같이 바꿔 쓸 때 빈칸에 들어갈 알맞은 말을 쓰시오.

➡ I was ________ and ________ to see beautiful autumn leaves.

단원별 예상문제

출제율 90%

01 다음 짝지어진 두 단어의 관계가 같도록 주어진 철자로 시작하여 빈칸에 알맞은 단어를 쓰시오.

amazing : incredible – c________ : state

[02~03] 밑줄 친 단어와 바꿔 쓸 수 있는 단어를 쓰시오.

출제율 90%

02

I'm not sure if I can do it.

➡ ____________________ (3 단어)

출제율 95%

03

The beach is only five minutes away by walking.

➡ ____________________

출제율 100%

04 다음 빈칸에 공통으로 들어갈 말로 알맞은 것을 쓰시오.

- It will ________ a long time to download data to my computer.
- Did you hear that we're going to ________ a field trip?

출제율 85%

05 주어진 문장 이후에 올 대화의 순서가 올바르게 배열된 것을 고르시오.

We have a long holiday this month. Do you have any plans?

(A) That's also a good idea!
(B) Oh, really? That's nice. What are you planning to do with them?
(C) I'm going to visit my grandparents in Jeonju.
(D) I'm planning to go to Hanok Village with them. How about you? What are your plans for the holiday?
(E) I'm going to stay home and relax.`

① (B) – (A) – (C) – (D) – (E)
② (B) – (C) – (D) – (A) – (E)
③ (C) – (A) – (B) – (E) – (D)
④ (C) – (B) – (D) – (E) – (A)
⑤ (C) – (B) – (E) – (A) – (D)

[06~09] 다음 대화를 읽고 물음에 답하시오.

B: Wow, these pictures are so beautiful. Where did you take them?
G: At Riverside Park. There were lots ⓐ______ flowers. You should go there!
B: I want to. How do I get there ⓑ______ our school?
G: Get on bus number 135 and get ⓒ______ at the Riverside Stadium (A)stop. You can see the park ⓓ______ front ⓔ______ the bus stop.
B: (B)거기까지 가는 데 얼마나 걸려?
G: It takes 30 minutes.
B: Thanks. I'll go there next weekend.

출제율 90%

06 다음 영영풀이에 해당하는 단어를 위 대화에서 찾아 쓰시오.

a large sports field

➡ ____________________

출제율 100%

07 빈칸 ⓐ~ⓔ에 알맞은 말을 〈보기〉에서 골라 쓰시오.

보기
from in of off

➡ ⓐ ________, ⓑ ________, ⓒ ________,
ⓓ ________, ⓔ ________

출제율 95%

08 밑줄 친 (A)stop과 다른 의미로 쓰인 문장을 모두 고르시오.

① He decided to stop using it.
② I get off at the next stop.
③ Is there a bus stop near the hotel?
④ Drop me at the next stop, please.
⑤ This elevator only stops at the fifth floor and above.

출제율 90%

09 밑줄 친 (B)의 우리말을 주어진 말을 이용하여 영작하시오. (long, get)

➡ ______________________________

[10~12] 다음 대화를 읽고 물음에 답하시오.

B: Excuse me. ①How do I get from Hanguk University to here?
W: You can go there (A)_____ bus or (B)_____ foot.
B: ②How long does it take to get there?
W: It takes five minutes (A)_____ bus and 20 minutes (B)_____ foot.
B: ③Oh, then I will walk there. ④Can you tell me how to get there?
W: ⑤Go straight for two blocks, and then turn left. You will see Hanguk University on your right.
B: Go straight for two blocks and turn left. Thank you!

출제율 95%

10 위 대화의 ①~⑤ 중에서 문맥상 어색한 부분을 고르시오.

① ② ③ ④ ⑤

출제율 90%

11 빈칸 (A)와 (B)에 적절한 것을 쓰시오.

➡ (A) __________, (B) __________

출제율 100%

12 위 대화의 내용과 일치하지 않는 것을 고르시오.

① The boy wants to go to Hanguk University.
② The boy is going to walk to Hanguk University.
③ The woman knows how to get to Hanguk University.
④ When you go to Hanguk University from here, walking is more faster than taking a bus.
⑤ It takes twenty minutes by walking to get to Hanguk University.

출제율 95%

13 다음 중 어법상 옳은 것은?

① It is fun to speaking in front of people.
② It is difficult say which way the wind is blowing.
③ It was great for seeing the historical sites of this city from the park.
④ It was scary to play the game on the big rock.
⑤ It is important make plans in advance.

출제율 90%

14 다음을 간접의문문을 이용하여 한 문장으로 쓰시오.

(1) Do you know? Who is that tall guy over there?
➡ ______________________________
(2) Tell me. Who made this chocolate cake?
➡ ______________________________
(3) I wonder. Did Marianne get married?
➡ ______________________________
(4) Do you think? Where is Snow White?
➡ ______________________________

출제율 95%

15 다음 그림을 보고 주어진 어휘를 이용하여 자신의 생각을 쓰시오.

(for him, do dunk shot, to)

➡ ____________________

출제율 100%

16 다음 밑줄 친 부분의 쓰임이 어색한 것은?

① Do you know why leaves turn red in autumn?
② Luke's mother knew where he kept the comic books.
③ I wonder what there's an easy way to improve my grade.
④ Do you know how many books your brother has?
⑤ I asked her when she had left her home country.

[17~19] 다음 글을 읽고 물음에 답하시오.

Teacher: Good morning, everyone! ⓐHow was your field trips last week? Please tell us about them!

Busan, Market Heaven

Do you like traditional markets? Then go to Gukje Market in Busan. It is one of the most famous markets in Busan. Do you know what it is famous for? It is famous for selling a variety of goods from different countries. It was interesting to see all the international goods there. We also ate many kinds of street food, such as *Gimbap*, fish cake, and *Hotteok*. Then we walked to Bosu-dong Book Street. Many bookstores there sell used books. We were really excited because we found some old comic books! It was nice ⓑto relax in a café and read them.

출제율 90%

17 위 글의 밑줄 친 ⓐ에서 어법상 틀린 부분을 찾아 고치시오.

➡ ____________________

출제율 95%

18 아래 <보기>에서 위 글의 밑줄 친 ⓑto relax와 to부정사의 용법이 다른 것의 개수를 고르시오.

보기
① They promised to meet in front of the museum at 5.
② I have nothing to write with.
③ She must be a fool to believe such a thing.
④ I wanted to go to so Spain.
⑤ This book was too difficult to read.

① 1개 ② 2개 ③ 3개 ④ 4개 ⑤ 5개

출제율 100%

19 위 글을 읽고 대답할 수 없는 질문은?

① When did the students go on field trips?
② What was interesting about Gukje Market?
③ What street food did the students eat at Gukje Market?
④ How long did it take to go to Bosu-dong Book Street from Gukje Market?
⑤ What do the bookstores on Bosu-dong Book Street sell?

[20~22] 다음 글을 읽고 물음에 답하시오.

Gangwon-do, Full of Natural Beauty

There is no place ⓐlike Gangwon-do for beautiful nature. First, we went to Baengnyong Cave. This (A)[1.8-kilometer-long / 1.8-kilometes-long] cave is still in good condition. It was so amazing to see its natural beauty. Near the end of our cave tour, the guide turned off the lights in the cave for a minute. Everything became very dark, so we were able to focus on the sounds there. It was the most amazing experience of the tour! Our next stop was Donggang. We went (B)[to raft / rafting]! It was exciting to ride on the rough water and enjoy the view (C)[at the same time / one by one].

출제율 95%

20 위 글의 밑줄 친 ⓐlike와 같은 의미로 쓰인 것을 고르시오.

① She's wearing a dress like mine.
② How did you like the book?
③ There are many things of like shape.
④ I like my coffee strong.
⑤ He responded in like manner.

출제율 90%

21 위 글의 괄호 (A)~(C)에서 문맥이나 어법상 알맞은 낱말을 골라 쓰시오.

➡ (A) ________
(B) ________
(C) ________

출제율 90%

22 Why did the guide turn off the lights in the cave for a minute near the end of the cave tour? Fill in the blanks with the suitable words.

➡ Because he[she] wanted to make everything become ________ ________ so that the students could ________ ________ the sounds in the cave.

[23~24] 다음 글을 읽고 물음에 답하시오.

A Perfect Day in Anmyeon-do

Last summer, I went to Anmyeon-do with my family. I swam in the sea with my brothers. Then we caught some crabs on the beach. ⓐ It was awful and fantastic to see the beautiful sunset there.

출제율 90%

23 글쓴이가 지난 여름 안면도에서 한 일을 우리말로 쓰시오. (세 가지)

➡ (1) ________________
(2) ________________
(3) ________________

출제율 90%

24 위 글의 밑줄 친 ⓐ에서 흐름상 어색한 부분을 찾아 고치시오.

➡ ________________

서술형 실전문제

[01~02] 다음 대화를 읽고 물음에 답하시오.

A: (A)Where will you go?
B: I will go to Sydney.
A: How long does it take to get there?
B: (B)________________(10시간 반)
A: What are you planning to do there?
B: I'm planning to go surfing.

중요
01 밑줄 친 (A)와 의미가 같도록 주어진 단어를 이용해서 영작하시오.

➡ ______________________________ (plan)
______________________________ (go)
______________________________ (think)

02 주어진 정보를 이용해 빈칸 (B)에 알맞은 말을 쓰시오.

➡ ______________________________

[03~04] 다음 대화를 읽고 물음에 답하시오.

A: (A)(going, your, where, you, trip, are, for)?
B: I'm going to Seoul.
A: What are you planning to do there?
B: (B)______________________________
A: That sounds great!

03 괄호 안에 주어진 단어를 알맞게 배열하시오.

➡ ______________________________

04 주어진 영영풀이의 단어의 복수형을 이용해 빈칸 (B)를 채우시오.

a building where historical or artistic objects are displayed

➡ ______________________________

05 두 문장이 같은 뜻이 되도록 to부정사를 이용하여 문장을 완성하시오.

(1) My grandma has difficulty remembering names.
→ It is difficult ________________.
(2) Studying English is boring for most of students.
→ It is boring ________________.

중요
06 주어진 두 문장을 한 문장으로 연결하시오.

(1) It is doubtful.
+ Does Anna love me?
➡ ______________________________
(2) I'm not sure.
+ Why was Kate so surprised?
➡ ______________________________
(3) Cathy knows.
Who broke the window yesterday?
➡ ______________________________
(4) Can you imagine?
Which book did Jennifer buy?
➡ ______________________________

07 중요 다음 문장에서 어법상 어색한 것을 찾아 바르게 고치시오.

(1) It is necessary for John takes another science class.

_______________ ➡ _______________

(2) That was amazing and exciting to see beautiful autumn leaves!

_______________ ➡ _______________

(3) Write an interesting storybook is my dream.

_______________ ➡ _______________

(4) Do you know when does the show start?

_______________ ➡ _______________

(5) Please let me know if does the bag have some pockets.

_______________ ➡ _______________

(6) Do you think who runs fastest?

_______________ ➡ _______________

[08~10] 다음 글을 읽고 물음에 답하시오.

Teacher: Good morning, everyone! (A)[How / What] were your field trips last week? Please tell us about them!

Busan, Market Heaven

Do you like traditional markets? Then go to Gukje Market in Busan. It is one of the most famous (B)[market / markets] in Busan. Do you know what it is famous for? It is famous for selling a variety of goods from different countries. ⓐIt was interesting to see all the international goods there. We also ate many kinds of street food, such as *Gimbap*, fish cake, and *Hotteok*. Then we walked to Bosu-dong Book Street. Many bookstores there sell used books. We were really excited because we (C)[found / founded] some old comic books! It was nice to relax in a café and read them.

08 중요 위 글의 괄호 (A)~(C)에서 문맥이나 어법상 알맞은 낱말을 골라 쓰시오.

➡ (A)________ (B)________ (C)________

09 위 글의 밑줄 친 ⓐ를 다음과 같이 바꿔 쓸 때 빈칸에 들어갈 알맞은 한 단어를 쓰시오.

➡ ________ all the international goods there was interesting.

10 다음 빈칸 (A)와 (B)에 알맞은 단어를 넣어 국제시장에 대한 소개를 완성하시오.

It is a good place for those who like to visit (A)________ ________, and it is well known for selling various goods which are imported from (B)________ ________.

창의사고력 서술형 문제

01 주어진 조건을 이용하여 대화의 흐름에 맞게 빈칸을 완성하시오.

조건

다음 주말에 대한 계획 / 영화 보기 / 영화관은 걸어서 5분

A: ______________________________
B: I'm planning ____________________ alone.
A: I don't have any plans for next weekend. Can I join?
B: Of course.
A: ______________________________
B: You can go there by walking.
A: ______________________________
B: It ____________________.

02 주어진 어구를 활용하여 자신의 생각을 쓰시오.

It is important … / It is necessary … / Do you know …? / I wonder …

(1) ______________________________
(2) ______________________________
(3) ______________________________
(4) ______________________________

03 다음 내용을 바탕으로 자신의 여행기를 쓰시오.

1. Where: Anmyeon-do
2. When: last summer
3. With whom: with my family
4. Activities:
   - swim in the sea
   - catch crabs on the beach
   - see the beautiful sunset
5. Feelings: awesome, fantastic

A Perfect Day in Anmyeon-do

(A)____________, I went to Anmyeon-do with my family. I (B)____________ in the sea with my brothers. Then we (C)____________ some crabs on the beach. It was (D)____________ and fantastic to see the (E)____________ there.

단원별 모의고사

01 빈칸에 알맞은 단어를 고르시오.

She turned __________ her cell phone before the movie started.

① off ② out ③ of
④ in ⑤ at

02 다음 제시된 의미에 맞는 단어를 주어진 철자로 시작하여 빈칸에 쓰고, 알맞은 것을 골라 문장을 완성하시오.

- h__________: events that have happened in the past
- s__________: a beautiful view of nature
- W__________: a particular way or form relating to Western countries

(1) We enjoyed the __________ at the beach.
(2) I want to know about the __________ of the Eiffel Tower.
(3) I like __________ houses better than Eastern-style houses.

[03~06] 다음 대화를 읽고 물음에 답하시오.

B: Hi, Nuri. ⓐWhat is your class going for the field trip tomorrow?
G: Hello, Mike. (①) We ⓑare going to the art museum.
B: Sounds ⓒinteresting. (②) ⓓWhere are you planning to see there?
G: (③) There are three art shows right now. I'm planning to see Vincent van Gogh's paintings. Where is your class going?
B: (④) I'm ⓔexciting to ride a roller coaster!
G: That sounds fun. (⑤) Have a good trip!

03 위 대화의 ①~⑤ 중 주어진 문장이 들어갈 알맞은 곳은?

We are going to the amusement park.

① ② ③ ④ ⑤

04 다음 영영풀이에 해당하는 단어를 위 대화에서 찾아 쓰시오.

a visit made by students and teachers to learn about something

➡ ____________________

05 ⓐ~ⓔ 중 문법상 또는 흐름상 어색한 부분이 모두 몇 개인지 고르시오.

① 1개 ② 2개 ③ 3개 ④ 4개 ⑤ 5개

06 위의 대화를 읽고 대답할 수 없는 질문을 고르시오.

① When are they going on the field trip?
② Where is the boy going on the field trip?
③ Where is the girl going on the field trip?
④ How will the boy go to the amusement park?
⑤ How many art shows are there in the art museum now?

[07~09] 다음 대화를 읽고 물음에 답하시오.

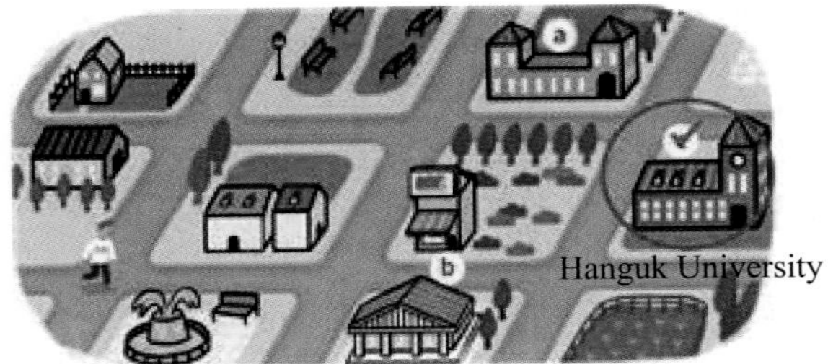

B: Excuse me. 여기서 한국 대학교까지 어떻게 가나요?(get, how)
W: You can go there by bus or on foot.
B: How long does it take to get there?
W: It takes five minutes by bus and 20 minutes on foot.
B: Oh, then I will walk there. Can you tell me how to get there?
W: (A)__________________ You will see Hanguk University on (B)________.
B: (A)__________________ Thank you!

07 남자의 이동 수단과 소요 시간이 바르게 짝지어진 것을 고르시오.

① 버스 - 5분
② 지하철 - 5분
③ 걷기 - 12분
④ 버스 - 20분
⑤ 걷기 - 20분

08 밑줄 친 우리말을 괄호 안에 주어진 말을 이용하여 영작하시오.

➡ ______________________________

09 그림을 참고하여 빈칸 (A)와 (B)에 들어갈 말을 쓰시오.

➡ (A) ______________________________
(B) ______________________________

10 다음 빈칸에 들어갈 말이 바르게 짝지어진 것은?

• It is difficult ________ 1 km without a rest.
• Melinda knows ________ the man is.

① run – that
② to run – if
③ to run – who
④ running – who
⑤ running – if

11 다음 밑줄 친 부분의 쓰임이 나머지 넷과 다른 것은?

① I wonder if my child expresses himself well in English.
② You can catch the train if you go now.
③ Let's wait and see if the market improves.
④ Please tell me if there's anything I can do to help.
⑤ Alex asked me if I wanted a massage.

12 다음 중 어법상 바르지 않은 것은?

① It was not easy to play soccer after it rained lot.
② These days it is essential to learn English.
③ It is exciting to meet a famous person.
④ Is it possible breathe under the water?
⑤ It is important to drink a lot of water for our health.

13 다음 두 문장을 간접의문문을 이용하여 한 문장으로 쓰시오.

(1) I know. + Who won the race?

➡ ______________________

(2) Do you know? + When will the bus come?

➡ ______________________

(3) The man is asking her. + How long does it take to get to the mart?

➡ ______________________

(4) I have no idea. + Do they like it or not?

➡ ______________________

(5) Do you think? + Who will win the game?

➡ ______________________

(6) Do you guess? + What does she want to buy?

➡ ______________________

14 주어진 어휘를 이용하여 다음 우리말을 영작하시오. (to부정사나 간접의문문을 이용하여 쓸 것.)

(1) 우리의 환경을 보호하는 것은 중요하다. (environment, protect, it)

➡ ______________________

(2) 전통 시장을 구경하는 것은 재미있다. (the traditional market, look around, it)

➡ ______________________

(3) 롤러코스터를 타는 것은 신나는 일이다. (the roller coaster, exciting, it)

➡ ______________________

(4) 잠을 충분히 자는 것이 필요하다. (enough sleep, necessary, get, it)

➡ ______________________

(5) 나는 그 소녀가 어디에 살았었는지 기억하지 못한다. (remember, live)

➡ ______________________

(6) Anna는 내게 내가 Angelina를 사랑하는지 물었다. (ask, love)

➡ ______________________

[15~16] 다음 글을 읽고 물음에 답하시오.

Busan, Market Heaven

Do you like traditional markets? Then go to Gukje Market in Busan. It is one of the most famous markets in Busan. ⓐ그곳이 무엇으로 유명한지 아세요? It is famous for selling ⓑ a variety of goods from different countries. It was interesting to see all the international goods there. We also ate many kinds of street food, such as *Gimbap*, fish cake, and *Hotteok*. Then we walked to Bosu-dong Book Street. Many bookstores there sell used books. We were really excited because we found some old comic books! It was nice to relax in a café and read them.

15 위 글의 밑줄 친 ⓐ의 우리말에 맞게 한 단어를 보충하여, 주어진 어휘를 알맞게 배열하시오.

it / what / famous / you / is / know / do / ?

➡ ______________________

16 위 글의 밑줄 친 ⓑa variety of와 바꿔 쓸 수 있는 단어를 모두 고르시오.

① familiar ② diverse
③ various ④ same
⑤ common

[17~19] 다음 글을 읽고 물음에 답하시오.

______Ⓐ______

ⓐThere is no place like Gangwon-do for beautiful nature. ⓑFirst, we went to Baengnyong Cave. This 1.8-kilometer-long cave is still in good condition. It was so amazing to see its natural beauty. ⓒNear the end of our cave tour, the guide turned off the lights in the cave for a minute. Everything became very dark, so we were able to focus on the sounds Ⓑthere. It was the most amazing experience of the tour! ⓓOur next stop was Donggang. We went rafting! ⓔIt was exciting to ride on the rough water and enjoy the view at the same time.

17 위 글의 빈칸 Ⓐ에 들어갈 제목으로 알맞은 것을 고르시오.

① Gangwon-do, Seafood Heaven
② Baengnyong Cave in Good Condition
③ Focus on the Sounds of Nature
④ Gangwon-do, Full of Natural Beauty
⑤ How about Going Rafting?

18 위 글의 밑줄 친 문장 ⓐ~ⓔ를 사실(Fact)과 견해(Opinion)로 구분하시오.

➡사실(Fact): ____________________
견해(Opinion): ____________________

19 위 글의 밑줄 친 Ⓑthere가 가리키는 것을 본문에서 찾아 쓰시오.

➡ ____________________

[20~22] 다음 글을 읽고 물음에 답하시오.

Incheon, A City of Firsts
Do you know where the first train station in Korea is? How about the first *Jajangmyeon*? The answer is Incheon! This place has (A)[many / much] of Korea's firsts. To (B)[get / get to] there, we went to Incheon Station. (①) The Jajangmyeon Museum is next to the station. (②) We learned about the history of *Jajangmyeon* there. (③) The view from the park was awesome! (④) It was great to see the historical sites of this city from the park. (⑤)
Teacher: Wow, these places sound (C)[great / greatly]! You all have done a wonderful job on your presentations!

20 위 글의 흐름으로 보아, 주어진 문장이 들어가기에 가장 적절한 곳은?

Later, we walked around Jayu Park, the first Western-style park in Korea.

① ② ③ ④ ⑤

21 위 글의 괄호 (A)~(C)에서 어법상 알맞은 낱말을 골라 쓰시오.

(A)________ (B)________ (C)________

22 위 글의 내용과 일치하지 않는 것은?

① The first train station in Korea is in Incheon.
② Incheon has many of Korea's firsts.
③ The Jajangmyeon Museum is next to Incheon Station.
④ Jayu Park is the first Eastern-style park in Korea.
⑤ Seeing the historical sites of Incheon from Jayu Park was great.

On My Way to the Future

의사소통 기능

- 능력 표현하기
  I'm good at drawing pictures.
- 조언 구하고 답하기
  A: What do I need to do?
  B: You need to read a lot of books.

언어 형식

- to부정사를 목적격보어로 취하는 동사
  Taeho wants more people to use 3D printed products in the future.
- 조건을 나타내는 접속사 if
  If you keep looking ahead and dreaming big, your future will be bright.

교과서

Words & Expressions

Key Words

- □ **advice**[ædváis] 명 충고, 조언
- □ **allow**[əláu] 동 허락하다
- □ **amazing**[əméiziŋ] 형 대단한, 멋진
- □ **amount**[əmáunt] 명 양, 총액
- □ **analyze**[ǽnəlàiz] 동 분석하다
- □ **appear**[əpíər] 동 나타나다, 보이기 시작하다
- □ **apply**[əplái] 동 지원하다, 신청하다
- □ **artificial**[ɑ́:rtəfíʃəl] 형 인공적인, 인조의
- □ **career**[kəríər] 명 진로, 직업
- □ **cartoonist**[kɑ:rtú:nist] 명 만화가
- □ **collaborate**[kəlǽbərèit] 동 협력하다
- □ **collaboration**[kəlæ̀bəréiʃən] 명 공동 작업, 협동
- □ **collect**[kəlékt] 동 모으다, 수집하다
- □ **consultant**[kənsʌ́ltənt] 명 상담가
- □ **counseling**[káunsəliŋ] 명 상담
- □ **creative**[kriéitiv] 형 창의적인
- □ **creativity**[krì:eitívəti] 명 창의력, 독창력
- □ **customer**[kʌ́stəmər] 명 손님, 고객
- □ **decorate**[dékərèit] 동 꾸미다, 장식하다
- □ **designer**[dizáinər] 명 디자이너, 설계자
- □ **develop**[divéləp] 동 발달시키다, 발전하다
- □ **emotion**[imóuʃən] 명 감정
- □ **float**[flout] 동 (물 위에) 뜨다, 떠다니다
- □ **following**[fálouiŋ] 형 다음[아래]에 나오는[언급되는]
- □ **improve**[imprú:v] 동 개선하다, 향상시키다
- □ **interpreter**[intə́:rpritər] 명 통역사
- □ **kind**[kaind] 명 종류
- □ **late-night**[léitnàit] 형 심야의
- □ **modeler**[mádlər] 명 모형 제작자
- □ **P.E.** 명 체육(**physical education**)
- □ **patient**[péiʃənt] 명 환자
- □ **photographer**[fətágrəfər] 명 사진작가, 사진사
- □ **problem-solving** 형 문제 해결의
- □ **reason**[rí:zn] 명 이유, 원인
- □ **reduce**[ridjú:s] 동 줄이다, 감소시키다
- □ **reviewer**[rivjú:ər] 명 (책 · 영화 등의) 논평가
- □ **route**[ru:t] 명 경로, 노선
- □ **scientist**[sáiəntist] 명 과학자
- □ **self-driving car** 자율주행차
- □ **skill**[skil] 명 기능, 기술
- □ **software**[sɔ́:ftwὲər] 명 소프트웨어
- □ **space**[speis] 명 우주, 공간
- □ **specialist**[spéʃəlist] 명 전문가
- □ **strength**[streŋkθ] 명 힘, 강점, 장점
- □ **talent**[tǽlənt] 명 (타고난) 재능, 재주
- □ **upcycle**[ʌ́psaikl] 동 (폐품 등을) 다시 쓸 수 있게 만들다
- □ **waste material** 쓰레기, 폐기물

Key Expressions

- □ **be good at** ~을 잘하다
- □ **be planning to 동사원형** ~할 계획이다
- □ **come true** 이루어지다, 실현되다
- □ **fill out** (서식 등을) 작성하다, (정보를) 기입하다, 채우다
- □ **first of all** 무엇보다도
- □ **help out** 도와주다, 거들다
- □ **keep a diary** 일기를 쓰다
- □ **look ahead** (앞일을) 내다보다, 예견하다
- □ **need to 동사원형** ~할 필요가 있다
- □ **print out** 출력하다
- □ **take care of** ~을 돌보다
- □ **wait for** ~을 기다리다
- □ **what else** 그 외에, 그 밖에

Word Power

※ 명사 – 동사

□ **advice**(충고, 조언) – **advise**(충고하다)

□ **analysis**(분석) – **analyze**(분석하다)

※ 서로 비슷한 뜻을 가진 어휘

□ **allow**(허락하다) – **permit**(허락하다, 허가하다)

□ **space**(우주) – **universe**(우주)

□ **strength**(강점, 장점) – **strong point**(장점)

□ **collaborate**(협력하다) – **work together**(함께 일하다)

□ **specialist**(전문가) – **expert**(전문가)

※ 동사 – 행위자

□ **design**(디자인하다, 설계하다) – **designer**(디자이너, 설계자)

□ **consult**(상담하다) – **consultant**(상담가)

□ **interpret**(해석하다, 통역하다) – **interpreter**(통역사)

□ **model**(모형[견본]을 만들다) – **modeler**(모형 제작자)

□ **photograph**(~의 사진을 찍다, 촬영하다) – **photographer**(사진작가, 사진사)

□ **review**(논평[비평]하다) – **reviewer**((책 · 영화 등의) 논평가)

English Dictionary

□ **analyze** 분석하다
→ to study in detail 자세히 연구하다

□ **apply** 지원하다, 신청하다
→ to give someone papers that say you want to do something
어떤 것을 하기를 원한다고 말하는 서류를 제출하다

□ **artificial** 인공적인, 인조의
→ not natural; created by humans
자연적이지 않은, 인간에 의해 만들어진

□ **career** 진로, 직업
→ a job that requires special skills or training
특별한 기술이나 훈련을 요구하는 직업

□ **counseling** 상담
→ advice that is given to someone to help them with their problems
문제 해결을 돕기 위해 누군가에게 주어지는 조언

□ **creativity** 창의력, 독창력
→ the ability to think of or create something new
새로운 것을 생각해 내거나 만들어 내는 능력

□ **develop** 발달시키다, 발전하다
→ to grow or become more advanced
좀 더 진보된 상태로 되거나 변화되다

□ **fill out** (서식 등을) 작성하다, (정보를) 기입하다, 채우다
→ to write down information on a form
서식에 정보를 적어 넣다

□ **float** (물 위에) 뜨다, 떠다니다
→ to stay up on water 물 위에 머무르다

□ **improve** 개선하다, 향상시키다
→ to make something better
어떤 것을 더 좋게 만들다

□ **late-night** 심야의
→ late at night 밤 늦게

□ **look ahead** (앞일을) 내다보다, 예견하다
→ to think about what might happen in the future
미래에 발생할지도 모르는 것에 대해 생각하다

□ **modeler** 모형 제작자
→ a person who makes something based on something else
다른 어떤 것에 기초해서 어떤 것을 만들어 내는 사람

□ **patient** 환자
→ a person who receives medical care
치료를 받는 사람

□ **reviewer** (책 · 영화 등의) 논평가
→ a person who writes opinions about the quality of a book, movie, or product 책, 영화, 상품의 질에 대한 의견을 쓰는 사람

□ **route** 경로, 노선
→ a way between two places 두 장소 사이의 길

□ **specialist** 전문가
→ a person who has a special skill
특별한 기술을 가진 사람

□ **strength** 강점, 장점
→ an advantageous quality or ability
유리한 특성이나 능력

□ **talent** (타고난) 재능, 재주
→ a natural ability to do something well
어떤 것을 잘하는 타고난 능력

Words & Expressions **시험대비 실력평가**

중요
01 다음 중 성격이 다른 하나를 고르시오.

① cartoonist ② customer
③ photographer ④ consultant
⑤ designer

[02~04] 다음 빈칸에 들어갈 말로 가장 적절한 것은?

02

This food contains no ______ colors.

① annual ② cheerful ③ fake
④ creative ⑤ artificial

03

How can I ______ my writing skills?

① require ② design ③ develop
④ expect ⑤ allow

중요
04

______ a diary is a good way to practice writing.

① Keeping ② Improving ③ Reducing
④ Decorating ⑤ Allowing

05 다음 영영풀이에 해당하는 단어를 고르시오.

a person who writes opinions about the quality of a book, movie, or product

① judge ② writer ③ artist
④ reviewer ⑤ movie director

중요
06 다음 대화의 빈칸에 들어갈 말을 고르시오.

A: Can you sing?
B: Yes. I'm pretty ______ at singing.

① able ② proud ③ work
④ good ⑤ bad

중요
07 다음 중 밑줄 친 부분의 뜻풀이가 바르지 않은 것은?

① Sam likes to collect fallen leaves every autumn. (모으다)
② A balloon modeler showed an airplane made with balloons only. (모델)
③ Chess seems to improve problem-solving skills. (문제 해결의)
④ The leaves on trees reduce pollution. (줄이다)
⑤ I think my talent is taking pictures of people. (재능, 재주)

08 다음 밑줄 친 단어와 바꿔 쓸 수 있는 것을 고르시오.

Weather specialists said the rainy season will last for a little more than 10 days.

① experiences ② scientists
③ experts ④ professions
⑤ strangers

중요
01 다음 밑줄 친 부분과 의미가 비슷한 것을 주어진 철자로 시작하여 쓰시오.

The strong point of my job is high paycheck.

➡ s____________________

[02~03] 다음 빈칸에 공통으로 들어갈 말을 쓰시오.

02

- The park's officials want to ________ them safe.
- ________ a diary so that you can write down your thoughts.

중요
03

- I need someone to take care ________ my little girl after school.
- First ________ all, you need to calm down.

고난이도
04 다음 빈칸에 들어갈 말을 <보기>에서 찾아 쓰시오.

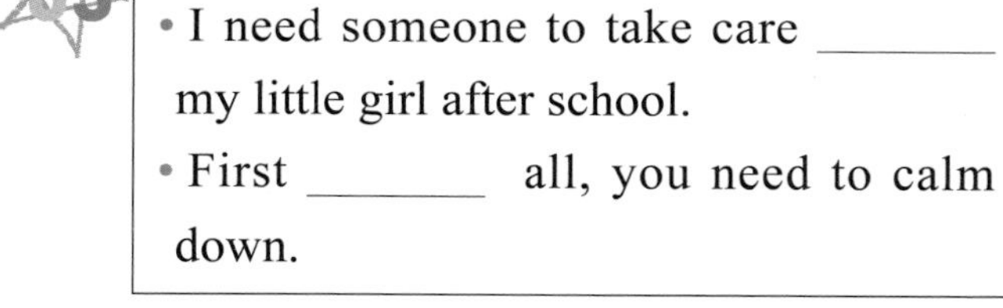

보기
amount career emotion reason

(1) You need to control your __________s.
(2) Recycling can save large __________s of energy.
(3) The man chose acting as a(n) __________.
(4) What is the __________ for your visit?

05 다음 그림을 보고 대화의 빈칸을 알맞게 채우시오. (한 칸에 한 단어임)

A: Would you please ________ ________ your information?
B: Sure.

06 다음 우리말에 맞게 주어진 단어를 바르게 배열하시오.

(1) 우리는 실패의 원인을 분석할 필요가 있다. (need, of, we, failure, analyze, to, the, the, cause)
➡ ______________________________

(2) 너는 영어 실력을 향상시킬 필요가 있다. (you, your, English, improve, need, to)
➡ ______________________________

(3) 나의 장점은 나 자신을 믿는다는 것이다. (in, strength, that, I, my, is, myself, believe)
➡ ______________________________

(4) 내 아들은 노래에 재능이 있다. (has, singing, my, a, for, son, talent)
➡ ______________________________

(5) 너 야식 먹고 싶니? (late-night, you, snack, want, a, do)
➡ ______________________________

교과서

Conversation

1 능력 표현하기

I'm good at drawing pictures. 나는 그림을 잘 그려.

- 능력을 말할 때 'be good at ~'을 사용해서 '~을 잘한다'는 의미를 나타낼 수 있다. 전치사 at 다음에는 math, baseball 등의 명사나 dancing, playing the piano 등 동명사(구)를 쓰면 된다.
- '내 생각에는 ~'이라는 의미의 'I think ~.'를 활용하면 자신의 능력을 좀 더 겸손하게 표현할 수 있다.
- 자신이 '~에 능숙하지 못하다'고 능력을 부정할 때는 be동사 뒤에 not을 붙여 부정문을 만들며 'be not good at ~ing'의 형태가 된다.

능력 여부 묻기

- Are you good at (동)명사? (너는 ~하는 것을 잘하니?)
- Can you 동사원형 (well)? (너는 ~을 (잘) 할 수 있니?)
- Are you able to 동사원형? (너는 ~을 할 수 있니?)
- Do you know how to 동사원형? (너는 ~하는 방법을 아니?)

능력 표현하기

- Yes, I am. / Yes, I can 동사원형.
- I know how to 동사원형.
- I am able to 동사원형.
- I'm (pretty) good at ~.

능력 부인하기

- (No,) I'm not. / (No,) I can't 동사원형 (well).
- I don't know how to 동사원형.
- Not really.
- I'm not able to 동사원형.
- I'm not good at ~.
- I'm poor at ~.

핵심 Check

1. 다음 우리말을 보고 대화의 빈칸을 채우시오.

A: Are you ________________ the piano? (너는 피아노 연주를 잘하니?)

B: Yeah, I think so. (응, 그렇다고 생각해.)

2. 다음 주어진 단어를 이용하여 대화를 완성하시오.

A: ________________________________? (taking, good, pictures, are, at, you)

B: No, but ___________________________. (good, it, is, my, brother, at)

2 조언 구하고 답하기

A What do I need to do? 뭘 해야 하니?
B You need to read a lot of books. 책을 많이 읽어야 해.

- 상대방에게 조언을 구할 때는 'What do I need to do?', 'What do you suggest?', 'What should I do to 동사원형?' 등의 표현을 쓸 수 있다.
- 조언을 구하는 질문에 대해 답할 때는 'You need to 동사원형', 'I suggest (that) you ~.', '(I think) you have to[should] 동사원형 ~.'을 이용하여 답을 할 수 있다. 이때 조동사 have to나 must는 어투가 다소 강한 느낌을 줄 수 있다는 것을 유의한다.

조언을 구할 때

- What do I need to do?
- What do you suggest?
- What should I do to ~?
- How can I ~?
- What can I do to ~?

조언을 할 때

- You need to ~.
- I suggest (that) you ~.
- (I think (that)) You should/have to ~.
- Make sure you ~.

- I suggest (that) ~.에서 접속사 that은 생략할 수 있으며, 뒤따르는 절의 동사는 동사원형을 쓴다.
- 'Why don't you ~?'나 'How[What] about ~?'의 제안하는 표현을 이용하여 조언을 할 수도 있다.

핵심 Check

3. 다음 우리말을 보고 대화의 빈칸을 채우시오.

A: What do I ________________ lose weight? (살을 빼기 위해서 뭘 해야 하니?)

B: You should exercise every day. (매일 운동을 해야 해.)

4. 다음 대화의 밑줄 친 부분과 같은 의미가 되도록, 주어진 단어를 이용하여 영작하시오.

A: <u>What do I need to do to improve my English skills?</u>

B: You need to keep a diary in English.

➡ (can, how) ____

(suggest, what) ____

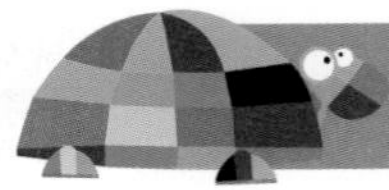

Conversation 교과서 대화문 익히기

Listen & Talk 1 A

G: ❶Let's play basketball.
B: Well… ❷I'm not good at playing basketball. Are you?
G: Yes, ❸I think I am. ❹What are you good at?
B: ❺I'm good at playing soccer.
G: Okay, then let's play soccer.

G: 우리 농구하자.
B: 음... 나는 농구를 잘하지 못해. 너는 잘하니?
G: 응, 내 생각에 나는 잘하는 것 같아. 넌 어떤 것을 잘해?
B: 나는 축구를 잘해.
G: 그래, 그러면 축구를 하자.

❶ 'Let's ~'는 '~하자'라고 제안을 할 때 사용된다. 이 외에도 'Why don't we ~?'의 표현을 쓸 수 있다.
❷ 능력을 말하는 'be good at(~을 잘하다)'에서 자신이 '~에 능숙하지 못하다'라고 능력을 부정할 때는 be동사 뒤에 not을 붙여 부정문을 만들어 'be not good at ~ing'의 형태가 된다.
❸ 'I think I am.' 뒤에 'good at playing basketball'이 생략되어 있다.
❹ 무엇을 잘하는지 묻는 표현으로 'What can you do (well)?', 'What are you able to do?'로 바꿔 쓸 수 있다.
❺ 능력을 말할 때 'be good at ~'을 사용해서 '~을 잘한다'는 의미를 나타낼 수 있다. 전치사 at 다음에는 (동)명사가 나올 수 있다.

Check(√) True or False

(1) The boy can play basketball well. T ☐ F ☐
(2) The girl is going to play basketball. T ☐ F ☐
(3) The girl is good at playing basketball. T ☐ F ☐

Listen & Talk 2 A

B: ❶I want to be a scientist. ❷What do I need to do?
W: ❸You need to study science. ❹And you need to develop your problem-solving skills.

B: 저는 과학자가 되고 싶어요. 저는 어떤 것을 해야 할까요?
W: 과학 공부를 해야 돼요. 그리고 문제 해결 능력을 개발할 필요가 있어요.

❶ be a scientist: 과학자가 되다
❷ 'What do I need to do?'는 '저는 어떤 것을 해야 할까요?'의 뜻으로 의미상 뒤에 'to be a scientist'가 생략되어 있다. 같은 의미로 쓸 수 있는 문장으로는 'What do you suggest?', 'What should I do?', 'How can I be a scientist?' 등이 있다.
❸ need to 동사원형: ~할 필요가 있다
❹ develop: 발달시키다, 발전하다 problem-solving: 문제 해결의

Check(√) True or False

(4) Problem-solving skills are important to become a scientist. T ☐ F ☐
(5) The boy wants to be a science teacher. T ☐ F ☐
(6) The woman suggests that the boy should study science. T ☐ F ☐

Listen & Talk 1 B

B: Jessica, ❶what are you going to do for the school talent show?
G: ❷I didn't decide yet. ❸What am I good at?
B: You're good at dancing, aren't you?
G: Not really. But I think I'm good at singing. I like singing very much.
B: Really? Actually, ❹I'm planning to play rock music with my band. ❺Why don't you sing for us?
G: Sure, I'd love to.

❶ be going to 동사원형: ~할 것이다 What are you going to do?: 뭐 할 거야? talent: (타고난) 재능, 재주
❷ decide: 결정하다 yet: 아직
❸ What am I good at?: 나 어떤 것을 잘하지?
❹ be planning to 동사원형: ~할 계획이다(= be going to 동사원형)
❺ 어떤 일을 하기를 제안하거나 권유하고자 할 때, '~하는 게 어때?'라는 의미로 'Why don't you+동사원형 ~?'을 쓴다.

Listen & Talk 2 B

G: Jason, I read your paper. It was so ❶amazing!
B: ❷Thank you for saying that. I'm trying hard ❸to improve my writing skills. I want to be a writer someday.
G: Really? I want to write well ❹like you. ❺What do I need to do?
B: You need to read a lot of books. Reading makes your writing better.
G: What else do I need to do?
B: Well, I write almost every day. Why don't you start ❻keeping a diary?
G: Thank you for your advice. I'll start today.

❶ amazing: 대단한, 멋진
❷ Thank you 뒤의 전치사 for 다음에는 고마워하는 이유가 나온다. Thank you for saying that.: 그렇게 말해 줘서 고마워.
❸ to부정사의 부사적 용법(목적)으로 '~하기 위해서'의 의미로 사용되었다.
❹ like는 전치사로 '~처럼'의 의미이다.
❺ 'What do I need to do?'는 '뭘 해야 하니?' 의미로 조언을 구할 때 하는 표현이다.
❻ keep a diary: 일기를 쓰다

Listen & Talk 1 C

B: Mom, ❶I need to fill out this form for tomorrow's career counseling program. Could you help me?
W: Sure. Let me see. You already wrote your dream job and hobby.
B: Yes, ❷I want to be a P.E. teacher, and my hobby is watching sports games. But writing my strengths is hard. What am I good at?
W: Well, I think you have lots of strengths. ❸First of all, you are good at playing baseball, aren't you?
B: Oh, yes. I'm good at playing baseball.
W: And you have many other strengths.
B: You're right. I also work well with other people. And I'm good at listening to people.
W: Right! You're good at so many things.
B: Thanks, Mom.

❶ need to 동사원형: ~할 필요가 있다 fill out: (서식 등을) 작성하다, (정보를) 기입하다, 채우다
❷ P.E.: 체육(physical education) 'my hobby is watching sports games.'에서 'watching sports games'는 'is'의 보어로 사용되었다.
❸ first of all: 무엇보다도

Listen & Talk 2 C

G: Hello, Mr. Watson! Thank you for doing this interview.
M: Sure, no problem.
G: This interview is for students ❶who want to be food stylists. ❷Can you tell me about your job?
M: Sure. You may see pictures of food in books or on TV. A food stylist decorates food to look good for pictures or movies.
G: I want to be a food stylist like you. What do I need to do?
M: You need to learn about many kinds of food.
G: ❸What else do I need to do?
M: You need to study art, too. ❹Creativity is important.
G: All right! Thank you for your time, Mr. Watson.

❶ who는 주격 관계대명사로 앞의 students를 수식하고 있다.
❷ 어떤 것에 대한 설명을 요청할 때 'Can you tell me about ~?'이나 'Can you explain ~?'으로 말할 수 있다.
❸ What else: 그 외에 무엇을
❹ creativity: 창의력, 독창력

Conversation 교과서 확인학습

• 다음 우리말과 일치하도록 빈칸에 알맞은 말을 쓰시오. (주어진 철자가 있으면 그 철자로 시작할 것)

Listen & Talk 1 A

G: Let's ________ basketball.

B: Well… I'm ________ ________ at playing basketball. Are you?

G: Yes, I think I am. ________ ________ ________ good at?

B: I'm good ________ ________ soccer.

G: Okay, then ________ play soccer.

해석

G: 우리 농구하자.
B: 음... 나는 농구를 잘하지 못해. 너는 잘하니?
G: 응, 내 생각에 나는 잘하는 것 같아. 넌 어떤 것을 잘해?
B: 나는 축구를 잘해.
G: 그래, 그러면 축구를 하자.

Listen & Talk 1 B

B: Jessica, what are you going ________ ________ for the school talent show?

G: I didn't ________ yet. ________ ________ I good at?

B: You're ________ ________ dancing, aren't you?

G: Not really. But I think I'm ________ ________ ________. I like singing very much.

B: Really? Actually, I'm planning ________ ________ rock music with my band. ________ ________ ________ sing for us?

G: Sure, I'd love to.

B: Jessica, 학교 재능 발표회에서 뭐 할 거야?
G: 아직 결정 안 했어. 나 어떤 것을 잘하지?
B: 너 춤 잘 추잖아, 그렇지 않니?
G: 사실은 그렇지 않아. 하지만 내 생각에는 나는 노래를 잘해. 나는 노래하는 것을 매우 좋아해.
B: 정말? 사실 나 우리 밴드와 록 음악을 연주할 계획이야. 우리를 위해 노래해 주는 게 어때?
G: 그래, 좋아.

Listen & Talk 1 C

B: Mom, I ________ ________ ________ ________ this form for tomorrow's career counseling program. Could you help me?

W: Sure. Let me see. You already ________ your dream job ________hobby.

B: Yes, I want to ________ a ________ ________, and my hobby is ________ sports games. But ________ my ________ is hard. ________ ________ ________ ________ at?

W: Well, I think you have ________ of strengths. ________ ________ all, you ________ ________ ________ playing baseball, ________ ________?

B: Oh, yes. ________ ________ ________ ________ ________.

W: And you have many other ________.

B: You're right. I also ________ well with other people. And I'm good ________ ________ ________ people.

W: Right! ________ ________ ________ so many things.

B: Thanks, Mom.

B: 엄마, 저 내일 있을 진로 상담 프로그램을 준비하기 위해 이 양식을 작성해야 해요. 저 좀 도와주시겠어요?
W: 물론이지. 어디 보자. 이미 하고 싶은 직업과 취미는 적었구나.
B: 네. 저는 체육 선생님이 되고 싶어요. 제 취미는 스포츠 경기 보는 거예요. 하지만, 제 강점을 적는 것은 어려워요. 저는 무엇을 잘하죠?
W: 음, 나는 네게 많은 강점이 있다고 생각해. 무엇보다도 너는 야구를 잘하잖니, 그렇지 않니?
B: 아, 맞아요. 저는 야구를 잘해요.
W: 그리고 너는 다른 강점들도 가지고 있단다.
B: 맞아요. 저는 다른 사람들과 협업을 잘해요. 그리고 사람들의 이야기를 잘 들어 줘요.
W: 그렇지! 너는 아주 많은 것들을 잘한단다.
B: 감사해요, 엄마.

Listen & Talk 2 A

B: I ________ ________ ________ a scientist. ________ do I need to do?

W: You ________ ________ study science. And you need to ________ your ____________ skills.

Listen & Talk 2 B

G: Jason, I read your paper. It was so ________!

B: Thank you for saying that. I'm ________ hard ________ ________ my writing skills. I want to be a ________ someday.

G: Really? I ________ to write well ________ you. ________ ________ ________ need ________ do?

B: You need to read a lot of books. ________ ________ ________ ________ ________.

G: What ________ do I need to do?

B: Well, I write almost every day. Why ________ you start ________ a diary?

G: Thank you for your ________. I'll start today.

Listen & Talk 2 C

G: Hello, Mr. Watson! Thank you ________ doing this interview.

M: Sure, no problem.

G: This interview is for students ________ ________ ________ ________ ________ stylists. Can you tell me about your job?

M: Sure. You may see pictures of food in books or on TV. A food stylist ________ food ________ ________ good for pictures or movies.

G: I want ________ ________ ________ ________ ________ like you. ________ do I ________ to do?

M: You ________ ________ ________ about many ________ of food.

G: What ________ do I need to do?

M: You need to study art, too. ________ is important.

G: All right! ________ you ________ your time, Mr. Watson.

해석

B: 저는 과학자가 되고 싶어요. 저는 어떤 것을 해야 할까요?
W: 과학 공부를 해야 돼요. 그리고 문제 해결 능력을 개발할 필요가 있어요.

G: Jason, 나 너의 글을 읽었어. 아주 놀라웠어!
B: 그렇게 말해 줘서 고마워. 나는 내 글쓰기 기량을 발전시키려고 노력하고 있어. 언젠가 작가가 되고 싶어.
G: 정말? 나도 너처럼 글을 잘 쓰고 싶어. 뭘 해야 하니?
B: 책을 많이 읽어야 해. 독서가 네 글쓰기를 더 좋게 만들거든.
G: 다른 건 또 뭘 해야 할까?
B: 음, 나는 거의 매일 글을 쓰고 있어. 일기 쓰기를 시작하는 건 어때?
G: 조언 고마워. 오늘부터 시작할게.

G: 안녕하세요, Watson 씨! 오늘 인터뷰 감사해요.
M: 네, 문제 없어요.
G: 이 인터뷰는 푸드 스타일리스트가 되고 싶어 하는 학생들을 위한 것이에요. 당신의 직업에 대해 말씀해 주시겠어요?
M: 그럼요. 아마 여러분은 책이나 TV에서 음식 사진을 보셨을 겁니다. 푸드 스타일리스트는 사진이나 영화에서 음식이 맛있어 보이도록 장식하는 일을 합니다.
G: 저도 Watson 씨와 같은 푸드 스타일리스트가 되고 싶어요. 뭘 해야 하나요?
M: 많은 종류의 음식에 대해 배워야 해요.
G: 다른 건 뭘 해야 하죠?
M: 미술 공부도 해야 해요. 창의력이 중요하거든요.
G: 알겠습니다! 시간 내 주셔서 감사합니다, Watson 씨.

01 다음 대화의 빈칸에 알맞지 않은 것은?

> B: I want to be a scientist. ______________________
> W: You need to study science. And you need to develop your problem-solving skills.

① What can I do?
② Is there something else to do?
③ What should I do?
④ What do you suggest?
⑤ What do I need to do?

[02~03] 다음 대화의 빈칸에 알맞은 것은?

02

> G: I want to be a food stylist like you. What do I need to do?
> M: ______________________________

① You have to make a shopping list.
② You need to learn about many kinds of food.
③ You should exercise every day.
④ You need to design a blog about Korean culture.
⑤ You should explain the styles about cultures.

03

> A: What are you good at?
> B: ________________

① I don't like sports.
② I'm not good at drawing.
③ I'm not a talented cook.
④ I will be a good teacher.
⑤ I'm good at playing soccer.

04 다음 대화의 밑줄 친 부분의 의도로 적절한 것을 고르시오.

> G: Jason, I read your paper. It was so amazing!
> B: Thank you for saying that. I'm trying hard to improve my writing skills. I want to be a writer someday.
> G: Really? I want to write well like you. What do I need to do?
> B: You need to read a lot of books. Reading makes your writing better.

① 희망이나 소망 묻기
② 능력 여부 묻기
③ 설명 요청하기
④ 하고 싶은 것 묻기
⑤ 조언 구하기

[01~02] 다음 짝지어진 대화가 어색한 것은?

01 ① A: What are you good at?
B: I'm good at fixing things.
② A: Are you good at soccer?
B: Yes, I think so.
③ A: What should we do?
B: We need to find water to drink first.
④ A: You are so good at drawing.
B: No, thanks. Do you draw pictures, too?
⑤ A: How can I get better grades?
B: You should study harder.

중요
02 ① A: Are you good at telling jokes?
B: No, I'm not good at it.
② A: Jiho, what do I need to do to play the piano like you?
B: Well, I think you're right.
③ A: What's your advice?
B: You should exercise every day.
④ A: What should I do to become a good writer?
B: You need to read many books first.
⑤ A: What can I do to get better grades?
B: You need to take good notes in class.

[03~06] 다음 대화를 읽고 물음에 답하시오.

B: Mom, I need to fill (A)_______ this form for tomorrow's career counseling program. Could you help me?
W: Sure. Let me see. You already wrote your dream job and hobby.
B: Yes, I want to be a P.E. teacher, and my hobby is watching sports games. But writing my strengths is hard. What am I good at?
W: Well, I think you have lots of (B)strengths. First of all, you are good at playing baseball, aren't you?
B: Oh, yes. I'm good at playing baseball.
W: And you have many other strengths.
B: You're right. I also work well with other people. And I'm good at listening to people.
W: Right! (C)너는 아주 많은 것들을 잘한단다. (so, things, at, you, good, many, are)
B: Thanks, Mom.

03 빈칸 (A)에 들어갈 말로 적절한 것을 고르시오.

① at ② on ③ out
④ with ⑤ from

04 밑줄 친 (B)와 같은 의미로 쓰이지 않은 것은?

① Focus on your strengths to boost your self-confidence.
② A person using strengths is creative, energetic, and productive.
③ Climbing an ice wall requires much physical strength.
④ His strength lies in his honesty.
⑤ His height is his strength in basketball.

서답형
05 밑줄 친 (C)의 우리말에 맞게 괄호 안에 주어진 단어를 알맞게 배열하시오

➡ ______________________

서답형
06 다음 영영풀이에 해당하는 단어를 대화에서 찾아 쓰시오.

advice that is given to someone to help them with their problems

➡ ______________

[07~10] 다음 대화를 읽고 물음에 답하시오.

G: Jason, I read your paper. It was so amazing!
B: Thank you for saying that. I'm trying hard to improve my writing skills. (①) I want to be a (A)______ someday.
G: Really? I want to write well like you. What do I need to do? (②)
B: You need to read a lot of books. Reading makes your writing better. (③)
G: (B)____________________
B: Well, I write almost every day. (④) Why don't you start keeping a diary?
G: (⑤) I'll start today.

중요
07 위 대화의 ①~⑤ 중 주어진 문장이 들어갈 알맞은 곳은?

Thank you for your advice.

① ② ③ ④ ⑤

08 빈칸 (A)에 들어갈 적절한 말을 고르시오.

① writer ② designer ③ singer
④ painter ⑤ lawyer

09 빈칸 (B)에 들어갈 말로 적절한 것을 고르시오.

① How can I write?
② What do you need to do?
③ What else do I need to do?
④ How often do you draw?
⑤ What skills do I need to develop?

중요
10 위 대화의 내용과 일치하지 않는 것은?

① The girl thinks Jason is good at writing.
② Jason thinks reading lots of books is helpful to improve writing skills.
③ Jason doesn't write every day.
④ The girl's writing is not as good as the boy's.
⑤ The girl thinks Jason's paper is excellent.

서답형
11 빈칸 (A)와 (B)에 들어갈 말로 적절한 것을 고르시오.

A: (A)____________________
B: I'm good at drawing pictures.
A: (B)____________________
B: I want to be an artist.

ⓐ What do I need to do?
ⓑ What are you good at?
ⓒ Why don't you draw pictures?
ⓓ What am I good at?
ⓔ What do you want to be in the future?
ⓕ How about becoming an artist?

➡ (A) ____________________
(B) ____________________

[01~02] 다음 대화의 순서를 바르게 배열하시오.

01

(A) I want to be a food stylist like you. What do I need to do?
(B) What else do I need to do?
(C) You need to study art, too. Creativity is important.
(D) You need to learn about many kinds of food.

➡ ______________________

02

(A) You need to learn about the human body.
(B) Then how about becoming a nurse?
(C) What are you good at?
(D) That sounds good. What do I need to do to become a nurse?
(E) I'm good at taking care of people.

➡ ______________________

[03~04] 다음 대화를 읽고 물음에 답하시오.

G: Let's play basketball.
B: Well... I'm not good at playing basketball. (A)Are you?
G: Yes, I think I am. What are you good at?
B: (B)______________________
G: Okay, then let's play soccer.

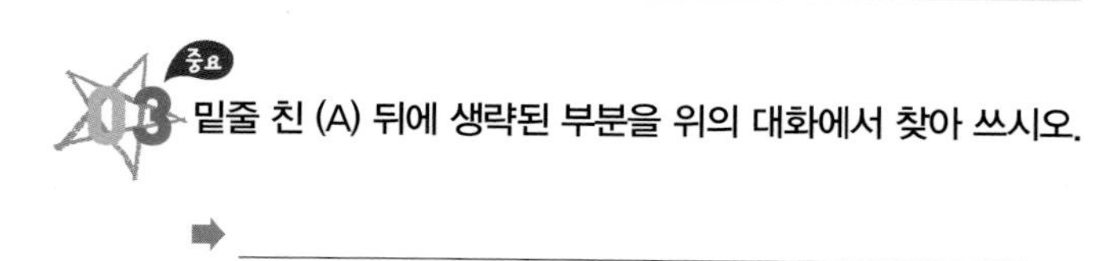

03 밑줄 친 (A) 뒤에 생략된 부분을 위의 대화에서 찾아 쓰시오.

➡ ______________________

04 빈칸 (B)에 들어갈 적절한 말을 위의 대화의 단어를 이용하여 쓰시오.

➡ ______________________

[05~06] 다음 대화를 읽고 물음에 답하시오.

G: Jason, I read your paper. It was so amazing!
B: Thank you for saying that. I'm trying hard to improve my writing skills. I want to be a writer someday.
G: Really? I want to write well like you. (A) 내가 뭘 해야 하니?
B: You need to read a lot of books. (B)독서가 네 글쓰기를 더 좋게 만들거든.(better, makes, reading, writing, your)
G: What else do I need to do?
B: Well, I write almost every day. Why don't you start keeping a diary?
G: Thank you for your advice. I'll start today.

05 밑줄 친 (A)의 우리말을 주어진 단어를 이용하여 영작하시오.

➡ ______________________ (need, what)

중요

06 밑줄 친 (B)의 우리말에 맞게 괄호 안에 주어진 단어를 알맞게 배열하시오.

➡ ______________________

07 밑줄 친 우리말을 주어진 단어를 이용하여 영작하시오.

G: Let's play badminton.
B: Well... 나는 배드민턴을 잘하지 못해. (good, play) Are you?
G: Yes, I think I am.

➡ ______________________

교과서

Grammar

1 to부정사를 목적격보어로 취하는 동사

- Taeho **wants** more people **to use** 3D printed products in the future. 태호는 미래에 더 많은 사람이 3D 프린터로 출력된 제품들을 사용하기를 원합니다.
- Would you **ask** her **to call** me tonight? 오늘밤 저에게 전화해 달라고 그녀에게 부탁해 주시겠어요?

■ 동사 다음에 목적어와 to부정사가 쓰여 '목적어가 …하는 것을 ~하다'라는 의미를 나타낸다. 이때 목적어를 설명해 주는 to부정사를 목적격보어라고 하고 이런 문장 유형을 5형식이라고 한다. 동사에 따라 목적격보어로 to부정사를 쓰기도 하고, 동사원형을 쓰기도 한다.

■ 목적격보어로 to부정사를 쓰는 동사에는 advise, allow, ask, tell, cause, enable, encourage, expect, force, get, help, need, order, persuade, require, teach, want, would like 등이 있다.

- I **asked** him **to mail** the letter. 나는 그에게 편지를 부쳐달라고 부탁했다.
- I **expect** her **to help** me. 나는 그녀가 나를 도와줄 것으로 기대하고 있다.

■ 목적격보어로 쓰인 to부정사의 부정형은 'not to 동사원형'으로 쓴다.

- He **advised** me **not to go** there. 그는 나에게 거기에 가지 말라고 충고했다.

■ 목적격보어로 동사원형을 쓰는 동사에는 make, have, let 등이 있다.

- I will **have** him **do** it. 나는 그가 그것을 하게 할 것이다.

핵심 Check

1. 괄호 안에서 알맞은 것을 고르시오.
   (1) I want Sumin (to be / be) nicer to me.
   (2) She told me (to return / returned) this book by Friday.
   (3) Will you help him (to clear / clearing) the table?
2. 다음 우리말에 맞게 빈칸에 알맞은 말을 쓰시오.
   - 그녀의 성공에 힘입어 나도 똑같은 걸 시도했다.
   ➡ Her success encouraged me ________ ________ the same thing.

2 조건을 나타내는 접속사 if

- **If** you keep looking ahead and dreaming big, your future will be bright. 만약 당신이 계속 앞을 내다보고 꿈을 크게 꾼다면, 당신의 미래는 밝을 것입니다.
- I will start tomorrow **if** it is fine. 나는 날씨가 좋으면 내일 출발하겠다.

■ if는 '만약 ~한다면'이라는 뜻의 조건을 나타내는 부사절을 이끄는 접속사로 한 문장을 다른 문장에 연결해 준다. 접속사가 사용된 문장에서 접속사가 붙은 절을 종속절, 접속사가 붙지 않은 나머지 절을 주절이라고 하는데, 주절이 먼저 나올 수도 있고 종속절이 먼저 나올 수도 있다. if절이 앞에 올 경우, 부사절 뒤에 쉼표(,)를 붙인다.

- **If** you want, you can look around.
  = You can look around **if** you want. 원한다면 둘러보아도 좋아.

■ 시간이나 조건의 접속사가 이끄는 부사절에서는 실제로는 미래의 일을 나타내더라도 will을 쓰지 않고 현재시제를 쓴다.

- **If** it rains tomorrow, we will stay home. 내일 비가 오면 우리는 집에 있을 거예요.
- **After** I find out, I'll let you know at the next class. 확인해서 다음 수업시간에 알려 줄게요.

■ 접속사 unless
'만약 ~하지 않는다면'의 뜻으로 'if ~ not'과 같은 의미이다.

- You'll miss the bus **unless** you walk more quickly.
  = You'll miss the bus **if** you **don't** walk more quickly. 더 빨리 걷지 않으면 버스를 놓칠 거야.

■ if절이 명사 역할을 하는 경우도 있으며 (이때 if는 whether와 같은 의미이다.) 이때는 '~인지 아닌지'로 해석하며 미래를 나타낼 때에는 미래시제를 써야 한다.

- I wonder **if** he **will** come. 나는 그가 올지 궁금하다.

핵심 Check

3. 괄호 안에서 알맞은 것을 고르시오.

(1) You can catch the train (if / unless) you leave now.
(2) If it (will rain / rains) tomorrow, we will put off the picnic.
(3) I don't know if he (will come / comes) tomorrow.

01 다음 문장에서 어법상 어색한 부분을 바르게 고치시오.

(1) When can I expect you be back?

_____________ ➡ _____________

(2) He told me to not lose heart.

_____________ ➡ _____________

(3) It is difficult to do unless you aren't a professional.

_____________ ➡ _____________,

_____________ ➡ _____________

(4) You will fail if you won't work harder.

_____________ ➡ _____________

02 다음 우리말을 영어로 옮길 때, 빈칸에 알맞은 것이 순서대로 짝지어진 것은?

> • 그가 그녀를 거기로 태워다 주면 그녀는 그에게 돈을 줄 것이다.
> → She _______ him some money if he _______ her there.

① will give – will drive
② will give – drives
③ gives – will drive
④ gives – drives
⑤ gave – drove

03 괄호 안의 동사를 어법에 맞게 빈칸에 쓰시오.

(1) She asked me ________ her advice. (give)
(2) I want you ________ us. (join)
(3) I told him ________ it immediately. (do)
(4) The teacher made me ________ my homework. (do)

04 다음 우리말에 맞게 빈칸에 알맞은 말을 쓰시오.

(1) 그들은 내가 더 노력하기를 기대한다.

➡ They expect me ________ ________ harder.

(2) 네가 아무런 계획이 없다면, 우리는 쇼핑을 갈 수 있다.

➡ ________ you don't have any plans, we can go shopping.

01 다음 중 어법상 어색한 문장은?

① My mom let me eat ice cream for dessert.
② Why don't you go home if you feel ill?
③ Are you going to allow us to ask personal questions?
④ If Jina comes to my birthday party, I will be happy.
⑤ They advised him leave the place as soon as possible

중요
02 다음 우리말을 바르게 영작한 것은?

유나는 나에게 그녀와 함께 수학 동아리에 가입하자고 했다.

① Yuna asked me join the math club with her.
② Yuna asked me joined the math club with her.
③ Yuna asked me to join the math club with her.
④ Yuna asked me joining the math club with her.
⑤ Yuna asked me to joining the math club with her.

서답형
03 다음 괄호 안에서 알맞은 것을 고르시오.

(1) Mr. Lee told his children (to be / be) quiet.
(2) I want Mijin (to study / studying) harder.
(3) If you (will smile /smile) at people, they will smile back at you.

중요
04 빈칸에 들어갈 말을 순서대로 바르게 연결한 것은?

• ________ you speak too fast, your classmates will not understand you.
• Don't smoke in front of elders ________ you are invited to do so.

① If – if
② If – unless
③ Unless – if
④ Unless – unless
⑤ When – however

05 다음 빈칸에 알맞은 것은?

I ordered him ________ silent in the hall.

① be ② was ③ is
④ to be ⑤ being

중요
06 다음 중 어법상 어색한 문장을 고르시오.

① If Hanbin will join our soccer club, I will play soccer with him.
② I will close this meeting unless you have further questions.
③ If you feel sick, take this medicine quickly.
④ If help is needed, what can people do?
⑤ Unless you start now, you'll be late.

07 다음 문장의 빈칸에 알맞지 않은 것은?

Her mom ________ her to marry him.

① wanted ② made ③ asked
④ advised ⑤ expected

[08~09] 다음 중 어법상 옳은 것을 고르시오.

08 ① I asked the man take my suitcase to the room.
② He advised me seeing a doctor right away.
③ I want you to share your ideas with your classmates.
④ His mom allowed them watched TV after dinner.
⑤ They made me to say the same thing over and over again.

09 ① If I'm wrong, you should tell me the right answer.
② Unless you go to the aquarium, you can see a lot of fish and sea animals.
③ If you won't have lunch, you will feel hungry soon.
④ I don't know if she comes home next weekend.
⑤ The work will not be done if you do it now.

중요
10 다음 빈칸에 공통으로 들어갈 말을 쓰시오.

• I wonder ______ she received my letter or not.
• You should visit there ______ you want to enjoy a beautiful view of Toronto.

➡ ____________________

11 괄호 안에 주어진 동사를 어법에 맞게 빈칸에 쓰시오.

(A) My teacher advised us ______ some rest. (get)
(B) What will big data allow us ______ in the future? (do)

중요
12 다음 밑줄 친 부분의 의미가 다른 하나는?

① I would like to hear it if there is a good reason for that.
② Do you happen to know if there's a pay phone around here?
③ If you don't use your smartphone before bed, you can sleep well.
④ If you have any questions, call me right away.
⑤ If Ella makes some mistakes, will Chris help her?

서답형
13 주어진 어구를 이용하여 다음 우리말을 영어로 쓰시오.

(1) 나는 네가 아무한테도 그것에 관해 말을 안 했으면 좋겠어. (want, tell, anybody, that)
➡ ____________________
(2) 그 의사는 나에게 패스트푸드를 그만 먹으라고 조언했다. (advise, eat, junk food)
➡ ____________________
(3) 오늘 밤에 비가 오면, 나는 집에 머물 것이다. (rain, home, it, stay, at)
➡ ____________________
(4) 답을 모르겠다면, 저에게 물어보세요. (the answer, know, ask, unless)
➡ ____________________

[14~15] 다음 중 어법상 어색한 부분을 찾아 바르게 고친 것은?

14

> Jessie ①told me ②send an email ③to Mr. Smith as ④soon ⑤as possible.

① told → tells
② send → to send
③ to → for
④ soon → sooner
⑤ as → than

15 중요

> ①If Jimin ②will come to school ③early, I ④will exercise with ⑤her.

① If → Unless
② will come → comes
③ early → lately
④ will exercise → exercise
⑤ her → she

서답형
16 다음 빈칸에 들어갈 괄호 안에 주어진 동사의 형태가 다른 하나는?

① When do you want me ________ the package? (send)
② He made me ________ in the street for an hour last night. (stand)
③ Ann didn't allow them ________ a taxi. (take)
④ She got her two boys ________ a cake exactly in half. (divide)
⑤ Jenny asked him ________ the ants away from the food. (keep)

17 다음 중 어법상 바르지 않은 것은?

> ①He ②got ③his car ④to wash ⑤yesterday.

① ② ③ ④ ⑤

서답형
18 다음 우리말과 같은 뜻이 되도록 if를 이용하여 두 문장을 연결하시오.

> 단어를 좋아하면 십자말풀이가 재미있어.
> • Crossword puzzles are fun to do.
> • You enjoy words.

➡ ______________________________
____

서답형
19 다음 문장에서 어법상 어색한 부분을 찾아 바르게 고쳐 다시 쓰시오.

(1) My family expects me come home by 9 p.m.
➡ ______________________________

(2) His illness forced him canceling his visit.
➡ ______________________________

(3) Yesterday my boss even had me to walk his dog.
➡ ______________________________

(4) We don't have enough people to get the work do.
➡ ______________________________

(5) If Mina will teach me English, I will help her with math.
➡ ______________________________

(6) If you will keep looking ahead and dreaming big, your future is bright.
➡ ______________________________
____

(7) I forget things if I mark them down.
➡ ______________________________

01 다음 두 문장이 비슷한 의미를 갖도록 빈칸을 알맞은 말로 채우시오.

(1) Mr. Taylor let her go back home early.
➡ Mr. Taylor allowed her __________ back home early.

(2) She said that I should focus on my studies.
➡ She advised me __________ on my studies.

(3) The doctor told me that I should stop smoking.
➡ The doctor advised me __________ smoking.

(4) Juliet said to her, "Don't go out late at night."
➡ Juliet warned her __________ out late at night.

(5) Steve said to Donald, "Great. Keep writing a diary in English."
➡ Steve encouraged Donald __________ writing a diary in English.

02 중요 괄호 안에 주어진 어휘를 이용하여 문장을 완성하시오.

(1) ______________________, I will cook some food for her. (come, Juhee, my birthday party, 7 단어)

(2) ______________________, I will buy you a new computer. (volunteer, a month, work, do, for, 8 단어)

(3) ______________________, you'll be late for the meeting. (the subway, take, 5 단어)

03 중요 다음 중 어법상 어색한 부분을 찾아 바르게 고쳐 다시 쓰시오.

(1) I want Jimin coming to school early.
➡ ______________________

(2) The teacher told the students respected each other.
➡ ______________________

(3) How much would it cost to have the camera repair?
➡ ______________________

(4) Her little black dress and pretty hat made her to look chic.
➡ ______________________
____

(5) If you won't hurry, you will miss the train.
➡ ______________________

(6) You will achieve everything you want if you will work hard.
➡ ______________________

(7) Unless you don't have anything to wear, wear my coat.
➡ ______________________
____

04 괄호 안에 주어진 동사를 어법에 맞게 빈칸에 쓰시오.

When would you like me __________ work? (start)

고난이도

05 다음 두 문장이 같은 의미가 되도록 빈칸에 알맞은 말을 쓰시오.

(1) Amanda told him that he must not forget to turn off the machine.
➡ Amanda warned him __________ to turn off the machine.

(2) I think that Sumi had better join our soccer club.
➡ I want Sumi __________ our soccer club.

(3) The captain told his soldiers that they should leave the city immediately.
➡ The captain ordered his soldiers __________ the city immediately.

(4) Morris told Joseph that he should exercise regularly.
➡ Morris advised Joseph __________ regularly.

(5) Her parents hoped that she would become a good figure skater.
➡ Her parents expected her __________ a good figure skater.

06 다음 괄호 안에 주어진 동사를 어법에 맞게 빈칸에 쓰시오.

(1) If Sumi __________ our soccer club, I __________ her my soccer ball. (join, give)

(2) I'm not sure if Santa __________ me a nice gift or not. (give)

(3) Unless you __________ it up, I __________ you give it up. (give, make)

중요

07 다음 두 문장의 뜻이 같도록 빈칸에 알맞은 말을 쓰시오.

(1) Sign the paper, and the bank will lend you money.
➡ __________ you sign the paper, the bank will lend you money.

(2) Hold the bar tight, or you will fall to the ground.
➡ __________ you hold the bar tight, you will fall to the ground.

08 다음 우리말을 괄호 안에 주어진 어휘를 이용하여 주어진 단어 수대로 영작하시오.

(1) 내가 내일 6시에 나오지 않으면, 나를 깨워줘. (come out, wake up, 12 단어) (종속절로 시작할 것)
➡ ______________________________

(2) 내가 전화를 받지 않으면, 내 동생에게 전화해라. (my phone, answer, call, sister, 8 단어) (종속절로 시작할 것)
➡ ______________________________

(3) 우리가 밤새 걸으면, 내일 그곳에 도착할 거야. (get, all night, 10 단어) (주절로 시작할 것)
➡ ______________________________

(4) 나는 나의 엄마가 나에게 새 휴대전화를 사주시길 원한다. (my mom, cell phone, 11 단어)
➡ ______________________________

(5) 그녀는 나에게 자기와 친구가 되어 달라고 요청했다. (ask, become friends, 8 단어)
➡ ______________________________

(6) 그녀는 대학에 가라고 아들을 격려했다. (encourage, go, college, 8 단어)
➡ ______________________________

(7) 그를 5시에 여기로 오게 하시오. (have, 6 단어)
➡ ______________________________

교과서

Reading

Jobs of the Future

2020s: Self-driving cars will be on the market.

2030s: People will have robots that(주격 관계대명사) do everything for them.

2030s: 3D printers in every home(every + 단수명사) will print out(출력하다) almost everything.

2050s: People will take space trips.

2050s: People will live under the sea or in floating cities.

Look at the pictures above(위에 있는). Do these ideas surprise you?(=Are you surprised at these ideas?) You can see that(접속사) our lives will be very different in the future(미래에는). As(~함에 따라(비례)) our lives(life의 복수형) change, many new jobs will appear. What kind of job do you want? What will your future life be like(~와 같다)? The following(다음의) people looked ahead((앞일을) 내다보았다) and chose jobs that(=which) will be important in the future.
Let's read about their jobs!

Do you see the flower pot that(목적격 관계대명사(=which)) Sujin made? It was made(과거수동태) from old street flags. She is an upcycling designer. She works with waste materials to make(부사적 용법(목적)) new products. Her products show people that(접속사 that이 명사절을 이끌어 show의 목적어 역할을 하고 있다.) old materials can be useful in new ways. Upcycling can reduce the amount of waste in the future. To become(부사적 용법의 to부정사 (목적)) an upcycling designer, you should be creative and learn about art.

market 시장
almost 거의
float: 떠다니다
appear: 나타나다, 보이기 시작하다
look ahead: (앞일을) 내다보다, 예견하다
product 제품
in the future 미래에
amount 양
creative 창의적인

확인문제

● 다음 문장이 본문의 내용과 일치하면 T, 일치하지 않으면 F를 쓰시오.

1 In 2020s, self-driving cars will be on the market. ☐

2 In 2050s, people will live under the sea or in the universe. ☐

3 Sujin works with new materials to make new products. ☐

4 Upcycling can reduce the amount of waste in the future. ☐

Have you ever heard of 3D modelers? Taeho, a 3D modeler, works
현재완료 경험 용법 / └ 동격 관계 ┘
for a company that makes artificial hands and legs. Taeho uses special
주격 관계대명사(=which)
software to print out new hands and legs. They are made specially for
부사적 용법(목적) / 수동태
patients. If you are good at computer programming and art, you can
~을 잘하다
be a 3D modeler. Taeho wants more people to use 3D printed products
want는 to부정사를 목적격 보어로 취하는 동사: 동사+목적어+to V
in the future.

Jihye is a big data specialist. She works on many projects. For example, last year, she made bus routes. To find the best night routes,
예를 들어 / 부사적 용법의 to부정사(목적)
she needed to collect smartphone use data and taxi use patterns from
datum의 복수형
late-night travelers. Then she analyzed this information to create the
부사적 용법의 to부정사(목적)
most useful routes. Now Jihye is working with an online shopping
useful의 최상급
mall. She is collecting data from customers to find out the best styles
부사적 용법의 to부정사(목적)
for them. She knows big data allows us to learn more about our daily
allow+목적어+to부정사: ~가 …하도록 허락하다
lives. If you want to become a big data specialist, you should develop
조건절을 이끄는 접속사
your math and problem-solving skills!

Think about yourself and prepare for your future. If you keep
재귀대명사 / 조건의 부사절에서 현재시제가 미래시제를 대신한다.
looking ahead and dreaming big, your future will be bright.
keep ~ing: 계속해서 ~하다

modeler: 모형 제작자
artificial: 인위적인, 인조의
patient: 환자
specialist: 전문가(= expert)
route: 길, 경로
collect: 모으다, 수집하다
data: 데이터
late-night: 심야의
analyze: 분석하다
develop: 개발하다, 성장[발달]시키다

확인문제

- 다음 문장이 본문의 내용과 일치하면 T, 일치하지 않으면 F를 쓰시오.

1 Taeho is a 3D modeler. ☐

2 Taeho uses a special hardware to print out new hands and legs. ☐

3 Though you aren't good at computer programming and art, you can be a 3D modeler. ☐

4 Jihye, a big data specialist, works on many projects. ☐

5 Last year, Jihye made bus routes. ☐

6 Jihye knows big data allows us to learn more about our future. ☐

Reading 교과서 확인학습 A

• 우리말을 참고하여 빈칸에 알맞은 말을 쓰시오.

1 Jobs ________ ________ ________

2 2020s: Self-driving cars will ________ ________ ________ ________.

3 2030s: People will have robots ________ do everything for them.

4 2030s: 3D printers in every home ________ ________ ________ almost everything.

5 2050s: People will ________ ________ ________.

6 2050s: People will live ________ ________ ________ or ________ ________ ________.

7 Look at the pictures ________.

8 Do these ideas ________ you?

9 You can see that our lives will be very different ________ ________ ________.

10 ________ our lives change, many new jobs ________ ________.

11 ________ ________ ________ ________ do you want?

12 What will your future life ________ ________?

13 The following people ________ ________ and ________ ________ that will be important in the future.

14 ________ ________ about their jobs!

15 Do you see the flower pot ________ ________ ________?

16 It ________ ________ ________ old street flags.

17 She is an ________ ________.

18 She works with ________ ________ to make new products.

19 Her products show people that old materials can be useful ________ ________ ________.

20 Upcycling can reduce ________ ________ ________ ________ in the future.

21 ________ ________ an upcycling designer, you should be ________ and learn about art.

1 미래의 직업
2 2020년대: 자율주행차들이 시장에 나올 것이다.
3 2030년대: 사람들은 그들을 위하여 모든 것을 하는 로봇을 갖게 될 것이다.
4 2030년대: 모든 가정의 3D 프린터가 거의 모든 것을 출력해 낼 것이다.
5 2050년대: 사람들은 우주여행을 할 것이다.
6 2050년대: 사람들은 바다 밑이나 수상 도시에서 살 것이다.
7 위의 그림들을 보세요.
8 이 생각들이 놀랍습니까?
9 당신은 미래에 우리의 삶이 매우 달라질 것을 볼 수 있습니다.
10 우리의 삶이 변화함에 따라 새로운 직업들이 많이 생겨날 것입니다.
11 당신은 어떤 직업을 원하세요?
12 미래의 당신 삶은 어떤 모습일까요?
13 다음의 사람들은 앞을 내다보고 미래에 중요하게 될 직업을 선택하였습니다.
14 그들의 직업에 관하여 읽어 봅시다!
15 수진이 만든 화분이 보이시나요?
16 이것은 거리의 낡은 깃발들로 만들어졌습니다.
17 그녀는 업사이클링 디자이너입니다.
18 그녀는 새로운 제품을 만들기 위해 폐기물을 가지고 작업합니다.
19 그녀의 제품들은 낡은 재료가 새로운 방식으로 유용해질 수 있다는 것을 사람들에게 보여줍니다.
20 업사이클링은 미래에 쓰레기의 양을 줄일 수 있습니다.
21 업사이클링 디자이너가 되려면 당신은 창의적이어야 하며 미술을 배워야 합니다.

22 ________ ________ ________ ________ of 3D modelers?

23 Taeho, a 3D modeler, ________ ________ a company ________ ________ artificial hands and legs.

24 Taeho uses ________ ________ to print out new hands and legs.

25 They are made ________ ________ ________.

26 If you ________ ________ ________ computer programming and art, you can be a 3D modeler.

27 Taeho wants more people ________ ________ 3D printed products in the future.

28 Jihye is a ________ ________ ________.

29 She ________ ________ many projects.

30 ________ ________, last year, she made bus routes.

31 To find the best night routes, she needed to collect smartphone use data and ________ ________ ________ from ________ ________.

32 Then she ________ this information ________ ________ the most useful routes.

33 Now Jihye is ________ ________ an online shopping mall.

34 She is ________ ________ ________ customers to find out the best styles for them.

35 She knows big data ________ ________ ________ ________ more about our daily lives.

36 If you want to become a big data specialist, you should ________ your math and ____________ ________!

37 Think about ________ and ________ ________ your future.

38 If you ________ ________ ahead and ________ big, your future will be bright.

22 3D 모형 제작자에 관하여 들어 본 적이 있으신가요?

23 3D 모형 제작자인 태호는 인공 손과 다리를 만드는 회사에서 일합니다.

24 태호는 새 손과 다리를 출력하기 위하여 특별한 소프트웨어를 사용합니다.

25 그것들은 환자를 위하여 특별히 제작됩니다.

26 만약 당신이 컴퓨터 프로그래밍이나 미술을 잘한다면, 3D 모형 제작자가 될 수 있습니다.

27 태호는 미래에 더 많은 사람들이 3D 프린터로 출력된 제품들을 사용하기를 원합니다.

28 지혜는 빅데이터 전문가입니다.

29 그녀는 많은 프로젝트에서 일합니다.

30 예를 들어, 작년에 그녀는 버스 노선을 만들었습니다.

31 최적의 심야 노선을 찾기 위하여, 그녀는 심야에 이동하는 사람들의 스마트폰 이용 정보와 택시 이용 패턴을 수집할 필요가 있었습니다.

32 그런 다음 그녀는 그 정보를 분석하여 가장 유용한 노선을 만들었습니다.

33 현재 지혜는 온라인 쇼핑몰과 작업하고 있습니다.

34 그녀는 소비자들에게 맞는 최적의 스타일을 찾기 위하여 그들로부터 데이터를 수집하고 있습니다.

35 그녀는 빅데이터가 우리에게 일상생활에 관하여 더 많이 알게 해 준다는 것을 알고 있습니다.

36 만약 당신이 빅데이터 전문가가 되고 싶다면, 수학과 문제 해결 능력을 계발해야 합니다!

37 자신에 대하여 생각해 보고 미래를 준비하세요.

38 만약 당신이 계속 앞을 내다보고 꿈을 크게 꾼다면, 당신의 미래는 밝을 것입니다.

Reading 교과서 확인학습 B

• 우리말을 참고하여 본문을 영작하시오.

1 미래의 직업

➡ ______________________

2 2020년대: 자율주행차들이 시장에 나올 것이다.

➡ ______________________

3 2030년대: 사람들은 그들을 위하여 모든 것을 하는 로봇을 갖게 될 것이다.

➡ ______________________

4 2030년대: 모든 가정의 3D 프린터가 거의 모든 것을 출력해 낼 것이다.

➡ ______________________

5 2050년대: 사람들은 우주여행을 할 것이다.

➡ ______________________

6 2050년대: 사람들은 바다 밑이나 수상 도시에서 살 것이다.

➡ ______________________

7 위의 그림들을 보세요.

➡ ______________________

8 이 생각들이 놀랍습니까?

➡ ______________________

9 당신은 미래에 우리의 삶이 매우 달라질 것을 볼 수 있습니다.

➡ ______________________

10 우리의 삶이 변화함에 따라 새로운 직업들이 많이 생겨날 것입니다.

➡ ______________________

11 당신은 어떤 직업을 원하세요?

➡ ______________________

12 미래의 당신 삶은 어떤 모습일까요?

➡ ______________________

13 다음의 사람들은 앞을 내다보고 미래에 중요하게 될 직업을 선택하였습니다.

➡ ______________________

14 그들의 직업에 관하여 읽어 봅시다!

➡ ______________________

15 수진이 만든 화분이 보이시나요?

➡ ______________________

16 이것은 거리의 낡은 깃발들로 만들어진 것입니다.

➡ ______________________

17 그녀는 업사이클링 디자이너입니다.

➡ ______________________

18 그녀는 새로운 제품을 만들기 위해 폐기물을 가지고 작업합니다.
➡ ______

19 그녀의 제품들은 낡은 재료가 새로운 방식으로 유용해질 수 있다는 것을 사람들에게 보여줍니다.
➡ ______

20 업사이클링은 미래에 쓰레기의 양을 줄일 수 있습니다.
➡ ______

21 업사이클링 디자이너가 되려면 당신은 창의적이어야 하며 미술을 배워야 합니다.
➡ ______

22 3D 모형 제작자에 관하여 들어 본 적이 있으신가요?
➡ ______

23 3D 모형 제작자인 태호는 인공 손과 다리를 만드는 회사에서 일합니다.
➡ ______

24 태호는 새 손과 다리를 출력하기 위하여 특별한 소프트웨어를 사용합니다.
➡ ______

25 그것들은 환자를 위하여 특별히 제작됩니다.
➡ ______

26 만약 당신이 컴퓨터 프로그래밍이나 미술을 잘한다면, 3D 모형 제작자가 될 수 있습니다.
➡ ______

27 태호는 미래에 더 많은 사람들이 3D 프린터로 출력된 제품들을 사용하기를 원합니다.
➡ ______

28 지혜는 빅데이터 전문가입니다.
➡ ______

29 그녀는 많은 프로젝트에서 일합니다.
➡ ______

30 예를 들어, 작년에 그녀는 버스 노선을 만들었습니다.
➡ ______

31 최적의 심야 노선을 찾기 위하여, 그녀는 심야에 이동하는 사람들의 스마트폰 이용 정보와 택시 이용 패턴을 수집할 필요가 있었습니다.
➡ ______

32 그런 다음 그녀는 그 정보를 분석하여 가장 유용한 노선을 만들었습니다.
➡ ______

33 현재 지혜는 온라인 쇼핑몰과 작업하고 있습니다.
➡ ______

34 그녀는 소비자들에게 맞는 최적의 스타일을 찾기 위하여 그들로부터 데이터를 수집하고 있습니다.
➡ ______

35 그녀는 빅데이터가 우리에게 일상생활에 관하여 더 많이 알게 해 준다는 것을 알고 있습니다.
➡ ______

36 만약 당신이 빅데이터 전문가가 되고 싶다면, 수학과 문제 해결 능력을 계발해야 합니다!
➡ ______

37 자신에 대하여 생각해 보고 미래를 준비하세요.
➡ ______

38 만약 당신이 계속 앞을 내다보고 꿈을 크게 꾼다면, 당신의 미래는 밝을 것입니다.
➡ ______

Reading 시험대비 실력평가

[01~04] 다음 글을 읽고 물음에 답하시오.

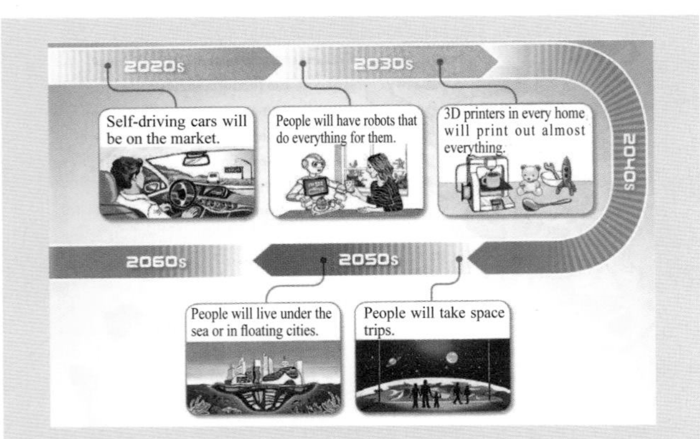

Look at the pictures above. Do these ideas surprise you? You can see that our lives will be very different in the future. ⓐAs our lives change, many new jobs will (A)[appear / disappear]. What kind of job do you want? (B)[How / What] will your future life be like? The following people looked (C)[ahead / behind] and chose jobs that will be important in the future. Let's read about their jobs!

01 위 글의 밑줄 친 ⓐAs와 같은 의미로 쓰인 것을 고르시오.

① As he is honest, everyone trusts him.
② He runs as fast as you run.
③ Her anger grew as she talked.
④ They treat him as a child.
⑤ Do in Rome as the Romans do.

서답형

02 위 글의 괄호 (A)~(C)에서 문맥이나 어법상 알맞은 낱말을 골라 쓰시오.

➡ (A)________ (B)________ (C)________

서답형

03 Where will people be able to live in the 2050s? Fill in the blanks with the suitable words.

➡ They will be able to live not only on land but also ______________ or ______________.

중요

04 위 글의 내용과 일치하지 않는 것은?

① They will begin to sell self-driving cars in the 2020s.
② In the 2030s, robots will do everything for people.
③ In the 2030s, we will be able to print out almost everything with our 3D printers in our home.
④ Our lives will always be the same in the future, too.
⑤ We will see many new jobs appear in the future.

[05~07] 다음 글을 읽고 물음에 답하시오.

Have you ever heard of 3D modelers? ⓐ Taeho, a 3D modeler, works for a company what makes artificial hands and legs. Taeho uses special software ⓑto print out new hands and legs. They are made specially for patients. If you are good at computer programming and art, you can be a 3D modeler. Taeho wants more people to use 3D printed products in the future.

서답형

05 위 글의 밑줄 친 ⓐ에서 어법상 틀린 부분을 찾아 고치시오.

➡ ______________________________

06 위 글의 밑줄 친 ⓑto print와 to부정사의 용법이 다른 것을 고르시오. (3개)

① I need someone to help me.
② It is difficult for me to answer the question.
③ This book is easy to read.
④ Do you know how to use this machine?
⑤ She must be smart to solve the problem.

서답형
07 다음 빈칸 (A)~(C)에 알맞은 단어를 넣어 태호의 직업에 대한 소개를 완성하시오.

His Job: He is (A)________________. About the Job: He (B)________________ ________________. To Get the Job: You (C)________________ ________________.

[08~10] 다음 글을 읽고 물음에 답하시오.

Jihye is a big data ⓐspecialist. She works on many projects. For example, last year, she made bus routes. To find the best night routes, she needed to collect smartphone use data and taxi use patterns from late-night travelers. Then she analyzed this information to create the most useful routes. Now Jihye is working with an online shopping mall. She is collecting data from customers to find out the best styles for ⓑthem. She knows big data allows us to learn more about our daily lives. If you want to become a big data specialist, you should develop your math and problem-solving skills!

Think about yourself and prepare for your future. ⓒIf you will keep looking ahead and dreaming big, your future will be bright.

08 위 글의 밑줄 친 ⓐspecialist와 바꿔 쓸 수 있는 말을 모두 고르시오.

① expert ② amateur
③ beginner ④ professional
⑤ outsider

서답형
09 위 글의 밑줄 친 ⓑthem이 가리키는 것을 본문에서 찾아 쓰시오.

➡ ________________

서답형
10 위 글의 밑줄 친 ⓒ에서 어법상 틀린 부분을 찾아 고치시오.

➡ ________________

[11~13] 다음 글을 읽고 물음에 답하시오.

Do you see the flower pot that Sujin made? It was made from old street flags. She is a(an) ____ⓐ____. She works with waste materials to make new products. Her products show people that old materials can be useful in new ways. Upcycling can reduce the amount of waste in the future. To become an upcycling designer, you should be creative and learn about art.

11 위 글의 빈칸 ⓐ에 들어갈 알맞은 말을 고르시오.

① florist
② upcycling designer
③ garbage collector
④ recycling programmer
⑤ garbage bag designer

12 위 글의 내용과 어울리는 표어를 고르시오.

① No more environmental pollution!
② Let's buy recycled products.
③ Don't waste waste.
④ Be a wise consumer.
⑤ Don't buy disposable products.

중요
13 위 글을 읽고 알 수 없는 것을 고르시오.

① 수진이 만든 화분의 재료
② 화분 제작에 걸린 시간
③ 수진이 하는 일
④ 수진의 제품이 사람들에게 보여주는 것
⑤ 수진의 직업에 필요한 자격 요건

[14~16] 다음 글을 읽고 물음에 답하시오.

Hello, everyone. My name is Soin Kim. I'm ⓐ(excite) to tell you about my job. I am a computer programmer, and I work at a software company. I develop new software for computers there. I work with many people from different countries. I chose this job because I am ⓑ(interest) in math and science. To become a computer programmer, I studied computer science and developed my problem-solving skills. If you have a dream, work hard for ⓒit. Then it will come true someday.

서답형
14 위 글의 밑줄 친 ⓐ와 ⓑ에 주어진 단어를 각각 알맞은 형태로 쓰시오.

➡ ⓐ ____________ ⓑ ____________

서답형
15 위 글의 밑줄 친 ⓒit이 가리키는 것을 본문에서 찾아 쓰시오.

➡ ____________________

중요
16 위 글을 읽고 대답할 수 없는 질문은?

① What is Soin's job and where does she work?
② What does Soin usually do at the company?
③ Who does Soin work with?
④ When did Soin begin to work?
⑤ What did Soin do to get this job?

[17~19] 다음 글을 읽고 물음에 답하시오.

2020s • Self-driving cars will be on the market.
2030s • People will have robots that do everything for ⓐthem.
• 3D printers in every home will print out almost everything.
2050s • People will take space trips.
• People will live under the sea or in floating cities.

Look at the pictures above. Do these ideas surprise you? You can see that our lives will be very __(A)__ in the future. As our lives change, many new jobs will appear. What kind of job do you want? What will your future life be like? The following people looked ahead and chose jobs that will be important in the future. Let's read about their jobs!

17 위 글의 빈칸 (A)에 들어갈 알맞은 말을 고르시오.

① difficult ② simple
③ similar ④ common
⑤ different

서답형
18 위 글의 밑줄 친 ⓐthem이 가리키는 것을 본문에서 찾아 쓰시오.

➡ ____________________

19 중요 위 글을 읽고, 다음 중 자신의 미래 모습에 대한 설명이 옳지 않은 사람을 고르시오.

수민: I don't like driving, so I will buy a self-driving car in the 2020s.
희정: I'm a little bit lazy, so in the 2030s, I'm willing to buy a robot to do everything for me.
진수: I will live forever because 3D printers that can print out everything will print out me, too.
호진: I'm adventurous, so I'm looking forward to taking a trip to the universe in the 2050s.
지혜: I like the blue sky, so I will move to the floating city in the 2050s.

① 수민 ② 희정 ③ 진수 ④ 호진 ⑤ 지혜

[20~22] 다음 글을 읽고 물음에 답하시오.

Jihye is a big data specialist. She works on many projects. For example, last year, she made bus routes. To find the best night routes, she needed to collect smartphone use data and taxi use patterns from late-night travelers. Then she analyzed this information to create the most useful routes. Now Jihye is working with an online shopping mall. She is collecting data from customers to find out the best styles __ⓐ__ them. She knows big data allows us __ⓑ__ more about our daily lives. If you want to become a big data specialist, you should develop your math and problem-solving skills!

Think about yourself and prepare __ⓒ__ your future. If you keep looking ahead and dreaming big, your future will be bright.

20 위 글의 빈칸 ⓐ와 ⓒ에 공통으로 들어갈 전치사를 고르시오.

① from ② to ③ in
④ for ⑤ on

21 서답형 위 글의 빈칸 ⓑ에 learn을 알맞은 형태로 쓰시오.

➡ ______________

22 서답형 What did Jihye do as a big data specialist last year? Answer in English in a full sentence. (4 words)

➡ ______________

[23~25] 다음 글을 읽고 물음에 답하시오.

Hello, everyone. My name is Soin Kim. I'm excited to tell you about my job. I am a computer programmer, and I work at a software company. I develop new software for computers ⓐthere. I work with many people from different countries. I chose this job because I am interested in math and science. To become a computer programmer, I studied computer science and developed my problem-solving skills. If you have a dream, work hard for it. ⓑThen it will come true someday.

23 서답형 위 글의 밑줄 친 ⓐthere와 바꿔 쓸 수 있는 말을 본문에서 찾아 쓰시오.

➡ ______________

24 서답형 위 글의 밑줄 친 문장 ⓑ를 다음과 같이 바꿔 쓸 때 빈칸에 들어갈 알맞은 단어를 쓰시오.

➡ Then it will be ________ someday.

25 서답형 Why did Soin choose her job? Answer in English in a full sentence.

➡ ______________
____

[01~03] 다음 글을 읽고 물음에 답하시오.

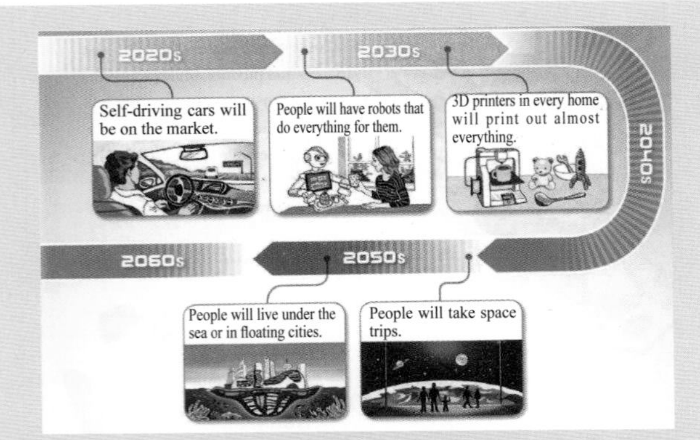

Look at the pictures above. ⓐDo these ideas surprise you? You can see that our lives will be very different in the future. As our lives change, many new jobs will appear. What kind of job do you want? What will your future life be like? The following people (A)looked ( ) and chose jobs that will be important in the future. Let's read about their jobs!

01 중요 위 글의 밑줄 친 (A)가 다음과 같은 뜻이 되도록 빈칸에 철자 a로 시작하는 단어를 쓰시오.

- considered what would happen in the future
- foresaw

➡ ____________________

02 What changes will come to us in the 2030s? Answer in English in a full sentence.

➡ ____________________

____

____

03 중요 위 글의 밑줄 친 문장 ⓐ를 수동태로 바꾸시오.

➡ ____________________

[04~06] 다음 글을 읽고 물음에 답하시오.

Do you see the flower pot that Sujin made? It was made from old street flags. She is an upcycling designer. She works with ⓐwaste materials to make ⓑnew products. ⓒHer products show people that new materials can be useful in old ways. Upcycling can reduce the amount of waste in the future. To become an upcycling designer, you should be creative and learn about art.

04 위 글의 밑줄 친 ⓐwaste materials와 ⓑnew products의 예를 본문에서 찾아 쓰시오.

➡ ⓐ __________ ⓑ __________

05 중요 위 글의 밑줄 친 ⓒ에서 흐름상 어색한 부분을 찾아 고치시오.

➡ ____________________

06 고난이도 다음 빈칸 (A)~(C)에 알맞은 단어를 넣어 수진의 직업에 대한 소개를 완성하시오.

Her Job: She is (A)____________________.
About the Job: She (B)____________________
____________________.
To Get the Job: You (C)____________________
____________________.

[07~09] 다음 글을 읽고 물음에 답하시오.

Have you ever heard of 3D modelers? Taeho, a 3D modeler, (A)[work / works] for a company (B)[that / where] makes artificial hands and legs. Taeho uses special software to print out new hands and legs. They are made specially for patients. If you are good (C)[at / for] computer programming and art, you can be a 3D modeler. ⓐTaeho wants more people using 3D printed products in the future.

중요
07 위 글의 괄호 (A)~(C)에서 문맥이나 어법상 알맞은 낱말을 골라 쓰시오.

➡ (A) ________ (B) ________ (C) ________

08 위 글에서 man-made와 같은 뜻의 단어를 찾아 쓰시오.

➡ ________________________

09 위 글의 밑줄 친 ⓐ에서 어법상 틀린 부분을 찾아 고치시오.

________________ ➡ ________________

[10~13] 다음 글을 읽고 물음에 답하시오.

Jihye is a big data specialist. She works on many projects. For example, last year, she made bus routes. ⓐTo find the best night routes, she needed to collect smartphone use data and taxi use patterns from late-night travelers. Then she analyzed this information to create the most useful routes. Now Jihye is working with an online shopping mall. She is collecting data from customers to find out the best styles for them. ⓑ그녀는 빅데이터가 우리에게 일상생활에 관하여 더 많이 알게 해 준다는 것을 알고 있습니다. If you want to become a big data specialist, you should develop your math and problem-solving skills!

Think about yourself and prepare for your future. If you keep __(A)__ ahead and __(B)__ big, your future will be bright.

10 위 글의 빈칸 (A)와 (B)에 look과 dream을 각각 알맞은 형태로 쓰시오.

➡ (A) ______________ (B) ______________

고난이도
11 위 글의 밑줄 친 ⓐ를 다음과 같이 바꿔 쓸 때 빈칸에 들어갈 알맞은 말을 쓰시오.

(1) ______________ the best night routes
(2) ______________ the best night routes

중요
12 위 글의 밑줄 친 ⓑ의 우리말에 맞게 한 단어를 보충하여, 주어진 어휘를 알맞게 배열하시오.

big data / our daily lives / us / learn / she / about / allows / more / knows

➡ ________________________________
____

고난이도
13 Answer in English in a full sentence.

(1) What did Jihye need to do to find the best night routes?
(2) What did Jihye do to create the most useful routes?

➡ (1) ________________________________
____
(2) ________________________________

교과서

구석구석

After You Read D

Taehun Kim is a movie reviewer. He writes articles about new movies. He chose this job because (= as, since) he loves watching (= to watch) movies. To get (부사적 용법의 to부정사(목적)) this job, he read many books to improve his writing skills. He also (be동사, 조동사 뒤, 일반동사 앞에 위치) watched many different types of movies.

구문해설 • reviewer: (책 · 연극 · 영화 등의) 논평가[비평가] • article: (신문 · 잡지의) 글, 기사
• chose: choose의 과거 • improve: 향상시키다

해석
김태훈은 영화 비평가이다. 그는 새로운 영화에 대한 기사를 쓴다. 그는 영화 보는 것을 매우 좋아하기 때문에 이 직업을 선택했다. 이 직업을 얻기 위해 그는 글쓰기 기술을 향상시키려고 많은 책들을 읽었다. 그는 또한 많은 다른 유형의 영화들을 보았다.

Culture Link

Personal Brand Consultant

A personal brand consultant creates (=makes) a personal brand for ([대리 · 대용] ~ 대신, ~을 위해) their customers. They find the customer's unique strengths. Then they build a personal brand by using (전치사 뒤에 동명사 by -ing: ~함으로써) the customer's personality, knowledge, and skills. To get (to부정사의 부사적 용법(목적)) this job, you need to have (need의 목적어) great communication skills.

구문해설 • unique: 유일(무이)한, 독특한 • knowledge: 지식 • skill: 기술

개인 브랜드 상담가
개인 브랜드 상담가는 한 개인의 브랜드를 그들의 고객들을 위해 만든다. 그들은 고객의 독특한 장점을 찾는다. 그러고 나서 그들은 고객의 개성, 지식 그리고 기술을 사용하여 개인 브랜드를 만든다. 이 직업을 갖기 위해서 당신은 훌륭한 의사소통 기술을 갖출 필요가 있다.

Do It Yourself A

B: Hey, Mandy. What are you looking at? (look at ~을 보다)

G: Hey, Edward. Look! Some volunteers are needed for the school festival. (자원봉사자가 학교 축제에 필요한 것이므로 수동태(be+p.p)를 사용한다.)

B: Really? I want to help out. You know I'm good at drawing pictures. I think I can do something for the festival. (want는 to동사원형을 목적어로 받는다 / 접속사 that 생략 (know와 I'm 사이))

G: I think you can help out at the cartoon event. (도와주다)

B: Right! Why don't we apply together? ('Why don't we ~?': 상대방에게 제안하는 표현)

G: Well, I am not good at drawing pictures. But I'm good at playing board games.

B: You can help out at the game event then.

G: Okay. Let's go and apply to become volunteers. (go와 apply가 and로 연결되어 있는 병렬구조이다.)

구문해설 • volunteer: 자원 봉사자 • help out: 도와주다, 거들다 • be good at: ~을 잘하다
• cartoon: 만화 • apply: 지원하다, 신청하다

B: 안녕, Mandy. 무엇을 보고 있니?
G: 안녕, Edward. 봐! 자원봉사자들이 학교 축제에서 필요하대.
B: 정말? 나 돕고 싶다. 너도 알다시피 내가 그림을 잘 그리잖아. 내 생각엔 내가 축제에서 어떤 것을 할 수 있을 것 같아.
G: 나는 네가 만화 행사에서 도움이 될 수 있을 거라고 생각해.
B: 맞아! 우리 함께 지원해 보는 게 어때?
G: 음, 나는 그림을 잘 그리지 못해. 하지만, 나는 보드게임을 잘해.
B: 그러면 너는 게임 행사에서 도울 수 있겠다.
G: 좋아. 우리 가서 함께 자원 봉사자에 지원하자.

영역별 핵심문제

Words & Expressions

01 다음 짝지어진 단어의 관계가 같도록 빈칸에 알맞은 말을 쓰시오.

design : designer – consult : __________

02 밑줄 친 부분과 의미가 가장 가까운 것을 고르시오.

They work together as a team.

① lead ② enforce ③ allow
④ apply ⑤ collaborate

03 빈칸에 들어갈 알맞은 말을 <보기>에서 골라 쓰시오. (형태 변화 가능)

보기
allow apply decorate float

(1) Will you help me __________ the Christmas tree?
(2) Nobody is __________ to smoke here.
(3) I'm very happy to __________ for the overseas volunteer program.
(4) They will __________ if you drop them in the water.

04 다음 영영풀이에 해당하는 단어를 고르시오.

a way between two places

① route ② street ③ travel
④ destination ⑤ chance

Conversation

[05~07] 다음 대화를 읽고 물음에 답하시오.

B: Hey, Mandy. ①What are you looking at?
G: Hey, Edward. Look! ②Some volunteers are needed for the school festival.
B: Really? I want to help out. You know I'm good at drawing pictures. ③I think I can do something for the festival.
G: I think you can help out at the cartoon event.
B: Right! ④Why don't we apply together?
G: Well, ⑤I am good at drawing pictures. But I'm good at playing board games.
B: You can help out at the game event then.
G: Okay. Let's go and apply to become volunteers.

05 위 대화의 ①~⑤ 중 흐름상 어색한 부분을 고르시오.

① ② ③ ④ ⑤

06 다음 영영풀이에 해당하는 단어를 대화에서 찾아 쓰시오.

to give someone papers that say you want to do something

➡ __________

07 대화의 내용과 일치하지 않는 것은?

① They will apply for volunteer work.
② They want to help out at the same event for the school festival.
③ The boy can draw pictures well.
④ The boy is looking at something about the school festival.
⑤ The girl is good at playing board games.

[08~09] 다음 대화를 읽고 물음에 답하시오.

B: I want to be a scientist. (A)______________
W: You need to study science. And (B)문제 해결 능력을 개발할 필요가 있어요.

08 빈칸 (A)에 들어갈 수 없는 것을 고르시오.

① What do I need to do?
② What do I want to do?
③ What do you suggest?
④ What should I do to be a scientist?
⑤ How can I be a scientist?

09 주어진 단어를 이용하여 밑줄 친 (B)의 우리말을 영작하시오.

➡ ______________________________
(solve, develop, need, skills)

[10~12] 다음 대화를 읽고 물음에 답하시오.

B: Jessica, what are you going to do for the school talent show?
G: I didn't decide yet. (①) (A)______________
B: You're good at dancing, aren't you? (②)
G: Not really. (③) But I think I'm good at (B)________. I like singing very much. (④)
B: Really? (⑤) Why don't you (C)________ for us?
G: Sure, I'd love to.

10 위 대화의 ①~⑤ 중 주어진 문장이 들어갈 알맞은 곳은?

Actually, I'm planning to play rock music with my band.

① ② ③ ④ ⑤

11 빈칸 (A)에 들어갈 수 있는 말을 모두 고르시오.

① Do you know how to dance?
② What are you planning to do?
③ What am I good at?
④ What are you able to do?
⑤ What can I do well?

12 빈칸 (B)와 (C)에 sing을 알맞게 채우시오.

➡ (B) ____________ (C) ____________

Grammar

13 다음 중 어법상 올바른 것은?

① We expect you to winning the singing contest.
② The son asked his mom give him more pocket money.
③ I want Juhee coming to my birthday party.
④ He ordered us finished the project by Monday.
⑤ Good health enabled him to carry out the plan.

14 다음 중 어법상 어색한 것은?

① If you know Mr. Lee, please introduce me to him.
② If the weather is fine, take a trip somewhere.
③ If you will miss it, you'll regret it.
④ You must not drink if you drive.
⑤ Let's go for a picnic if it doesn't rain.

15 주어진 어구를 바르게 배열하여 문장을 완성하시오.

(1) the pool, a shower, you, you, can't, don't, go, take, first, if, into

➡ ______________________________

(2) if, you, you, an upcycling designer, art, be, learn, become, want, should, creative, and, to, about

➡ ______________________________

____

(3) the grandfather, his grandson, this weekend, him, wanted, visit, to

➡ ______________________________

____

(4) I, me, him, tomorrow, asked, call, back, to

➡ ______________________________

(5) a, I, me, you, favor, do, need, to

➡ ______________________________

16 다음 문장의 밑줄 친 부분과 쓰임이 같은 것은?

> • If you want to help me, please give me a rope, too.

① Would you please check if I filled out this card right?

② If you take a taxi, you can get there in ten minutes.

③ Some people wonder if another writer just used his name.

④ The police weren't sure if he could catch a thief.

⑤ If he were here, he would be very pleased by your words.

17 다음 그림을 보고 주어진 어휘를 이용하여 빈칸을 알맞게 채우시오.

➡ The teacher told them ____________ again. If they fight again, they ____________. (fight, punish)

18 다음 빈칸에 들어갈 수 없는 것을 고르시오.

> • Daniel ________ his son to study science harder.

① advised ② wanted ③ got

④ had ⑤ encouraged

19 주어진 표현을 이용하여 문장을 완성하시오.

(1) You won't be late for school ____________ ____________. (the bus, miss, unless)

(2) You will be in trouble ____________. (a lie, tell, if)

20 If를 사용하여 한 문장으로 연결하시오.

> • Go to Europe.
> • You can see many old structures.

➡ ______________________________

Reading

[21~23] 다음 글을 읽고 물음에 답하시오.

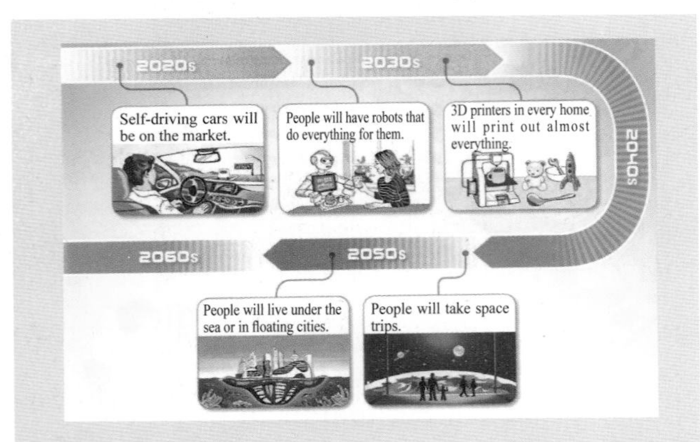

Look at the pictures above. Do ⓐthese ideas surprise you? You can see that our lives will be very different in the future. As our lives change, many new jobs will appear. What kind of job do you want? What will your future life be ⓑlike? The following people looked ahead and chose jobs that will be important in the future. Let's read about their jobs!

21 위 글의 밑줄 친 ⓐthese ideas에 해당되지 않는 것을 고르시오.

① Self-driving cars will be offered for sale in the 2020s.
② In the 2030s, people will be able to make robots do everything for them.
③ In the 2030s, almost everything will be printed out by 3D printers in every home.
④ People will go on space trips in the 2050s.
⑤ People will live in space in the 2050s.

22 위 글의 밑줄 친 ⓑlike와 문법적 쓰임이 다른 것을 모두 고르시오.

① He just looks like his father.
② How did you like the book?
③ She's wearing a dress like yours.
④ They sell various things of like shape.
⑤ The boy was like a son to me.

23 위 글의 뒤에 올 내용으로 가장 알맞은 것을 고르시오.

① 미래에 달라질 삶의 모습에 대한 소개
② 미래의 사람들이 선호할 직업 소개
③ 미래에 중요하게 될 직업을 선택한 사람들과 그들의 직업
④ 미래에 사라질 직업 소개
⑤ 미래에도 꾸준히 인기 있을 직업들 소개

[24~25] 다음 글을 읽고 물음에 답하시오.

Do you see the flower pot that Sujin made? ⓐIt was made from old street flags. She is an ___(A)___ designer. She works with waste materials to make new products. Her products show people that old materials can be useful in new ways. ___(A)___ can reduce the amount of waste in the future. To become an ___(A)___ designer, you should be creative and learn about art.

24 주어진 영영풀이를 참고하여 빈칸 (A)에 철자 u로 시작하는 단어를 쓰시오. (대・소문자 무시)

the process of transforming by-products, waste materials, useless, or unwanted products into new materials or products of better quality and environmental value

➡ ____________________

25 위 글의 밑줄 친 ⓐ를 능동태로 고치시오.

➡ ______________________

[26~27] 다음 글을 읽고 물음에 답하시오.

ⓐ<u>Have you ever heard of 3D modelers?</u> Taeho, a 3D modeler, works for a company that makes artificial hands and legs. Taeho uses special software to print out new hands and legs. They are made specially for patients. If you are good at computer programming and art, you can be a 3D modeler. Taeho wants more people to use 3D printed products in the future.

26 다음 중 3D 모형 제작자가 될 수 있는 사람을 고르시오.

보람: I'm good at computer programming and art. 정호: I always want to help handicapped people but my computer programming is not good yet. 이슬: I'm good at computer programming but I don't like art. 창수: I have an excellent problem-solving skills. 민규: I'm not good at computer programming but I like art.

① 보람 ② 정호 ③ 이슬
④ 창수 ⑤ 민규

27 위 글의 밑줄 친 문장 ⓐ의 현재완료와 용법이 같은 것을 모두 고르시오.

① She <u>has gone</u> to New York.
② Tom <u>has</u> just <u>eaten</u> breakfast.
③ How many times <u>have</u> you <u>met</u> her?
④ How long <u>have</u> they <u>known</u> each other?
⑤ I <u>have visited</u> Paris before.

[28~30] 다음 글을 읽고 물음에 답하시오.

Jihye is a big data specialist. She works on many projects. ___ⓐ___, last year, she made bus routes. To find the best night routes, she needed to collect smartphone use data and taxi use patterns from late-night travelers. Then she analyzed this information to create the most useful routes. Now Jihye is working with an online shopping mall. She is collecting data from customers to find out the best styles for them. She knows big data allows us to learn more about our daily lives. If you want to become a big data specialist, you should develop your math and problem-solving skills!

Think about yourself and prepare for your future. If you keep looking ahead and dreaming big, your future will be bright.

28 위 글의 빈칸 ⓐ에 들어갈 알맞은 말을 고르시오.

① Therefore ② For example
③ However ④ In addition
⑤ Moreover

29 What is Jihye doing as a big data specialist now? Fill in the blanks with the suitable words.

➡ Now she is ________ ________ from customers of an online shopping mall ________ ________ ________ the best styles for them.

30 본문의 내용과 일치하도록 다음 빈칸 (A)와 (B)에 알맞은 단어를 쓰시오.

According to Jihye, (A)________ ________ allows us to learn more about (B)________ ________ ________.

단원별 예상문제

출제율 90%

01 다음 짝지어진 두 단어의 관계가 같도록 빈칸에 알맞은 단어를 쓰시오.

analysis : analyze – ________ : advise

출제율 100%

02 다음 빈칸에 공통으로 들어갈 말로 알맞은 것을 쓰시오.

- I'd like to help ________ if I can.
- Could you please print ________ this document for me?

출제율 95%

03 다음 중 밑줄 친 부분의 뜻풀이가 바르지 않은 것은?

① These artificial roses are quite lifelike. (인조의)
② Scientists have sent people out into space. (공간)
③ Terry suggested many kinds of movies. (종류)
④ She always gets creative ideas from children. (창조적인)
⑤ One of my strengths is that I never give up. (장점)

출제율 85%

04 대화의 순서를 올바르게 배열하시오.

(A) You're good at dancing, aren't you?
(B) I didn't decide yet. What am I good at?
(C) Jessica, what are you going to do for the school talent show?
(D) Not really. But I think I'm good at singing. I like singing very much.

➡ ________________

출제율 90%

05 다음 영영풀이에 해당하는 단어를 쓰시오.

to stay up on water

➡ ________________

[06~08] 다음 대화를 읽고 물음에 답하시오.

G: Jason, I read your paper. It was so (A)[amazing / amazed]!
B: Thank you for saying that. (①) I'm trying hard to improve my writing skills. I want to be a writer someday.
G: Really? (②) I want to write well like you. What do I need to do?
B: You need to read a lot of books. (③)
G: What else do I need to do?
B: Well, I write almost every day. (④) Why don't you (B)[to start / start] keeping a diary?
G: Thank you for your advice. (⑤) I'll start today.

출제율 100%

06 위 대화의 ①~⑤ 중 주어진 문장이 들어갈 알맞은 곳은?

Reading makes your writing better.

① ② ③ ④ ⑤

출제율 90%

07 괄호 (A)와 (B)에서 적절한 것을 고르시오.

➡ (A) ________________ (B) ________________

출제율 85%

08 다음 영영풀이에 해당하는 단어를 대화에서 찾아 쓰시오.

to make something better

➡ ________________

출제율 95%

09 다음 짝지어진 대화 중 어색한 것은?

① A: What do I need to do to become a painter?
B: Well, I need to study art history.

② A: Do you know how to do magic tricks?
B: No, I have no idea about it.

③ A: What do you suggest to get better grades?
B: I think you should take good notes in class.

④ A: How can I get better from this cold?
B: You need to drink a lot of water.

⑤ A: What do I need to do not to be late?
B: You should sleep early.

[10~12] 다음 대화를 읽고 물음에 답하시오.

G: Hello, Mr. Watson! Thank you for doing this interview. (①)
M: Sure, no problem.
G: This interview is for students (A)[what / which / who] want to be food stylists. (②)
M: Sure. You may see pictures of food in books or on TV. (③) A food stylist (B)[decorates / has / likes] food to look good for pictures or movies.
G: I want to be a food stylist like you. What do I need to do?
M: (④) You need to learn about many kinds of food.
G: What else do I need to do?
M: You need to study art, too. (⑤) Creativity is important.
G: All right! Thank you for your time, Mr. Watson.

출제율 90%

10 위 대화의 ①~⑤ 중 주어진 문장이 들어갈 알맞은 곳은?

Can you tell me about your job?

① ② ③ ④ ⑤

출제율 90%

11 괄호 (A)와 (B)에서 적절한 것을 고르시오.

➡ (A) ____________ (B) ____________

출제율 100%

12 위 대화의 내용으로 대답할 수 없는 질문을 고르시오.

① What does the girl want to be in the future?
② What does the girl need to do to become a food stylist?
③ What is the most important thing to become a food stylist?
④ What does a food stylist do?
⑤ What does the man do?

출제율 95%

13 다음 중 어법상 바르지 않은 것은?

She ①knows big data ②allows us ③learn ④more about our daily ⑤lives.

출제율 100%

14 다음 중 어법상 바른 것은?

① The father told his daughter did her homework.
② I want Seri watching the movie with us.
③ Because something happens tomorrow, call me immediately.
④ I'll do it after I finish here.
⑤ I didn't expect you get home so fast.

출제율 95%

15 다음 문장에서 어법상 잘못된 것을 고치시오.

(1) The teacher requested her go back to her seat.

➡ ______________________

(2) His dad won't let him to do it again in the future.

➡ ______________________

[16~18] 다음 글을 읽고 물음에 답하시오.

Do you see the flower pot that Sujin made? It was made from (A)[new / old] street flags. She is an upcycling designer. She works with (B)[useful / waste] materials to make new products. Her products show people that old materials can be (C)[useful / useless] in new ways. Upcycling can reduce the amount of waste in the future. To become an upcycling designer, you should be creative and learn about art.

출제율 100%

16 위 글의 괄호 (A)~(C)에서 문맥상 알맞은 낱말을 골라 쓰시오.

➡ (A)________ (B)________ (C)________

출제율 85%

17 본문의 내용을 참고하여 다음 빈칸 (A)와 (B)에 알맞은 단어를 쓰시오.

> We can say that upcycling is good for protecting environment because it can (A)__________ the amount of (B)__________.

출제율 90%

18 위 글의 내용과 일치하지 않는 것은?

① 수진은 화분을 만들었다.
② 수진은 업사이클링 디자이너이다.
③ 수진의 제품들은 낡은 재료를 새로운 방식으로 만든 것들이다.
④ 업사이클링으로 인해 미래에는 쓰레기의 종류가 늘어날 것이다.
⑤ 업사이클링 디자이너가 되려면 당신은 창의적이어야 하며 미술을 배워야 한다.

[19~21] 다음 글을 읽고 물음에 답하시오.

2020s • Self-driving cars will be on the market.
2030s • People will have robots __ⓐ__ do everything for them.
• 3D printers in every home will print out almost everything.
2050s • People will take space trips.
• People will live under the sea or in floating cities.

Look at the pictures above. Do these ideas surprise you? You can see __ⓑ__ our lives will be very different in the future. As our lives change, many new jobs will ⓒappear. What kind of job do you want? What will your future life be like? The following people looked ahead and chose jobs that will be important in the future. Let's read about their jobs!

출제율 100%

19 위 글의 빈칸 ⓐ와 ⓑ에 공통으로 들어갈 알맞은 단어를 고르시오.

① which ② what ③ while
④ that ⑤ as

출제율 85%

20 위 글의 밑줄 친 ⓒappear와 바꿔 쓸 수 없는 말을 고르시오.

① show up ② emerge
③ come along ④ turn up
⑤ encounter

출제율 90%

21 How will our lives be different in the 2020s? Fill in the blanks with the suitable words.

➡ ________________ __________ will be sold in the 2020s.

[22~23] 다음 글을 읽고 물음에 답하시오.

Have you ever heard of 3D modelers? Taeho, a 3D modeler, works for a company that makes artificial hands and legs. Taeho uses special software to print out new hands and legs. ⓐThey are made specially for patients. If you are good at computer programming and art, you can be a 3D modeler. Taeho wants more people to use 3D printed products in the future.

출제율 90%

22 위 글의 밑줄 친 ⓐThey가 가리키는 것을 본문에서 찾아 쓰시오.

➡ ________________________________

출제율 100%

23 위 글을 읽고 대답할 수 없는 질문은?

① What is Taeho's job?
② Where does Taeho work?
③ What does Taeho make at the company?
④ Who does Taeho work with?
⑤ What do you need to do well to become a 3D modeler?

[24~26] 다음 글을 읽고 물음에 답하시오.

Jihye is a big data specialist. She works on many projects. For example, last year, she made bus routes. To find the best night routes, she needed to collect smartphone use data and taxi use patterns from late-night travelers. Then she analyzed this information to create the most useful routes. Now Jihye is working with an online shopping mall. She is collecting data from customers to find out the best styles for them. She knows big data allows us ⓐto learn more about our daily lives. If you want to become a big data specialist, you should develop your math and problem-solving skills!

Think about yourself and prepare for your future. If you keep looking ahead and dreaming big, your future will be bright.

출제율 95%

24 위 글에 나온 big data 수집의 예 두 가지를 우리말로 쓰시오.

➡ (1) ________________________________
(2) ________________________________
____

출제율 90%

25 아래 〈보기〉에서 위 글의 밑줄 친 ⓐto learn과 to부정사의 용법이 다른 것의 개수를 고르시오. (2개)

보기
① She has a few friends to play with.
② I found it difficult to do so.
③ My goal is to become a great physicist.
④ She was sorry to hear that.
⑤ I told her to do it next.

① 1개 ② 2개 ③ 3개 ④ 4개 ⑤ 5개

출제율 90%

26 If you want to make your future bright, what do you need to do? Answer in English in a full sentence. (9 words)

➡ ________________________________
____

서술형 실전문제

[01~02] 다음 대화를 읽고 물음에 답하시오.

B: Jessica, what are you (A)going to do for the school talent show?
G: I didn't decide yet. (B)__________
B: You're good at dancing, aren't you?
G: Not really. But I think I'm good at singing. I like singing very much.
B: Really? Actually, I'm planning to play rock music with my band. Why don't you sing for us?
G: Sure, I'd love to.

01 밑줄 친 (A)와 바꿔 쓸 수 있는 말을 대화에서 찾아 쓰시오.

➡ __________

02 중요 빈칸 (B)에 들어갈 말을 주어진 단어를 이용하여 완성하시오.

➡ __________ (good, at)

03 다음 대화의 ①~⑤ 중 어색한 곳을 골라 바르게 고치시오.

A: ①What are you good at?
B: ②I'm good at took care of people.
A: Then how about becoming a nurse?
B: That sounds good. ③What do I need to do to become a nurse?
A: ④You need to learn about the human body.
B: ⑤What skills do I need to develop?
A: You need to develop your communication skills.

➡ __________
____

04 다음 빈칸을 알맞은 말로 채워 같은 뜻을 갖는 문장으로 바꾸어 쓰시오.

(1) Mary told her son that he should clean his room for himself.
➡ Mary asked __________.

(2) The doctor told him that he should stop smoking to live a life without pain.
➡ The doctor warned __________
__________.

(3) We hope that John will pass the entrance exam.
➡ We expect __________.

05 중요 다음 문장에서 어법상 어색한 부분을 찾아 바르게 고쳐 다시 쓰시오.

(1) What do you want me doing for you?
➡ __________

(2) Can you ask my prince comes to this tower?
➡ __________

(3) If you want to save us throw a rope down to us.
➡ __________

(4) If Seri will watch the movie with us, I will buy her some popcorn.
➡ __________
____

06 다음 우리말에 맞게 빈칸에 알맞은 말을 쓰시오.

• ________ you want, I ________ ________ there.
네가 원하지 않으면, 나는 거기 안 갈 거야.

[07~09] 다음 글을 읽고 물음에 답하시오.

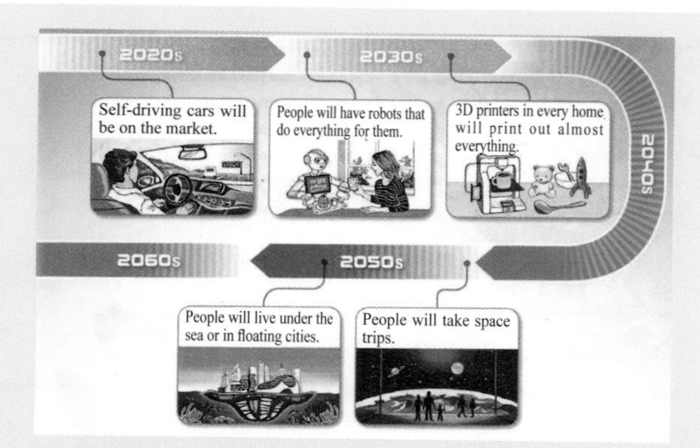

Look at the pictures above. Do these ideas surprise you? You can see that our lives will be very different in the future. As our lives change, many new jobs will appear. What kind of job do you want? ⓐ미래의 당신 삶은 어떤 모습일까요? The following people looked ahead and chose jobs that will be important in the future. Let's read about their jobs!

중요
07 위 글의 밑줄 친 ⓐ의 우리말에 맞게 한 단어를 보충하여, 주어진 어휘를 알맞게 배열하시오.

future / be / will / life / what / your / ?

➡ ______________________________

08 In the 2040s, will it be possible for you to take a space trip? Answer in English. (3 words)

➡ ____________________

09 다음 빈칸에 알맞은 단어를 넣어 위 글의 요지를 완성하시오.

In the future, our lives will not be the same as those of today. As our lives change, there will be many ________ ________.

[10~12] 다음 글을 읽고 물음에 답하시오.

Jihye is a big data specialist. She works on many projects. For example, last year, she made bus routes. To find the best night routes, she needed to (A)[collect / correct] smartphone use data and taxi use patterns from late-night travelers. Then she analyzed ⓐthis information to create the most useful routes. Now Jihye is working with an online shopping mall. She is collecting data from customers to find out the best styles for them. She knows big data allows us to learn more about our (B)[daily / dairy] lives. If you want to become a big data specialist, you should develop your math and problem-solving skills!

Think about (C)[you / yourself] and prepare for your future. If you keep looking ahead and dreaming big, your future will be bright.

10 위 글의 괄호 (A)~(C)에서 문맥이나 어법상 알맞은 낱말을 골라 쓰시오.

➡ (A)________ (B)________ (C)________

중요
11 위 글의 밑줄 친 ⓐthis information이 가리키는 것을 본문에서 찾아 쓰시오.

➡ ______________________________
____

12 다음 빈칸 (A)와 (B)에 알맞은 단어를 넣어 지혜의 직업에 대한 소개를 완성하시오.

Her Job: She is (A)________________. To Get the Job: You should develop your (B)________________.

창의사고력 서술형 문제

01 다음 그림의 상황을 보고, 조언을 구하고 답하는 대화를 주어진 단어를 이용하여 완성하시오.

A: Can I ask you something?
B: Sure. What is it?
A: ____________________ a good cook? (need)
B: ____
A: ____________________ (need)
B: You should try to make new dishes.

02 다음 기대 사항과 일치하도록 expect를 이용하여 어법에 맞게 쓰시오.

Mom's expectations
(1) me: get good grades
(2) my sister: become a scientist
(3) my dad: do not smoke

(1) ____
(2) ____
(3) ____

03 다음 내용을 바탕으로 20년 뒤 자신의 직업에 관해 강연할 원고를 작성하시오.

1. What is your job and where do you work?
   I am a computer programmer and work at a software company.
2. What do you usually do at work?
   I develop new software for computers.
3. Who do you work with?
   I work with people from different countries.
4. Why did you choose your job?
   I chose this job because I am interested in math and science.
5. What did you do to get this job?
   I studied computer science and developed my problem-solving skills.

Hello, everyone. My name is Soin Kim. I'm excited to tell you about my job. I am (A)____________________, and I work at a software company. I develop (B)____________________ for computers there. I work with many people (C)____________________. I chose this job because I am interested in (D)____________________. To become a computer programmer, I studied (E)____________________ and developed my problem-solving skills. If you have a dream, work hard for it. Then it will come true someday.

단원별 모의고사

[01~02] 다음 빈칸에 알맞은 단어를 고르시오.

01

There was a large ______ of information.

① average ② numbers
③ amount ④ order
⑤ much

02 우리말에 맞게 주어진 단어를 이용하여 빈칸을 채우시오.

(1) The team project needs everyone's __________. (collaborate) (그 팀 프로젝트는 모든 사람들의 협동을 필요로 한다.)

(2) __________ is the key to success. (creative) (창의력은 성공의 비결이다.)

03 다음 우리말과 일치하도록 빈칸을 채우시오. (주어진 철자로 시작할 것)

(1) 해가 하늘에 나타났다.
➡ The sun a__________ in the sky.

(2) 그녀는 그 일자리에 지원했다.
➡ She a__________ for the job.

(3) 나는 나의 담임선생님께 상담을 받았다.
➡ I received some c__________ from my homeroom teacher.

(4) 지금은 미래를 내다봐야 할 시기이다.
➡ Now is the time to l__________ a__________.

04 다음 영영풀이에 해당하는 단어를 고르시오.

a natural ability to do something well

① career ② knowledge ③ talent
④ job ⑤ artificial

[05~07] 다음 대화를 읽고 물음에 답하시오.

G: Hello, Mr. Watson! Thank you for doing this interview.
M: Sure, no problem.
G: This interview is for students who want to be food stylists. (A)__________________
M: Sure. You may see pictures of food in books or on TV. A food stylist decorates food to look good for pictures or movies.
G: I want to be a food stylist like you. (B)__________________
M: 많은 종류의 음식에 대해 배워야 해요. (need)
G: (C)__________________
M: You need to study art, too. Creativity is important.
G: All right! Thank you for your time, Mr. Watson.

05 위 대화의 빈칸 (A)~(C)에 알맞은 말을 <보기>에서 골라 순서대로 배열한 것은?

보기
ⓐ What else do I need to do?
ⓑ What do I need to do?
ⓒ Can you tell me about your job?

① ⓐ – ⓒ – ⓑ ② ⓑ – ⓐ – ⓒ
③ ⓑ – ⓒ – ⓐ ④ ⓒ – ⓐ – ⓑ
⑤ ⓒ – ⓑ – ⓐ

06 다음 영영풀이에 해당하는 단어를 대화에서 찾아 쓰시오.

the ability to think of or create something new

➡ __________________

07 밑줄 친 우리말을 주어진 단어를 이용하여 영작하시오.

➡ __________________

[08~10] 다음 대화를 읽고 물음에 답하시오.

A: What are you good (A)______?
B: I'm good at taking care (B)______ people.
A: Then how (C)______ becoming a nurse?
B: That sounds good. What do I need to do to become a nurse?
A: You need to learn (D)_____ the human body.
B: (do, skills, develop, what, to, I, need)?
A: You need to develop your communication skills.

08 빈칸 (A)~(D)에 들어갈 알맞은 말을 〈보기〉에서 골라 쓰시오. (중복 가능)

보기
about at from of to

➡ (A)________ (B)________
(C)________ (D)________

09 다음 영영풀이에 해당하는 단어를 대화에서 찾아 쓰시오.

to grow or become more advanced

➡ ________________

10 괄호 안의 단어를 알맞게 배열하여 영작하시오.

➡ ________________________

[11~12] 다음 대화를 읽고 물음에 답하시오.

B: Hey, Mandy. What are you ⓐ________ at?
G: Hey, Edward. Look! Some volunteers ⓑ________ for the school festival.
B: Really? I want ⓒ________ out. You know I'm good at ⓓ________ pictures. I think I can do something for the festival.
G: I think you can help out at the cartoon event.
B: Right!
G: Well, 나는 그림을 잘 그리지 못해. But I'm good at playing board games.
B: You can help out at the game event then.
G: Okay. Let's go and ⓔ________ to become volunteers.

11 빈칸 ⓐ~ⓔ에 들어갈 말로 올바르게 짝지어진 것을 모두 고르시오.

① ⓐ looked
② ⓑ need
③ ⓒ to help
④ ⓓ drawing
⑤ ⓔ to apply

12 밑줄 친 우리말을 주어진 말을 이용해 영작하시오. (good, draw)

➡ ________________________

13 다음 중 밑줄 친 부분의 쓰임이 바르지 못한 것은?

① I want you to listen to your father.
② You can persuade him do it again.
③ What made you think about it?
④ I need you to help me.
⑤ She advised me not to do it.

14 다음 빈칸에 들어갈 말로 어법상 적절한 것을 모두 고르시오.

__________ you get enough sleep, you will feel tired.

① Unless ② Until ③ As
④ When ⑤ Because

15 다음 상황에 알맞은 말을 어법에 맞게 빈칸에 쓰시오.

(1) Jack was very disappointed. Then, Paul told him that he could win the contest.
→ Paul encouraged Jack ________ ________ the contest.

(2) Today Mike was late for work. His boss said to him, "Don't be late again."
→ His boss ordered Mike ________ ________ ________ ________ again.

16 어법상 어색한 것을 고쳐 문장을 다시 쓰시오.

(1) The mother wanted her son cleans his room.
➡ ______________________

(2) I expect Juho exercising more.
➡ ______________________

(3) The doctor advised me stop eating junk food.
➡ ______________________

(4) Unless you show us your hand, we will open the door.
➡ ______________________

(5) If you won't sleep enough, you will be very tired.
➡ ______________________

17 괄호 안에 주어진 동사를 어법에 맞게 빈칸에 쓰시오.

(1) The boy told the woman ________ first. (go)

(2) If it ________ tomorrow, I will stay home. (rain)

[18~20] 다음 글을 읽고 물음에 답하시오.

Jihye is a big data specialist. She works on many projects. (①) For example, last year, she made bus routes. (②) To find the best night routes, she needed to collect smartphone use data and taxi use patterns from late-night travelers. (③) Now Jihye is working with an online shopping mall. (④) She is collecting data from customers to find out the best styles for them. (⑤) She knows big data allows us to learn more about our daily lives. If you want to become a big data specialist, you should develop your math and problem-solving skills!

Think about yourself and prepare for your future. ⓐ만약 당신이 계속 앞을 내다보고 꿈을 크게 꾼다면, your future will be bright.

18 위 글의 흐름으로 보아, 주어진 문장이 들어가기에 가장 적절한 곳은?

Then she analyzed this information to create the most useful routes.

① ② ③ ④ ⑤

19 위 글의 밑줄 친 ⓐ의 우리말에 맞게 주어진 어휘를 이용하여 8 단어로 영작하시오.

keep, ahead, big

➡ ______________________

20 위 글의 내용과 일치하지 않는 것은?

① 지혜는 빅데이터 전문가이다.
② 지혜는 작년에 버스 노선을 만들었다.
③ 현재 지혜는 온라인 쇼핑몰과 작업하고 있다.
④ 지혜는 빅데이터가 미래에 관하여 더 많이 알게 해 준다는 것을 알고 있다.
⑤ 빅데이터 전문가가 되고 싶다면, 수학과 문제 해결 능력을 계발해야 한다.

[21~22] 다음 글을 읽고 물음에 답하시오.

Do you see the flower pot that Sujin made? It was made from old street flags. She is an upcycling designer. She works with waste materials to make new products. Her products show people that old materials can be useful in new ways. Upcycling can reduce the amount of ⓐwaste in the future. To become an upcycling designer, you should be __(A)__ and learn about art.

21 위 글의 빈칸 (A)에 create를 알맞은 형태로 쓰시오.

➡ ____________________

22 위 글의 밑줄 친 ⓐwaste와 같은 의미로 쓰인 것을 고르시오.

① Don't waste your energy on useless things.
② The cause of pollution is industrial waste.
③ You should not waste a good opportunity.
④ It's a waste of time to do such a thing.
⑤ Waste water is pumped from the factory into a nearby river.

[23~25] 다음 글을 읽고 물음에 답하시오.

2020s • Self-driving cars will be on the market.
2030s • People will have robots that do everything for them.
• 3D printers in every home will print out almost everything.
2050s • People will take space trips.
• People will live under the sea or in floating cities.

Look at the pictures above. Do these ideas surprise you? You can see that our lives will be very different in the future. As our lives change, many new jobs will appear. What kind of job do you want? What will your future life be like? The following people looked ahead and chose jobs ⓐthat will be important in the future. Let's read about ⓑtheir jobs!

23 위 글의 밑줄 친 ⓐthat과 문법적 쓰임이 같은 것을 모두 고르시오.

① He is the greatest novelist that has ever lived.
② It's true that we were a little late.
③ There was no hope that she would recover her health.
④ The watch that you gave me keeps perfect time.
⑤ She said that the story was true.

24 위 글의 밑줄 친 ⓑtheir가 가리키는 것을 본문에서 찾아 쓰시오.

➡ ____________________

25 위 글을 읽고 대답할 수 없는 질문은?

① What will happen in the 2020s?
② How will our lives be different in the 2030s?
③ When will people be able to live in floating cities?
④ What will our lives be like in the 2060s?
⑤ Why will many new jobs appear in the future?

교과서 파헤치기

단어 Test

Step1

※ 다음 영어를 우리말로 쓰시오.

01 accident ____________
02 fame ____________
03 beauty ____________
04 moment ____________
05 spirit ____________
06 collect ____________
07 elderly ____________
08 survive ____________
09 respect ____________
10 following ____________
11 goodwill ambassador ____________
12 statue ____________
13 realize ____________
14 blind ____________
15 international ____________
16 alive ____________
17 worldwide ____________
18 feed ____________
19 item ____________
20 medicine ____________
21 donate ____________
22 luckily ____________
23 serve ____________
24 nursing home ____________
25 volunteer ____________
26 homeless ____________
27 praise ____________
28 mission ____________
29 raise ____________
30 honor ____________
31 turning point ____________
32 saying ____________
33 favor ____________
34 support ____________
35 all the time ____________
36 fall down ____________
37 hand out ____________
38 pass away ____________
39 thanks to ____________
40 clean up ____________
41 give a hand ____________
42 search for ____________
43 take care of ____________

단어 Test

Step2

※ 다음 우리말을 영어로 쓰시오.

01 존경하다 ______________

02 눈 먼, 장님의 ______________

03 속담, 격언 ______________

04 (음식을) 제공하다 ______________

05 세계적인 ______________

06 아름다움, 미(美) ______________

07 임무, 사명 ______________

08 순간, 잠깐 ______________

09 친선 대사 ______________

10 호의, 친절 ______________

11 (그) 다음의 ______________

12 조각상 ______________

13 열다, 개최하다 ______________

14 사고 ______________

15 들어 올리다, (자금을) 모으다 ______________

16 나이가 지긋한 ______________

17 깨닫다, 알아차리다 ______________

18 모으다, 수집하다 ______________

19 양로원 ______________

20 마음, 정신, 영혼 ______________

21 명성 ______________

22 예우하다, 존중하다 ______________

23 살아 있는, 존속하는 ______________

24 전환점 ______________

25 지지하다, 원조하다 ______________

26 칭찬하다 ______________

27 운이 좋게도, 다행스럽게도 ______________

28 풀, 잔디 ______________

29 약 ______________

30 살아남다, 생존하다 ______________

31 기부하다 ______________

32 집 없는, 노숙자의 ______________

33 자원봉사의, 자원 봉사자 ______________

34 먹이를 주다 ______________

35 사망하다 ______________

36 넘어지다 ______________

37 ~을 돌보다 ______________

38 나누어 주다 ______________

39 ~ 덕분에 ______________

40 ~을 돕다 ______________

41 어려움에 처한 ______________

42 ~을 치우다, 청소하다 ______________

43 늘, 내내 ______________

단어 Test

Step3

※ 다음 영영풀이에 알맞은 단어를 <보기>에서 골라 쓴 후, 우리말 뜻을 쓰시오.

1 __________: the state of being famous: __________

2 __________: not able to see anything: __________

3 __________: a sudden event that causes damage: __________

4 __________: to put things together in one place: __________

5 __________: to say nice things about someone: __________

6 __________: to suddenly know something: ____________

7 __________: to provide with assistance: ____________

8 __________: to admire or look up to somebody: __________

9 __________: to give something to help people: __________

10 __________: a time when a huge change takes place: __________

11 __________: to treat someone with respect: ____________

12 __________: a special task to be accomplished: __________

13 __________: a sculpture of a person made from stone or metal: __________

14 __________: to continue to live after something bad happens: ____________

15 __________: someone who is willing to do a job without getting paid: __________

16 __________: a place where people who are too old or sick to take care of themselves live: __________

보기

statue	fame	turning point	support
blind	nursing home	praise	volunteer
mission	collect	respect	realize
accident	survive	honor	donate

Step1

※ 다음 우리말과 일치하도록 빈칸에 알맞은 말을 쓰시오.

Listen & Talk 1 A

B: Mia, ________ you ________ ________ ________ these books?

G: Sure. ________ ________ you ________ ________ do with them?

B: I'm ________ ________ ________ them to a children's library.

B: Mia, 이 책들 옮기는 거 도와줄 수 있어?
G: 그럼. 너 이 책으로 뭐 할 거야?
B: 나는 이 책을 어린이 도서관에 기부할 거야.

Listen & Talk 1 B

B: Hey, Minji! What's ________ ________ your leg?

G: I ________ ________ last week.

B: Really? What ________?

G: I was in ________ ________ ________ ________ a train. But I ________ ________ in the street.

B: Oh, that's ________! ________ ________ anything I ________ ________ for you?

G: Well, ________ ________ ________ ________ ________ this bag?

B: Sure.

B: 민지야! 너 다리에 무슨 문제가 있니?
G: 지난주에 부러졌어.
B: 그래? 무슨 일이야?
G: 기차를 타려고 서두르고 있었어. 그런데 길에 넘어졌어.
B: 오, 정말 끔찍하다! 내가 너를 위해 해 줄 게 있니?
G: 음, 이 가방을 드는 걸 도와줄 수 있니?
B: 그럼.

Listen & Talk 1 C

B1: Wow! These dogs are so dirty. Jay, ________ ________ ________ me ________ ________?

B2: Allen, I'm sorry, ________ I ________. I have ________ ________ the cats now. ________ ________ ________ ________ Nicky?

B1: Okay! Nicky, can I ________ ________ ________ ________?

G: Sure, Allen. ________ is it?

B1: ________ ________ ________ me ________ these dogs?

G: Sure. But I ________ ________ ________ these dogs first. After that, I will help you.

B1: All right! ________ ________.

B1: 와! 이 개들 정말 더럽다. Jay, 이 개들 씻기는 거 도와줄 수 있니?
B2: Allen, 미안한데 못할 거 같아. 지금 이 고양이들에게 밥 줘야 해. Nicky한테 물어보는 게 어때?
B1: 알겠어! Nicky, 나 좀 도와줄 수 있니?
G: 물론이지, Allen. 뭔데?
B1: 이 개들 씻기는 거 도와줄 수 있니?
G: 그럼. 근데 나 이 개들 산책 먼저 시켜야 해. 끝나고 나서 도와줄게.
B1: 그래! 고마워.

Listen & Talk 2 A

G: ________ ________ ________ ________ activities can we do?

B: Why ________ ________ ________ ________ our town's streets?

G: All ________! ________ do it.

G: 우리 어떤 종류의 봉사 활동을 할 수 있을까?
B: 우리 동네 길거리를 청소하는 게 어때?
G: 좋아! 그러자.

Listen & talk 2 B

G: Good morning, students! ________ ________ ________, there ________ a big fire in Mapletown. ________ ________ ________ ________ money and help the people there? Come to our special event ________ the school grounds ________ ________ 3! Please ________ ________ ________ and ________ them. We will sell your items. Then, we will ________ ________ ________ ________ ________ Mapletown. Please ________ ________ ________ to people ________ ________.

G: 좋은 아침입니다, 학생 여러분! 아시다시피, Mapletown에 큰 화재가 있었습니다. 우리 돈을 모금해서 그 곳 사람들을 도와주는 게 어떨까요? 5월 3일 학교 운동장에서 열리는 특별 행사에 오세요! 물품들을 가져와서 그것들을 기부해 주세요. 우리는 여러분의 물품들을 팔 것입니다. 그리고, 모든 돈을 Mapletown에 기부할 것입니다. 어려운 사람들에게 도움을 줍시다.

Listen & Talk 2 C

B1: Next Wednesday is Volunteer Day. We ________ ________the park last time. What are ________ ________ ________ do this time?

G: Why ________ ________ ________ a ________ ________ and ________ ________ ________?

B2: That's not a ________ ________. But I want ________ ________ ________ ________. ________ ________ ________ ________ a party for the people there?

G: That's a good idea. ________ can we do at the party?

B1: We ________ ________ some food.

B2: And ________ ________ ________ some music? I can play the piano.

G: And I ________ ________ ________ ________.

B1: It ________ ________ a good plan.

B1: 다음 주 수요일이 봉사 활동 날이네. 우리 저번에는 공원을 청소했지. 이번엔 뭘 할까?
G: 양로원 가서 청소하는 건 어때?
B2: 나쁜 생각은 아니야. 근데 좀 재미있는 걸 하고 싶어. 거기 계신 분들을 위해 파티를 여는 게 어떨까?
G: 좋은 생각이야. 우리가 파티에서 뭘 할 수 있지?
B1: 음식을 대접할 수 있지.
B2: 그리고 연주를 하는 게 어때? 나 피아노 칠 수 있어.
G: 나는 첼로를 켤 수 있어.
B1: 아주 좋은 계획 같아.

Do It Yourself A

G1: We have a class activity day next Friday. What do you ________ ________ ________ ________ ________ ________?

B: ________ ________ we do some ________ ________? We can ________ ________ and ________ our community ________.

G1: That ________ ________, but choosing a good place ________ not easy.

B: We need someone ________ ________ ________ ________ ________.

G1: I know Sumin ________ ________ a lot. Sumin, can you ________ ________ ________ some good places?

G2: Sure. I ________ ________ ________ information on the internet. Why ________ ________ ________ the volunteering website for teens?

B: That's a ________ ________.

G1:우리 다음 주 금요일에 학급 활동이 있어. 그 날 어떤 것을 하고 싶니?
B: 우리 자원 봉사 활동들을 해 보는 게 어때? 우리가 다른 사람들을 도울 수 있고, 우리의 지역 사회를 더 좋게 만들 수 있어.
G1:그거 좋다, 하지만 좋은 장소를 고르는 건 쉽지 않아.
B: 우리는 봉사 활동을 많이 해본 사람이 필요해.
G1:나는 수민이가 봉사 활동을 많이 한 것을 알고 있어. 수민아, 우리가 좋은 장소들을 찾는 것을 도와주겠니?
G2:물론. 나는 주로 인터넷에서 정보를 찾아. 십대들을 위한 자원 봉사 웹사이트를 확인해 보는 게 어떠니?
B: 좋은 생각이다.

대화문 Test

Step2

※ 다음 우리말에 맞도록 대화를 영어로 쓰시오.

Listen & Talk 1 A

B: ______________________

G: ______________________

B: ______________________

B: Mia, 이 책들 옮기는 거 도와줄 수 있어?
G: 그럼. 너 이 책으로 뭐 할 거야?
B: 나는 이 책을 어린이 도서관에 기부할 거야.

Listen & Talk 1 B

B: ______________________

G: ______________________

B: ______________________

G: ______________________

B: ______________________

G: ______________________

B: ______________________

B: 민지야! 너 다리에 무슨 문제가 있니?
G: 지난주에 부러졌어.
B: 그래? 무슨 일이야?
G: 기차를 타려고 서두르고 있었어. 그런데 길에 넘어졌어.
B: 오, 정말 끔찍하다! 내가 너를 위해 해 줄 게 있니?
G: 음, 이 가방을 드는 걸 도와줄 수 있니?
B: 그럼.

Listen & Talk 1 C

B1: ______________________

B2: ______________________

____

B1: ______________________

G: ______________________

B1: ______________________

G: ______________________

B1: ______________________

B1: 와! 이 개들 정말 더럽다. Jay, 이 개들 씻기는 거 도와줄 수 있니?
B2: Allen, 미안한데 못할 거 같아. 지금 이 고양이들에게 밥 줘야 해. Nicky한테 물어보는 게 어때?
B1: 알겠어! Nicky, 나 좀 도와줄 수 있니?
G: 물론이지, Allen. 뭔데?
B1: 이 개들 씻기는 거 도와줄 수 있니?
G: 그럼. 근데 나 이 개들 산책 먼저 시켜야 해. 끝나고 나서 도와줄게.
B1: 그래! 고마워.

Listen & Talk 2 A

G: ______________________

B: ______________________

G: ______________________

G: 우리 어떤 종류의 봉사 활동을 할 수 있을까?
B: 우리 동네 길거리를 청소하는 게 어때?
G: 좋아! 그러자.

Listen & talk 2 B

G: ______________________________

G: 좋은 아침입니다, 학생 여러분! 아시다시피, Mapletown에 큰 화재가 있었습니다. 우리 돈을 모금해서 그 곳 사람들을 도와주는 게 어떨까요? 5월 3일 학교 운동장에서 열리는 특별 행사에 오세요! 물품들을 가져와서 그것들을 기부해 주세요. 우리는 여러분의 물품들을 팔 것입니다. 그리고, 모든 돈을 Mapletown에 기부할 것입니다. 어려운 사람들에게 도움을 줍시다.

Listen & Talk 2 C

B1: ______________________________

G: ______________________________

B2: ______________________________

G: ______________________________

B1: ______________________________

B2: ______________________________

G: ______________________________

B1: ______________________________

B1: 다음 주 수요일이 봉사 활동 날이네. 우리 저번에는 공원을 청소했지. 이번엔 뭘 할까?
G: 양로원 가서 청소하는 건 어때?
B2: 나쁜 생각은 아니야. 근데 좀 재미있는 걸 하고 싶어. 거기 계신 분들을 위해 파티를 여는 게 어떨까?
G: 좋은 생각이야. 우리가 파티에서 뭘 할 수 있지?
B1: 음식을 대접할 수 있지.
B2: 그리고 연주를 하는 게 어때? 나 피아노 칠 수 있어.
G: 나는 첼로를 켤 수 있어.
B1: 아주 좋은 계획 같아.

Do It Yourself A

G1: ______________________________

B: ______________________________

G1: ______________________________

B: ______________________________

G1: ______________________________

G2: ______________________________

B: ______________________________

G1:우리 다음 주 금요일에 학급 활동이 있어. 그 날 어떤 것을 하고 싶니?
B: 우리 자원 봉사 활동들을 해 보는 게 어때? 우리가 다른 사람들을 도울 수 있고, 우리의 지역 사회를 더 좋게 만들 수 있어.
G1:그거 좋다, 하지만 좋은 장소를 고르는 건 쉽지 않아.
B: 우리는 봉사 활동을 많이 해본 사람이 필요해.
G1:나는 수민이가 봉사 활동을 많이 한 것을 알고 있어. 수민아, 우리가 좋은 장소들을 찾는 것을 도와주겠니?
G2:물론. 나는 주로 인터넷에서 정보를 찾아. 십대들을 위한 자원 봉사 웹사이트를 확인해 보는 게 어떠니?
B: 좋은 생각이다.

본문 Test

Step1

※ 다음 우리말과 일치하도록 빈칸에 알맞은 것을 골라 쓰시오.

1 The ________ of ________
A. Audrey B. Spirit

1 오드리의 정신

2 ________ World War II, a ________ girl and her mother ________ hungry and sick.
A. little B. during C. were

2 제2차 세계 대전 동안, 한 어린 소녀와 그녀의 어머니는 굶주리고 아팠다.

3 The only food ________ they could ________ ________ grass.
A. that B. was C. find

3 그들이 찾을 수 있었던 유일한 음식은 풀뿐이었다.

4 The little girl ________ ________ all the ________.
A. scared B. felt C. time

4 어린 소녀는 내내 겁에 질려 있었다.

5 ________, the girl survived, ________ ________ the help of others.
A. to B. luckily C. thanks

5 다행히도, 소녀는 다른 사람들의 도움 덕분에 살아남았다.

6 One of the ________ that ________ her ________ UNICEF.
A. helped B. was C. groups

6 그녀를 도왔던 단체 중 하나는 유니세프(국제 연합 아동 기금)였다.

7 ________, the girl ________ a ________ movie star.
A. worldwide B. became C. later

7 후에, 소녀는 세계적인 영화배우가 되었다.

8 ________ ________ was Audrey Hepburn.
A. name B. her

8 그녀의 이름은 오드리 헵번이었다.

9 ________ she grew ________, Hepburn became a symbol of ________.
A. beauty B. up C. when

9 그녀가 자랐을 때, 헵번은 아름다움의 상징이 되었다.

10 She was very popular ________ ________ her hit movies, ________ ________ *My Fair Lady* and *Roman Holiday*.
A. of B. as C. such D. because

10 그녀는 〈마이 페어 레이디〉와 〈로마의 휴일〉과 같은 흥행 영화들로 인해 매우 인기가 있었다.

11 The little black dress ________ she ________ in a movie is famous ________ today.
A. wore B. even C. which

11 그녀가 영화에서 입었던 아담한 검은 드레스는 심지어 오늘날까지도 유명하다.

12 Many people ________ ________ her ________.
A. style B. love C. still

12 많은 사람이 여전히 그녀의 스타일을 사랑한다.

13 The autumn of 1987 was a ________ ________ in Hepburn's ________.
A. life B. point C. turning

13 1987년 가을은 헵번의 인생 전환점이었다.

14 She ________ to an ________ music ________ in Macau.
A. went B. festival C. international

14 그녀는 마카오의 한 국제 음악 축제에 갔다.

15 Many people ________ ________ at the festival, and the money ________ to UNICEF.
A. money B. went C. donated

15 많은 사람이 축제에서 돈을 기부했고, 그 돈은 유니세프로 보내졌다.

16 ________ ________ her fame, UNICEF collected ________ money ________ ever before.

A. than B. to C. more D. thanks

17 Hepburn ________ that her ________ could help ________, so she became a UNICEF Goodwill Ambassador.

A. realized B. others C. fame

18 First, Hepburn ________ ________ Ethiopia ________ 1988.

A. to B. in C. went

19 ________, she ________ food ________ hungry children.

A. brought B. to C. there

20 She was ________ ________ their ________ were very difficult.

A. lives B. because C. shocked

21 ________ that, she ________ in ________ countries.

A. after B. other C. volunteered

22 In 1990, she ________ Vietnam to ________ ________ medicine and ________ clean drinking water programs.

A. out B. visited C. support D. hand

23 Her last trip was ________ Somalia in 1992, and she ________ ________ the ________ year.

A. away B. to C. following D. passed

24 Many people ________ her ________ and style, but Hepburn's ________ was her ________.

A. beauty B. heart C. real D. praised

25 ________ ________ her, UNICEF made a ________, *The Spirit of Audrey*.

A. honor B. statue C. to

26 People who ________ her ________ her mission ________.

A. alive B. keep C. respect

27 Her ________ ________ shows her ________.

A. saying B. favorite C. mission

28 ________ *you* ________ *older,* ________ *you have two hands.*

A. remember B. get C. as

29 ________ *is for helping* ________, *and the* ________ *is for helping* ________.

A. other B. one C. others D. yourself

16 그녀의 명성 덕분에, 유니세프는 어느 때보다도 더 많은 돈을 모았다.

17 헵번은 자신의 명성이 다른 사람들을 도울 수 있다는 것을 깨닫고, 유니세프 친선 대사가 되었다.

18 먼저, 헵번은 1988년에 에티오피아로 갔다.

19 그곳에서, 그녀는 굶주린 아이들에게 음식을 가져다주었다.

20 그녀는 그들의 삶이 매우 어려웠기 때문에 충격을 받았다.

21 그 후, 그녀는 다른 나라들에서도 봉사하였다.

22 1990년, 그녀는 의약품을 나눠 주고 깨끗한 식수 프로그램을 지원하기 위하여 베트남을 방문하였다.

23 그녀의 마지막 여행은 1992년 소말리아에 간 것이었으며, 이듬해 그녀는 사망하였다.

24 많은 사람이 그녀의 아름다움과 스타일을 칭송했지만, 헵번의 진정한 아름다움은 그녀의 마음이었다.

25 그녀를 기리기 위해, 유니세프는 '오드리의 정신'이라는 동상을 만들었다.

26 그녀를 존경하는 사람들이 그녀의 사명을 이어 나가고 있다.

27 그녀가 가장 좋아했던 구절은 그녀의 사명을 보여 준다.

28 나이가 들어갈수록, 당신에게 손이 두 개가 있다는 것을 기억하라.

29 한 손은 자신을 돕기 위한 것이고, 다른 한 손은 타인을 돕기 위한 것이다.

본문 Test

Step2

※ 다음 우리말과 일치하도록 빈칸에 알맞은 말을 쓰시오.

1 The ________ ________ ________

2 ________ World War II, a ________ girl and her mother ________ ________ and ________.

3 ________ ________ food ________ they could find ________ grass.

4 The little girl ________ ________ ________ ________ ________.

5 ________, the girl survived, ________ ________ the help of ________.

6 ________ ________ ________ ________ ________ helped her ________ UNICEF.

7 Later, the girl became ________ ________ ________ ________.

8 ________ ________ ________ Audrey Hepburn.

9 When she ________ ________, Hepburn became ________ ________ ________ ________.

10 She was very popular ________ ________ her hit movies, ________ ________ *My Fair Lady* and *Roman Holiday*.

11 The little black dress ________ ________ ________ in a movie ________ ________ even today.

12 Many people ________ ________ ________ ________.

13 The autumn of 1987 was ________ ________ ________ in Hepburn's life.

14 She went to ________ ________ ________ ________ in Macau.

15 Many people ________ ________ at the festival, and the money went ________ ________.

1 오드리의 정신

2 제2차 세계 대전 동안, 한 어린 소녀와 그녀의 어머니는 굶주리고 아팠다.

3 그들이 찾을 수 있었던 유일한 음식은 풀뿐이었다.

4 어린 소녀는 내내 겁에 질려 있었다.

5 다행히도, 소녀는 다른 사람들의 도움 덕분에 살아남았다.

6 그녀를 도왔던 단체 중 하나는 유니세프(국제 연합 아동 기금)였다.

7 후에, 소녀는 세계적인 영화배우가 되었다.

8 그녀의 이름은 오드리 헵번이었다.

9 그녀가 자랐을 때, 헵번은 아름다움의 상징이 되었다.

10 그녀는 〈마이 페어 레이디〉와 〈로마의 휴일〉과 같은 흥행 영화들로 인해 매우 인기가 있었다.

11 그녀가 영화에서 입었던 아담한 검은 드레스는 심지어 오늘날까지도 유명하다.

12 많은 사람이 여전히 그녀의 스타일을 사랑한다.

13 1987년 가을은 헵번의 인생 전환점이었다.

14 그녀는 마카오의 한 국제 음악 축제에 갔다.

15 많은 사람이 축제에서 돈을 기부했고, 그 돈은 유니세프로 보내졌다.

16 _______ _______ her fame, UNICEF _______ _______ money _______ ever before.

17 Hepburn _______ _______ her fame could _______ _______, so she became _______ _______ _______ _______.

18 First, Hepburn _______ _______ _______ in 1988.

19 There, she _______ food _______ _______ _______.

20 She _______ _______ _______ their _______ were very difficult.

21 After that, she _______ _______ _______ _______.

22 In 1990, she visited Vietnam _______ _______ _______ _______ and _______ clean drinking water programs.

23 Her last trip was _______ Somalia in 1992, and she _______ _______ the _______ _______.

24 Many people _______ her beauty and style, but Hepburn's _______ _______ _______ _______ _______.

25 _______ _______ her, UNICEF _______ _______ _______, *The Spirit of Audrey*.

26 People _______ _______ her _______ her mission _______.

27 Her _______ _______ shows _______ _______.

28 _______ *you* _______ _______, *remember you have two hands.*

29 _______ *is for helping* _______, *and* _______ _______ *is for helping* _______.

16 그녀의 명성 덕분에, 유니세프는 어느 때보다도 더 많은 돈을 모았다.

17 헵번은 자신의 명성이 다른 사람들을 도울 수 있다는 것을 깨닫고, 유니세프 친선 대사가 되었다.

18 먼저, 헵번은 1988년에 에티오피아로 갔다.

19 그곳에서, 그녀는 굶주린 아이들에게 음식을 가져다주었다.

20 그녀는 그들의 삶이 매우 어려웠기 때문에 충격을 받았다.

21 그 후, 그녀는 다른 나라들에서도 봉사하였다.

22 1990년, 그녀는 의약품을 나눠 주고 깨끗한 식수 프로그램을 지원하기 위하여 베트남을 방문하였다.

23 그녀의 마지막 여행은 1992년 소말리아에 간 것이었으며, 이듬해 그녀는 사망하였다.

24 많은 사람이 그녀의 아름다움과 스타일을 칭송했지만, 헵번의 진정한 아름다움은 그녀의 마음이었다.

25 그녀를 기리기 위해, 유니세프는 '오드리의 정신'이라는 동상을 만들었다.

26 그녀를 존경하는 사람들이 그녀의 사명을 이어 나가고 있다.

27 그녀가 가장 좋아했던 구절은 그녀의 사명을 보여 준다.

28 나이가 들어갈수록, 당신에게 손이 두 개가 있다는 것을 기억하라.

29 한 손은 자신을 돕기 위한 것이고, 다른 한 손은 타인을 돕기 위한 것이다.

본문 Test

Step3

※ 다음 문장을 우리말로 쓰시오.

1 The Spirit of Audrey

➡ ______________________________

2 During World War II, a little girl and her mother were hungry and sick.

➡ ______________________________

3 The only food that they could find was grass.

➡ ______________________________

4 The little girl felt scared all the time.

➡ ______________________________

5 Luckily, the girl survived, thanks to the help of others.

➡ ______________________________

6 One of the groups that helped her was UNICEF.

➡ ______________________________

7 Later, the girl became a worldwide movie star.

➡ ______________________________

8 Her name was Audrey Hepburn.

➡ ______________________________

9 When she grew up, Hepburn became a symbol of beauty.

➡ ______________________________

10 She was very popular because of her hit movies, such as *My Fair Lady* and *Roman Holiday*.

➡ ______________________________

11 The little black dress which she wore in a movie is famous even today.

➡ ______________________________

12 Many people still love her style.

➡ ______________________________

13 The autumn of 1987 was a turning point in Hepburn's life.

➡ ______________________________

14 She went to an international music festival in Macau.

➡ ______________________________

15 Many people donated money at the festival, and the money went to UNICEF.

➡ ______________________________

16 Thanks to her fame, UNICEF collected more money than ever before.

➡ ______________________________

17 Hepburn realized that her fame could help others, so she became a UNICEF Goodwill Ambassador.

➡ ______________________________

18 First, Hepburn went to Ethiopia in 1988.

➡ ______________________________

19 There, she brought food to hungry children.

➡ ______________________________

20 She was shocked because their lives were very difficult.

➡ ______________________________

21 After that, she volunteered in other countries.

➡ ______________________________

22 In 1990, she visited Vietnam to hand out medicine and support clean drinking water programs.

➡ ______________________________

23 Her last trip was to Somalia in 1992, and she passed away the following year.

➡ ______________________________

24 Many people praised her beauty and style, but Hepburn's real beauty was her heart.

➡ ______________________________

25 To honor her, UNICEF made a statue, *The Spirit of Audrey*.

➡ ______________________________

26 People who respect her keep her mission alive.

➡ ______________________________

27 Her favorite saying shows her mission.

➡ ______________________________

28 *As you get older, remember you have two hands.*

➡ ______________________________

29 *One is for helping yourself, and the other is for helping others.*

➡ ______________________________

본문 Test

Step4

※ 다음 괄호 안의 단어들을 우리말에 맞도록 바르게 배열하시오.

1 (Spirit / The / Audrey / of)
➡ ______________________________

2 (World / II, / During / War / little / a / girl / and / mother / her / were / sick. / and / hungry)
➡ ______________________________

3 (only / the / that / food / they / find / could / grass. / was)
➡ ______________________________

4 (little / the / girl / scared / felt / time. / the / all)
➡ ______________________________

5 (the / luckily / girl / survived, / to / thanks / the / of / others. / help)
➡ ______________________________

6 (of / one / groups / the / helped / that / UNICEF. / was / her)
➡ ______________________________

7 (the / later, / girl / became / worldwide / a / star. / movie)
➡ ______________________________

8 (name / her / Hepburn. / Audrey / was)
➡ ______________________________

9 (she / when / up, / grew / became / Hepburn / symbol / a / beauty. / of)
➡ ______________________________

10 (was / she / popular / very / of / because / her / movies, / hit / as / such / *Lady* / *Fair* / *My* / and / *Holiday*. / *Roman*)
➡ ______________________________
____

11 (little / the / dress / black / she / which / wore / a / in / movie / is / today. / even / famous)
➡ ______________________________

12 (people / many / love / still / style. / her)
➡ ______________________________

13 (autumn / the / 1987 / of / was / turning / a / point / life. / Hepburn's / in)
➡ ______________________________

14 (went / she / to / international / an / festival / music / Macau. / in)
➡ ______________________________

15 (people / many / money / donated / the / at / festival, / and / money / the / UNICEF. / to / went)
➡ ______________________________
____

1 오드리의 정신

2 제2차 세계 대전 동안, 한 어린 소녀와 그녀의 어머니는 굶주리고 아팠다.

3 그들이 찾을 수 있었던 유일한 음식은 풀뿐이었다.

4 어린 소녀는 내내 겁에 질려 있었다.

5 다행히도, 소녀는 다른 사람들의 도움 덕분에 살아남았다.

6 그녀를 도왔던 단체 중 하나는 유니세프(국제 연합 아동 기금)였다.

7 후에, 소녀는 세계적인 영화배우가 되었다.

8 그녀의 이름은 오드리 헵번이었다.

9 그녀가 자랐을 때, 헵번은 아름다움의 상징이 되었다.

10 그녀는 〈마이 페어 레이디〉와 〈로마의 휴일〉과 같은 흥행 영화들로 인해 매우 인기가 있었다.

11 그녀가 영화에서 입었던 아담한 검은 드레스는 심지어 오늘날까지도 유명하다.

12 많은 사람이 여전히 그녀의 스타일을 사랑한다.

13 1987년 가을은 헵번의 인생 전환점이었다.

14 그녀는 마카오의 한 국제 음악 축제에 갔다.

15 많은 사람이 축제에서 돈을 기부했고, 그 돈은 유니세프로 보내졌다.

Step4

16 (to / thanks / fame, / her / UNICEF / more / collected / money / ever / before. / than)

➡ ____________________

17 (realized / Hepburn / that / fame / her / help / could / others, / she / so / became / UNICEF / a / Ambassador. / Goodwill)

➡ ____________________

____

18 (Hepburn / first, / to / went / 1988 / in / Ethiopia)

➡ ____________________

19 (she / there, / brought / to / food / children. / hungry)

➡ ____________________

20 (was / she / because / shocked / lives / their / difficult. / very / were)

➡ ____________________

21 (that, / after / volunteered / she / countries. / other / in)

➡ ____________________

22 (1990, / in / visited / she / Vietnam / hand / to / medicine / out / and / clean / support / drinking / programs. / water)

➡ ____________________

____

23 (last / her / trip / to / was / Somalia / 1992, / in / she / and / away / passed / year. / following / the)

➡ ____________________

____

24 (people / many / her / praised / beauty / and / style, / but / real / Hepburn's / beauty / heart. / her / was)

➡ ____________________

____

25 (honor / to / her, / made / UNICEF / statue, / a / *of* / *Spirit* / *Audrey.* / *The*)

➡ ____________________

26 (who / people / her / respect / keep / alive. / mission / her)

➡ ____________________

27 (favorite / her / shows / mission. / her / saying)

➡ ____________________

28 (you / as / older, / get / you / remember / hands. / two / have)

➡ ____________________

29 (is / one / helping / for / yourself, / the / and / other / for / is / others. / helping)

➡ ____________________

16 그녀의 명성 덕분에, 유니세프는 어느 때보다도 더 많은 돈을 모았다.

17 헵번은 자신의 명성이 다른 사람들을 도울 수 있다는 것을 깨닫고, 유니세프 친선 대사가 되었다.

18 먼저, 헵번은 1988년에 에티오피아로 갔다.

19 그곳에서, 그녀는 굶주린 아이들에게 음식을 가져다주었다.

20 그녀는 그들의 삶이 매우 어려웠기 때문에 충격을 받았다.

21 그 후, 그녀는 다른 나라들에서도 봉사하였다.

22 1990년, 그녀는 의약품을 나눠 주고 깨끗한 식수 프로그램을 지원하기 위하여 베트남을 방문하였다.

23 그녀의 마지막 여행은 1992년 소말리아에 간 것이었으며, 이듬해 그녀는 사망하였다.

24 많은 사람이 그녀의 아름다움과 스타일을 칭송했지만, 헵번의 진정한 아름다움은 그녀의 마음이었다.

25 그녀를 기리기 위해, 유니세프는 '오드리의 정신'이라는 동상을 만들었다.

26 그녀를 존경하는 사람들이 그녀의 사명을 이어 나가고 있다.

27 그녀가 가장 좋아했던 구절은 그녀의 사명을 보여 준다.

28 나이가 들어갈수록, 당신에게 손이 두 개가 있다는 것을 기억하라.

29 한 손은 자신을 돕기 위한 것이고, 다른 한 손은 타인을 돕기 위한 것이다.

본문 Test

Step5

※ 다음 우리말을 영어로 쓰시오.

1 오드리의 정신

➡ ______________________________

2 제2차 세계 대전 동안, 한 어린 소녀와 그녀의 어머니는 굶주리고 아팠다.

➡ ______________________________

3 그들이 찾을 수 있었던 유일한 음식은 풀뿐이었다.

➡ ______________________________

4 어린 소녀는 내내 겁에 질려 있었다.

➡ ______________________________

5 다행히도, 소녀는 다른 사람들의 도움 덕분에 살아남았다.

➡ ______________________________

6 그녀를 도왔던 단체 중 하나는 유니세프(국제 연합 아동 기금)였다.

➡ ______________________________

7 후에, 소녀는 세계적인 영화배우가 되었다.

➡ ______________________________

8 그녀의 이름은 오드리 헵번이었다.

➡ ______________________________

9 그녀가 자랐을 때, 헵번은 아름다움의 상징이 되었다.

➡ ______________________________

10 그녀는 〈마이 페어 레이디〉와 〈로마의 휴일〉과 같은 흥행 영화들로 인해 매우 인기가 있었다.

➡ ______________________________

11 그녀가 영화에서 입었던 아담한 검은 드레스는 심지어 오늘날까지도 유명하다.

➡ ______________________________

12 많은 사람이 여전히 그녀의 스타일을 사랑한다.

➡ ______________________________

13 1987년 가을은 헵번의 인생 전환점이었다.

➡ ______________________________

14 그녀는 마카오의 한 국제 음악 축제에 갔다.

➡ ______________________________

15 많은 사람이 축제에서 돈을 기부했고, 그 돈은 유니세프로 보내졌다.

➡ ______________________________

16 그녀의 명성 덕분에, 유니세프는 어느 때보다도 더 많은 돈을 모았다.

➡ ______________________________

17 헵번은 자신의 명성이 다른 사람들을 도울 수 있다는 것을 깨닫고, 유니세프 친선 대사가 되었다.

➡ ______________________________

18 먼저, 헵번은 1988년에 에티오피아로 갔다.

➡ ______________________________

19 그곳에서, 그녀는 굶주린 아이들에게 음식을 가져다주었다.

➡ ______________________________

20 그녀는 그들의 삶이 매우 어려웠기 때문에 충격을 받았다.

➡ ______________________________

21 그 후, 그녀는 다른 나라들에서도 봉사하였다.

➡ ______________________________

22 1990년, 그녀는 의약품을 나눠 주고 깨끗한 식수 프로그램을 지원하기 위하여 베트남을 방문하였다.

➡ ______________________________

23 그녀의 마지막 여행은 1992년 소말리아에 간 것이었으며, 이듬해 그녀는 사망하였다.

➡ ______________________________

24 많은 사람이 그녀의 아름다움과 스타일을 칭송했지만, 헵번의 진정한 아름다움은 그녀의 마음이었다.

➡ ______________________________

25 그녀를 기리기 위해, 유니세프는 '오드리의 정신'이라는 동상을 만들었다.

➡ ______________________________

26 그녀를 존경하는 사람들이 그녀의 사명을 이어 나가고 있다.

➡ ______________________________

27 그녀가 가장 좋아했던 구절은 그녀의 사명을 보여 준다.

➡ ______________________________

28 나이가 들어갈수록, 당신에게 손이 두 개가 있다는 것을 기억하라.

➡ ______________________________

29 한 손은 자신을 돕기 위한 것이고, 다른 한 손은 타인을 돕기 위한 것이다.

➡ ______________________________

※ 다음 우리말과 일치하도록 빈칸에 알맞은 말을 쓰시오.

Presentation Time

1. Lee Taeseok was ________ ________ ________.
2. He was a ________ and ________ a doctor.
3. He ________ hospitals and schools ________ the people of Tonj.
4. He ________ ________ ________ them and ________ ________.
5. ________ this person, I learned ________ I ________ ________ people ________ ________.

1. 이태석은 위대한 사람이었다.
2. 그는 성직자이고 또한 의사였다.
3. 그는 톤즈의 사람들을 위해 병원과 학교를 세웠다.
4. 그는 그들을 돌보고 수업을 했다.
5. 이 사람으로부터, 나는 어려움에 처한 사람들을 도와야 한다고 배웠다.

After You Read B

1. Reporter: ________ was your life ________ World War II?
2. Can you ________ ________ ________ it?
3. Audrey: It was ________. My family and I ________ ________ and ________.
4. We ________ ________ ________ the help of ________.
5. Reporter: How did you ________ ________ ________ for UNICEF?
6. Audrey: In 1987, a musical festival in Macau ________ ________ ________.
7. I learned ________ my fame ________ ________ ________ ________.
8. Reporter: ________ ________, what ________ you ________?
9. Audrey: I ________ ________ ________ in Africa and Asia and ________ ________.

1. 리포터: 제2차 세계 대전 동안 당신의 삶은 어땠습니까?
2. 그것에 대해 말해주실 수 있나요?
3. 오드리: 끔찍했어요. 제 가족과 저는 굶주리고 아팠어요.
4. 우리는 다른 사람들의 도움 덕분에 살아남았어요.
5. 리포터: 당신은 어떻게 유니세프를 위해 일하게 되었나요?
6. 오드리: 1987년에, 마카오의 한 음악 축제가 제 삶을 바꿨어요.
7. 저는 제 명성이 다른 사람들을 도울 수 있다는 것을 알게 되었어요.
8. 리포터: 그 다음에, 무엇을 했나요?
9. 오드리: 아프리카와 아시아의 몇몇 나라들을 방문해서 그곳에서 자원 봉사를 했어요.

Culture Link

1. ________ ________ Program
2. This is a ________ ________ ________ audiobooks for ________ people.
3. It ________ ________ in 1931 in the United States.
4. You just read books and ________ ________ ________.
5. These audiobooks ________ ________ to blind people ________ ________.

1. 말하는 책 프로그램
2. 이것은 시각장애인을 위한 오디오북을 만드는 프로그램이다.
3. 이것은 1931년 미국에서 시작되었다.
4. 당신은 책을 읽고 당신의 목소리를 녹음하기만 하면 된다.
5. 이러한 오디오북들은 시각장애인들에게 무료로 주어진다.

※ 다음 우리말을 영어로 쓰시오.

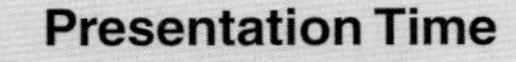

Presentation Time

1. 이태석은 위대한 사람이었다.
   ➡ ____________________
2. 그는 성직자이고 또한 의사였다.
   ➡ ____________________
3. 그는 톤즈의 사람들을 위해 병원과 학교를 세웠다.
   ➡ ____________________
4. 그는 그들을 돌보고 수업을 했다.
   ➡ ____________________
5. 이 사람으로부터, 나는 어려움에 처한 사람들을 도와야 한다고 배웠다.
   ➡ ____________________

After You Read B

1. 리포터: 제2차 세계 대전 동안 당신의 삶은 어땠습니까?
   ➡ ____________________
2. 그것에 대해 말해주실 수 있나요?
   ➡ ____________________
3. 오드리: 끔찍했어요. 제 가족과 저는 굶주리고 아팠어요.
   ➡ ____________________
4. 우리는 다른 사람들의 도움 덕분에 살아남았어요.
   ➡ ____________________
5. 리포터: 당신은 어떻게 유니세프를 위해 일하게 되었나요?
   ➡ ____________________
6. 오드리: 1987년에, 마카오의 한 음악 축제가 제 삶을 바꿨어요.
   ➡ ____________________
7. 저는 제 명성이 다른 사람들을 도울 수 있다는 것을 알게 되었어요.
   ➡ ____________________
8. 리포터: 그 다음에, 무엇을 했나요?
   ➡ ____________________
9. 오드리: 아프리카와 아시아의 몇몇 나라들을 방문해서 그곳에서 자원 봉사를 했어요.
   ➡ ____________________

Culture Link

1. 말하는 책 프로그램
   ➡ ____________________
2. 이것은 시각장애인을 위한 오디오북을 만드는 프로그램이다.
   ➡ ____________________
3. 이것은 1931년 미국에서 시작되었다.
   ➡ ____________________
4. 당신은 책을 읽고 당신의 목소리를 녹음하기만 하면 된다.
   ➡ ____________________
5. 이러한 오디오북들은 시각장애인들에게 무료로 주어진다.
   ➡ ____________________

단어 Test

Step1

※ 다음 영어를 우리말로 쓰시오.

01 presentation ______
02 view ______
03 relax ______
04 awesome ______
05 stop ______
06 comic book ______
07 condition ______
08 field trip ______
09 amazing ______
10 art museum ______
11 history ______
12 purpose ______
13 amusement park ______
14 foreign ______
15 street food ______
16 hike ______
17 straight ______
18 holiday ______
19 international ______
20 village ______
21 art show ______
22 historical ______
23 site ______
24 natural ______
25 painting ______
26 goods ______
27 plan ______
28 rafting ______
29 autumn ______
30 rough ______
31 scenery ______
32 university ______
33 museum ______
34 visit ______
35 at the same time ______
36 on foot ______
37 be able to 동사원형 ______
38 get off ______
39 no longer ______
40 a variety of ______
41 focus on ______
42 in front of ______
43 by bus ______

단어 Test

Step2

※ 다음 우리말을 영어로 쓰시오.

01 만화책 ______________
02 풍경, 경치 ______________
03 국제적인 ______________
04 똑바로, 일직선으로 ______________
05 상태, 상황 ______________
06 발표 ______________
07 박물관 ______________
08 놀라운, 멋진 ______________
09 미술관 ______________
10 전망 ______________
11 정거장, (여행 중) 머무른 곳 ______________
12 거친, 파도가 심한 ______________
13 견학 여행, 현장 학습 ______________
14 도보 여행하다 ______________
15 휴식을 취하다, 느긋이 쉬다 ______________
16 역사 ______________
17 마을 ______________
18 외국의 ______________
19 대학교 ______________
20 목적, 목표 ______________
21 가을 ______________
22 방문하다, 찾아가다 ______________
23 역사적인, 역사상의 ______________
24 장소 ______________
25 휴가, 공휴일, 휴일 ______________
26 놀이공원 ______________
27 길거리 음식 ______________
28 상품, 물건 ______________
29 미술 전시회 ______________
30 자연의 ______________
31 래프팅, 급류 타기 ______________
32 매우 멋진 ______________
33 그림 ______________
34 계획하다; 계획 ______________
35 (~에) 집중하다, 초점을 맞추다 ______________
36 걸어서, 도보로 ______________
37 내리다, 하차하다 ______________
38 여러 가지의, 다양한 ______________
39 버스로 ______________
40 ~ 앞에서 ______________
41 더 이상 ~하지 않는 ______________
42 ~할 수 있다 ______________
43 동시에, 한꺼번에 ______________

단어 Test

Step3

※ 다음 영영풀이에 알맞은 단어를 <보기>에서 골라 쓴 후, 우리말 뜻을 쓰시오.

1 __________: the state of something: __________

2 __________: wonderful or impressive: __________

3 __________: products for sale: __________

4 __________: a beautiful view of nature: __________

5 ____________: a place that has many games and rides: __________

6 __________: the season after summer and before winter: __________

7 __________: not to do anything: ________________

8 __________: a large sports field: ____________

9 __________: from another country: __________

10 __________: events that have happened in the past: __________

11 __________: the reason why something is used or done: __________

12 __________: having a bumpy surface: __________

13 __________: traveling down a river in a small, flat boat: ____________

14 __________: a place where one stops during a trip: ____________

15 __________: a visit made by students and teachers to learn about something: ____________

16 __________: a building where historical or artistic objects are displayed: __________

보기

foreign	awesome	stadium	history
goods	purpose	scenery	stop
field trip	relax	autumn	condition
rough	museum	rafting	amusement park

대화문 Test

※ 다음 우리말과 일치하도록 빈칸에 알맞은 말을 쓰시오.

Listen & Talk 1 A

B: ________ ________ ________ going to do ________ ________?

G: I'm ________ ________ ________ to Jeju-do.

B: ________ are ________ ________ ________ ________ there?

G: ________ ________ ________ go hiking on Hallasan.

남: 너 이번 주말에 뭐 할 거야?
여: 제주도에 갈 거야.
남: 거기서 뭐 할 계획이야?
여: 한라산에 올라갈 계획이야.

Listen & Talk 1 B

B: We ________ a long holiday ________ month. Do you ________ ________ plans?

G: I'm ________ to visit my grandparents in Jeonju.

B: Oh, really? That's nice. ________ are you ________ ________ do ________ them?

G: ________ ________ to go to Hanok Village ________ ________. How ________ you? What are your ________ ________ the holiday?

B: I'm ________ to ________ ________ and ________.

G: That's also a ________ ________!

남: 우리 이번 달에 긴 휴가가 있어. 무슨 계획이라도 있니?
여: 나는 전주에 있는 나의 조부모님을 방문할 예정이야.
남: 아, 그래? 좋다. 그분들과 어떤 것을 할 계획이야?
여: 그분들과 한옥 마을에 갈 계획이야. 너는 어때? 휴가 때 무슨 계획 있어?
남: 나는 집에 머물면서 쉴 거야.
여: 그것도 좋은 아이디어다!

Listen & Talk 1 C

B: Hi, Nuri. ________ is your class going for the ________ ________ tomorrow?

G: Hello, Mike. ________ ________ ________ ________ the art museum.

B: Sounds ________. What are you ________ ________ ________ there?

G: There ________ three art shows ________ ________. ________ ________ ________ ________ Vincent van Gogh's paintings. ________ is your class ________?

B: ________ ________ ________ ________ the ________ park. I'm ________ ________ ________ a roller coaster!

G: That ________ ________. Have a ________ ________!

남: 안녕, 누리야. 너희 반은 내일 현장 학습으로 어디 가니?
여: 안녕, 마이크. 우리는 미술관에 갈 거야.
남: 재미있겠다. 너 거기서 뭐 볼 계획이니?
여: 지금 3개의 전시회가 있어. 나는 빈센트 반 고흐의 그림을 볼 거야. 너희 반은 어디로 가니?
남: 우리는 놀이동산에 갈 거야. 롤러코스터를 타게 되어 신나!
여: 재미있겠다. 좋은 여행하길 바라!

Listen & Talk 2 A

G: ________ do you ________ ________ ________?

B: I go to school ________ ________.

G: ________ ________ does it ________ ________ ________ there?

B: ________ ________ 15 minutes.

여: 너 학교에 어떻게 가니?
남: 버스 타고 가.
여: 거기까지 가는 데 얼마나 걸려?
남: 15분 걸려.

Listen & Talk 2 B

B: Wow, these ________ are so ________. ________ did you ________ them?

G: At Riverside Park. There ________ ________ ________ flowers. You ________ go there!

B: I want ________. ________ do I ________ there ________ our school?

G: ________ ________ bus number 135 and ________ ________ at the Riverside Stadium stop. You can ________ the park ________ ________ ________ the bus stop.

B: How ________ does it ________ ________ ________ there?

G: It ________ 30 ________.

B: Thanks. I'll go there ________ ________.

남: 와, 이 사진들 너무 예쁘다. 어디서 찍었어?
여: Riverside Park에서. 꽃이 많았어. 넌 거기 꼭 가 봐야 해!
남: 나도 가고 싶어. 학교에서 거기까지 어떻게 가니?
여: 135번 버스를 타고 Riverside Stadium 정류장에서 내리면 돼. 버스 정류장 앞에 공원이 보일 거야.
남: 거기까지 가는 데 얼마나 걸려?
여: 30분 걸려.
남: 고마워. 다음 주말에 그곳에 가야겠다.

Listen & Talk 2 C

B: Excuse me. ________ ________ ________ ________ ________ Hanguk University from here?

W: You can ________ ________ ________ ________ ________ ________ ________.

B: ________ ________ does it ________ ________ ________ there?

W: It takes five minutes ________ bus and 20 minutes ________ ________.

B: Oh, then I ________ ________ there. ________ ________ ________ me ________ ________ ________ there?

W: ________ ________ for two blocks, and then ________ left. You will see Hanguk University ________ ________ ________.

B: ________ straight ________ two blocks and ________ ________. Thank you!

남: 실례합니다. 여기서 한국 대학교까지 어떻게 가나요?
여: 버스 타고 가거나 걸어서 갈 수 있어요.
남: 거기까지 가는 데 얼마나 걸리나요?
여: 버스 타면 5분 걸리고, 걸어서는 20분 걸려요.
남: 아, 그러면 걸어서 갈래요. 어떻게 가는지 말해 줄 수 있나요?
여: 2블록 직진한 다음에 좌회전하세요. 그러면 오른쪽에 한국 대학교가 보일 거예요.
남: 2블록 직진해서 좌회전이요. 감사합니다!

Do It Yourself A

G: ________ are you ________ ________ ________ ________ weekend?

B: I'm planning ________ ________ ________ a baseball game in Daegu.

G: ________ ________ going ________ ________ the All-Star Game?

B: Yes. It ________ be fun. Also, ________ ________ ________ ________ my friend there.

G: Nice. ________ ________ does it take ________ ________ there?

B: It takes ________ ________ ________ ________ ________ ________ express train.

G: Wow, it's ________ ________ ________ I thought. I hope you ________ a ________ ________!

B: Thank you.

여: 이번 주말에 너는 무엇을 할 계획이니?
남: 나는 대구에 야구 경기를 보러 갈 계획이야.
여: 올 스타 경기를 보러 갈 예정이야?
남: 응. 재미있을 거야. 또한, 그곳에서 내 친구를 만날 계획이야.
여: 좋다. 거기까지 가는 데 얼마나 걸리니?
남: 급행열차로 1시간 40분이 걸려.
여: 와, 내가 생각한 것보다 훨씬 더 빠르다. 즐거운 여행이 되길 바랄게.
남: 고마워.

대화문 Test

※ 다음 우리말에 맞도록 대화를 영어로 쓰시오.

Listen & Talk 1 A

B: ____________________

G: ____________________

B: ____________________

G: ____________________

남: 너 이번 주말에 뭐 할 거야?
여: 제주도에 갈 거야.
남: 거기서 뭐 할 계획이야?
여: 한라산에 올라갈 계획이야.

Listen & Talk 1 B

B: ____________________

G: ____________________

B: ____________________

G: ____________________

____

B: ____________________

G: ____________________

남: 우리 이번 달에 긴 휴가가 있어. 무슨 계획이라도 있니?
여: 나는 전주에 있는 나의 조부모님을 방문할 예정이야.
남: 아, 그래? 좋다. 그분들과 어떤 것을 할 계획이야?
여: 그분들과 한옥 마을에 갈 계획이야. 너는 어때? 휴가 때 무슨 계획 있어?
남: 나는 집에 머물면서 쉴 거야.
여: 그것도 좋은 아이디어다!

Listen & Talk 1 C

B: ____________________

G: ____________________

B: ____________________

G: ____________________

____

B: ____________________

G: ____________________

남: 안녕, 누리야. 너희 반은 내일 현장 학습으로 어디 가니?
여: 안녕, 마이크. 우리는 미술관에 갈 거야.
남: 재미있겠다. 너 거기서 뭐 볼 계획이니?
여: 지금 3개의 전시회가 있어. 나는 빈센트 반 고흐의 그림을 볼 거야. 너희 반은 어디로 가니?
남: 우리는 놀이동산에 갈 거야. 롤러코스터를 타게 되어 신나!
여: 재미있겠다. 좋은 여행하길 바라!

Listen & Talk 2 A

G: ____________________

B: ____________________

G: ____________________

B: ____________________

여: 너 학교에 어떻게 가니?
남: 버스 타고 가.
여: 거기까지 가는 데 얼마나 걸려?
남: 15분 걸려.

Listen & Talk 2 B

B: ____________________

G: ____________________

B: ____________________

G: ____________________

____

B: ____________________

G: ____________________

B: ____________________

남: 와, 이 사진들 너무 예쁘다. 어디서 찍었어?
여: Riverside Park에서. 꽃이 많았어. 넌 거기 꼭 가 봐야 해!
남: 나도 가고 싶어. 학교에서 거기까지 어떻게 가니?
여: 135번 버스를 타고 Riverside Stadium 정류장에서 내리면 돼. 버스 정류장 앞에 공원이 보일 거야.
남: 거기까지 가는 데 얼마나 걸려?
여: 30분 걸려.
남: 고마워. 다음 주말에 그곳에 가야겠다.

Listen & Talk 2 C

B: ____________________

W: ____________________

B: ____________________

W: ____________________

B: ____________________

W: ____________________

____

B: ____________________

남: 실례합니다. 여기서 한국 대학교까지 어떻게 가나요?
여: 버스 타고 가거나 걸어서 갈 수 있어요.
남: 거기까지 가는 데 얼마나 걸리나요?
여: 버스 타면 5분 걸리고, 걸어서는 20분 걸려요.
남: 아, 그러면 걸어서 갈래요. 어떻게 가는지 말해 줄 수 있나요?
여: 2블록 직진한 다음에 좌회전하세요. 그러면 오른쪽에 한국 대학교가 보일 거예요.
남: 2블록 직진해서 좌회전이요. 감사합니다!

Do It Yourself A

G: ____________________

B: ____________________

G: ____________________

B: ____________________

G: ____________________

B: ____________________

G: ____________________

B: ____________________

여: 이번 주말에 너는 무엇을 할 계획이니?
남: 나는 대구에 야구 경기를 보러 갈 계획이야.
여: 올 스타 경기를 보러 갈 예정이야?
남: 응. 재미있을 거야. 또한, 그곳에서 내 친구를 만날 계획이야.
여: 좋다. 거기까지 가는 데 얼마나 걸리니?
남: 급행열차로 1시간 40분이 걸려.
여: 와, 내가 생각한 것보다 훨씬 더 빠르다. 즐거운 여행이 되길 바랄게.
남: 고마워.

본문 Test

※ 다음 우리말과 일치하도록 빈칸에 알맞은 것을 골라 쓰시오.

1 The ________ ________ of the ________ Trip
A. Field　B. Moment　C. Best

2 Teacher: Good morning, everyone! ________ were your field ________ last week? Please ________ ________ about them!
A. how　B. tell　C. trips　D. us

3 Busan, ________ ________
A. Heaven　B. Market

4 Do you like ________ ________?
A. markets　B. traditional

5 ________ ________ to Gukje Market ________ Busan.
A. go　B. in　C. then

6 It is ________ of the ________ ________ ________ in Busan.
A. most　B. one　C. markets　D. famous

7 Do you know ________ it is ________ ________?
A. for　B. what　C. famous

8 It is famous for ________ a ________ ________ goods from ________ countries.
A. different　B. variety　C. selling　D. of

9 It was ________ to see ________ the ________ ________ there.
A. international　B. interesting　C. goods　D. all

10 We also ate many ________ ________ street food, ________ ________ *Gimbap*, fish cake, and *Hotteok*.
A. kinds　B. as　C. of　D. such

11 ________ we ________ ________ Bosu-dong Book Street.
A. walked　B. then　C. to

12 ________ ________ there sell ________ ________.
A. used　B. many　C. bookstores　D. books

13 We were really ________ ________ we ________ some old comic books!
A. found　B. excited　C. because

14 It was ________ to ________ in a café and ________ them.
A. relax　B. nice　C. read

15 Gangwon-do, ________ of ________ ________
A. Beauty　B. Full　C. Natural

16 There is no ________ ________ Gangwon-do for beautiful ________.
A. nature　B. like　C. place

17 ________, we ________ ________ Baengnyong Cave.
A. went　B. to　C. first

18 This 1.8-kilometer-long ________ is still ________ good ________.
A. condition　B. in　C. cave

19 It was so ________ to see its ________ ________.
A. beauty　B. amazing　C. natural

---

1 수학여행에서의 가장 좋았던 순간
2 교사: 안녕하세요, 여러분! 지난 주 수학여행은 어땠나요? 얘기해 봅시다!
3 부산, 시장 천국
4 전통 시장을 좋아하세요?
5 그렇다면 부산에 있는 국제시장으로 가세요.
6 그곳은 부산에서 가장 유명한 시장 중 하나입니다.
7 그곳이 무엇으로 유명한지 아세요?
8 그 시장은 여러 나라에서 온 다양한 제품들을 파는 것으로 유명합니다.
9 그곳에서 세계 곳곳의 제품들을 모두 볼 수 있어서 흥미로웠습니다.
10 우리는 또한 김밥, 어묵 그리고 호떡과 같은 여러 종류의 길거리 음식을 먹었습니다.
11 그러고 나서 우리는 보수동 책방 거리로 걸어갔습니다.
12 그곳의 많은 서점에서는 중고 책을 팝니다.
13 우리는 몇 권의 오래된 만화책을 발견해서 정말 신이 났습니다!
14 카페에서 휴식을 취하며 그 책들을 읽는 것이 좋았습니다.
15 강원도, 자연의 아름다움으로 가득한 곳
16 아름다운 자연에 관한 한 강원도만 한 곳이 없습니다.
17 우선, 우리는 백룡동굴로 갔습니다.
18 이 1.8킬로미터 길이의 동굴은 여전히 잘 보존된 상태입니다.
19 그곳의 자연의 아름다움을 보는 것은 매우 놀라웠습니다.

20 ________ the end of our cave tour, the guide ________ ________ the lights in the cave for a ________.
A. off B. minute C. turned D. near

21 Everything ________ very dark, so we were ________ to ________ ________ the sounds there.
A. able B. became C. focus D. on

22 It was the ________ ________ ________ of the tour!
A. experience B. most C. amazing

23 ________ ________ ________ was Donggang.
A. stop B. next C. our

24 We ________ ________!
A. rafting B. went

25 It was ________ to ride on the ________ water and enjoy the ________ at the ________ time.
A. rough B. exciting C. same D. view

26 Incheon, A ________ ________ ________
A. Firsts B. of C. City

27 Do you know ________ the ________ train station in Korea ________?
A. is B. first C. where

28 ________ ________ the first *Jajangmyeon*?
A. about B. how

29 The ________ ________ Incheon!
A. answer B. is

30 This ________ has ________ of Korea's ________.
A. firsts B. many C. place

31 ________ ________ there, we ________ to Incheon Station.
A. get B. went C. to

32 The Jajangmyeon Museum is ________ ________ the ________.
A. station B. to C. next

33 We ________ ________ the ________ of *Jajangmyeon* there.
A. history B. learned C. about

34 Later, we ________ ________ Jayu Park, the first ________ park in Korea.
A. around B. Western-style C. walked

35 The ________ ________ the park was ________!
A. from B. awesome C. view

36 It was ________ to see the ________ ________ of this city from the park.
A. great B. sites C. historical

37 Teacher: Wow, these ________ ________ ________!
A. great B. sound C. places

38 You ________ have ________ a wonderful job ________ your ________!
A. presentations B. done C. on D. all

20 동굴 관광의 끝 무렵, 안내인이 동굴 안의 불을 잠시 껐습니다.

21 모든 것이 매우 어두워져서, 우리는 그곳의 소리에 집중할 수 있었습니다.

22 그것은 여행에서 가장 경이로운 경험이었습니다!

23 우리의 다음 여행지는 동강이었습니다.

24 우리는 래프팅을 하러 갔습니다!

25 급류를 타면서 동시에 경치를 즐기는 것은 흥미진진했습니다.

26 인천, '최초의 것'들의 도시

27 한국 최초의 기차역이 어디인지 아세요?

28 첫 번째 자장면은요?

29 그 답은 인천입니다!

30 이곳에는 한국의 최초의 것들이 많이 있습니다.

31 그곳으로 가기 위하여, 우리는 인천역으로 갔습니다.

32 자장면 박물관은 역 옆에 있습니다.

33 우리는 그곳에서 자장면의 역사에 대하여 배웠습니다.

34 다음에는, 한국 최초의 서구식 공원인 자유 공원을 거닐었습니다.

35 공원에서 바라본 경치는 정말 멋있었습니다!

36 공원에서 이 도시의 역사적인 장소들을 바라보는 것은 아주 좋았습니다.

37 교사: 와, 이 장소들은 멋지게 들리네요!

38 여러분 모두 발표를 훌륭하게 잘했어요!

본문 Test

※ 다음 우리말과 일치하도록 빈칸에 알맞은 말을 쓰시오.

1 ________ ________ ________ of the ________ ________

2 Teacher: Good morning, everyone! ________ ________ your field trips ________ ________? ________ ________ ________ about them!

3 Busan, ________ ________

4 Do you like ________ ________?

5 ________ ________ ________ Gukje Market in Busan.

6 It is ________ ________ ________ ________ ________ ________ in Busan.

7 Do you know ________ ________ ________ ________ ________?

8 It ________ ________ ________ selling ________ ________ ________ ________ from different countries.

9 ________ was interesting ________ ________ ________ ________ ________ ________ there.

10 We ________ ________ ________ ________ ________ street food, ________ ________ *Gimbap*, fish cake, and *Hotteok*.

11 ________ we ________ ________ Bosu-dong Book Street.

12 Many bookstores there ________ ________ ________.

13 We were ________ ________ ________ we ________ some old comic books!

14 It was nice ________ ________ in a café and ________ them.

15 Gangwon-do, ________ ________ ________ ________

16 There is ________ ________ ________ Gangwon-do for ________ ________.

17 ________, we ________ ________ Baengnyong Cave.

18 This 1.8-kilometer-long cave is still ________ ________ ________.

19 It was ________ ________ to see its ________ ________.

1 수학여행에서의 가장 좋았던 순간

2 교사: 안녕하세요, 여러분! 지난 주 수학여행은 어땠나요? 얘기해 봅시다!

3 부산, 시장 천국

4 전통 시장을 좋아하세요?

5 그렇다면 부산에 있는 국제시장으로 가세요.

6 그곳은 부산에서 가장 유명한 시장 중 하나입니다.

7 그곳이 무엇으로 유명한지 아세요?

8 그 시장은 여러 나라에서 온 다양한 제품들을 파는 것으로 유명합니다.

9 그곳에서 세계 곳곳의 제품들을 모두 볼 수 있어서 흥미로웠습니다.

10 우리는 또한 김밥, 어묵 그리고 호떡과 같은 여러 종류의 길거리 음식을 먹었습니다.

11 그러고 나서 우리는 보수동 책방 거리로 걸어갔습니다.

12 그곳의 많은 서점에서는 중고 책을 팝니다.

13 우리는 몇 권의 오래된 만화책을 발견해서 정말 신이 났습니다!

14 카페에서 휴식을 취하며 그 책들을 읽는 것이 좋았습니다.

15 강원도, 자연의 아름다움으로 가득한 곳

16 아름다운 자연에 관한 한 강원도만 한 곳이 없습니다.

17 우선, 우리는 백룡동굴로 갔습니다.

18 이 1.8킬로미터 길이의 동굴은 여전히 잘 보존된 상태입니다.

19 그곳의 자연의 아름다움을 보는 것은 매우 놀라웠습니다.

20 Near the end of our ________ ________, the guide ________ ________ the lights in the cave ________ ________ ________.

21 Everything became very dark, so we ________ ________ ________ ________ ________ the sounds there.

22 It was ________ ________ ________ ________ of the tour!

23 ________ ________ ________ was Donggang.

24 We ________ ________!

25 It was ________ ________ ________ on the rough water and enjoy the view ________ ________ ________ ________.

26 Incheon, A City of ________

27 Do you know ________ the first train station in Korea ________?

28 ________ ________ the first *Jajangmyeon*?

29 ________ ________ is Incheon!

30 This place has ________ ________ ________ ________.

31 ________ ________ ________, we ________ to Incheon Station.

32 The Jajangmyeon Museum is ________ ________ the station.

33 We learned about ________ ________ ________ ________ there.

34 Later, we walked around Jayu Park, ________ ________ ________ ________ in Korea.

35 The ________ ________ the park was ________!

36 It was great ________ ________ ________ ________ ________ of this city from the park.

37 Teacher: Wow, these places ________ ________!

38 You all have done a wonderful job ________ ________ ________!

20 동굴 관광의 끝 무렵, 안내인이 동굴 안의 불을 잠시 껐습니다.

21 모든 것이 매우 어두워져서, 우리는 그곳의 소리에 집중할 수 있었습니다.

22 그것은 여행에서 가장 경이로운 경험이었습니다!

23 우리의 다음 여행지는 동강이었습니다.

24 우리는 래프팅을 하러 갔습니다!

25 급류를 타면서 동시에 경치를 즐기는 것은 흥미진진했습니다.

26 인천, '최초의 것'들의 도시

27 한국 최초의 기차역이 어디인지 아세요?

28 첫 번째 자장면은요?

29 그 답은 인천입니다!

30 이곳에는 한국의 최초의 것들이 많이 있습니다.

31 그곳으로 가기 위하여, 우리는 인천역으로 갔습니다.

32 자장면 박물관은 역 옆에 있습니다.

33 우리는 그곳에서 자장면의 역사에 대하여 배웠습니다.

34 다음에는, 한국 최초의 서구식 공원인 자유 공원을 거닐었습니다.

35 공원에서 바라본 경치는 정말 멋있었습니다!

36 공원에서 이 도시의 역사적인 장소들을 바라보는 것은 아주 좋았습니다.

37 교사: 와, 이 장소들은 멋지게 들리네요!

38 여러분 모두 발표를 훌륭하게 잘했어요!

본문 Test

※ 다음 문장을 우리말로 쓰시오.

1 The Best Moment of the Field Trip
➡ ______________________________

2 Teacher: Good morning, everyone! How were your field trips last week? Please tell us about them!
➡ ______________________________

3 Busan, Market Heaven
➡ ______________________________

4 Do you like traditional markets?
➡ ______________________________

5 Then go to Gukje Market in Busan.
➡ ______________________________

6 It is one of the most famous markets in Busan.
➡ ______________________________

7 Do you know what it is famous for?
➡ ______________________________

8 It is famous for selling a variety of goods from different countries.
➡ ______________________________

9 It was interesting to see all the international goods there.
➡ ______________________________

10 We also ate many kinds of street food, such as *Gimbap*, fish cake, and *Hotteok*.
➡ ______________________________

11 Then we walked to Bosu-dong Book Street.
➡ ______________________________

12 Many bookstores there sell used books.
➡ ______________________________

13 We were really excited because we found some old comic books!
➡ ______________________________

14 It was nice to relax in a café and read them.
➡ ______________________________

15 Gangwon-do, Full of Natural Beauty
➡ ______________________________

16 There is no place like Gangwon-do for beautiful nature.
➡ ______________________________

17 First, we went to Baengnyong Cave.
➡ ______________________________

18 This 1.8-kilometer-long cave is still in good condition.
➡ ______________________________

19 It was so amazing to see its natural beauty.
➡ ______________________________

20 Near the end of our cave tour, the guide turned off the lights in the cave for a minute.
➡ ______

21 Everything became very dark, so we were able to focus on the sounds there.
➡ ______

22 It was the most amazing experience of the tour!
➡ ______

23 Our next stop was Donggang.
➡ ______

24 We went rafting!
➡ ______

25 It was exciting to ride on the rough water and enjoy the view at the same time.
➡ ______

26 Incheon, A City of Firsts
➡ ______

27 Do you know where the first train station in Korea is?
➡ ______

28 How about the first *Jajangmyeon*?
➡ ______

29 The answer is Incheon!
➡ ______

30 This place has many of Korea's firsts.
➡ ______

31 To get there, we went to Incheon Station.
➡ ______

32 The Jajangmyeon Museum is next to the station.
➡ ______

33 We learned about the history of *Jajangmyeon* there.
➡ ______

34 Later, we walked around Jayu Park, the first Western-style park in Korea.
➡ ______

35 The view from the park was awesome!
➡ ______

36 It was great to see the historical sites of this city from the park.
➡ ______

37 Teacher: Wow, these places sound great!
➡ ______

38 You all have done a wonderful job on your presentations!
➡ ______

본문 Test

※ 다음 괄호 안의 단어들을 우리말에 맞도록 바르게 배열하시오.

1. (Best / of / Moment / The / Trip / Field / the)
➡ ______________________________

2. (Teacher: / morning, / good / everyone! // were / how / field / your / week? / last / trips // tell / please / about / us / them!)
➡ ______________________________
____

3. (Busan, / Heaven / Market)
➡ ______________________________

4. (like / you / do / markets? / traditional)
➡ ______________________________

5. (go / then / Gukje / to / Busan. / in / Market)
➡ ______________________________

6. (is / it / of / one / the / famous / most / Busan. / in / markets)
➡ ______________________________

7. (know / you / do / it / what / for? / famous / is)
➡ ______________________________

8. (is / it / for / famous / selling / variety / a / goods / of / countries. / different / from)
➡ ______________________________

9. (was / it / to / interesting / see / the / all / there. / goods / international)
➡ ______________________________

10. (also / we / many / ate / kinds / of / food, / street / as / such / *Gimbap*, / cake, / fish / *Hotteok*. / and)
➡ ______________________________

11. (we / then / to / walked / Book / Street. / Bosu-dong)
➡ ______________________________

12. (bookstores / many / sell / there / books. / used)
➡ ______________________________

13. (were / we / excited / really / we / because / some / found / books! / comic / old)
➡ ______________________________

14. (was / it / to / nice / in / relax / a / café / and / them. / read)
➡ ______________________________

15. (Full / Gangwon-do, / Beauty / Natural / of)
➡ ______________________________

16. (is / there / place / no / Gangwon-do / like / nature. / beautiful / for)
➡ ______________________________

17. (we / first, / to / went / Cave. / Baengnyong)
➡ ______________________________

18. (1.8-kilometer-long / is / this / cave / in / still / condition. / good)
➡ ______________________________

19. (was / it / amazing / so / see / to / its / beauty. / natural)
➡ ______________________________

1 수학여행에서의 가장 좋았던 순간
2 교사: 안녕하세요, 여러분! 지난 주 수학여행은 어땠나요? 얘기해 봅시다!
3 부산, 시장 천국
4 전통 시장을 좋아하세요?
5 그렇다면 부산에 있는 국제시장으로 가세요.
6 그곳은 부산에서 가장 유명한 시장 중 하나입니다.
7 그곳이 무엇으로 유명한지 아세요?
8 그 시장은 여러 나라에서 온 다양한 제품들을 파는 것으로 유명합니다.
9 그곳에서 세계 곳곳의 제품들을 모두 볼 수 있어서 흥미로웠습니다.
10 우리는 또한 김밥, 어묵 그리고 호떡과 같은 여러 종류의 길거리 음식을 먹었습니다.
11 그러고 나서 우리는 보수동 책방 거리로 걸어갔습니다.
12 그곳의 많은 서점에서는 중고 책을 팝니다.
13 우리는 몇 권의 오래된 만화책을 발견해서 정말 신이 났습니다!
14 카페에서 휴식을 취하며 그 책들을 읽는 것이 좋았습니다.
15 강원도, 자연의 아름다움으로 가득한 곳
16 아름다운 자연에 관한 한 강원도만 한 곳이 없습니다.
17 우선, 우리는 백룡동굴로 갔습니다.
18 이 1.8킬로미터 길이의 동굴은 여전히 잘 보존된 상태입니다.
19 그곳의 자연의 아름다움을 보는 것은 매우 놀라웠습니다.

20 (the / near / end / our / of / tour, / cave / guide / the / off / turned / lights / the / the / in / cave / minute. / a / for)
➡ ______________________________
____

21 (became / everythiing / dark, / very / we / so / able / were / to / on / focus / the / there. / sounds)
➡ ______________________________

22 (was / is / most / the / amazing / of / experience / tour! / the)
➡ ______________________________

23 (next / our / was / Donggang. / stop)
➡ ______________________________

24 (went / rafting! / we)
➡ ______________________________

25 (was / it / to / exciting / on / ride / rough / the / and / water / enjoy / view / the / at / time. / same / the)
➡ ______________________________

26 (A / Incheon, / of / City / Firsts)
➡ ______________________________

27 (you / do / where / know / first / the / station / train / is? / Korea / in)
➡ ______________________________

28 (about / how / first / the / *Jajangmyeon*?)
➡ ______________________________

29 (answer / the / Incheon! / is)
➡ ______________________________

30 (place / this / many / has / firsts. / Korea's / of)
➡ ______________________________

31 (get / to / there, / went / we / Incheon / to / Station.)
➡ ______________________________

32 (Jajangmyeon / The / Museum / next / is / station. / the / to)
➡ ______________________________

33 (learned / we / the / about / of / history / there. / *Jajangmyeon*)
➡ ______________________________

34 (we / later, / around / walked / Park, / Jayu / first / the / park / Western-style / Korea. / in)
➡ ______________________________

35 (view / the / from / park / the / awesome! / was)
➡ ______________________________

36 (was / it / to / great / see / historical / the / sites / this / of / city / from / park. / the)
➡ ______________________________

37 (Teacher: / these / wow, / places / great! / sound)
➡ ______________________________

38 (all / you / done / have / wonderful / a / job / presentations! / your)
➡ ______________________________

20 동굴 관광의 끝 무렵, 안내인이 동굴 안의 불을 잠시 껐습니다.

21 모든 것이 매우 어두워져서, 우리는 그곳의 소리에 집중할 수 있었습니다.

22 그것은 여행에서 가장 경이로운 경험이었습니다!

23 우리의 다음 여행지는 동강이었습니다.

24 우리는 래프팅을 하러 갔습니다!

25 급류를 타면서 동시에 경치를 즐기는 것은 흥미진진했습니다.

26 인천, '최초의 것'들의 도시

27 한국 최초의 기차역이 어디인지 아세요?

28 첫 번째 자장면은요?

29 그 답은 인천입니다!

30 이곳에는 한국의 최초의 것들이 많이 있습니다.

31 그곳으로 가기 위하여, 우리는 인천역으로 갔습니다.

32 자장면 박물관은 역 옆에 있습니다.

33 우리는 그곳에서 자장면의 역사에 대하여 배웠습니다.

34 다음에는, 한국 최초의 서구식 공원인 자유 공원을 거닐었습니다.

35 공원에서 바라본 경치는 정말 멋있었습니다!

36 공원에서 이 도시의 역사적인 장소들을 바라보는 것은 아주 좋았습니다.

37 교사: 와, 이 장소들은 멋지게 들리네요!

38 여러분 모두 발표를 훌륭하게 잘했어요!

본문 Test

※ 다음 우리말을 영어로 쓰시오.

1 수학여행에서의 가장 좋았던 순간

➡ ____________________

2 교사: 안녕하세요, 여러분! 지난주 수학여행은 어땠나요? 얘기해 봅시다!

➡ ____________________

3 부산, 시장 천국

➡ ____________________

4 전통 시장을 좋아하세요?

➡ ____________________

5 그렇다면 부산에 있는 국제시장으로 가세요.

➡ ____________________

6 그곳은 부산에서 가장 유명한 시장 중 하나입니다.

➡ ____________________

7 그곳이 무엇으로 유명한지 아세요?

➡ ____________________

8 그 시장은 여러 나라에서 온 다양한 제품들을 파는 것으로 유명합니다.

➡ ____________________

9 그곳에서 세계 곳곳의 제품들을 모두 볼 수 있어서 흥미로웠습니다.

➡ ____________________

10 우리는 또한 김밥, 어묵 그리고 호떡과 같은 여러 종류의 길거리 음식을 먹었습니다

➡ ____________________

11 그러고 나서 우리는 보수동 책방 거리로 걸어갔습니다.

➡ ____________________

12 그곳의 많은 서점에서는 중고 책을 팝니다.

➡ ____________________

13 우리는 몇 권의 오래된 만화책을 발견해서 정말 신이 났습니다!

➡ ____________________

14 카페에서 휴식을 취하며 그 책들을 읽는 것이 좋았습니다.

➡ ____________________

15 강원도, 자연의 아름다움으로 가득한 곳

➡ ____________________

16 아름다운 자연에 관한 한 강원도만 한 곳이 없습니다.

➡ ____________________

17 우선, 우리는 백룡동굴로 갔습니다.

➡ ____________________

18 이 1.8킬로미터 길이의 동굴은 여전히 잘 보존된 상태입니다.

➡ ____________________

19 그곳의 자연의 아름다움을 보는 것은 매우 놀라웠습니다.

➡ ____________________

Step5

20 동굴 관광의 끝 무렵, 안내인이 동굴 안의 불을 잠시 껐습니다.

➡ ______

21 모든 것이 매우 어두워져서, 우리는 그곳의 소리에 집중할 수 있었습니다.

➡ ______

22 그것은 여행에서 가장 경이로운 경험이었습니다!

➡ ______

23 우리의 다음 여행지는 동강이었습니다.

➡ ______

24 우리는 래프팅을 하러 갔습니다!

➡ ______

25 급류를 타면서 동시에 경치를 즐기는 것은 흥미진진했습니다.

➡ ______

26 인천, '최초의 것'들의 도시

➡ ______

27 한국 최초의 기차역이 어디인지 아세요?

➡ ______

28 첫 번째 자장면은요?

➡ ______

29 그 답은 인천입니다!

➡ ______

30 이곳에는 한국의 최초의 것들이 많이 있습니다.

➡ ______

31 그곳으로 가기 위하여, 우리는 인천역으로 갔습니다.

➡ ______

32 자장면 박물관은 역 옆에 있습니다.

➡ ______

33 우리는 그곳에서 자장면의 역사에 대하여 배웠습니다.

➡ ______

34 다음에는, 한국 최초의 서구식 공원인 자유 공원을 거닐었습니다.

➡ ______

35 공원에서 바라본 경치는 정말 멋있었습니다!

➡ ______

36 공원에서 이 도시의 역사적인 장소들을 바라보는 것은 아주 좋았습니다.

➡ ______

37 교사: 와, 이곳들은 멋지게 들리네요!

➡ ______

38 여러분 모두 발표를 훌륭하게 잘했어요!

➡ ______

구석구석 지문 Test

Step1

※ 다음 우리말과 일치하도록 빈칸에 알맞은 말을 쓰시오.

After You Read D

1. I ________ ________ Hang-dong, Seoul.
2. ________ ________ an old ________.
3. It is ________ ________ ________.
4. You can walk there and ________ ________ ________ beautiful ________.

1. 나는 서울의 항동에 산다.
2. 오래된 철도가 있다.
3. 이것은 더 이상 사용되지 않는다.
4. 너는 그 철길을 걸을 수 있고 예쁜 풍경 사진을 찍을 수도 있다.

Think & Write Step 3

1. ________ ________ in Naejangsan
2. ________ ________, I ________ ________ Naejangsan ________ my family.
3. I ________ a cable car ________ ________ ________ ________ the mountain.
4. ________, I ________ ________ the top.
5. ________ ________ ________, I saw beautiful ________ ________. I ________ many ________.
6. ________ was ________ and ________ ________ ________ beautiful autumn leaves.

1. 내장산에서의 가을 산행
2. 지난 가을, 나는 가족과 함께 내장산에 갔다.
3. 나는 산의 중간까지 케이블 카를 타고 갔다.
4. 그러고 나서, 나는 정상까지 하이킹을 갔다.
5. 정상에서, 나는 아름다운 가을 경치를 보았다. 나는 많은 사진을 찍었다.
6. 아름다운 가을 나뭇잎을 보는 것은 놀랍고 흥미진진했다.

Culture Link

1. ________ Trip
2. Some people ________ ________ in nature ________ ________ the environment.
3. They think ________ is important ________ ________ ________.
4. ________ Trip
5. Some people ________ ________ ________ for ________ ________.
6. They travel ________ ________ ________ ________.
7. They help ________ ________ or wild animals ________ their trips.
8. ________ ________
9. ________ ________ ________, people visit ________ ________ and ________ ________ history.
10. ________ this trip, people ________ ________ the ________ of people ________ ________ ________.

1. 생태 여행
2. 몇몇 사람들은 자연 속에서 환경을 해치지 않고 여행을 합니다.
3. 그들은 자연을 보호하는 것이 중요하다고 생각합니다.
4. 자원봉사 여행
5. 몇몇 사람들은 특별한 목적을 위해 여행을 갑니다.
6. 그들은 자원봉사를 하기 위해 여행합니다.
7. 그들은 그들의 여행 중에 지역 사회와 야생 동물들을 돕습니다.
8. 역사 여행
9. 이 여행에서 사람들은 역사적인 유적들을 방문하고 역사에 대해 배웁니다.
10. 이 여행 동안 사람들은 과거의 사람들의 삶을 이해할 수 있습니다.

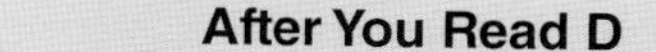

※ 다음 우리말을 영어로 쓰시오.

After You Read D

1. 나는 서울의 항동에 산다.
➡ ______________________
2. 오래된 철도가 있다.
➡ ______________________
3. 이것은 더 이상 사용되지 않는다.
➡ ______________________
4. 너는 그 철길을 걸을 수 있고 예쁜 풍경 사진을 찍을 수도 있다.
➡ ______________________

Think & Write Step 3

1. 내장산에서의 가을 산행
➡ ______________________
2. 지난 가을, 나는 가족과 함께 내장산에 갔다.
➡ ______________________
3. 나는 산의 중간까지 케이블 카를 타고 갔다.
➡ ______________________
4. 그러고 나서, 나는 정상까지 하이킹을 갔다.
➡ ______________________
5. 정상에서, 나는 아름다운 가을 경치를 보았다. 나는 많은 사진을 찍었다.
➡ ______________________
6. 아름다운 가을 나뭇잎을 보는 것은 놀랍고 흥미진진했다.
➡ ______________________

Culture Link

1. 생태 여행
➡ ______________________
2. 몇몇 사람들은 자연 속에서 환경을 해치지 않고 여행을 합니다.
➡ ______________________
3. 그들은 자연을 보호하는 것이 중요하다고 생각합니다.
➡ ______________________
4. 자원봉사 여행
➡ ______________________
5. 몇몇 사람들은 특별한 목적을 위해 여행을 갑니다.
➡ ______________________
6. 그들은 자원봉사를 하기 위해 여행합니다.
➡ ______________________
7. 그들은 그들의 여행 중에 지역 사회와 야생 동물들을 돕습니다.
➡ ______________________
8. 역사 여행
➡ ______________________
9. 이 여행에서 사람들은 역사적인 유적들을 방문하고 역사에 대해 배웁니다.
➡ ______________________
10. 이 여행 동안 사람들은 과거의 사람들의 삶을 이해할 수 있습니다.
➡ ______________________

단어 Test

Step1

※ 다음 영어를 우리말로 쓰시오.

01 amount ____________

02 career ____________

03 collaboration ____________

04 self-driving car ____________

05 collect ____________

06 appear ____________

07 consultant ____________

08 develop ____________

09 emotion ____________

10 analyze ____________

11 float ____________

12 counseling ____________

13 artificial ____________

14 improve ____________

15 interpreter ____________

16 strength ____________

17 late-night ____________

18 apply ____________

19 talent ____________

20 patient ____________

21 waste material ____________

22 specialist ____________

23 collaborate ____________

24 route ____________

25 decorate ____________

26 creativity ____________

27 reduce ____________

28 space ____________

29 customer ____________

30 problem-solving ____________

31 following ____________

32 upcycle ____________

33 reviewer ____________

34 creative ____________

35 first of all ____________

36 take care of ____________

37 look ahead ____________

38 be good at ____________

39 what else ____________

40 come true ____________

41 fill out ____________

42 keep a diary ____________

43 print out ____________

단어 Test

Step2

※ 다음 우리말을 영어로 쓰시오.

01 충고, 조언 ____________

02 진로, 직업 ____________

03 기능, 기술 ____________

04 줄이다, 감소시키다 ____________

05 (타고난) 재능, 재주 ____________

06 (책, 영화 등의) 논평가 ____________

07 상담 ____________

08 전문가 ____________

09 협력하다 ____________

10 지원하다, 신청하다 ____________

11 꾸미다, 장식하다 ____________

12 통역사 ____________

13 분석하다 ____________

14 감정 ____________

15 상담가 ____________

16 인공적인, 인조의 ____________

17 (물 위에) 뜨다, 떠다니다 ____________

18 힘, 강점, 장점 ____________

19 공동 작업, 협동 ____________

20 다음에 나오는[언급되는] ____________

21 개선하다, 향상시키다 ____________

22 심야의 ____________

23 창의적인 ____________

24 환자 ____________

25 양, 총액 ____________

26 문제 해결의 ____________

27 허락하다 ____________

28 이유, 원인 ____________

29 손님, 고객 ____________

30 경로, 노선 ____________

31 발달시키다, 발전하다 ____________

32 나타나다, 보이기 시작하다 ____________

33 창의력, 독창력 ____________

34 우주, 공간 ____________

35 일기를 쓰다 ____________

36 (앞일을) 내다보다, 예견하다 ____________

37 출력하다 ____________

38 ~을 돌보다 ____________

39 그 외에, 그 밖에 ____________

40 (서식 등을) 작성하다 ____________

41 이루어지다, 실현되다 ____________

42 ~을 잘하다 ____________

43 무엇보다도 ____________

단어 Test

Step3

※ 다음 영영풀이에 알맞은 단어를 <보기>에서 골라 쓴 후, 우리말 뜻을 쓰시오.

1 __________: late at night: __________

2 __________: to study in detail: __________

3 __________: a way between two places: __________

4 __________: to make something better: __________

5 __________: a person who has a special skill: __________

6 __________: a person who receives medical care: __________

7 __________: to stay up on water: __________

8 __________: not natural; created by humans: __________

9 __________: an advantageous quality or ability: __________

10 __________: advice that is given to someone to help them with their problems: __________

11 __________: a natural ability to do something well: __________

12 __________: the ability to think of or create something new: __________

13 __________: to grow or become more advanced: __________

14 __________: a job that requires special skills or training: __________

15 __________: to give someone papers that say you want to do something: __________

16 __________: a person who writes opinions about the quality of a book, movie, or product: __________

보기

artificial	late-night	analyze	improve
route	reviewer	strength	develop
creativity	apply	career	counseling
float	patient	specialist	talent

대화문 Test

Step1

※ 다음 우리말과 일치하도록 빈칸에 알맞은 말을 쓰시오.

Listen & Talk 1 A

G: ________ ________ basketball.

B: Well… I'm ________ ________ ________ playing basketball. Are you?

G: Yes, I think I am. ________ ________ ________ ________ ________?

B: I'm ________ ________ ________ soccer.

G: Okay, then ________ ________ soccer.

G: 우리 농구하자.
B: 음... 나는 농구를 잘하지 못해. 너는 잘하니?
G: 응, 내 생각에 나는 잘하는 것 같아. 넌 어떤 것을 잘해?
B: 나는 축구를 잘해.
G: 그래, 그러면 축구를 하자.

Listen & Talk 1 B

B: Jessica, what ________ you ________ ________ ________ for the school talent show?

G: I didn't ________ yet. ________ ________ I ________ ________?

B: You're ________ ________ ________, ________ you?

G: Not really. But I think I'm ________ ________ ________. I like ________ very much.

B: Really? Actually, I'm ________ ________ ________ rock music with my band. ________ ________ ________ sing for us?

G: Sure, I'd ________ ________.

B: Jessica, 학교 재능 발표회에서 뭐 할 거야?
G: 아직 결정 안 했어. 나 어떤 것을 잘하지?
B: 너 춤 잘 추잖아, 그렇지 않니?
G: 사실은 그렇지 않아. 하지만 내 생각에는 나는 노래를 잘해. 나는 노래하는 것을 매우 좋아해.
B: 정말? 사실 나 우리 밴드와 록 음악을 연주할 계획이야. 우리를 위해 노래해 주는 게 어때?
G: 그래, 좋아.

Listen & Talk 1 C

B: Mom, I ________ ________ ________ ________ this form for tomorrow's ________ ________ program. Could you help me?

W: Sure. Let me see. You already ________ your dream job ________hobby.

B: Yes, I want to ________ a ________ ________, and my hobby is ________ sports games. But ________ my ________ is hard. ________ ________ ________ ________ at?

W: Well, I think you have ________ of strengths. ________ ________ all, you ________ ________ ________ playing baseball, ________ ________?

B: Oh, yes. ________ ________ ________ ________ ________.

W: And you have many ________ ________.

B: You're right. I also ________ well with ________ ________. And I'm good ________ ________ ________ people.

W: Right! ________ ________ ________ so many things.

B: ________, Mom.

B: 엄마, 저 내일 있을 진로 상담 프로그램을 준비하기 위해 이 양식을 작성해야 해요. 저 좀 도와주시겠어요?
W: 물론이지. 어디 보자. 이미 하고 싶은 직업과 취미는 적었구나.
B: 네. 저는 체육 선생님이 되고 싶어요. 제 취미는 스포츠 경기 보는 거예요. 하지만, 제 강점을 적는 것은 어려워요. 저는 무엇을 잘하죠?
W: 음, 나는 네게 많은 강점이 있다고 생각해. 무엇보다도 너는 야구를 잘하잖니, 그렇지 않니?
B: 아, 맞아요. 저는 야구를 잘해요.
W: 그리고 너는 다른 강점들도 가지고 있단다.
B: 맞아요. 저는 다른 사람들과 협업을 잘해요. 그리고 사람들의 이야기를 잘 들어 줘요.
W: 그렇지! 너는 아주 많은 것들을 잘한단다.
B: 감사해요, 엄마.

Listen & Talk 2 A

B: I ________ ________ ________ a scientist. ________ do I ________ ________ ________?

W: You ________ ________ study science. And you need to ________ your ____________ ________.

B: 저는 과학자가 되고 싶어요. 저는 어떤 것을 해야 할까요?
W: 과학 공부를 해야 돼요. 그리고 문제 해결 능력을 개발할 필요가 있어요.

Listen & Talk 2 B

G: Jason, I read your paper. It was so ________!

B: ________ you ________ ________ that. I'm ________ hard ________ ________ my ________ ________. I want to be a ________ someday.

G: Really? I ________ to write well ________ you. ________ ________ ________ need ________ do?

B: You need to read ________ ________ ________ books. ________ ________ ________ ________ ________.

G: What ________ do I ________ ________ do?

B: Well, I write almost ________ ________. Why ________ you start ________ a diary?

G: ________ you ________ your ________. I'll start today.

G: Jason, 나 너의 글을 읽었어. 아주 놀라웠어!
B: 그렇게 말해 줘서 고마워. 나는 내 글쓰기 기량을 발전시키려고 노력하고 있어. 언젠가 작가가 되고 싶어.
G: 정말? 나도 너처럼 글을 잘 쓰고 싶어. 뭘 해야 하니?
B: 책을 많이 읽어야 해. 독서가 네 글쓰기를 더 좋게 만들거든.
G: 다른 건 또 뭘 해야 할까?
B: 음, 나는 거의 매일 글을 쓰고 있어. 일기 쓰기를 시작하는 건 어때?
G: 조언 고마워. 오늘부터 시작할게.

Listen & Talk 2 C

G: Hello, Mr. Watson! ________ you ________ doing this interview.

M: Sure, no ________.

G: This interview is for students ________ ________ ________ ________ ________ stylists. Can you tell me ________ ________ ________?

M: Sure. You may see pictures of food in books or on TV. A food stylist ________ food ________ ________ good for pictures or movies.

G: I want ________ ________ ________ ________ ________ like you. ________ do I ________ to do?

M: You ________ ________ ________ about many ________ of food.

G: ________ ________ do I ________ ________ ________?

M: You need to study art, ________. ________ is important.

G: All right! ________ you ________ your time, Mr. Watson.

G: 안녕하세요, Watson 씨! 오늘 인터뷰 감사해요.
M: 네, 문제 없어요.
G: 이 인터뷰는 푸드 스타일리스트가 되고 싶어 하는 학생들을 위한 것이에요. 당신의 직업에 대해 말씀해 주시겠어요?
M: 그럼요. 아마 여러분은 책이나 TV에서 음식 사진을 보셨을 겁니다. 푸드 스타일리스트는 사진이나 영화에서 음식이 맛있어 보이도록 장식하는 일을 합니다.
G: 저도 Watson 씨와 같은 푸드 스타일리스트가 되고 싶어요. 뭘 해야 하나요?
M: 많은 종류의 음식에 대해 배워야 해요.
G: 다른 건 뭘 해야 하죠?
M: 미술 공부도 해야 해요. 창의력이 중요하거든요.
G: 알겠습니다! 시간 내 주셔서 감사합니다, Watson 씨.

대화문 Test

Step2

※ 다음 우리말에 맞도록 대화를 영어로 쓰시오.

Listen & Talk 1 A

G: ____________________
B: ____________________
G: ____________________
B: ____________________
G: ____________________

G: 우리 농구하자.
B: 음... 나는 농구를 잘하지 못해. 너는 잘하니?
G: 응, 내 생각에 나는 잘하는 것 같아. 넌 어떤 것을 잘해?
B: 나는 축구를 잘해.
G: 그래, 그러면 축구를 하자.

Listen & Talk 1 B

B: ____________________
G: ____________________
B: ____________________
G: ____________________
B: ____________________
____
G: ____________________

B: Jessica, 학교 재능 발표회에서 뭐 할 거야?
G: 아직 결정 안 했어. 나 어떤 것을 잘하지?
B: 너 춤 잘 추잖아, 그렇지 않니?
G: 사실은 그렇지 않아. 하지만 내 생각에는 나는 노래를 잘해. 나는 노래하는 것을 매우 좋아해.
B: 정말? 사실 나 우리 밴드와 록 음악을 연주할 계획이야. 우리를 위해 노래해 주는 게 어때?
G: 그래, 좋아.

Listen & Talk 1 C

B: ____________________
____
W: ____________________
B: ____________________
____
W: ____________________
____
B: ____________________
W: ____________________
B: ____________________
W: ____________________
B: ____________________

B: 엄마, 저 내일 있을 진로 상담 프로그램을 준비하기 위해 이 양식을 작성해야 해요. 저 좀 도와주시겠어요?
W: 물론이지. 어디 보자. 이미 하고 싶은 직업과 취미는 적었구나.
B: 네. 저는 체육 선생님이 되고 싶어요. 제 취미는 스포츠 경기 보는 거예요. 하지만, 제 강점을 적는 것은 어려워요. 저는 무엇을 잘하죠?
W: 음, 나는 네게 많은 강점이 있다고 생각해. 무엇보다도 너는 야구를 잘하잖니, 그렇지 않니?
B: 아, 맞아요. 저는 야구를 잘해요.
W: 그리고 너는 다른 강점들도 가지고 있단다.
B: 맞아요. 저는 다른 사람들과 협업을 잘해요. 그리고 사람들의 이야기를 잘 들어 줘요.
W: 그렇지! 너는 아주 많은 것들을 잘한단다.
B: 감사해요, 엄마.

Listen & Talk 2 A

B: ____

W: ____

B: 저는 과학자가 되고 싶어요. 저는 어떤 것을 해야 할까요?
W: 과학 공부를 해야 돼요. 그리고 문제 해결 능력을 개발할 필요가 있어요.

Listen & Talk 2 B

G: ____

B: ____

____

G: ____

B: ____

G: ____

B: ____

G: ____

G: Jason, 나 너의 글을 읽었어. 아주 놀라웠어!
B: 그렇게 말해 줘서 고마워. 나는 내 글쓰기 기량을 발전시키려고 노력하고 있어. 언젠가 작가가 되고 싶어.
G: 정말? 나도 너처럼 글을 잘 쓰고 싶어. 뭘 해야 하니?
B: 책을 많이 읽어야 해. 독서가 네 글쓰기를 더 좋게 만들거든.
G: 다른 건 또 뭘 해야 할까?
B: 음, 나는 거의 매일 글을 쓰고 있어. 일기 쓰기를 시작하는 건 어때?
G: 조언 고마워. 오늘부터 시작할게.

Listen & Talk 2 C

G: ____

M: ____

G: ____

____

M: ____

____

G: ____

M: ____

G: ____

M: ____

G: ____

G: 안녕하세요, Watson 씨! 오늘 인터뷰 감사해요.
M: 네, 문제 없어요.
G: 이 인터뷰는 푸드 스타일리스트가 되고 싶어 하는 학생들을 위한 것이에요. 당신의 직업에 대해 말씀해 주시겠어요?
M: 그럼요. 아마 여러분은 책이나 TV에서 음식 사진을 보셨을 겁니다. 푸드 스타일리스트는 사진이나 영화에서 음식이 맛있어 보이도록 장식하는 일을 합니다.
G: 저도 Watson 씨와 같은 푸드 스타일리스트가 되고 싶어요. 뭘 해야 하나요?
M: 많은 종류의 음식에 대해 배워야 해요.
G: 다른 건 뭘 해야 하죠?
M: 미술 공부도 해야 해요. 창의력이 중요하거든요.
G: 알겠습니다! 시간 내 주셔서 감사합니다, Watson 씨.

본문 Test

Step1

※ 다음 우리말과 일치하도록 빈칸에 알맞은 것을 골라 쓰시오.

1 ______ ______ the ______
A. Future B. of C. Jobs

2 2020s: Self-driving cars will ______ ______ the ______.
A. market B. on C. be

3 2030s: People will have ______ ______ do ______ for them.
A. that B. everything C. robots

4 2030s: 3D printers in ______ home will ______ ______ ______ everything.
A. almost B. print C. every D. out

5 2050s: People will ______ ______ ______.
A. trips B. space C. take

6 2050s: People will live ______ the sea or in ______ ______.
A. floating B. under C. cities

7 ______ ______ the pictures ______.
A. at B. above C. look

8 ______ these ______ ______ you?
A. ideas B. surprise C. do

9 You can see that our ______ will be very ______ in the ______.
A. different B. lives C. future

10 ______ our lives ______, many new jobs will ______.
A. appear B. as C. change

11 ______ ______ of ______ do you want?
A. kind B. job C. what

12 What ______ your future life ______ ______?
A. like B. be C. will

13 The ______ people ______ ______ and ______ jobs that will be important in the future.
A. chose B. ahead C. following D. looked

14 ______ ______ about ______ jobs!
A. read B. their C. let's

15 Do you see the flower ______ ______ Sujin ______?
A. made B. that C. pot

16 It was ______ ______ old street ______.
A. made B. flags C. from

17 She is an ______ ______.
A. designer B. upcycling

18 She works with ______ ______ to make new ______.
A. waste B. products C. materials

19 Her products show people ______ old materials can be ______ ______ new ______.
A. ways B. useful C. in D. that

20 ______ can ______ the amount of ______ in the future.
A. waste B. upcycling C. reduce

21 To ______ an upcycling designer, you should be ______ and ______ about art.
A. creative B. become C. learn

1 미래의 직업
2 2020년대: 자율주행차들이 시장에 나올 것이다.
3 2030년대: 사람들은 그들을 위하여 모든 것을 하는 로봇을 갖게 될 것이다.
4 2030년대: 모든 가정의 3D 프린터가 거의 모든 것을 출력해 낼 것이다.
5 2050년대: 사람들은 우주여행을 할 것이다.
6 2050년대: 사람들은 바다 밑이나 수상 도시에서 살 것이다.
7 위의 그림들을 보세요.
8 이 생각들이 놀랍습니까?
9 당신은 미래에 우리의 삶이 매우 달라질 것을 볼 수 있습니다.
10 우리의 삶이 변화함에 따라 새로운 직업들이 많이 생겨날 것입니다.
11 당신은 어떤 직업을 원하세요?
12 미래의 당신 삶은 어떤 모습일까요?
13 다음의 사람들은 앞을 내다보고 미래에 중요하게 될 직업을 선택하였습니다.
14 그들의 직업에 관하여 읽어 봅시다!
15 수진이 만든 화분이 보이시나요?
16 이것은 거리의 낡은 깃발들로 만들어졌습니다.
17 그녀는 업사이클링 디자이너입니다.
18 그녀는 새로운 제품을 만들기 위해 폐기물을 가지고 작업합니다.
19 그녀의 제품들은 낡은 재료가 새로운 방식으로 유용해질 수 있다는 것을 사람들에게 보여줍니다.
20 업사이클링은 미래에 쓰레기의 양을 줄일 수 있습니다.
21 업사이클링 디자이너가 되려면 당신은 창의적이어야 하며 미술을 배워야 합니다.

22 ________ you ________ ________ of 3D modelers?
A. heard B. ever C. have

23 Taeho, a 3D modeler, ________ ________ a company that ________ ________ hands and legs.
A. artificial B. works C. makes D. for

24 Taeho uses ________ ________ to ________ ________ new hands and legs.
A. out B. special C. print D. software

25 They are ________ ________ for ________.
A. patients B. specially C. made

26 If you are ________ ________ computer programming and art, you can be a 3D ________.
A. at B. good C. modeler

27 Taeho wants more people to ________ 3D ________ products in the ________.
A. printed B. use C. future

28 Jihye is a ________ ________ ________.
A. data B. big C. specialist

29 She ________ ________ many ________.
A. on B. works C. projects

30 ________ ________, ________ year, she made bus ________.
A. routes B. last C. example D. for

31 To find the best night routes, she needed to ________ smartphone use data and taxi ________ patterns from ________ ________.
A. collect B. late-night C. use D. travelers

32 Then she ________ this information to ________ the most ________ routes.
A. useful B. analyzed C. create

33 Now Jihye is ________ ________ an ________ shopping mall.
A. with B. online C. working

34 She is ________ data ________ customers to ________ ________ the best styles for them.
A. find B. collecting C. out D. from

35 She knows big data ________ us to ________ more about our ________ lives.
A. daily B. learn C. allows

36 If you want to become a big data ________, you should ________ your math and ____________ skills!
A. develop B. problem-solving C. specialist

37 ________ about ________ and ________ ________ your future.
A. yourself B. for C. think D. prepare

38 If you ________ ________ ________ and ________ big, your future will be bright.
A. keep B. ahead C. dreaming D. looking

22 3D 모형 제작자에 관하여 들어 본 적이 있으신가요?

23 3D 모형 제작자인 태호는 인공 손과 다리를 만드는 회사에서 일합니다.

24 태호는 새 손과 다리를 출력하기 위하여 특별한 소프트웨어를 사용합니다.

25 그것들은 환자를 위하여 특별히 제작됩니다.

26 만약 당신이 컴퓨터 프로그래밍이나 미술을 잘한다면, 3D 모형 제작자가 될 수 있습니다.

27 태호는 미래에 더 많은 사람들이 3D 프린터로 출력된 제품들을 사용하기를 원합니다.

28 지혜는 빅데이터 전문가입니다.

29 그녀는 많은 프로젝트에서 일합니다.

30 예를 들어, 작년에 그녀는 버스 노선을 만들었습니다.

31 최적의 심야 노선을 찾기 위하여, 그녀는 심야에 이동하는 사람들의 스마트폰 이용 정보와 택시 이용 패턴을 수집할 필요가 있었습니다.

32 그런 다음 그녀는 그 정보를 분석하여 가장 유용한 노선을 만들었습니다.

33 현재 지혜는 온라인 쇼핑몰과 작업하고 있습니다.

34 그녀는 소비자들에게 맞는 최적의 스타일을 찾기 위하여 그들로부터 데이터를 수집하고 있습니다.

35 그녀는 빅데이터가 우리에게 일상생활에 관하여 더 많이 알게 해 준다는 것을 알고 있습니다.

36 만약 당신이 빅데이터 전문가가 되고 싶다면, 수학과 문제 해결 능력을 계발해야 합니다!

37 자신에 대하여 생각해 보고 미래를 준비하세요.

38 만약 당신이 계속 앞을 내다보고 꿈을 크게 꾼다면, 당신의 미래는 밝을 것입니다.

본문 Test

Step2

※ 다음 우리말과 일치하도록 빈칸에 알맞은 말을 쓰시오.

1 Jobs ________ ________ ________

2 2020s: ________ cars will ________ ________ ________ ________.

3 2030s: People will have robots ________ do ________ for them.

4 2030s: 3D printers in every home ________ ________ ________ ________ ________.

5 2050s: People will ________ ________ ________.

6 2050s: People will live ________ ________ ________ or ________ ________ ________.

7 ________ ________ the pictures ________.

8 Do ________ ideas ________ you?

9 You can see that ________ ________ will be very different ________ ________ ________.

10 ________ our lives ________, many new jobs ________ ________.

11 ________ ________ ________ ________ do you want?

12 ________ ________ your future life ________ ________?

13 ________ ________ people ________ ________ and ________ ________that will ________ ________ in the future.

14 ________ ________ about their jobs!

15 Do you see the ________ ________ ________ ________ ________?

16 It ________ ________ ________ old street ________.

17 She is an ________ ________.

18 She works with ________ ________ to make new ________.

19 Her products show people that old materials ________ ________ ________ ________ ________ ________.

20 Upcycling can ________ ________ ________ ________ ________ in the future.

21 ________ ________ an ________ ________, you should be ________ and learn about art.

1 미래의 직업

2 2020년대: 자율주행차들이 시장에 나올 것이다.

3 2030년대: 사람들은 그들을 위하여 모든 것을 하는 로봇을 갖게 될 것이다.

4 2030년대: 모든 가정의 3D 프린터가 거의 모든 것을 출력해 낼 것이다.

5 2050년대: 사람들은 우주여행을 할 것이다.

6 2050년대: 사람들은 바다 밑이나 수상 도시에서 살 것이다.

7 위의 그림들을 보세요.

8 이 생각들이 놀랍습니까?

9 당신은 미래에 우리의 삶이 매우 달라질 것을 볼 수 있습니다.

10 우리의 삶이 변화함에 따라 새로운 직업들이 많이 생겨날 것입니다.

11 당신은 어떤 직업을 원하세요?

12 미래의 당신 삶은 어떤 모습일까요?

13 다음의 사람들은 앞을 내다보고 미래에 중요하게 될 직업을 선택하였습니다.

14 그들의 직업에 관하여 읽어 봅시다!

15 수진이 만든 화분이 보이시나요?

16 이것은 거리의 낡은 깃발들로 만들어졌습니다.

17 그녀는 업사이클링 디자이너입니다.

18 그녀는 새로운 제품을 만들기 위해 폐기물을 가지고 작업합니다.

19 그녀의 제품들은 낡은 재료가 새로운 방식으로 유용해질 수 있다는 것을 사람들에게 보여줍니다.

20 업사이클링은 미래에 쓰레기의 양을 줄일 수 있습니다.

21 업사이클링 디자이너가 되려면 당신은 창의적이어야 하며 미술을 배워야 합니다.

22 ________ ________ ________ ________ of 3D ________?

23 Taeho, a 3D modeler, ________ ________ a company ________ ________ ________ hands and legs.

24 Taeho uses ________ ________ to print out new hands and legs.

25 They are made ________ ________ ________.

26 If you ________ ________ ________ computer programming and art, you can ________ ________ ________ ________.

27 Taeho ________ more people ________ ________ 3D printed products ________ ________ ________.

28 Jihye is a ________ ________ ________.

29 She ________ ________ many projects.

30 ________ ________, last year, she made ________ ________.

31 To find the best night routes, she needed to collect smartphone use data and ________ ________ ________ from ________ ________.

32 Then she ________ this information ________ ________the most ________ ________.

33 Now Jihye is ________ ________ an online shopping mall.

34 She is ________ ________ ________ customers to ________ ________ the best styles for them.

35 She knows big data ________ ________ ________ ________ more about ________ ________ ________.

36 If you want to become a big data ________, you should ________ your math and ____________ ________!

37 ________ about ________ and ________ ________ your future.

38 If you ________ ________ ahead and ________ big, your future will ________ ________.

22 3D 모형 제작자에 관하여 들어 본 적이 있으신가요?

23 3D 모형 제작자인 태호는 인공 손과 다리를 만드는 회사에서 일합니다.

24 태호는 새 손과 다리를 출력하기 위하여 특별한 소프트웨어를 사용합니다.

25 그것들은 환자를 위하여 특별히 제작됩니다.

26 만약 당신이 컴퓨터 프로그래밍이나 미술을 잘한다면, 3D 모형 제작자가 될 수 있습니다.

27 태호는 미래에 더 많은 사람들이 3D 프린터로 출력된 제품들을 사용하기를 원합니다.

28 지혜는 빅데이터 전문가입니다.

29 그녀는 많은 프로젝트에서 일합니다.

30 예를 들어, 작년에 그녀는 버스 노선을 만들었습니다.

31 최적의 심야 노선을 찾기 위하여, 그녀는 심야에 이동하는 사람들의 스마트폰 이용 정보와 택시 이용 패턴을 수집할 필요가 있었습니다.

32 그런 다음 그녀는 그 정보를 분석하여 가장 유용한 노선을 만들었습니다.

33 현재 지혜는 온라인 쇼핑몰과 작업하고 있습니다.

34 그녀는 소비자들에게 맞는 최적의 스타일을 찾기 위하여 그들로부터 데이터를 수집하고 있습니다.

35 그녀는 빅데이터가 우리에게 일상생활에 관하여 더 많이 알게 해 준다는 것을 알고 있습니다.

36 만약 당신이 빅데이터 전문가가 되고 싶다면, 수학과 문제 해결 능력을 계발해야 합니다!

37 자신에 대하여 생각해 보고 미래를 준비하세요.

38 만약 당신이 계속 앞을 내다보고 꿈을 크게 꾼다면, 당신의 미래는 밝을 것입니다.

본문 Test

Step3

※ 다음 문장을 우리말로 쓰시오.

1 Jobs of the Future

➡ ____________________

2 2020s: Self-driving cars will be on the market.

➡ ____________________

3 2030s: People will have robots that do everything for them.

➡ ____________________

4 2030s: 3D printers in every home will print out almost everything.

➡ ____________________

5 2050s: People will take space trips.

➡ ____________________

6 2050s: People will live under the sea or in floating cities.

➡ ____________________

7 Look at the pictures above.

➡ ____________________

8 Do these ideas surprise you?

➡ ____________________

9 You can see that our lives will be very different in the future.

➡ ____________________

10 As our lives change, many new jobs will appear.

➡ ____________________

11 What kind of job do you want?

➡ ____________________

12 What will your future life be like?

➡ ____________________

13 The following people looked ahead and chose jobs that will be important in the future.

➡ ____________________

14 Let's read about their jobs!

➡ ____________________

15 Do you see the flower pot that Sujin made?

➡ ____________________

16 It was made from old street flags.

➡ ____________________

17 She is an upcycling designer.

➡ ____________________

18 She works with waste materials to make new products.
➡ ______

19 Her products show people that old materials can be useful in new ways.
➡ ______

20 Upcycling can reduce the amount of waste in the future.
➡ ______

21 To become an upcycling designer, you should be creative and learn about art.
➡ ______

22 Have you ever heard of 3D modelers?
➡ ______

23 Taeho, a 3D modeler, works for a company that makes artificial hands and legs.
➡ ______

24 Taeho uses special software to print out new hands and legs.
➡ ______

25 They are made specially for patients.
➡ ______

26 If you are good at computer programming and art, you can be a 3D modeler.
➡ ______

27 Taeho wants more people to use 3D printed products in the future.
➡ ______

28 Jihye is a big data specialist.
➡ ______

29 She works on many projects.
➡ ______

30 For example, last year, she made bus routes.
➡ ______

31 To find the best night routes, she needed to collect smartphone use data and taxi use patterns from late-night travelers.
➡ ______

______

32 Then she analyzed this information to create the most useful routes.
➡ ______

33 Now Jihye is working with an online shopping mall.
➡ ______

34 She is collecting data from customers to find out the best styles for them.
➡ ______

35 She knows big data allows us to learn more about our daily lives.
➡ ______

36 If you want to become a big data specialist, you should develop your math and problem-solving skills!
➡ ______

37 Think about yourself and prepare for your future.
➡ ______

38 If you keep looking ahead and dreaming big, your future will be bright.
➡ ______

본문 Test

Step4

※ 다음 괄호 안의 단어들을 우리말에 맞도록 바르게 배열하시오.

1 (of / Future / the / Jobs)
➡ ____________________

2 (2020s: / cars / self-driving / be / will / the / market. / on)
➡ ____________________

3 (2030s: / will / people / robots / have / do / that / for / everything / them.)
➡ ____________________

4 (2030s: / printers / 3D / every / in / will / home / out / print / everything. / almost)
➡ ____________________

5 (2050s: / will / people / space / take / trips.)
➡ ____________________

6 (2050s: / people / live / will / the / under / sea / or / in / cities. / floating)
➡ ____________________

7 (at / look / above. / pictures / the)
➡ ____________________

8 (these / do / surprise / you? / ideas)
➡ ____________________

9 (can / you / see / lives / our / that / will / be / different / very / future. / the / in)
➡ ____________________

10 (our / as / change, / lives / new / many / jobs / appear. / will)
➡ ____________________

11 (kind / what / job / of / do / want? / you)
➡ ____________________

12 (will / what / future / your / like? / be / life)
➡ ____________________

13 (following / the / looked / people / ahead / and / jobs / chose / will / that / be / in / important / the / future.)
➡ ____________________
____

14 (read / let's / their / jobs! / about)
➡ ____________________

15 (you / do / see / flower / the / pot / made? / Sujin / that)
➡ ____________________

16 (was / it / from / made / street / flags. / old)
➡ ____________________

17 (is / she / designer. / upcycling / an)
➡ ____________________

18 (works / she / waste / with / to / materials / make / products. / new)
➡ ____________________

19 (products / her / people / show / old / that / materials / be / can / useful / ways. / new / in)
➡ ____________________

20 (can / upcycling / reduce / amount / the / waste / of / future. / the / in)
➡ ____________________

21 (become / to / upcycling / an / designer, / should / you / creative / be / and / about / learn / art.)
➡ ____________________

1 미래의 직업
2 2020년대: 자율주행차들이 시장에 나올 것이다.
3 2030년대: 사람들은 그들을 위하여 모든 것을 하는 로봇을 갖게 될 것이다.
4 2030년대: 모든 가정의 3D 프린터가 거의 모든 것을 출력해 낼 것이다.
5 2050년대: 사람들은 우주여행을 할 것이다.
6 2050년대: 사람들은 바다 밑이나 수상 도시에서 살 것이다.
7 위의 그림들을 보세요.
8 이 생각들이 놀랍습니까?
9 당신은 미래에 우리의 삶이 매우 달라질 것을 볼 수 있습니다.
10 우리의 삶이 변화함에 따라 새로운 직업들이 많이 생겨날 것입니다.
11 당신은 어떤 직업을 원하세요?
12 미래의 당신 삶은 어떤 모습일까요?
13 다음의 사람들은 앞을 내다보고 미래에 중요하게 될 직업을 선택하였습니다.
14 그들의 직업에 관하여 읽어 봅시다!
15 수진이 만든 화분이 보이시나요?
16 이것은 거리의 낡은 깃발들로 만들어졌습니다.
17 그녀는 업사이클링 디자이너입니다.
18 그녀는 새로운 제품을 만들기 위해 폐기물을 가지고 작업합니다.
19 그녀의 제품들은 낡은 재료가 새로운 방식으로 유용해질 수 있다는 것을 사람들에게 보여줍니다.
20 업사이클링은 미래에 쓰레기의 양을 줄일 수 있습니다.
21 업사이클링 디자이너가 되려면 당신은 창의적이어야 하며 미술을 배워야 합니다.

22 (you / have / ever / heard / 3D / modelers? / of)
➡ ______________________________

23 (a / Taeho, / modeler, / 3D / for / works / company / a / makes / that / hands / legs. / and / artificial)
➡ ______________________________

24 (uses / Taeho / software / special / print / to / out / hands / new / legs. / and)
➡ ______________________________

25 (are / they / specially / made / patients. / for)
➡ ______________________________

26 (you / if / good / are / at / programming / computer / and / art, / can / you / be / a / modeler. / 3D)
➡ ______________________________

27 (wants / Taeho / people / more / use / to / printed / 3D / products / future. / the / in)
➡ ______________________________

28 (a / Jihye / is / big / specialist. / data)
➡ ______________________________

29 (works / she / many / on / projects.)
➡ ______________________________

30 (example, / for / year, / last / made / she / routes. / bus)
➡ ______________________________

31 (find / to / best / the / routes, / night / needed / she / collect / to / use / smartphone / data / and / use / taxi / from / patterns / travelers. / late-night)
➡ ______________________________
____

32 (she / then / analyzed / information / this / create / to / most / the / routes. / useful)
➡ ______________________________

33 (now / Jihye / working / is / with / online / an / mall. / shopping)
➡ ______________________________

34 (is / she / collecting / from / data / customers / find / to / out / best / the / for / styles / them.)
➡ ______________________________

35 (knows / she / data / big / us / allows / learn / to / about / more / lives. / daily / our)
➡ ______________________________

36 (you / if / become / to / want / a / data / big / specialist, / should / you / your / develop / math / and / skills! / problem-solving)
➡ ______________________________
____

37 (about / think / yourself / and / for / prepare / future. / your)
➡ ______________________________

38 (you / if / keep / ahead / looking / and / big, / dreaming / future / your / will / bright. / be)
➡ ______________________________

22 3D 모형 제작자에 관하여 들어 본 적이 있으신가요?

23 3D 모형 제작자인 태호는 인공 손과 다리를 만드는 회사에서 일합니다.

24 태호는 새 손과 다리를 출력하기 위하여 특별한 소프트웨어를 사용합니다.

25 그것들은 환자를 위하여 특별히 제작됩니다.

26 만약 당신이 컴퓨터 프로그래밍이나 미술을 잘한다면, 3D 모형 제작자가 될 수 있습니다.

27 태호는 미래에 더 많은 사람들이 3D 프린터로 출력된 제품들을 사용하기를 원합니다.

28 지혜는 빅데이터 전문가입니다.

29 그녀는 많은 프로젝트에서 일합니다.

30 예를 들어, 작년에 그녀는 버스 노선을 만들었습니다.

31 최적의 심야 노선을 찾기 위하여, 그녀는 심야에 이동하는 사람들의 스마트폰 이용 정보와 택시 이용 패턴을 수집할 필요가 있었습니다.

32 그런 다음 그녀는 그 정보를 분석하여 가장 유용한 노선을 만들었습니다.

33 현재 지혜는 온라인 쇼핑몰과 작업하고 있습니다.

34 그녀는 소비자들에게 맞는 최적의 스타일을 찾기 위하여 그들로부터 데이터를 수집하고 있습니다.

35 그녀는 빅데이터가 우리에게 일상생활에 관하여 더 많이 알게 해 준다는 것을 알고 있습니다.

36 만약 당신이 빅데이터 전문가가 되고 싶다면, 수학과 문제 해결 능력을 계발해야 합니다!

37 자신에 대하여 생각해 보고 미래를 준비하세요.

38 만약 당신이 계속 앞을 내다보고 꿈을 크게 꾼다면, 당신의 미래는 밝을 것입니다.

본문 Test

Step5

※ 다음 우리말을 영어로 쓰시오.

1 미래의 직업
➡ ______________________________

2 2020년대: 자율주행차들이 시장에 나올 것이다.
➡ ______________________________

3 2030년대: 사람들은 그들을 위하여 모든 것을 하는 로봇을 갖게 될 것이다.
➡ ______________________________

4 2030년대: 모든 가정의 3D 프린터가 거의 모든 것을 출력해 낼 것이다.
➡ ______________________________

5 2050년대: 사람들은 우주여행을 할 것이다.
➡ ______________________________

6 2050년대: 사람들은 바다 밑이나 수상 도시에서 살 것이다.
➡ ______________________________

7 위의 그림들을 보세요.
➡ ______________________________

8 이 생각들이 놀랍습니까?
➡ ______________________________

9 당신은 미래에 우리의 삶이 매우 달라질 것을 볼 수 있습니다.
➡ ______________________________

10 우리의 삶이 변화함에 따라 새로운 직업들이 많이 생겨날 것입니다.
➡ ______________________________

11 당신은 어떤 직업을 원하세요?
➡ ______________________________

12 미래의 당신 삶은 어떤 모습일까요?
➡ ______________________________

13 다음의 사람들은 앞을 내다보고 미래에 중요하게 될 직업을 선택하였습니다.
➡ ______________________________

14 그들의 직업에 관하여 읽어 봅시다!
➡ ______________________________

15 수진이 만든 화분이 보이시나요?
➡ ______________________________

16 이것은 거리의 낡은 깃발들로 만들어진 것입니다.
➡ ______________________________

17 그녀는 업사이클링 디자이너입니다.
➡ ______________________________

18 그녀는 새로운 제품을 만들기 위해 폐기물을 가지고 작업합니다.
➡ ____________________

19 그녀의 제품들은 낡은 재료가 새로운 방식으로 유용해질 수 있다는 것을 사람들에게 보여줍니다.
➡ ____________________

20 업사이클링은 미래에 쓰레기의 양을 줄일 수 있습니다.
➡ ____________________

21 업사이클링 디자이너가 되려면 당신은 창의적이어야 하며 미술을 배워야 합니다.
➡ ____________________

22 3D 모형 제작자에 관하여 들어 본 적이 있으신가요?
➡ ____________________

23 3D 모형 제작자인 태호는 인공 손과 다리를 만드는 회사에서 일합니다.
➡ ____________________

24 태호는 새 손과 다리를 출력하기 위하여 특별한 소프트웨어를 사용합니다.
➡ ____________________

25 그것들은 환자를 위하여 특별히 제작됩니다.
➡ ____________________

26 만약 당신이 컴퓨터 프로그래밍이나 미술을 잘한다면, 3D 모형 제작자가 될 수 있습니다.
➡ ____________________

27 태호는 미래에 더 많은 사람들이 3D 프린터로 출력된 제품들을 사용하기를 원합니다.
➡ ____________________

28 지혜는 빅데이터 전문가입니다.
➡ ____________________

29 그녀는 많은 프로젝트에서 일합니다.
➡ ____________________

30 예를 들어, 작년에 그녀는 버스 노선을 만들었습니다.
➡ ____________________

31 최적의 심야 노선을 찾기 위하여, 그녀는 심야에 이동하는 사람들의 스마트폰 이용 정보와 택시 이용 패턴을 수집할 필요가 있었습니다.
➡ ____________________

32 그런 다음 그녀는 그 정보를 분석하여 가장 유용한 노선을 만들었습니다.
➡ ____________________

33 현재 지혜는 온라인 쇼핑몰과 작업하고 있습니다.
➡ ____________________

34 그녀는 소비자들에게 맞는 최적의 스타일을 찾기 위하여 그들로부터 데이터를 수집하고 있습니다.
➡ ____________________

35 그녀는 빅데이터가 우리에게 일상생활에 관하여 더 많이 알게 해 준다는 것을 알고 있습니다.
➡ ____________________

36 만약 당신이 빅데이터 전문가가 되고 싶다면, 수학과 문제 해결 능력을 계발해야 합니다!
➡ ____________________

37 자신에 대하여 생각해 보고 미래를 준비하세요.
➡ ____________________

38 만약 당신이 계속 앞을 내다보고 꿈을 크게 꾼다면, 당신의 미래는 밝을 것입니다.
➡ ____________________

※ 다음 우리말과 일치하도록 빈칸에 알맞은 말을 쓰시오.

After You Read D

1. Taehun Kim is a movie ________. He ________ ________ about new movies.
2. He ________ this job ________ he loves ________ ________.
3. ________ ________ this job, he read many books to ________ his ________ ________.
4. He also watched ________ ________ ________ of movies.

1. 김태훈은 영화 비평가이다. 그는 새로운 영화에 대한 기사를 쓴다.
2. 그는 영화 보는 것을 매우 좋아하기 때문에 이 직업을 선택했다.
3. 이 직업을 얻기 위해 그는 글쓰기 기술을 향상시키려고 많은 책들을 읽었다.
4. 그는 또한 많은 다른 유형의 영화들을 보았다.

Culture Link

1. ________ Brand ________
2. A personal brand consultant ________ a personal brand for ________ ________.
3. They find the customer's ________ ________.
4. Then they build a personal brand ________ ________ the customer's ________, ________, and ________.
5. ________ ________ this job, you ________ ________ have great ________ ________.

1. 개인 브랜드 상담가
2. 개인 브랜드 상담가는 한 개인의 브랜드를 그들의 고객들을 위해 만든다.
3. 그들은 고객의 독특한 장점을 찾는다.
4. 그러고 나서 그들은 고객의 개성, 지식 그리고 기술을 사용하여 개인 브랜드를 만든다.
5. 이 직업을 갖기 위해서 당신은 훌륭한 의사소통 기술을 갖출 필요가 있다.

Do It Yourself A

1. B: Hey, Mandy. What are you ________ ________?
2. G: Hey, Edward. Look! Some volunteers ________ ________ for the school festival.
3. B: Really? I want to ________ ________. You know I'm ________ ________ ________ pictures. I think I can do something for the festival.
4. G: I think you can ________ ________ at the cartoon event.
5. B: Right! ________ ________ ________ ________ together?
6. G: Well, I am ________ ________ ________ drawing pictures. But I'm ________ ________ ________ board games.
7. B: You can ________ ________ at the game event then.
8. G: Okay. ________ go and ________ ________ ________ volunteers.

1. B: Mandy, 무엇을 보고 있니?
2. G: Edward, 봐! 자원봉사자들이 학교 축제에서 필요하대.
3. B: 정말? 나 돕고 싶다. 너도 알다시피 내가 그림을 잘 그리잖아. 내 생각엔 내가 축제에서 어떤 것을 할 수 있을 것 같아.
4. G: 나는 네가 만화 행사에서 도움이 될 수 있을 거로 생각해.
5. B: 맞아! 우리 함께 지원해 보는 게 어때?
6. G: 음, 나는 그림을 잘 그리지 못해. 하지만, 나는 보드게임을 잘해.
7. B: 그러면 너는 게임 행사에서 도울 수 있겠다.
8. G: 좋아. 우리 가서 함께 자원봉사자에 지원하자.

※ 다음 우리말을 영어로 쓰시오.

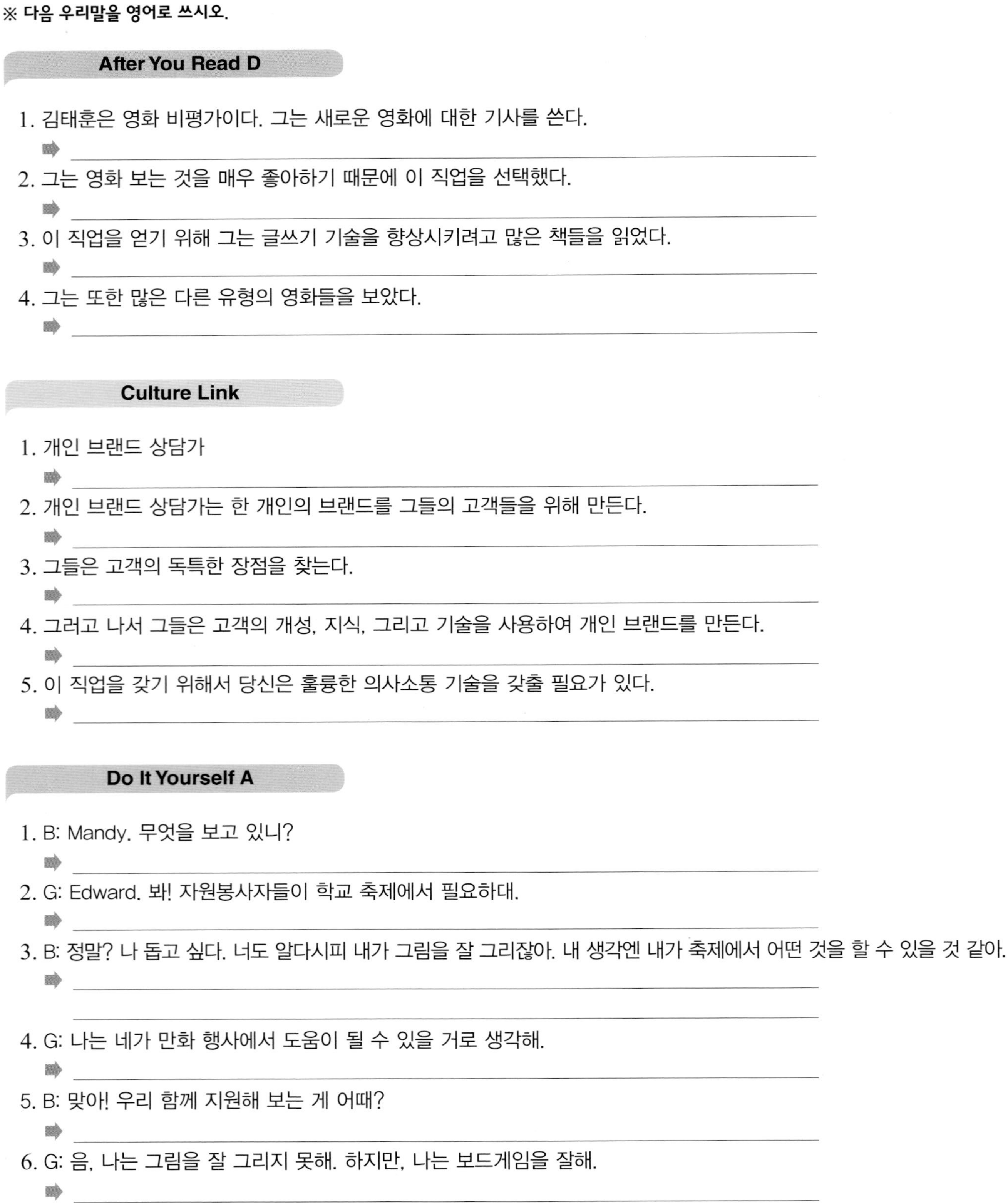

After You Read D

1. 김태훈은 영화 비평가이다. 그는 새로운 영화에 대한 기사를 쓴다.
   ➡ ______________________________
2. 그는 영화 보는 것을 매우 좋아하기 때문에 이 직업을 선택했다.
   ➡ ______________________________
3. 이 직업을 얻기 위해 그는 글쓰기 기술을 향상시키려고 많은 책들을 읽었다.
   ➡ ______________________________
4. 그는 또한 많은 다른 유형의 영화들을 보았다.
   ➡ ______________________________

Culture Link

1. 개인 브랜드 상담가
   ➡ ______________________________
2. 개인 브랜드 상담가는 한 개인의 브랜드를 그들의 고객들을 위해 만든다.
   ➡ ______________________________
3. 그들은 고객의 독특한 장점을 찾는다.
   ➡ ______________________________
4. 그러고 나서 그들은 고객의 개성, 지식, 그리고 기술을 사용하여 개인 브랜드를 만든다.
   ➡ ______________________________
5. 이 직업을 갖기 위해서 당신은 훌륭한 의사소통 기술을 갖출 필요가 있다.
   ➡ ______________________________

Do It Yourself A

1. B: Mandy, 무엇을 보고 있니?
   ➡ ______________________________
2. G: Edward, 봐! 자원봉사자들이 학교 축제에서 필요하대.
   ➡ ______________________________
3. B: 정말? 나 돕고 싶다. 너도 알다시피 내가 그림을 잘 그리잖아. 내 생각엔 내가 축제에서 어떤 것을 할 수 있을 것 같아.
   ➡ ______________________________
   ____
4. G: 나는 네가 만화 행사에서 도움이 될 수 있을 거로 생각해.
   ➡ ______________________________
5. B: 맞아! 우리 함께 지원해 보는 게 어때?
   ➡ ______________________________
6. G: 음, 나는 그림을 잘 그리지 못해. 하지만, 나는 보드게임을 잘해.
   ➡ ______________________________
7. B: 그러면 너는 게임 행사에서 도울 수 있겠다.
   ➡ ______________________________
8. G: 좋아. 우리 가서 함께 자원봉사자에 지원하자.
   ➡ ______________________________

MEMO

MEMO

영어 기출 문제집

적중100

2학기

정답 및 해설

능률 | 김성곤

중 2

적중100

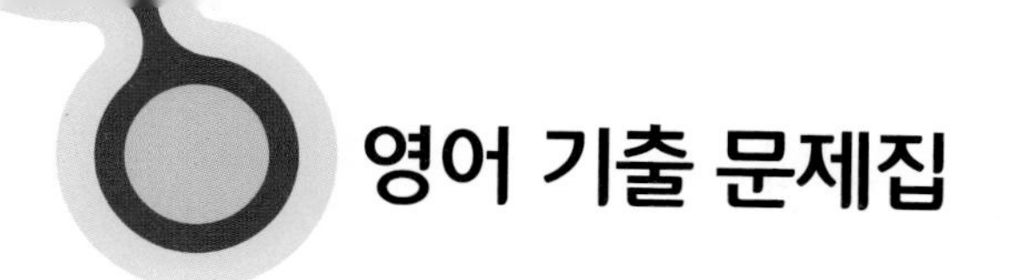

적중100

Lesson 5

Give a Helping Hand

시험대비 실력평가 p.08

01 ④	02 ①	03 ①	04 ③
05 ②	06 ③	07 ⑤	08 ①
09 ③			

01 ④ lucky(운이 좋은) 이외의 단어들은 사람의 성격을 묘사할 때 사용할 수 있는 단어이다. ① creative: 창의적인 ② generous: 관대한 ③ lively: 쾌활한 ⑤ passionate: 열정적인
02 feed: 먹이를 주다
03 carry: 나르다, 운반하다
04 item: 항목, 물품 goods: 상품, 물품
05 die: 죽다 pass away: 죽다, 사망하다
06 all over the world: 전 세계에 worldwide: 세계적인; 세계적으로 ① nationally: 전국적으로 ② internationally: 국제적으로 ④ global: 세계적인 ⑤ variously: 여러 가지로
07 raise money: 돈을 모금하다
08 turning point: 전환점 / 큰 변화가 발생하는 때
09 moment: 순간, 잠깐 / 시간 상의 특정한 시점

서술형 시험대비 p.09

01 (a)live
02 (s)pirit
03 in
04 gave
05 (1) take (2) broke (3) handed (4) search
06 (1) I feel better thanks to your advice.
(2) She passed away last month.
(3) The government planned to support the elderly.
(4) He gained both wealth and fame.
07 (1) (b)lind (2) (s)urvive (3) (h)onor

01 둘은 반의어 관계이다. luckily: 운이 좋게도 unluckily: 불행히도 alive: 살아 있는 dead: 죽은
02 soul: 영혼, 넋, 정신, 마음 spirit: 마음, 정신
03 be in a hurry: 급하다 in need: 어려움에 처한
04 give: 주다 give a hand: 돕다
05 (1) take care of: ~을 돌보다 (2) break one's arm: 팔이 부러지다 (3) hand out: 나누어 주다 (4) search for: ~을 찾다
06 (1) thanks to ~: ~ 덕분에 (2) pass away: 사망하다 (3) support: 지지하다, 원조하다 (4) fame: 명성
07 (1) blind: 눈 먼, 장님의 / 어떤 것도 볼 수 없는 (2) survive: 살아남다, 생존하다 / 나쁜 일이 일어난 후에 계속 살다 (3) honor: 예우하다, 존중하다 / 존경심을 가지고 누군가를 대하다

교과서
Conversation

핵심 Check p.10~11

1 favor / No problem
2 Can you help me to wash the dishes
3 Why don't we have some ice cream?
What about having some ice cream?
Let's have some ice cream.
4 Why don't we go to the movies tomorrow
5 How about playing soccer after school

교과서 대화문 익히기

Check(√) True or False p.12

1 F 2 T 3 T 4 T

교과서 확인학습 p.14~15

Listen & Talk 1 A
can, help me / What are, going / going to donate

Listen & Talk 1 B
with / broke it / a hurry, fell down / Is there, can do / can you help

Listen & Talk 1 C
can you help, wash them / but, to feed, don't you / ask you a favor / Can you help /have to

Listen & Talk 2 A
kinds of volunteer / don't we clean up

Listen & Talk 2 B
As, was, don't we raise, at, on, bring, donate, give a hand, need

Listen & Talk 2 C

cleaned up, we going to / don't we visit, it up / to do, hold / What / serve / about playing / like

Do It Yourself A

to do / don't, volunteer activities, make / is / who has volunteered / has volunteered, help us find / search for, don't we check

시험대비 기본평가 p.16

01 ② 02 ⑤ 03 ③ 04 ②

01 특정 행동을 같이 하자고 제안할 때는 'Why don't we ~?'로 시작하는 표현을 쓴다. 'How about ~?'이나 'What about ~?' 'Let's 동사원형 ~.' 등의 표현도 쓸 수 있는데 'Why don't you+동사 ~?'는 함께 하자는 것은 아니고 상대방에게만 권유하는 것이다.

02 ⑤는 '내가 도와줄까요?'의 의미이고, 나머지 보기들은 상대방에게 도움을 요청하는 말이다.

03 상대방에게 도움을 요청할 때는 'Can you help me ~?'로 시작하는 문장으로 표현할 수 있다. 이 때 can 대신 will을 쓸 수 있으며 would나 could를 써서 'Could you help me ~?'나 'Would you help me ~?'라고 말하면 공손하고 정중한 느낌을 준다.

04 what kinds of ~: 어떤 종류의 volunteer: 자원봉사의; 자원봉사자 / 어떤 종류의 봉사 활동을 할 수 있느냐는 질문을 했으므로, 구체적인 봉사 활동의 예시를 들며 같이 하자고 제안하는 것이 어울린다.

시험대비 실력평가 p.17~18

01 ①, ③ 02 ③ 03 ③ 04 ④ 05 ② 06 Can you help me buy a train ticket? 07 ③ 08 give 09 bring your items and donate them 10 ④ 11 ④ 12 And how about playing some music? 13 ②

01 help는 5형식 동사로 '~이 …하는 것을 돕다'의 의미로 사용된다. 목적격 보어로 to부정사와 동사원형을 쓸 수 있다.

02 (B) be going to 동사원형: ~할 것이다 (C) these books를 받는 인칭대명사가 와야 하므로, 복수형 them이 어울린다.

03 fall down: 넘어지다 / 기차를 타려고 서두르다가 길에 넘어졌다는 말이 연결되어야 자연스럽다.

04 ① 어떻게 남자아이가 여자아이를 도울 것인가? ② 언제 여자아이가 다쳤는가? ③ 왜 여자 아이가 서둘렀는가? ④ 그들은 어디를 갈 것인가? ⑤ 여자아이는 무엇을 부러뜨렸는가?

05 ② 도와준다는 말에 내가 할 수 없다고 말하는 것은 어색하다. Can I give you a hand? → Can you give me a hand?

06 help 목적어 (to) 동사원형: ~가 …하는 것을 돕다

07 as: (접) ~과 같이, ~하는 대로 as you know: 아시다시피

08 give: 주다 give a hand: ~을 돕다

09 item: 항목, 물품 donate: 기부하다

10 ① 특별 행사의 목적 ② 특별 행사가 어디서 열리는지 ③ 특별 행사가 언제 열리는지 ④ 어떤 품목을 기부할 수 없는지 ⑤ 특별 행사에서 모금한 돈이 어디로 주어지는지

11 양로원에서 청소를 하자고 제안하자 좀 더 재미있는 걸 하고 싶다고 이야기했으므로 ③은 답이 되지 않는다. 빈칸 (A) 다음 문장에서 여자아이가 'What can we do at the party?(우리가 파티에서 뭘 할 수 있지?)'라고 말했으므로 파티를 열자고 제안한 것을 추리할 수 있다.

12 How about (동)명사: ~하는 게 어떨까?

13 ① 여자아이는 무슨 악기를 연주할 수 있는가? ② 어떤 음식을 양로원에 있는 사람들에게 대접할 것인가? ③ 언제가 봉사 활동의 날인가? ④ 그들은 봉사활동을 위해 어디로 갈 것인가? ⑤ 양로원에서 그들은 무엇을 할 것인가?

서술형 시험대비 p.19

01 (D) → (B) → (A) → (C)
02 (A) → (C) → (B) → (D)
03 ④ which has volunteered a lot → who[that] has volunteered a lot
04 can you help us find some good places?
05 do
06 of

01 다리에 무슨 문제가 있는지 묻는 질문에 (D) 지난주에 부러졌다고 대답한다. (B) 어떻게 된 일인지 질문하자 (A) 기차를 타려고 서두르다가 길에 넘어졌다고 답한다. (C) 이에, 정말 끔찍하다고 말한다.

02 봉사 활동의 날에 무엇을 할 건지 묻는 질문에 (A) 양로원에 가서 청소를 하자고 제안한다. (C) 이 제안에 나쁜 생각은 아니지만 좀 재미있는 걸 하고 싶다고 말하며 파티를 여는 것을 제안하고 (B) 좋은 생각이라고 답하며, 파티에서 무엇을 할 수 있는지 질문하자 (D) 음식을 대접할 수 있다고 대답한다.

03 선행사인 수민이는 사람이므로 주격 관계대명사 who나 that이 적절하다.

04 Can you help 목적어 (to) 동사원형 ~?: 목적어가 ~하는 것을 도와주겠니?

05 do volunteer work: 자원 봉사를 하다

06 take care of: ~을 돌보다short: 짧은 / tail: 꼬리

교과서

Grammar

핵심 Check

p.20~21

1 (1) whom (2) which
2 (1) sleeping (2) exciting (3) written (4) excited

시험대비 기본평가

p.22

01 ①, ②, ③
02 ④
03 (1) who → which[that]
(2) which → who[whom/that]
(3) exciting → excited
04 The chicken salad which my mom made is very delicious.

01 선행사가 The only food로 사물이며 find의 목적어 역할을 할 수 있는 목적격 관계대명사 that이나 which가 적절하다.
02 감정을 나타내는 타동사의 과거분사는 '~한 감정을 느끼는'이라는 의미로, 주로 사람을 주어로 하며, 현재분사는 주로 사물을 주어로 하여 '~한 감정을 유발하는'의 의미를 나타낸다.
03 (1) 선행사가 동물이므로 who를 which나 that으로 고쳐야 한다. (2) 선행사가 사람이므로 which를 who나 whom 또는 that으로 고쳐야 한다. (3) 사람이 주어이며 '신나는 감정을 느끼는' 것이므로 과거분사가 적절하다.
04 '우리 엄마가 만든'을 관계대명사절로 하여 '치킨 샐러드'를 수식하는 구조로 쓴다. 선행사가 사물이므로 목적격 관계대명사로 which를 쓴다.

시험대비 실력평가

p.23~25

01 ② 02 ③ 03 ③
04 There is a dress in the box (which[that]) Alex sent (to) me.
05 (1) that (2) who (3) whom (4) interested (5) interesting
06 ④ 07 ① 08 ②
09 (1) scared (2) embarrassing (3) shocked 10 ③, ⑤
11 (1) who (2) that (3) which is 12 ④
13 (1) Audrey Hepburn is a person who[whom/that] my partner respects a lot.
(2) This is the ID which[that] the spy used before.
(3) The letter which[that] you sent to me last week made me happy.
(4) Do you remember the girl who[whom/that] I met at the party?
(5) I like the music to which I often listen. 또는 I like the music which[that] I often listen to.
(6) Do you know the girl to whom Ann is talking? / Do you know the girl who[whom/that] Ann is talking to?
14 ③ 15 ④
16 (1) She was shocked because their lives were very difficult.
(2) I can't forget the tiger which I saw on safari.
(3) Are you satisfied with your job as a tour guide?
17 (1) amazed (2) amazing

01 <보기>와 나머지는 목적격 관계대명사이지만 ②번은 주격 관계대명사이다.
02 모두 목적격으로 사용된 관계대명사 that이 들어갈 수 있지만 ③번은 소유격 관계대명사 whose가 들어가야 한다.
03 감정을 나타내는 타동사의 과거분사는 '~한 감정을 느끼는'이라는 의미로, 주로 사람을 주어로 한다.
04 'Alex가 나에게 보낸 박스'에서 목적격 관계대명사를 이용하여 '박스'를 'Alex가 나에게 보낸'이 수식하는 구조로 만들어 준다.
05 (1) 선행사가 사물이므로 that, (2) 선행사가 사람이므로 who, (3) 전치사 with가 있으므로 that은 쓸 수 없다. (4) 내가 흥미를 갖게 되는 '수동'의 의미이므로 과거분사 interested가 적절하다. (5) the game이 흥미롭게 만들어 주는 '능동'의 의미이므로 현재분사가 적절하다.
06 아이들이 놀라게 되는 것이므로 '능동'의 frightening이 아니라 '수동'의 의미를 나타내는 frightened가 되어야 한다.
07 ① 목적격 관계대명사는 생략될 수 있다. ②, ④ 관계대명사의 선행사가 사람이면 who, whom이나 that을 쓰고 사물이면 which나 that을 쓴다. ③ 관계대명사가 접속사와 대명사의 역할을 하므로 목적어로 쓴 it을 삭제해야 한다. ⑤ 전치사가 관계대명사 앞에 올 경우에는 관계대명사 that을 쓸 수 없으며, 관계대명사를 생략하지 않는다.
08 ②번은 접속사이지만 나머지는 모두 관계대명사이다.
09 감정을 나타내는 타동사의 과거분사는 '~한 감정을 느끼는'이라는 의미로, 주로 사람을 주어로 하며, 현재분사는 주로 사물을 주어로 하여 '~한 감정을 유발하는'의 의미를 나타낸다.
10 선행사가 사물이므로 which나 that을 이용하고 목적격이므로 목적어로 쓰인 it은 쓰지 말아야 한다. 또한 목적격 관계대명사는 생략될 수 있다.
11 목적격 관계대명사와 '주격 관계대명사+be동사'는 생략할 수 있다.
12 Everyone feels depressed at some time or another. 사람이 주어로 우울해지는 것이므로 과거분사가 적절하다. some time or another: 이런저런 때에, 언젠가
13 목적격 관계대명사는 선행사가 사람이면 who나 whom, that

을, 사람이나 동물이면 which나 that을 쓴다. 일반적으로 목적격 관계대명사는 생략될 수 있다. 목적격 관계대명사가 전치사의 목적어인 경우 전치사는 관계대명사절의 끝에 오거나 관계대명사 앞에 올 수 있다. 전치사가 관계대명사절의 끝에 올 경우에는 관계대명사를 생략할 수 있다. 전치사가 관계대명사 앞에 올 경우에는 관계대명사 that을 쓸 수 없으며, 관계대명사를 생략하지 않는다.

14 감정을 나타내는 타동사의 현재분사는 주로 사물을 주어로 하여 '~한 감정을 유발하는'의 의미를 나타낸다. 의미상 영어가 나를 '신나게 하는' 것이 아니라 '지루하게 만드는' 것이 자연스러우므로 boring이 적절하다.

15 관계대명사 that은 전치사 다음에는 쓸 수 없다. that → whom

16 (1) '충격을 받은'은 '수동'의 뜻이므로 과거분사를 쓴다. (2) '사파리에서 보았던 호랑이'를 '사파리에서 보았던'이 호랑이를 수식하는 관계대명사절로 수식하도록 한다. (3) be satisfied with: ~에 만족하다

17 감정을 나타내는 타동사가 '어떤 감정을 느끼게 하면' 주로 사물을 주어로 하여 현재분사를 쓰고, '어떤 감정을 느끼면' 주로 사람을 주어로 하여 과거분사를 쓴다.

서술형 시험대비 p.26~27

01 Playing, excited

02 (1) I didn't know you were interested in Latin dance.
(2) Emma was disappointed at her test score.
(3) I think these highway signs are very confusing.
(4) No one knows that I am worried about such a thing.
(5) For me he was not boring, so I was not bored.

03 that → which

04 (1) Jayu Park is a park which[that] my grandfather often visits.
(2) *Tom and Jerry* is a cartoon which[that] my little sister often watches.
(3) That is the girl who[whom/that] I saw this morning.
(4) The girl who[whom/that] I wanted to meet did not participate in the meeting.
(5) The woman who[whom/that] Mom is talking to is Ms. Larson. 또는 The woman to whom Mom is talking is Ms. Larson.
(6) Mariel took pictures of Ben and his car that were on the crime scene.

05 (1) King Sejong is a person who/whom/that my brother respects a lot.
(2) This is the bridge which/that they built about 20 years ago.
(3) The girl talked to a boy whom she met at the party.
(4) I don't like the movie which I saw yesterday.
(5) There are many subjects about which people feel little interest. 또는 There are many subjects (that/which) people feel little interest about.

06 (1) I felt very tired all day because I didn't sleep well last night.
(2) I was scared to be left home alone.
(3) Watching a baseball game makes me bored.

07 (1) *The Smurfs* is a cartoon.
(2) Let me introduce my friend.
(3) Laura was looking for the key all day long.
(4) I cannot speak about it for the reason.

08 (1) He put me in a very embarrassing situation.
(2) My mom was surprised at the news.
(3) It was shocking that he lied to me.
(4) We were all excited because my brother made a goal in the soccer game.

01 주어로 동명사 Playing을 쓰고 '내가 신이 나게 되는' 것이므로 과거분사 excited를 쓴다.

02 (1)~(4) 감정을 나타내는 타동사의 과거분사는 '~한 감정을 느끼는'이라는 의미로, 주로 사람을 주어로 하며, 현재분사는 주로 사물을 주어로 하여 '~한 감정을 유발하는'의 의미를 나타낸다. (5) 주어가 사람일 때도 현재분사를 쓸 수 있다. '나에게 그가 따분하게 만들지 않아서 내가 따분하지 않았다'는 의미이다.

03 관계대명사 that은 전치사와 함께 쓰이지 않는다.

04 (1), (2) 선행사가 사물이므로 관계대명사 which나 that, (3), (4) 선행사가 사람이므로 관계대명사 who, whom이나 that, (5) 목적격 관계대명사가 전치사의 목적어인 경우 전치사는 관계대명사절의 끝에 오거나 관계대명사 앞에 올 수 있으며 전치사가 관계대명사절의 끝에 올 경우에는 관계대명사를 생략할 수 있다. 전치사가 관계대명사 앞에 올 경우에는 관계대명사 that을 쓸 수 없다. (6) 선행사가 '사람+사물'이므로 관계대명사 that을 써야 한다. 목적격 관계대명사는 생략될 수 있다. crime scene: 범죄 현장

05 (1) 선행사가 사람이므로 who, whom이나 that, (2) 선행사가 사물이므로 which나 that, (3) 관계대명사가 접속사와 대명사의 역할을 하므로 him을 삭제해야 한다. (4) 관계대명사가 접속사와 대명사의 역할을 하므로 it을 삭제해야 한다. (5) 전치사가 관계대명사 앞에 올 경우에는 관계대명사 that을 쓸 수 없으며, 관계대명사를 생략하지 않는다.

06 감정을 나타내는 타동사의 과거분사는 '~한 감정을 느끼는'이라는 의미로, 주로 사람을 주어로 하며, 현재분사는 주로 사물을 주어로 하여 '~한 감정을 유발하는'의 의미를 나타낸다.

07 목적격 관계대명사는 접속사와 목적어 역할을 하며 선행사가

사람이면 who나 whom, that, 사물이나 동물이면 which나 that을 쓴다. 목적격 관계대명사절에는 동사 뒤에 목적어가 없다는 것에 주의한다.

08 (1), (3) '난처하게 만드는 상황', '충격을 주는'의 뜻이 자연스러우므로 현재분사, (2), (4) '놀라게 되는', '신나게 되는'이 자연스러우므로 과거분사가 적절하다.

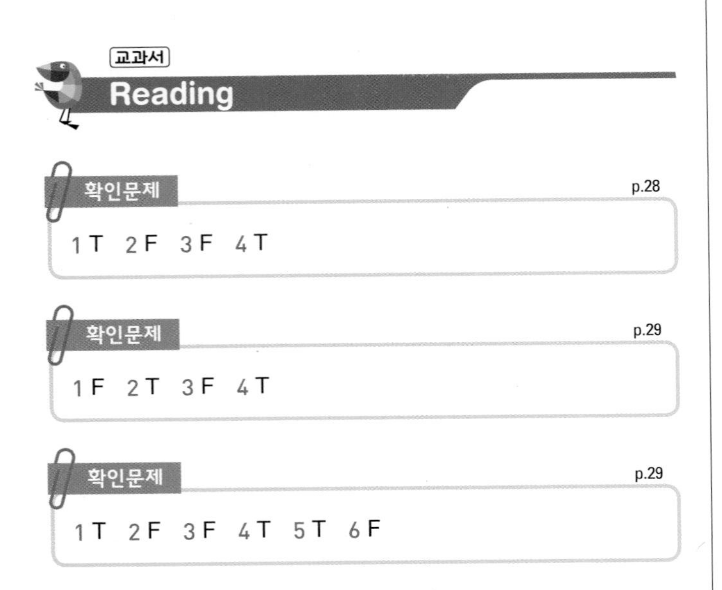

교과서

Reading

확인문제 p.28

1 T 2 F 3 F 4 T

확인문제 p.29

1 F 2 T 3 F 4 T

확인문제 p.29

1 T 2 F 3 F 4 T 5 T 6 F

교과서 확인학습 A p.30~31

01 Spirit 02 During, were
03 The only, that, was 04 felt scared
05 Luckily, thanks to
06 One of the groups that, was
07 a worldwide movie star
08 Her name 09 a symbol of beauty
10 because of, such as
11 which she wore 12 still love
13 a turning point
14 an international music festival
15 donated money
16 Thanks to, more, than
17 realized that, a UNICEF Goodwill Ambassador
18 went to 19 brought, to 20 shocked, lives
21 volunteered 22 to hand out, support
23 to, passed away, following
24 praised, real beauty 25 To honor
26 who, keep, alive 27 favorite saying
28 *As, get* 29 *One, yourself, the other, others*

교과서 확인학습 B p.32~33

1 The Spirit of Audrey
2 During World War II, a little girl and her mother were hungry and sick.
3 The only food that they could find was grass.
4 The little girl felt scared all the time.
5 Luckily, the girl survived, thanks to the help of others.
6 One of the groups that helped her was UNICEF.
7 Later, the girl became a worldwide movie star.
8 Her name was Audrey Hepburn.
9 When she grew up, Hepburn became a symbol of beauty.
10 She was very popular because of her hit movies, such as *My Fair Lady and Roman Holiday.*
11 The little black dress which she wore in a movie is famous even today.
12 Many people still love her style.
13 The autumn of 1987 was a turning point in Hepburn's life.
14 She went to an international music festival in Macau.
15 Many people donated money at the festival, and the money went to UNICEF.
16 Thanks to her fame, UNICEF collected more money than ever before.
17 Hepburn realized that her fame could help others, so she became a UNICEF Goodwill Ambassador.
18 First, Hepburn went to Ethiopia in 1988.
19 There, she brought food to hungry children.
20 She was shocked because their lives were very difficult.
21 After that, she volunteered in other countries.
22 In 1990, she visited Vietnam to hand out medicine and support clean drinking water programs.
23 Her last trip was to Somalia in 1992, and she passed away the following year.
24 Many people praised her beauty and style, but Hepburn's real beauty was her heart.
25 To honor her, UNICEF made a statue, *The Spirit of Audrey.*
26 People who respect her keep her mission alive.
27 Her favorite saying shows her mission.
28 *As you get older, remember you have two hands.*
29 *One is for helping yourself, and the other is for helping others.*

시험대비 실력평가 p.34~37

01 (A) During (B)was (C)was			02 a little
girl and her mother		03 ③	04 Later
05 like	06 fame	07 ①, ⑤	08 ③
09 ③	10 ②	11 ⑤	12 ②
13 ①	14 was → were		
15 before → after		16 ③	17 ②, ④
18 ③	19 ⑤	20 ②, ④	21 ②
22 ③	23 ②	24 ④, ⑤	
25 It made a statue, *The Spirit of Audrey.*			

01 (A) during+ 특정 기간을 나타내는 명사, while+주어+동사 (B) 주어 The only food를 서술하는 동사를 써야 하므로 was가 적절하다. that they could find는 주어를 수식하는 관계대명사절이다. (C) 문장의 주어는 groups가 아니라 One이므로 was가 적절하다.

02 '한 어린 소녀와 그녀의 어머니'를 가리킨다.

03 ⓑ: ~ 덕분에, ~ 때문에, ①, ②, ④, ⑤: ~ 때문에, ③ ~ 대신에

04 late: 늦은; 늦게 / later 나중에

05 such as = like: ~와 같은

06 famous의 명사 'fame'을 쓰는 것이 적절하다.

07 ⓒ와 ①, ⑤번은 접속사, 나머지는 다 관계대명사이다

08 ③ 1987년 가을은 헵번의 인생 '전환점'이었다.

09 주어진 문장의 that에 주목한다. ③번 앞 문장의 내용을 받고 있으므로 ③번이 적절하다.

10 ⓐ와 ①, ②, ④: 동명사, ③, ⑤: 현재분사

11 위 글은 ⑤ '전기'이다. ① (신문 · 잡지의) 기사, ③ 독후감, ④ 수필

12 ② 헵번은 에티오피아에서 '굶주린 아이들에게 음식을 가져다주었다.'

13 ① how: 어떻게, 어떠하게, ⓐ 제2차 세계 대전 중에 당신의 삶은 '어땠나요?' ⓒ '어떻게' 유니세프를 위해 일하기 시작했나요?

14 주어가 My family and I이기 때문에 were로 고치는 것이 적절하다.

15 1987년 마카오의 한 음악 축제가 오드리의 인생을 바꾼 것이기 때문에, 1987년 '이후에' 아프리카와 아시아의 몇 나라들을 방문해서 봉사했다고 고치는 것이 적절하다.

16 ⓐ bring A to B: B에게 A를 가져다주다, to Somalia: 소말리아에[로], ⓒ for helping: 돕기 위한

17 ⓑ 부사적 용법(목적), ① 부사적 용법(결과), ③ 부사적 용법(원인), ⑤ 부사적 용법(목적), ② 명사적 용법, ④ 형용사적 용법

18 ③ 헵번이 배우로서의 성공 여부는 본문에 언급되어 있지 않다.

19 ⑤ 유니세프가 '오드리의 정신'이라는 동상을 어디에 만들었는지는 대답할 수 없다. ① In 1988. ② She brought food to them. ③ To hand out medicine and support clean drinking water programs. ④ In 1992.

20 ② 실제로, ④ 적어도, ⓐ와 나머지: 마침내

21 ① 의지가 강한, ② 이기적인, ③ 다정한, ④ 자선을 베푸는, 궁핍한 사람들을 돕는, ⑤ 관대한

22 ③ 글쓴이의 엄마가 언제 행복하게 느끼는지는 알 수 없다. ① The writer's mom. ② She smiles a lot and tries to see the good in everything. ④ She had a serious car accident. She was in the hospital for six months. ⑤ Because she always helps people in need and she donates money and does volunteer work.

23 오드리 헵번이 방문한 국가와 그곳에서 한 활동을 소개함으로써 필자는 '헵번의 진정한 아름다움이 그녀의 마음이었음을' 설명하고 있다.

24 ⓐ와 ④, ⑤번은 동명사이다. 명사를 수식하더라도 목적이나 용도를 나타낼 때는 동명사이다. drinking water: 식수, be fond of: ~을 좋아하다, 나머지는 다 현재분사

25 그녀를 기리기 위해, 유니세프는 '오드리의 정신'이라는 동상을 만들었다.

서술형 시험대비 p.38~39

01 World War Two 또는 the second World War
02 that
03 (A) the help (B) movie star
04 (A) music festival (B) UNICEF Goodwill Ambassador
05 donated 06 (A)Thanks to (B)collected (C)than
07 As[Because]
08 (A)shocked (B)keep (C) *the other*
09 (A) volunteered (B)her heart
10 ⓐ died ⓑ *become* 또는 *grow*
11 your life during World War II
12 others
13 (A)help (B)help

01 로마 숫자를 포함하고 있는 단어를 영어로 읽을 때 '단어+기수' 또는 'the+서수+단어'로 읽는다. 단, Elizabeth II는 Elizabeth the second로 읽는다.

02 선행사에 수식어 the only가 있을 때에는 보통 관계대명사 that을 사용한다.

03 오드리 헵번은 다른 사람들의 '도움' 덕분에 제2차 세계 대전에서 살아남았고 후에 세계적인 '영화배우'가 되었다.

04 매우 인기 있는 여배우였던 헵번은 1987년 가을에 마카오의 한 국제 '음악 축제'에 갔다. 그 때 그녀는 자신의 명성이 다른 사람들을 도울 수 있다는 것을 깨닫고, '유니세프 친선 대사'가 되었다.

05 donate: 기부하다, 자선단체에 주다 / 과거시제로 쓰는 것이 적절하다.

06 (A) 그녀의 명성 '덕분에'라고 해야 하므로 Thanks to가 적절하다. in spite of: ~에도 불구하고, (B) 더 많은 돈을 '모았다'고 해야 하므로 collected가 적절하다. correct: 바로잡다, 정정하다, (C) 어느 때'보다도' 더 많은 돈이라고 해야 하므로 than이 적절하다. then: 그때, 그 다음에

07 'so' 대신에, 이유를 나타내는 접속사 'As[Because, Since]'를 맨 앞에 쓰는 것이 적절하다.

08 (A) 그녀가 '충격을 받은' 것이기 때문에 shocked가 적절하다. (B) 주어가 복수(People)이므로 동사는 keep이 적절하다. (C) 두 개의 손 중에 다른 한 손을 가리키므로 the other가 적절하다. the other: 둘 중 나머지 하나, another 셋 이상 중에서 두 번째 것을 가리킨다.

09 헵번이 많은 나라들을 방문하고 그곳에서 '봉사한' 것으로 판단하건대, 헵번의 진정한 아름다움은 '그녀의 마음'이었다. judging from ~으로 판단하건대[미루어 보아]

10 ⓐ pass away 죽다, ⓑ get[become, grow]+형용사의 비교급: 점점 ~해지다

11 '제2차 세계 대전 동안 당신의 삶'을 가리킨다.

12 other people은 others로 바꿔 쓸 수 있다.

13 제2차 세계 대전 동안, Audrey의 가족과 Audrey는 굶주리고 아팠고 다른 사람들의 '도움' 덕분에 살아남았다. 1987년 마카오의 한 음악 축제 이후, Audrey는 자신의 명성이 다른 사람들을 '도울 수 있다'는 것을 알게 되었고, 유니세프를 위해 일하기 시작했다.

영역별 핵심문제 p.41~45

01 ③ 02 (1) (m)oment (2) (p)raised (3) (r)ealized (4) (c)ollecting 03 ④
04 (1) hold (2) fell (3) clean (4) raise
05 can you help me wash them?
06 (A) Why, (B) What 07 ③
08 Shall we raise money and help the people there? Let's raise money and help the people there.
09 ⑤
10 can you help me (to) move these books?
11 donate 12 ②
13 Doing[To do] yoga makes me relaxed.
14 ③ 15 ④ 16 ②, ③ 17 ③, ⑤
18 (1) interesting, bored (2) tired
19 (1) The man (who/whom) I saw at the café was Park Jisung.
(2) I love the dog (which) my grandmother adopted.
(3) Jason didn't know about the party, so he was really surprised.
(4) We were so shocked when we heard about the accident. 20 which 21 ②
22 People who[that] respect her keep her mission alive. 23 ⑤
24 (1) 에티오피아(1988년), (2) 베트남(1990년), (3) 소말리아(1992년) 25 (A) terrible (B)changed (C)what
26 working 27 ④
28 helped young students with math homework
29 are → is

01 ① homeless: 집 없는, 노숙자의 ② elderly: 나이가 지긋한 ③ worldwide: 세계적인 ④ international: 국제적인 ⑤ following: (그) 다음의

02 (1) moment: 순간, 잠깐 (2) praise: 칭찬하다 (3) realize: 깨닫다, 알아차리다 (4) collect: 모으다, 수집하다

03 fame: 명성 / 유명한 상태

04 (1) hold a party: 파티를 열다 (2) fall down: 넘어지다 (3) clean up: ~을 치우다, ~을 청소하다 (4) raise money: 돈을 모금하다

05 Can you help 목적어 (to) 동사원형 ~?: 목적어가 ~하는 것을 도와주겠니?

06 Why don't you ~?: ~하지 그래? What: 무엇

07 남자아이 1이 'Can you help me wash these dogs?(이 개들 씻기는 거 도와줄 수 있니?)'라는 묻는 질문에 'Sure. But I have to walk these dogs first. After that, I will help you.(그럼. 근데 나 이 개들 산책 먼저 시켜야 해. 끝나고 나서 도와줄게.)'라고 대답했으므로, 개 산책을 시킬 것이다.

08 특정 행동을 제안할 때는 'Why don't we ~?'로 시작하는 표현을 쓴다. 'Shall we ~?', 'Let's ~' 등의 표현도 쓸 수 있다.

09 ① 어떻게 어려움에 처한 사람들을 위해 돈을 모금할 것인가? ② 어디서 특별 행사가 열리는가? ③ 언제 특별 행사가 열리는가? ④ 어디서 큰 불이 있었는가? ⑤ 언제 Mapletown에서 큰 불이 있었는가?

10 Can you help 목적어 (to) 동사원형 ~?: 목적어가 ~하는 것을 도와주겠니?

11 donate: 기부하다 / 사람들을 돕기 위해 무언가를 주다

12 오늘 오후에 무엇을 하기를 원하는지 묻는 질문에, 테니스를 같이 치자고 제안하는 것이 적절하다. Why don't we ~?: ~하는 게 어떨까?

13 내가 느긋해지는 것이므로 relaxed로 써야 한다.

14 감정을 나타내는 타동사의 과거분사는 '~한 감정을 느끼는'이라는 의미로, 주로 사람을 주어로 하며, 현재분사는 주로 사물을 주어로 하여 '~한 감정을 유발하는'의 의미를 나타낸다.

15 ④ Susan is the woman (who/whom/that) I helped on the street.

16 ① The little girl felt scared all the time. ④ Riding

a roller coaster makes me excited. ⑤ It was very exciting, and I became interested in hockey!

17 ③, ⑤번은 주격 관계대명사이고, 나머지는 모두 목적격 관계대명사이다. run into: ~을 우연히 만나다

18 감정을 나타내는 타동사의 과거분사는 '~한 감정을 느끼는'이라는 의미로, 주로 사람을 주어로 하며, 현재분사는 주로 사물을 주어로 하여 '~한 감정을 유발하는'의 의미를 나타낸다.

19 (1), (2) 관계대명사의 선행사가 사람이면 who, whom이나 that을, 사물이면 which나 that을 사용한다. (3), (4) 감정을 나타내는 타동사의 과거분사는 '~한 감정을 느끼는'이라는 의미로, 주로 사람을 주어로 한다.

20 목적격 관계대명사 which를 생략할 수 있다.

21 ② 많은 사람이 '여전히 그녀의 스타일을 사랑한다.'

22 주격 관계대명사 'who'나 'that'을 보충하면 된다.

23 ⓑ와 ⑤번은 (비례) ~함에 따라, ~할수록, As you get older: 나이가 들어갈수록, ① 같은 정도로, 마찬가지로, ② ~처럼, ~하는 대로, ③ ~할 때, ④ ~이므로, ~이기 때문에

24 에티오피아(1988년) → 베트남(1990년) → 소말리아(1992년) 순서로 방문했다.

25 (A) 제2차 세계 대전 동안 나의 삶은 '끔찍했다'고 해야 하므로 terrible이 적절하다. terrific: 아주 좋은, 멋진, 훌륭한, (B) 마카오의 한 음악 축제가 인생을 '바꿨다'고 해야 하므로 changed가 적절하다. exchange: 교환하다, (C) 당신은 '무엇을' 했습니까?'라고 해야 하므로 what이 적절하다. how를 쓰면 do 다음에 목적어를 써야 한다.

26 begin은 목적어로 to부정사와 동명사를 둘 다 쓸 수 있다.

27 ④ 마카오의 음악 축제에 Audrey가 참가한 이유는 알 수 없다. ① It was terrible. ② Thanks to the help of others. ③ In 1987, a musical festival in Macau changed her life and she learned that her fame could help other people. ⑤ Some countries in Africa and Asia.

28 앞 문장의 내용을 가리킨다.

29 주어가 동명사 helping이므로 단수로 취급해야 하고, helping 이하는 일반적인 사실을 나타내기 때문에 현재시제로 써야 하므로 is로 고치는 것이 적절하다.

단원별 예상문제

p.46~49

01 favor　02 ④　03 What　04 ②, ⑤
05 ③　06 ⑤　07 ①　08 ⑤
09 nursing home　10 ②　11 ③
12 Why don't we check the volunteering website for teens?
13 (1) This is the cell phone (which/that) I broke yesterday.
(2) The speed at which everything moved felt strange.
(3) The girl who I met the other day was very pretty.
(4) I was very worried about his health.
14 (1) excited (2) interested
15 ②번, excited → scared 또는 frightened　16 ③, ⑤
17 (A)because of (B)is (C)turning　18 ④
19 she realized (that) her fame could help others.
20 volunteered　21 helping others
22 *you* → *yourself*
23 We survived thanks to the help of others.
24 in some countries in Africa and Asia　25 ⑤

01 주어진 보기는 명사와 형용사의 관계이다. beauty: 아름다움, 미(美) beautiful: 아름다운 favor: 호의, 친절 favorable: 호의적인

02 friendly: 친절한 gentle: 온화한 curious: 호기심 많은 polite: 공손한 careful: 주의깊은 outgoing: 외향적인 patient: 끈기 있는

03 What kinds of ~: 어떤 종류의 What about 동명사 ~?: ~하는 게 어떨까?

04 thanks to: ~ 덕분에 because of: ~ 때문에 due to: ~ 때문에, ~ 덕분에

05 (B) 책을 옮기는 것을 도와줄 수 있느냐는 질문에 (C) 도와줄 수 있다고 대답하며 책으로 뭘 할지 질문하자 (A) 어린이 도서관에 기부할 거라고 대답한다.

06 (C) 어린이 병원에서 봉사 활동을 할 것을 제안하자 (B) 좋다고 대답하며, 거기서 뭘 할 수 있는지 질문한다. (A) 아픈 아이들을 위해 음악을 연주할 수 있다고 대답한다.

07 저번에 봉사 활동으로 공원을 청소했으므로 이번에는 무엇을 할지 묻는 질문이 연결되는 것이 자연스럽다. 또한 주어진 문장에 대해 양로원에 가서 청소하는 것을 제안하는 내용이 나오는 ①이 적절하다.

08 ⓐ visit ⓑ clean it up ⓒ to do ⓓ something fun ⓔ hold

09 nursing home: 양로원 / 너무 나이 들거나 병이 들어서 스스로를 돌볼 수 없는 사람들이 사는 장소

10 주어진 문장은 봉사활동에 대한 부가적 설명으로, 봉사활동을 제안하는 말에 이어 나오는 것이 적절하다.

11 do volunteer work: 자원 봉사를 하다

12 Why don't we ~?: ~하는 게 어떠니? check: 확인하다

13 (1) 선행사가 사물이므로 which나 that, (2) 전치사가 관계대명사 앞에 올 경우에는 관계대명사 that을 쓸 수 없으며, 관계대명사를 생략하지 않는다. (3) 관계대명사가 접속사와 대명사의 역할을 하므로 목적어 her를 삭제해야 한다. (4) 감정을 나타내는 타동사의 과거분사는 '~한 감정을 느끼는'이라는 의미로, 주로 사람을 주어로 한다.

14 (1) excite는 타동사로 '흥분시키다'라는 의미이다. 경기가 나를

흥분시키고 나는 흥분되는 것이므로 game을 주어로 할 때는 현재분사가, 나를 주어로 할 때는 과거분사가 적절하다. (2) 야구가 지루하다고 생각하는 것이므로 관심이 없다고 쓸 수 있다.

15 제2차 세계 대전 동안, 어린 소녀는 굶주리고 아팠기 때문에 내내 '겁에 질려 있었다.'로 고쳐야 한다. frightened: 겁먹은, 무서워하는

16 ③, ⑤번은 접속사, ⓐ와 나머지는 관계대명사이다.

17 (A) 뒤에 명사가 나오므로 because of가 적절하다. because of+명사나 동명사, because+주어+동사, (B) 주어 The little black dress를 서술하는 동사를 써야 하므로 is가 적절하다. which she wore in a movie는 주어를 수식하는 관계대명사절이다. (C) 인생의 '전환점'이라고 해야 하므로 turning이 적절하다. turning point: 전환점

18 주어진 문장의 UNICEF collected more money than ever before에 주목한다. ④번 앞 문장의 내용에 이어지는 말이므로 ④번이 적절하다.

19 헵번은 '자신의 명성이 다른 사람들을 도울 수 있다는 것을 깨닫고', 유니세프 친선 대사가 되었다.

20 volunteer: (어떤 일을 하겠다고) 자원[자진]하다 / 자원 봉사로 하다, 어떤 일을 하도록 강요받지 않고 해주다 / 과거시제로 쓰는 것이 적절하다.

21 '타인을 돕는 것'을 가리킨다.

22 자기 자신을 돕는 것으로 주어와 목적

23 survive: 살아남다, 생존하다, thanks to: ~ 덕택에, ~ 때문에

24 '아프리카와 아시아의 몇몇 나라들'을 가리킨다.

25 Audrey는 아프리카와 아시아의 몇몇 나라들에서 봉사하였다.

서술형 실전문제

p.50~51

01 ⓐ with ⓑ in ⓒ to ⓓ down

02 Is there anything (that) I can do for you?

03 (A) Why don't we raise money and help the people there?
(B) Please give a hand to people in need.

04 (1) I told you about her.
(2) I made it for my family.
(3) The food was delicious.
(4) You ate dinner with her last Sunday.

05 (1) disappointed (2) excited

06 because she was a UNICEF Goodwill Ambassador → because of her hit movies, such as *My Fair Lady* and *Roman Holiday*

07 The little black dress which she wore in a movie is famous even today.

08 a turning point

09 (A)shocked (B)last (C)alive

10 ②번, from Somalia → to Somalia

11 She passed away in 1993.

01 ⓐ What's wrong with ~?: ~에 무슨 문제가 있는 겁니까? ⓑ be in a hurry: 서두르다 ⓒ to부정사의 부사적 용법 중 목적(~하기 위해서) ⓓ fall down: 넘어지다

02 there is ~: ~가 있다 for: ~을 위해

03 (A) Why don't we ~?: ~하는 게 어떨까? raise money: 돈을 모금하다 (B) give a hand: ~을 돕다 in need: 어려움에 처한

04 목적격 관계대명사는 선행사가 사람이면 who나 whom, that을, 사람이 아니면 which나 that을 쓴다. 목적격 관계대명사는 생략될 수 있다. 목적격 관계대명사가 전치사의 목적어인 경우 전치사는 관계대명사절의 끝에 오거나 관계대명사 앞에 올 수 있으며 끝에 올 경우에는 관계대명사를 생략할 수 있다. 앞에 올 경우에는 관계대명사 that을 쓸 수 없으며, 관계대명사를 생략하지 않는다.

05 (1) disappoint는 타동사로 '실망시키다'라는 의미이다. 결과가 Nick을 실망시키고 Nick은 실망이 되는 것이므로 the result를 주어로 할 때는 현재분사가, Nick을 주어로 할 때는 과거분사가 적절하다. (2) Alita가 신난다고 생각하는 것이므로 Alita에 대해 신이 났다고 쓸 수 있다. 보통 과거분사는 사람을 주어로 하며 현재분사는 사물을 주어로 한다.

06 헵번은 '<마이 페어 레이디>와 <로마의 휴일>과 같은 흥행 영화들로 인해' 매우 인기가 있었다.

07 'even'을 보충하면 된다.

08 헵번의 인생에서 '전환점'이 된 행사는 1987년 가을에 열린 마카오의 한 국제 음악 축제였다.

09 (A) 그들의 삶이 매우 어려웠기 때문에 '충격을 받았다'고 해야 하므로 shocked가 적절하다. pleased: 기쁜, (B) 그녀의 '마지막' 여행이라고 해야 하므로 last가 적절하다. last: 마지막의, latest: 최근의, (C) 목적격보어로 쓰였고 뒤에 명사가 없기 때문에 alive가 적절하다. alive: 살아 있는, 존속하는(명사 앞에는 안 씀), live: 살아 있는(주로 명사 앞에 씀)

10 그녀의 마지막 여행은 1992년 '소말리아에' 간 것이었다고 해야 하므로 to Somalia로 고쳐야 한다.

11 그녀의 마지막 여행은 1992년 소말리아에 간 것이었으며, 이듬해 그녀는 사망하였다고 했으므로 1993년에 사망하였다.

창의사고력 서술형 문제

p.52

01 Why don't we / How about meeting at 1? / I'm afraid I can't. / What about meeting / Let's

|모범답안|

02 my mom / the good / car accident / in need / big hero

01 What[How] about 동명사 ~?: ~하는 게 어떨까? Why don't we ~?: ~하는 게 어떨까? I'm afraid I can't.: 유감이지만 할 수 없어.

단원별 모의고사

p.53~56

01 ⑤ 02 ③
03 (1) honor (2) broke, accident (3) mission (4) statue (5) survived
04 all the time
05 ⓒ am → was ⓔ terrific → terrible
06 can you help me (to) carry this bag?
07 ③ 08 Can you help me (to) solve a math problem[math problems]?
09 ⑤
10 We need someone who has volunteered a lot.
11 for 12 ② 13 ④
14 (1) relaxed (2) interesting
15 ①, ③, ④
16 (1) The book (which/that) she was reading is missing.
(2) The man (who/whom/that) I was having lunch with was Yoojin. 또는 The man with whom I was having lunch was Yoojin.
(3) We were amazed at the beautiful scenery.
(4) Dan is not a funny guy, but I'm not bored when I am with him.
17 ⑤ 18 thanks to Hepburn's fame 19 ③
20 hungry children 21 ⑤ 22 ②
23 ④
24 She was in the hospital for six months. 25 ③

01 collect: 모으다, 수집하다
02 hold: 열다, 개최하다
03 (1) honor: 존경하다, 존중하다 (2) break one's leg: 다리가 부러지다 accident: 사고 (3) mission: 임무, 사명 (4) statue: 조각상 (5) survive: 살아남다, 생존하다
04 always: 항상 all the time: 늘, 내내
05 'What happened?'는 과거에 무슨 일이 있었는지 질문하는 것이므로 과거시제로 써야 맞다. terrific: 멋진 terrible: 끔찍한
06 Can you help 목적어 (to) 동사원형 ~?: 목적어가 ~하는 것을 도와주겠니?
07 ⓐ can you help ⓑ move these books ⓒ Sure / Of course ⓓ What are you going ⓔ I'm going to
08 Can you help 목적어 (to) 동사원형 ~?: 목적어가 ~하는 것을 도와주겠니? solve a problem: 문제를 풀다 math: 수학
09 are → is / 동명사 주어는 단수 취급한다.
10 need: 필요하다 volunteer: 자원봉사를 하다 a lot: 많이
11 search for: ~을 찾다 for: ~을 위한
12 ② 수민이가 아니라 다른 여자아이의 생각이다.
13 관계대명사가 접속사와 대명사의 역할을 하므로 bought 다음에 목적어로 쓴 it을 삭제해야 한다.
14 영화를 보는 것이 '긴장이 풀어지도록 하는' 것이므로 과거분사, 게임이 '재미있게 해주는' 것이므로 현재분사를 쓴다.
15 선행사가 사람이므로 목적격 관계대명사로 who나 whom 또는 that을 써야 한다.
16 (1) 목적격 관계대명사를 이용하여 '그녀가 읽고 있던' 이 '책'을 수식하는 구조로 쓴다. (2) '내가 함께 점심을 먹고 있던'이 '남자'를 수식하는 구조로 쓴다. 목적격 관계대명사가 전치사 with의 목적어 역할을 한다. 목적격 관계대명사는 생략될 수 있다. (3), (4) 감정을 나타내는 타동사의 과거분사는 '~한 감정을 느끼는'이라는 의미로, 주로 사람을 주어로 한다.
17 ⑤ Someone was following me, and I felt scared. crocodile: 악어
18 '헵번의 명성 덕분에', 유니세프는 어느 때보다도 더 많은 돈을 모을 수 있었다.
19 이 글은 '헵번의 명성과 그녀의 인생 전환점'에 관한 글이다.
20 에티오피아의 '굶주린 아이들'의 삶을 가리킨다.
21 ⓑ 선행사 People을 수식하는 주격 관계대명사, ⑤ 선행사 Anyone을 수식하는 주격 관계대명사 나머지는 다 의문대명사(누구)
22 다른 한 손은 '타인'을 돕기 위한 것이라고 하는 것이 적절하다.
23 위 글은 필자가 존경하는 영웅에 대한 이야기이므로 제목으로는 '나의 작지만 거대한 영웅'이 적절하다.
24 글쓴이의 엄마는 '6개월' 동안 병원에 있었다.
25 ③ 그녀는 자동차 사고에서 '회복했다.'

Lesson 6

The Best Trip of Your Life

시험대비 실력평가

p.60

01 ③ 02 ③ 03 (1) scenery
(2) condition (3) autumn (5) amusement park
04 (a)wesome 05 (p)urpose 06 ④
07 ③ 08 ③ 09 ⑤

01 item: 물품 goods: 상품, 물건
02 a variety of: 여러 가지의, 다양한
03 (1) scenery: 풍경, 경치 / 나는 이 해변을 추천한다. 그것은 가장 아름다운 풍경을 가지고 있다. (2) condition: 상태, 상황 / 그 차는 상태가 좋다. (3) autumn: 가을 / 가을에 잎은 빨갛게 변한다. (4) amusement park: 놀이공원 / 그들은 놀이공원에서 재미있게 놀고 있다.
04 awesome: 매우 멋진 / 멋지거나 인상적인
05 purpose: 목적, 목표 / 어떤 것이 사용되거나 행해지는 이유
06 take: (얼마의 시간이) 걸리다
07 get to: (장소 · 위치에) 도착하다 / 우리는 곧 공항에 도착할 것이다.
08 rough: 거친, 파도가 심한 / 그 보트는 거친 파도를 헤치며 항해했다.

서술형 시험대비

p.61

01 goods
02 (p)laces
03 (1) Eugene's violin is old but still in good condition.
(2) The restaurant features a variety of desserts.
(3) You have to focus on your studies.
(4) I visited a foreign country last month.
04 (1) amazing (2) natural
05 get
06 how
07 (1) comic books (2) plans (3) block (4) cafe

01 goods: 상품, 물건 / 판매를 위한 물품 / 그들은 영국으로부터 비싼 상품들을 수입했다.
02 site: 장소 place: 장소, 곳 / 그 도시에는 중요한 역사적 장소들이 많다.
03 (1) condition: 상태, 상황 (2) a variety of: 여러 가지의, 다양한 (3) focus on: (~에) 집중하다, 초점을 맞추다 (4) foreign: 외국의 visit: 방문하다, 찾아가다
04 (1) amaze: 놀라게 하다 amazing: 놀라운, 멋진 (2) nature: 자연 natural: 자연의
05 get off: 내리다, 하차하다 get on: 타다, 승차하다
06 Can you tell me how to get ~?: ~에 어떻게 가는지 말해줄 수 있나요? How long does it take to go to ~?:~까지 가는 데 얼마나 걸리나요?
07 (1) comic book: 만화책 (2) plan: 계획 (3) block: 블록, 구역 (4) cafe: 카페, 커피숍

교과서

Conversation

핵심 Check

p.62~63

1 What are you, to do / I'm planning to do / What are you / going to see a movie
2 What are you planning to do this weekend? / I'm planning to visit my grandparents in Seoul.
3 (1) (C) → (A) → (B) → (D)
(2) (D) → (B) → (C) → (A) → (E)
4 How long does it take? / It takes 30 minutes by bus.

교과서 대화문 익히기

Check(√) True or False

p.64

1 T 2 F 3 F 4 T

교과서 확인학습

p.66~67

Listen & Talk 1 A

What are you, this / going, go / What, you, do / I'm planning to

Listen & Talk 1 B

have, this, have any / (g)oing / What, (p)lanning to, with / I'm (p)lanning, with them, about, plans for / (g)oing, stay, relax

Listen & Talk 1 C

Where, field trip / We are going to / (i)nteresting, (p)lanning to see / are, I'm (p)lanning to see, Where /

We are going to, amusement, excited

Listen & Talk 2 A

How, get / by / How long, take, get / It takes

Listen & Talk 2 B

pictures, beautiful, Where, take / were, of, should / to, How, get, from / Get on, off, see, front / long, take / takes / next weekend

Listen & Talk 2 C

How do I get to / go there by bus or on foot / How long, take / by, on foot / Can you tell, how to get / Go, turn, on / Go, for, turn left

Do It Yourself A

What, (p)lanning to do this / to go to / Are you, to see / will, I'm, to visit / How long / an hour and 40 minutes by / much, than, have

시험대비 기본평가 p.68

01 ②, ⑤	02 ④	03 ③	04 ③

01 What are you going to 동사원형 ~?: 너는 무엇을 할 거니? What are you planning to 동사원형 ~?: 너는 뭐 할 계획이니? be going to 동사원형: ~할 예정이다

02 특정 장소까지의 소요 시간을 물을 때는 'How long does it take to get ~?'이라고 묻는다. 시간이 얼마 걸린다는 표현이 나와야 한다. It takes (about) 시간: ~ (정도) 걸려.

03 계획을 대답할 때 'I'm going to 동사원형 ~.', 'I'm thinking of (동)명사 ~.', 'I'm planning to 동사원형 ~.' 또는 'I will 동사원형'을 사용하여 말할 수 있다.

04 ③번은 현재진행형을 사용해서 휴가 동안 무엇을 하고 있는 중인지 묻고 있는 질문이다. 이외의 문장들은 계획을 묻고 있는 것들이다.

시험대비 실력평가 p.69~70

01 ①	02 go there	03 ④	04 ④
05 ④	06 ④	07 ①	08 ②, ⑤
09 ④	10 have	11 ⑤	

12 I'm going to stay home and relax.

01 주어진 문장은 '(사진을) 어디서 찍었어?'란 의미이므로, 사진들이 예쁘다고 말한 이후에 질문하고, 여자아이가 Riverside Park에서 찍었다고 대답하는 것이 어울린다. 그러므로 ①이 적절하다.

02 여자아이의 'You should go there.(넌 거기 꼭 가 봐야 해.)'라는 말에 'I want to.'라고 대답하고 있으므로 '나도 거기 가 보고 싶다.'라는 말을 줄여서 쓴 것임을 알 수 있다.

03 ④ this weekend → next weekend 남자아이는 다음 주말에 Riverside Park에 갈 것이다.

04 ④ 소요 시간을 물어보는 질문에 거리를 말하는 것은 어색하다. How long does it take to get ~?: ~에 가는 데 얼마나 걸려?

05 (C) 학교에 어떻게 가는지 질문하자 (B) 버스를 타고 간다고 대답한다. (A) 거기(학교)까지 가는 데 얼마나 걸리는지 소요 시간을 묻자, (D) 15분 걸린다고 대답한다.

06 주어진 문장은 '거기(한국 대학교)에 어떻게 가는지 말해 줄 수 있나요?'란 뜻으로 다음에 버스를 타거나, 걸어서 갈 수 있다고 가는 방법을 안내해 주는 말이 나오는 ④번이 적절하다.

07 How do I get to 장소: ~에 어떻게 가나요? How long does it take to get ~?: ~까지 가는 데 얼마나 걸리나요?

08 ① 사진을 찍다 ③ 가져가다 ④ (버스를) 타다 ② 시간이 그렇게 많이 걸리지 않아요. ⑤ 그것을 준비하려면 많은 시간이 걸릴 것이다.

09 휴가 동안 여자아이의 계획은 조부모님을 방문해 한옥 마을에 갈 계획이라고 말하고, 이에 남자 아이는 휴가 때 무슨 계획이 있는지 질문해야 '나는 집에 머물면서 쉴 거야.'로 대답할 수 있으므로 ④번이 적절하다.

10 have a holiday: 휴가를 보내다 Do you have any plans?: 무슨 계획이라도 있니?

11 빈칸 다음에 남자아이가 'What are you planning to do with them?(그분들과 어떤 것을 할 계획이야?)'으로 말한 것으로 보아 여자아이는 them이라고 지칭할 만한 대상과 같이 무엇을 할 예정이다.

12 be going to 동사원형: ~할 예정이다 relax: 휴식을 취하다, 느긋이 쉬다

서술형 시험대비 p.71

01 to do
02 she is going to do this weekend, is going to go to, is planning to go hiking
03 (D) → (B) → (A) → (C)
04 (1) I will watch a soccer game.
(2) I am going to watch a soccer game.
(3) I am thinking of watching a soccer game.
05 (A) interesting (B) excited
06 What are you planning to see there?

01 be going to 동사원형: ~할 예정이다 be planning to 동사원형: ~할 계획이다 do: 하다

02 be going to 동사원형: ~할 예정이다 this weekend: 이번 주말에 여자아이는 제주도에 가서 한라산에 하이킹을 갈 계획을 가지고 있다.

03 어디 갈 것인지 묻는 질문에 → (D) 바르셀로나에 갈 것이라고 대답한다. → (B) 거기(바르셀로나)까지 가는 데 얼마나 걸리는지 소요시간을 묻고 → (A) 비행기를 타고 14시간이 걸린다고 대답한다. → (C) 그곳에서의 계획을 묻자 축구 경기를 볼 계획이라고 대답한다.

04 계획을 대답할 때 'I'm going to 동사원형 ~.', 'I'm thinking of (동)명사 ~.', 'I'm planning to 동사원형 ~.' 또는 'I will 동사원형'을 사용하여 말할 수 있다. be going to 동사원형: ~할 예정이다 be planning to 동사원형: ~할 계획이다 'I'm thinking of ~': 나는 ~을 할까 생각 중이다

05 감정을 나타내는 동사의 경우 현재분사는 '~하게 하는'의 뜻으로 감정을 유발하는 대상에 쓰이고, 과거분사는 '~하게 된'의 뜻으로 감정을 느끼는 대상에 쓰인다. (A)는 '미술관에 가는 것이 재미있겠다'라는 의미이므로 현재분사형, (B)는 남자아이가 롤러코스터 탈 생각으로 신나는 감정을 느끼는 것이므로 과거분사형을 쓴다.

06 be planning to 동사원형: ~할 계획이다 there: 거기에서

교과서

Grammar

핵심 Check

p.72~73

1 (1) it safe to (2) It, to (3) important not to
2 (1) what you bought (2) if[whether] you like
(3) Who do you think will

시험대비 기본평가

p.74

01 ② 02 ③ 03 ⑤
04 (1) It was nice to relax in a café and read the books.
(2) Do you know where the first train station in Korea is?

01 간접의문문은 '의문사+주어+동사'의 형태로 다른 문장 안에서 주어, 목적어, 보어 역할을 한다.

02 ③번은 거리를 나타내는 비인칭 주어이고, 나머지는 모두 가주어이다.

03 간접의문문은 '의문사+주어+동사'의 어순이다. It으로 받고 있으므로 단수가 적절하다.

04 (1) 가주어 it과 진주어로 to부정사를 이용하여 문장을 배열한다. (2) 간접의문문의 어순(의문사+주어+동사)에 주의하여 배열한다.

시험대비 실력평가

p.75~77

01 ② 02 ③ 03 (1) It (2) to win
(3) stand (4) she left (5) he is (6) if
04 ④ 05 ⑤
06 It is not difficult to use the Internet in Korea.
07 ④ 08 ⑤ 09 ④ 10 ③
11 ① 12 ② 13 ⑤ 14 ②
15 (1) To ride[Riding] a motorcycle without a helmet is dangerous. 또는 It is dangerous to ride a motorcycle without a helmet.
(2) It is great to make good friends in your life.
(3) It is not easy to keep a diary in English every day.
(4) It is important to learn the history of your country.
(5) The girl is asking where the nearest bus stop is.
(6) Do you know if[whether] the leaves will turn yellow in autumn?
(7) Will you tell me when you met her?
16 ④ 17 ⑤ 18 ①
19 why you couldn't[didn't]

01 가주어로는 that이 아니라 it을 쓴다.

02 간접의문문의 어순은 '의문사+주어+동사'의 형태임에 유의한다.

03 (1) 가주어로는 that이 아니라 it을 쓴다. (2), (3) 진주어로 to부정사가 적절하다. (4), (5) 간접의문문의 어순은 '의문사+주어+동사'이다. (6) 간접의문문에서 의문사가 없는 경우에는 의문사 대신에 if나 whether를 쓴다.

04 ④번은 인칭대명사로 '그것'이라고 해석하지만 나머지는 모두 가주어로 쓰인 it이다. bill: 계산서

05 간접의문문의 어순은 '의문사+주어+동사'의 형태임에 유의한다.

06 '한국에서 인터넷을 사용하는 것(to use the Internet in Korea)'을 진주어로 하고 가주어 It을 이용하여 'It ~ to ...' 형식으로 쓴다.

07 ④ 의문사가 없는 간접의문문의 어순은 'if[whether]+주어+동사'이며 if는 or not과 붙여 쓰지 않는다.

08 가주어로 it이 나와야 하며 진주어로 동명사가 나와야 한다.

09 진주어로 to부정사가 나와야 한다.

10 ⓐ to help로 진주어 ⓒ 의문사가 없으므로 if he will come ⓓ 의미상의 주어로 'for+목적격'이 나와 있으므로 진주어로 to부정사를 써야 한다. the elderly: 어르신들

11 간접의문문의 어순은 '의문사+주어+동사'이며 의문사가 없는 경우는 'if[whether]+주어+동사'로 쓴다.

12 ②번에는 Mastering 혹은 To master로 주어가 되도록 해야 하지만 나머지는 모두 가주어 It을 쓴다.

13 간접의문문의 어순은 '의문사+주어+동사'이다.

14 ② It was foolish of her to think so. to부정사가 진주어가 되도록 한다. Greek: 그리스어, 그리스 사람

15 (1) to부정사나 동명사가 주어가 되도록 하거나 가주어 it을 사용하고 진주어로 to부정사를 쓴다. (2), (4) 진주어로 to부정사를 쓴다. (3) 가주어로는 this가 아니라 it을 쓴다. (5), (6), (7) 간접의문문의 어순은 '의문사+주어+동사'이며 의문사가 없는 경우는 'if[whether]+주어+동사'로 쓴다.

16 의문사가 없는 간접의문문은 'if[whether]+주어+동사'로 쓴다.

17 가주어 it을 이용하여 바꿔 쓰는 것으로 to부정사를 진주어로 쓴다.

18 ①번은 진주어로 쓰인 명사적 용법이지만 나머지는 모두 to부정사의 부사적 용법으로 쓰였다.

19 이유를 답하고 있으므로 'why+주어+동사'를 쓰면 된다.

서술형 시험대비

p.78~79

01 (1) Tell me what you want for Christmas.
(2) She asked me how much sugar is there in the coke.
(3) Do you know where Greece is on the map?
(4) I wonder if[whether] he is a singer.
(5) I have no idea if[whether] he will join us soon.
(6) Where do you think your soul goes after you die?

02 (1) It is dangerous to climb that high mountain.
(2) It is not safe to walk on this road as it is very slippery.
(3) It is very smart of him to teach himself.

03 (1) what it is (2) where it is

04 (1) It was exciting to ride on the rough water and enjoy the view at the same time.
(2) It is no good trying to excuse yourself.
(3) It is wise not to take the car out during rush hours.
(4) It is no use continuing the search.
(5) It is highly regrettable for Laura to marry such a man.

05 (1) How long does it take to reach the top?
(2) Was the thief a man or a woman?
(3) What is the secret of his success?

06 (1) It is hard to read your handwriting.
(2) It is very dangerous to swim in this river.
(3) It is very easy to read and write Hangeul.
(4) It is impossible for me to run 1,000 meters in three minutes.
(5) It is unbelievable that she passed the exam.

07 (1) It is dangerous to cross this street at night.
(2) It is important not to give up.
(3) It was believed that Mike told a lie to his friends.
(4) The doctor will ask you what you ate for breakfast.
(5) Please let us know if[whether] you are able to attend.
(6) What do you suppose they are thinking?

08 (1) It was so amazing to see its natural beauty.
(2) It was necessary to take small risks.
(3) Daniel told us how he became a singer.
(4) It is doubtful whether he will come or not.

01 간접의문문의 어순은 '의문사+주어+동사'이며 의문사가 없는 경우는 'if[whether]+주어+동사'로 쓴다. think 동사가 주절에 있을 경우 간접의문문의 의문사를 문장 맨 앞에 놓는다.

02 (1) It을 가주어로 하고 진주어 to climb의 목적어로 that high mountain을 쓴다. (2) 전치사 on의 목적어로 this road를 쓴다. (3) to teach의 주어가 he이므로 of him으로 의미상의 주어를 나타내야 한다.

03 간접의문문의 어순은 '의문사+주어+동사'이며 (1)에는 무엇인지를 묻는 표현이, (2)에는 장소를 묻는 표현이 들어가는 것이 적절하다.

04 문장의 주어로 쓰인 to부정사를 뒤로 보내고 대신 주어 자리에 가주어 it을 쓴다. (5)번의 경우 For Laura는 to부정사의 의미상의 주어이다.

05 간접의문문의 어순은 '의문사+주어+동사'이며 의문사가 없는 경우는 'if[whether]+주어+동사'로 쓴다. (3)에서 believe 동사가 주절에 있을 경우 간접의문문의 의문사를 문장 맨 앞으로 배치한다.

06 (1)~(4) 문장의 주어로 쓰인 to부정사를 뒤로 보내고 대신 주어 자리에 가주어 it을 쓴다. (5) to부정사뿐만 아니라 주어로 쓰인 that절의 경우에도 긴 that절을 뒤로 보내고 주어 자리에 가주어 it을 쓴다. (4)번의 경우 For me는 to부정사의 의미상의 주어이다.

07 (1) 가주어로 it이 나와야 하며 진주어로 to부정사가 나와야 한다. (2) to부정사의 부정은 to부정사 앞에 not을 쓴다. (3) that절이 진주어인 경우이며 이때도 가주어로는 that이 아니라 it을 쓴다. (4), (5), (6) 간접의문문의 어순은 '의문사+주어+동사'이며 의문사가 없는 경우는 'if[whether]+주어+동사'로 쓴다. suppose 동사가 주절에 있을 경우 간접의문문의 의문사를 문장 맨 앞으로 배치한다.

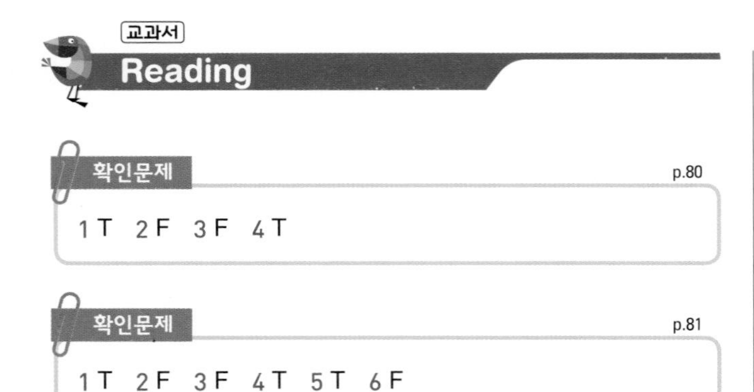

교과서

Reading

확인문제 p.80

1 T 2 F 3 F 4 T

확인문제 p.81

1 T 2 F 3 F 4 T 5 T 6 F

교과서 확인학습 A p.82~83

01 The Best Moment
02 How were, Please tell us
03 Market Heaven
04 traditional markets 05 Then
06 one of the most famous markets
07 what it is famous for
08 a variety of
09 all the international goods
10 many kinds of, such as 11 Then
12 used books 13 really excited
14 to relax 15 Full of Natural Beauty
16 no place like 17 First
18 in good condition 19 so amazing
20 turned off, for a minute 21 focus on
22 the most amazing experience
23 Our next stop 24 went rafting
25 at the same time 26 Firsts
27 where, is 28 How about 29 The answer
30 Korea's firsts 31 To get there 32 next to
33 the history of *Jajangmyeon*
34 the first Western-style park
35 from, awesome
36 the historical sites 37 sound great
38 on your presentations

교과서 확인학습 B p.84~85

1 The Best Moment of the Field Trip
2 Teacher: Good morning, everyone! How were your field trips last week? Please tell us about them!
3 Busan, Market Heaven
4 Do you like traditional markets?
5 Then go to Gukje Market in Busan.
6 It is one of the most famous markets in Busan.
7 Do you know what it is famous for?
8 It is famous for selling a variety of goods from different countries.
9 It was interesting to see all the international goods there.
10 We also ate many kinds of street food, such as *Gimbap*, fish cake, and *Hotteok*.
11 Then we walked to Bosu-dong Book Street.
12 Many bookstores there sell used books.
13 We were really excited because we found some old comic books!
14 It was nice to relax in a café and read them.
15 Gangwon-do, Full of Natural Beauty
16 There is no place like Gangwon-do for beautiful nature.
17 First, we went to Baengnyong Cave.
18 This 1.8-kilometer-long cave is still in good condition.
19 It was so amazing to see its natural beauty.
20 Near the end of our cave tour, the guide turned off the lights in the cave for a minute.
21 Everything became very dark, so we were able to focus on the sounds there.
22 It was the most amazing experience of the tour!
23 Our next stop was Donggang.
24 We went rafting!
25 It was exciting to ride on the rough water and enjoy the view at the same time.
26 Incheon, A City of Firsts
27 Do you know where the first train station in Korea is?
28 How about the first *Jajangmyeon?*
29 The answer is Incheon!
30 This place has many of Korea's firsts.
31 To get there, we went to Incheon Station.
32 The Jajangmyeon Museum is next to the station.
33 We learned about the history of *Jajangmyeon* there.
34 Later, we walked around Jayu Park, the first Western-style park in Korea.
35 The view from the park was awesome!
36 It was great to see the historical sites of this city from the park.
37 Teacher: Wow, these places sound great!
38 You all have done a wonderful job on your presentations!

시험대비 실력평가

p.86~89

01 ② 02 ① 03 ③, ④
04 What about
05 This place has many of Korea's firsts.
06 at the Jajangmyeon Museum 07 ②, ④
08 ②번, good → goods 09 ①, ④, ⑤
10 Gukje Market / Bosu–dong Book Street 11 ③
12 stop 13 ⑤
14 (A) Natural (B) off (C) rough 15 ②, ④
16 ① 17 Near the end of our cave tour, the guide turned off the lights in the cave for a minute. Everything became very dark, so we were able to focus on the sounds there. 18 ②
19 They learned about the history of *Jajangmyeon*.
20 (A) Incheon Station, (B) the Jajangmyeon Museum, (C) Jayu Park
21 ⓐ your field trips last week / ⓒ some old comic books
22 like 23 ⑤
24 People no longer use it.
25 ③, ⑤ 26 ②

01 부산의 재래시장인 국제시장을 중점적으로 소개하는 글이므로 제목으로는 '부산, 시장 천국'이 적절하다.
02 주어진 문장의 Then에 주목한다. ①번 앞 문장에 대한 긍정의 답을 가정하는 것이므로 ①번이 적절하다.
03 ⓐ와 ③, ④번: 가주어, ①, ⑤: 비인칭 주어, ② 가목적어
04 How about ~? = What about ~?: ~은 어때?
05 Korea's firsts: 한국의 최초의 것들
06 '자장면 박물관'을 가리킨다.
07 ⓓ와 ②, ④: 명사적 용법, ①, ⑤: 부사적 용법, ③ 형용사적 용법
08 그 시장은 여러 나라에서 온 다양한 '상품'들을 파는 것으로 유명하다고 해야 하므로, 'good'이 아니라 'goods'가 적절하다. goods: 상품, 제품, good: 선(善) 도움, 소용
09 ⓐ와 ②, ③번: 동명사, ①, ④, ⑤: 현재분사
10 '국제시장,' ⓒ '보수동 책방 거리'를 가리킨다.
11 '아름다운 자연'에 관한 한 강원도만 한 곳이 없다고 하는 것이 적절하다. ② 다양한 유적지, ④ 인공적인 구조물, ⑤ 전통적인 공연들
12 stop: (여행 도중에) 머무르기, 체재, 들르기
13 백룡동굴에서 동강까지 얼마나 먼지는 대답할 수 없다. ① They went to Baengnyong Cave first. ② It is 1.8 kilometers long. ③ He[She] turned off the lights in the cave for a minute. ④ They went to Donggang.
14 (A) '자연'의 아름다움으로 가득한 곳이라고 해야 하므로 Natural이 적절하다. artificial: 인공[인조]의, (B) 동굴 안의 불을 잠시 '껐다'고 해야 하므로 off가 적절하다. turn off: (전기·가스·수도 등을) 끄다, (C) '급류'라고 해야 하므로 rough가 적절하다. rough water: 격랑, 거친 물결, tough: 힘든, 어려운, (신체적으로) 억센[튼튼한]
15 가주어 자리에 to부정사나 동명사를 주어로 하여 고치는 것이 적절하다.
16 급류를 타면서 동시에 경치를 즐기는 것은 흥미진진했다고 했기 때문에, 학생들은 '만족한' 심경이었다고 하는 것이 적절하다. ② 놀란, ③ 지루한, ④ 실망한, ⑤ 속상한, 마음이 상한
17 동굴 관광의 끝 무렵, 안내인이 동굴 안의 불을 잠시 끄자 모든 것이 매우 어두워져서, 학생들은 그곳의 소리에 집중 할 수 있었다. 그것은 여행에서 가장 경이로운 경험이었다.
18 한국 최초의 기차역이 인천에 있고 첫 번째 자장면의 경우도 인천이라고 했고 한국 최초의 서구식 공원이 인천의 자유 공원이라고 했으므로, 한국의 '최초의 것들'이 많이 있다고 하는 것이 적절하다. ① 뜻밖의[놀라운] 일[소식], ③ 자원, ④ 발명, ⑤ 전통
19 '자장면의 역사'에 대하여 배웠다.
20 학생들은 '인천역', '자장면 박물관', '자유 공원'과 같은 한국의 최초의 것들과 관련이 있는 장소들에 갔다. be related to: …와 관계가 있다
21 ⓐ '지난주 수학여행' ⓒ '몇 권의 오래된 만화책들'을 가리킨다.
22 such as = like: …와 같은
23 중고 책을 파는 곳은 '보수동 책방 거리'이다.
24 People를 주어로 하여 고치는 것이 적절하다.
25 no longer = no more = not ~ any longer = not ~ any more: 더 이상 …아닌[하지 않는]
26 take pictures of: ~을 사진을 찍다

서술형 시험대비

p.90~91

01 If you like traditional markets,
02 It is one of the most famous markets in Busan.
03 (A) interesting (B) used (C) excited
04 where
05 There are many of Korea's firsts in this place.
06 (1) 한국 최초의 기차역 (2) 한국 최초의 자장면
(3) 한국 최초의 서구식 공원인 자유 공원
07 We can see the historical sites of this city from the park.
08 the most famous market → one of the most famous markets
09 (1) 세계 곳곳에서 온 상품들을 보았다.
(2) 김밥, 어묵 그리고 호떡과 같은 여러 종류의 길거리 음식을 먹었다.
10 used books
11 best
12 rafting
13 It was exciting to ride on the rough water and enjoy the view at the same time.
14 (A) see (B) the sounds

01 Then(그렇다면)은 '전통 시장을 좋아하면'이라는 뜻이다.

02 one of the 복수명사: ~ 중의 하나

03 (A) 감정을 나타내는 동사가 사물을 수식할 때는 보통 현재분사로 쓰므로 interesting이 적절하다. (B) '중고책'이라고 해야 하므로 used가 적절하다. (C) 감정을 나타내는 동사가 사람을 수식할 때는 보통 과거분사로 쓰므로 excited가 적절하다.

04 '첫 번째 자장면은요?'라는 말은 '한국 최초의 자장면이 어디에서 소개되었는지 아세요?'와 같은 뜻이다.

05 There are로 시작하여 고치는 것이 적절하다.

06 인천에는 '한국 최초의 기차역', '자장면', '자유 공원'과 같이 '한국의 최초의 것들'이 많이 있다.

07 공원에서 이 도시의 역사적인 장소들을 볼 수 있다.

08 국제시장은 부산에서 '가장 유명한 시장 중 하나'이다.

09 (1) 그곳에서 세계 곳곳에서 온 상품들을 모두 볼 수 있어서 흥미로웠다고 했다. (2) 우리는 또한 김밥, 어묵 그리고 호떡과 같은 여러 종류의 길거리 음식을 먹었다고 했다.

10 보수동 책방 거리의 많은 서점들은 '중고 책'을 파는 것으로 유명하다.

11 '아름다운 자연에 관한 한 강원도만 한 곳이 없다.'는 말은 아름다운 자연에 관한 한 강원도가 '제일 좋은' 장소라는 뜻이다.

12 go ~ing: ~하러 가다

13 'on'을 보충하면 된다.

14 안내인이 불을 껐을 때 모든 것이 매우 어두워져서 학생들은 동굴의 자연의 아름다움을 '볼 수' 없게 되었고, 그들은 그곳의 '소리'에만 집중할 수 있었다.

영역별 핵심문제 p.93~97

01 ③ 02 ④ 03 have 04 ④
05 ④ 06 ② 07 ⑤ 08 going
09 It takes an hour and 40 minutes by express train.
10 ⑤ 11 relax 12 ③
13 for you to pay attention to your teacher in class
14 ⑤ 15 ④ 16 ⑤
17 (1) Nobody knows. Why did Lauren leave the office early?
(2) It is difficult to understand. What does the teacher say?
(3) Steve didn't tell me. When did the movie begin?
(4) Do you think? What is the most typical Korean dish?
(5) Mariel wants to know. Is Kate going to meet Asako?
(6) They wonder. Can they borrow a few books today?
18 (1) I'll tell you where he has been since last Monday.
(2) I'd like to know if[whether] you met her.
(3) Where do you think I can find some fruit?
19 (1) It is abnormal to have the heart on the right side.
(2) It is hard to grab fish with your bare hands.
(3) I don't know where the girl lives.
(4) Could you tell me when the next train comes?
20 ①
21 After we (also) ate many kinds of street food, such as *Gimbap*, fish cake, and *Hotteok*
22 ④ 23 ②
24 ③
25 (A) Later (B) awesome (C) presentations
26 ④ 27 ②
28 **산의 중간까지 케이블 카를 타고 간 다음, 정상까지 걸어서 갔다.**
29 amazed, excited

01 ③의 get은 '얻다'의 의미로 사용되었다. 이외의 보기들은 '(장소 · 위치에) 도착하다'의 의미로 사용되었다. ① 너는 가능한 한 빨리 그곳에 도착해야 한다. ② 캐나다에 도착하자마자 너에게 편지를 보낼 것이다. ③ 너는 도서관에서 정보를 얻을 수 있다. ④ 택시를 타면, 그곳에 10분이면 도착할 수 있어요. ⑤ 아무래도 제시간에 학교에 도착하기는 틀린 것 같아요.

02 at the same time: 동시에, 한꺼번에

03 Do you have any plans?: 무슨 계획이라도 있니? Have a good trip.: 좋은 여행하길 바라.

04 ① rough: 거친 ② natural: 자연의 ③ Western-style: 서양풍의, 서양식의 ④ foreign: 외국의 ⑤ awesome: 매우 멋진

05 How long does it take to get ~?:~까지 가는 데 얼마나 걸리나요?(소요 시간 묻기)

06 What are you planning to 동사원형 ~?: 뭐 할 계획이야? be going to 동사원형: ~할 예정이다

07 주어진 문장은 '내가 생각한 것보다 훨씬 더 빠르다.'의 의미인데, 대구까지 가는 것에 대해 고속 열차로 1시간 40분 걸린다는 말에 대해 말한 것으로 볼 수 있다.

08 be going to 동사원형: ~할 예정이다 be planning to 동사원형: ~할 계획이다

09 It takes 시간: (시간이) ~ 걸린다 hour: 시간 minute: 분

10 ⑤ 남자아이가 친구와 같이 올 스타 경기를 보러 간다고는 언급하지 않았다. 남자아이는 올 스타 경기를 보고, 또한 친구를 만날 계획을 가지고 있다.

11 relax: 휴식을 취하다, 느긋이 쉬다 / 아무것도 하지 않다

12 ③ 휴가가 얼마나 긴지는 언급되어 있지 않았다. ① 그들은 무엇에 대해서 이야기하고 있는가? ② 여자아이의 조부모님은 어디에 사는가? ③ 휴가는 얼마나 긴가? ④ 여자아이는 그녀의 조부모님과 어디를 갈 계획인가? ⑤ 남자 아이의 휴가 계획은 무엇인가?

13 '~해야 한다'는 의미를 가주어 it을 이용하여 '~할 필요가 있다'라고 쓰려면 진주어로 to부정사를 이용한다. 이때 의미상의 주어를 빠뜨리지 않도록 주의한다.

14 의문사가 없는 간접의문문의 어순은 'if[whether]+주어+동사'이지만 if를 쓸 경우 or not을 바로 붙여 쓰지 않는다.

15 ④번은 강조 용법으로 쓰인 it이고 나머지는 모두 가주어로 쓰인 it이다.

16 'It ~ to부정사' 구문을 이용하고 to부정사의 의미상 주어는 'for+목적격'을 쓰지만, 사람의 태도나 성질에 관한 형용사가 올 경우 'of+목적격'을 쓴다.

17 간접의문문의 어순은 '의문사+주어+동사'이며 의문사가 없는 경우는 'if[whether]+주어+동사'로 쓴다. think 동사가 주절에 있을 경우 간접의문문의 의문사를 문장 맨 앞으로 배치한다.

18 간접의문문의 어순은 '의문사+주어+동사'이며 의문사가 없는 경우는 'if[whether]+주어+동사'로 쓴다. think 동사가 주절에 있을 경우 간접의문문의 의문사를 문장 맨 앞으로 배치한다.

19 (1), (2) 'It ~ to부정사'의 가주어·진주어 구문을 이용한다. (3), (4) 간접의문문의 어순은 '의문사+주어+동사'이다.

20 ⓐ, ⓑ, ⓒ는 Gukje Market, ⓓ는 to see all the international goods there, ⓔ는 to relax in a café and read them을 가리킨다.

21 Then(그러고 나서)은 '우리가 김밥, 어묵 그리고 호떡과 같은 여러 종류의 길거리 음식을 먹은 뒤에'라는 뜻이다.

22 ④번 다음 문장의 It에 주목한다. 주어진 문장의 내용을 받고 있으므로 ④번이 적절하다.

23 ⓐ for: (관련) …에 관해서(는), …의 점에서는, for beautiful nature: 아름다운 자연에 관한 한, ⓑ be in good condition: 상태가 좋다

24 동굴은 여전히 잘 보존된 상태이다.

25 (A) '나중에'라고 해야 하므로 Later가 적절하다. later: (지금 이야기 중인 시간보다) 후[뒤]에, latter: 후자의, (나열된 것들 중에서) 마지막의, (B) 경치는 정말 '멋있었다'고 해야 하므로 awesome이 적절하다. awesome: 경탄할 만한, 엄청난, awful: 끔찍한, 지독한, (C) '발표'를 훌륭하게 잘했다고 해야 하므로 presentations가 적절하다. presentation: 발표, preparation: 준비

26 부사적 용법(목적)의 to 부정사: in order to 동사원형 = so as to 동사원형 = in order that ~ may[can] = so that ~ may[can]

27 ② 누가 한국에서 첫 번째 자장면을 만들었는지는 대답할 수 없다. ① In Incheon. ③ At the Jajangmyeon Museum. ④ It is Jayu Park. ⑤ It was awesome.

28 산의 중간까지는 케이블 카를 타고 간 다음에, 정상까지 하이킹을 했다고 했다.

29 감정을 나타내는 동사의 경우 과거분사는 '~하게 된'의 뜻으로 보통 감정을 느끼는 대상에 쓰인다.

단원별 예상문제

p.98~101

01 (c)ondition 02 am able to 03 on foot 04 take
05 ④ 06 stadium
07 ⓐ of, ⓑ from, ⓒ off, ⓓ in, ⓔ of 08 ①, ⑤
09 How long does it take to get there? 10 ①
11 (A) by, (B) on 12 ④ 13 ④
14 (1) Do you know who that tall guy over there is?
(2) Tell me who made this chocolate cake.
(3) I wonder if[whether] Marianne got married.
(4) Where do you think Snow White is?
15 |모범답안| It is easy for him to do dunk shot.
16 ③ 17 was → were 18 ③
19 ④ 20 ①
21 (A) 1.8-kilometer-long (B) rafting
(C) at the same time
22 very dark, focus on
23 (1) 남자 형제들과 수영을 했다.
(2) 해변에서 게를 잡았다.
(3) 아름다운 일몰을 보았다.
24 awful → awesome

01 주어진 보기는 동의어 관계이다. amazing: 놀라운, 멋진 incredible: 믿을 수 없는 condition: 상태, 상황 state: 상태

02 be able to 동사원형: ~을 할 수 있다

03 on foot: 걸어서, 도보로

04 take: (얼마의 시간이) 걸리다 / 내 컴퓨터로 자료를 다운 받으려면 시간이 오래 걸릴 것이다. take a field trip: 현장 학습을 하다 / 우리 현장 학습 간다는 얘기 들었니?

05 긴 연휴에 대한 계획을 물으니 → (C) 전주에 있는 조부모님을 방문할 계획이라고 대답한다. → 이어서 (B) 그분들과 어떤 것을 할 계획인지 묻자 → (D) 한옥 마을에 갈 것이라고 대답하며, 상대방의 연휴 때 계획을 질문한다. → (E) 집에서 머물면서 쉴 거라는 대답에 → (A) 좋은 생각이라고 말한다.

06 stadium: 경기장, 스타디움 / 규모가 큰 운동 경기장

07 lots of: 많은 from: ~로부터 get off: 내리다, 하차하다 in front of: ~ 앞에서

08 (A)stop과 ②, ③, ④ 정류장, 정거장 ① 중단하다 ⑤ 멈추다

09 How long does it take to get ~?: ~에 가는 데 얼마나 걸리나요?

10 How do I get from Hanguk University to here? → How do I get to Hanguk University from here? 길을 알려주는 문장에서 'You will see Hanguk University on your right. (오른쪽에 한국 대학교가 보일 거예요.)'라는 것으로 보아 남자의 목적지는 한국 대학교이다.

11 (A) by bus: 버스로 on foot 걸어서, 도보로

12 ④ 한국 대학교에 가기 위해서 버스를 타면 5분 걸리고, 걸어서

20분 걸리므로 버스를 타는 것이 더 빠르다.

13 ① It is fun to speak in front of people. ② It is difficult to say which way the wind is blowing. ③ It was great to see the historical sites of this city from the park. ⑤ It is important to make plans in advance.

14 간접의문문의 어순은 '의문사+주어+동사'이며 의문사가 없는 경우는 'if[whether]+주어+동사'로 쓴다. 의문사가 주어인 경우에는 의문사가 주어 역할을 동시에 하므로 직접의문문처럼 '의문사+동사'의 어순임에 유의해야 하며, think 동사가 주절에 있을 경우 간접의문문의 의문사를 문장 맨 앞에 써야 함에도 유의한다.

15 'it ~ to 부정사' 구문을 이용하여 쓴다.

16 ③ 의문사 대신 if나 whether를 써야 한다.

17 주어가 'your field trips'이므로 were로 고치는 것이 적절하다.

18 ⓑ와 ①, ④: 명사적 용법, ② 형용사적 용법, ③, ⑤부사적 용법

19 국제시장에서 보수동 책방 거리까지 가는 데 얼마나 오래 걸렸는지는 대답할 수 없다. ① They went last week. ② It was interesting to see all the international goods there. ③ They ate many kinds of street food, such as Gimbap, fish cake, and Hotteok. ⑤ They sell used books.

20 ⓐ와 ①번: …와 같은(전치사), ②, ④: (…을) 좋아하다(동사), ③ [외관·형태·성질 등이] 같은(명사 shape를 수식하는 형용사), ⑤: 비슷한(명사 manner를 수식하는 형용사)

21 (A) '1.8-kilometer-long'이 형용사로 뒤에 나오는 명사를 꾸며주는 역할을 할 때는 단수로 써야 하므로 1.8-kilometer-long이 적절하다. (B) go ~ing: ~하러 가다 (C) 급류를 타면서 '동시에' 경치를 즐기는 것은 흥미진진했다고 해야 하므로 at the same time이 적절하다. at the same time: 동시에, one by one: 하나하나씩[차례차례]

22 학생들이 동굴 안의 소리에 '집중할 수' 있도록 모든 것을 '매우 어두워지게' 만들고 싶었기 때문이다.

23 남자 형제들과 수영을 했고, 해변에서 게를 좀 잡았고 아름다운 일몰을 보았다.

24 아름다운 일몰을 보는 것은 정말 '멋있었다'고 해야 하므로 awesome이 적절하다. awesome: 경탄할 만한, 어마어마한, 엄청난, awful: 끔찍한, 지독한

서술형 실전문제 p.102~103

01 Where are you planning to go?
Where are you going to go?
Where are you thinking of going?

02 It takes 10 and half hours.

03 Where are you going for your trip

04 I'm planning to visit[go to] museums.

05 (1) for my grandma to remember names
(2) for most of students to study English

06 (1) It is doubtful if[whether] Anna loves me.
(2) I'm not sure why Kate was so surprised.
(3) Cathy knows who broke the window yesterday.
(4) Which book can you imagine Jennifer bought?

07 (1) takes → to take (2) That → It
(3) Write → To write[Writing]
(4) when does the show start → when the show starts
(5) if does the bag have → if the bag has
(6) Do you think who → Who do you think

08 (A) How (B) markets (C) found

09 Seeing

10 (A) traditional markets, (B) different countries

01 Where are you planning to go?: 너는 어디에 갈 계획이니? Where are you going to go?: 너는 어디에 갈 거니? Where are you thinking of going?: 너는 어디에 갈 생각이니?

02 It takes 시간: (시간이) ~ 걸린다

03 where: 어디로 trip: 여행

04 museum: 박물관, 미술관 / 역사적이거나 예술적인 물건들이 전시되어 있는 건물 be planning to 동사원형: ~할 계획이다

05 (1) '이름을 기억하는 데 어려움이 있다'는 것을 '이름을 기억하기 어렵다'는 문장으로, (2) '영어 공부는 지루하다'는 것을 '영어를 공부하는 것은 지루하다'는 문장으로 'it ~ to 부정사' 구문을 이용하여 쓰고 to부정사의 의미상의 주어로 'for+목적격'을 쓴다.

06 간접의문문의 어순은 '의문사+주어+동사'이며 의문사가 없는 경우는 'if[whether]+주어+동사'로 쓴다. 의문사가 주어인 경우에는 직접의문문처럼 '의문사+동사'의 어순임에 유의해야 하며 imagine 동사가 주절에 있을 경우 간접의문문의 의문사를 문장 맨 앞에 써야 함에도 유의한다.

07 (1) 'it ~ to 부정사' 구문이 적절하다. (2) 가주어로는 that이 아니라 it을 쓴다. (3) to부정사나 동명사가 주어가 되도록 한다. (4) 간접의문문의 어순은 '의문사+주어+동사'이다. (5) 'if[whether]+주어+동사'의 어순이 되어야 한다. (6) think 동사가 주절에 있을 경우 간접의문문의 의문사를 문장 맨 앞에 써야 한다.

08 (A) 수학여행은 '어땠나요?'라고 해야 하므로 How가 적절하다. (B) one of the 복수명사: '~ 중의 하나'이므로 markets가 적절하다. (C) 만화책을 '발견했다'고 해야 하므로 found가 적절하다. find-found-found: 발견하다, found-founded-founded: 설립하다

09 진주어인 to부정사를 동명사 주어로 고치는 것이 적절하다.

10 그곳은 '전통 시장'을 방문하기를 좋아하는 사람들에게 좋은 장소이고, '여러 나라'에서 수입한 다양한 제품들을 파는 것으로 유명하다.

창의사고력 서술형 문제 p.104

|모범답안|

01 What are you going[planning] to do next weekend? / to watch a movie / How can I get to the movie theater? / How long does it take to get[go] there? / takes 5 minutes on foot

02 (1) It is important to save water for environment.
(2) It is necessary to prepare for the worst.
(3) Do you know who won the prize?
(4) I wonder if[whether] she loves me.

03 (A) Last summer (B) swam (C) caught
(D) awesome (E) beautiful sunset

01 next weekend: 다음 주말 What are you going to 동사원형 ~?: 너는 무엇을 할 거니? What are you planning to 동사원형 ~?: 뭐 할 계획이야? be planning to 동사원형: ~할 계획이다 How can[do] I get ~?: 어떻게 갈 수 있어? How long does it take to get ~?:~에 가는 데 얼마나 걸리나요? It takes 시간: (시간이) ~ 걸린다

단원별 모의고사 p.105~108

01 ①
02 (h)istory / (s)cenery / (W)estern-style
(1) scenery (2) history (3) Western-style
03 ④ 04 field trip 05 ③ 06 ④
07 ⑤
08 How do I get to Hanguk University from here?
09 (A) Go straight (for) two blocks, and then turn left.
(B) your right
10 ③ 11 ② 12 ④
13 (1) I know who won the race.
(2) Do you know when the bus will come?
(3) The man is asking her how long it takes to get to the mart.
(4) I have no idea if[whether] they like it or not.
(5) Who do you think will win the game?
(6) What do you guess she wants to buy?
14 (1) It is important to protect our environment.
(2) It is interesting to look around the traditional market.
(3) It is exciting to ride the roller coaster.
(4) It is necessary to get enough sleep.
(5) I don't remember where the girl lived.
(6) Anna asked me if[whether] I loved Angelina.
15 Do you know what it is famous for?
16 ②, ③ 17 ④ 18 ⓑ, ⓒ, ⓓ / ⓐ, ⓔ
19 in the cave 20 ③
21 (A) many (B) get (C) great 22 ④

01 turn off: (등, 전화기 등을) 끄다

02 (1) scenery: 풍경, 경치 / 자연의 아름다운 경치 / 우리는 해변에서 경치를 즐겼다. (2) history: 역사 / 과거에 발생한 사건들 / 나는 에펠탑의 역사를 알기 원한다. (3) Western-style: 서양풍의, 서양식의 / 서양 국가들과 관련된 특별한 방식이나 형식 / 나는 동양풍의 집보다 서양풍의 집을 선호한다.

03 여자아이는 현장 학습으로 미술관에 가고, 남자아이는 어디로 가는지 질문하자 놀이동산에 갈 것이라고 대답한다. 놀이동산에 가서 롤러코스터를 탈 생각으로 신난다고 하는 부분과 연결된다.

04 field trip: 견학 여행, 현장 학습 / 학생들과 선생님들이 무엇인가를 배우기 위해 방문하는 것

05 ⓐ Where ⓓ What ⓔ excited

06 ④ 남자아이가 놀이동산에 어떻게 갈 것인지는 언급되지 않았다. ① 언제 현장 학습에 가는가? ② 남자아이는 현장 학습으로 어디를 가는가? ③ 여자아이는 현장 학습으로 어디를 가는가? ⑤ 얼마나 많은 전시회가 지금 미술관에 있는가?

07 남자는 걸어서 가겠다고 말했다. 한국 대학교까지 버스를 타면 5분, 걸어가면 20분 걸린다.

08 How do I get to 장소: ~에 어떻게 가나요?

09 Go straight: 직진하세요 turn left: 좌회전하세요 It's on your right: 오른쪽에 있어요.

10 첫 문장에서는 진주어로 쓰인 to부정사가 적절하다. 두 번째 문장에서는 의문사 who가 적절하다.

11 ②번은 조건절에 쓰인 if이지만 나머지는 모두 간접의문문을 이끌고 있다.

12 ④ Is it possible to breathe under the water?

13 간접의문문의 어순은 '의문사+주어+동사'이며 의문사가 없는 경우는 'if[whether]+주어+동사'로 쓴다. think나 guess 동사가 주절에 있을 경우 간접의문문의 의문사를 문장 맨 앞으로 배치한다.

14 (1)~(4) 'it ~ to 부정사' 구문을 이용하여 쓴다. (5), (6) 간접의문문의 어순은 '의문사+주어+동사'이며 의문사가 없는 경우는 'if[whether]+주어+동사'로 쓴다.

15 'for'를 보충하고 간접의문문의 순서로 쓰는 것이 적절하다.

16 a variety of = various = diverse: 여러 가지의, 다양한, ① familiar: 익숙한, 친숙한, ⑤ common: 흔한

17 위 글은 강원도의 아름다운 자연에 관한 글이므로, 제목으로는 '강원도, 자연의 아름다움으로 가득한 곳'이 적절하다.

18 사실(fact)은 그것이 진실이라는 것을 입증할 수 있어야 한다. 반면에 견해(opinion)는 어떤 사람이 그렇게 믿거나 생각하고 있는 것이므로 그것이 진실이라는 보장이 없다. 따라서 사실은 모든 사람이 동일하게 인식하지만, 견해는 사람마다 다를 수 있다.

19 '동굴 안'을 가리킨다.

20 ③번 다음 문장의 the park에 주목한다. 주어진 문장의 Jayu Park를 가리키므로 ③번이 적절하다.

21 (A) 'Korea's firsts'가 복수이므로 many가 적절하다. (B) 'there'가 부사이므로 전치사 to 없이 get만 쓰는 것이 적절하다. get to+명사: ~에 도착하다, get there: 그곳에 도착하다, (C) 감각동사의 보어이므로 형용사 great이 적절하다.

22 ④ 자유 공원은 한국 최초의 '서구식' 공원이다. Eastern: 동양의

Lesson 7

On My Way to the Future

시험대비 실력평가 p.112

01 ②	02 ⑤	03 ③	04 ①
05 ④	06 ④	07 ②	08 ③

01 ② 이외의 보기는 직업에 관련된 단어들이다. ① cartoonist: 만화가 ② customer: 손님, 고객 ③ photographer: 사진작가, 사진사 ④ consultant: 상담가 ⑤ designer: 디자이너, 설계자

02 artificial: 인공적인, 인조의 / 이 음식에는 인공 색소가 들어 있지 않다.

03 develop: 발달시키다, 발전하다 / 어떻게 내 작문 실력을 발달시킬 수 있을까?

04 keep a diary: 일기를 쓰다 / 일기를 쓰는 것은 글 쓰는 연습을 하는 좋은 방법이다.

05 ① judge: 판사 ② writer: 작가 ③ artist: 예술가 ④ reviewer: (책·영화 등의) 논평가 ⑤ movie director: 영화감독

06 노래를 부를 수 있느냐는 질문에 긍정의 대답을 했으므로 노래를 잘 부른다는 내용이 나와야 어울린다. 'I am good at+(동)명사'로 ~을 잘할 수 있음을 표현할 수 있다.

07 ② modeler: 모형 제작자 ① Sam은 매년 가을에 낙엽을 모으는 것을 좋아한다. ② 풍선 모형 제작자는 풍선으로만 만들어진 비행기를 보여줬다. ③ 체스는 문제 해결 능력을 길러 주는 것 같다. ④ 나뭇잎들은 오염을 줄여준다. ⑤ 나는 사람들의 사진을 찍는 데 재주가 있다고 생각한다.

08 specialist: 전문가 expert: 전문가 / 기상 전문가들은 장마가 10일 이상 지속될 거라고 말했다.

서술형 시험대비 p.113

01 (s)trength
02 keep
03 of
04 (1) emotion(s) (2) amount(s) (3) career (4) reason
05 fill out
06 (1) We need to analyze the cause of the failure.
(2) You need to improve your English.
(3) My strength is that I believe in myself.
(4) My son has a talent for singing.
(5) Do you want a late-night snack?

01 strength: 강점, 장점 strong point: 장점 / 내 직업의 장점은 높은 급료다.

02 keep+목적어+목적격보어(형용사): ~가 …한 상태로 유지하다 / 그 공원의 직원들은 그것들을 안전하게 보호하고 싶어 한다. keep a diary: 일기를 쓰다 / 너의 생각을 적을 수 있도록 일기를 써라.

03 take care of: ~을 돌보다 / 방과 후에 작은 딸을 보살펴 줄 사람이 필요하다 first of all: 무엇보다도 / 무엇보다도, 진정할 필요가 있다.

04 (1) emotion: 감정 / 너는 감정을 조절할 필요가 있다. (2) amount: 양, 총액 / 재활용은 많은 양의 에너지를 절약할 수 있다. (3) career: 진로, 직업 / 그 남자는 연기를 직업으로 선택했다. (4) reason: 이유, 원인 / 방문한 이유가 무엇입니까?

05 fill out: (서식 등을) 작성하다, (정보를) 기입하다, 채우다

06 (1) analyze: 분석하다 (2) improve: 개선하다, 향상시키다 (3) strength: 힘, 강점, 장점 (4) talent: (타고난) 재능, 재주 (5) late-night: 심야의

교과서

Conversation

핵심 Check p.114~115

1 good at playing
2 Are you good at taking pictures / my brother is good at it
3 need to do to
4 How can I improve my English skills? / What do you suggest to improve my English skills?

교과서 대화문 익히기

Check(√) True or False p.116

1 F 2 F 3 T 4 T 5 F 6 T

교과서 확인학습 p.118~119

Listen & Talk 1 A

play / not good / What are you / at playing / let's

Listen & Talk 1 B

to do / decide, What am / good at / good at singing / to play, Why don't you

Listen & Talk 1 C

need to fill out / wrote, and / be, P.E. teacher, watching, writing, strengths, What am I good / lots, First of, are good at, aren't you / I'm good at playing baseball / strengths / work, at listening to / You're good at

Listen & Talk 2 A

want to be, What / need to, develop, problem-solving

Listen & Talk 2 B

amazing / trying, to improve, writer / want, like, What do I, to / Reading makes your writing better / else / don't, keeping / advice

Listen & Talk 2 C

for / who want to be food / decorates, to look / to be a food stylist, What, need / need to learn, kinds / else / Creativity / Thank, for

시험대비 기본평가

p.120

01 ② 02 ② 03 ⑤ 04 ⑤

01 상대방에게 조언을 구하는 질문에는 'What do I need to do?', 'What do you suggest?', 'What should I do?', 'What can I do?' 등이 있다.

02 푸드 스타일리스트가 되고 싶다는 상대방에게 어울리는 조언으로 다양한 종류의 음식에 대해서 배우라고 하는 것이 어울린다. ① 너는 쇼핑 리스트를 만들어야 해. ② 너는 많은 종류의 음식에 대해 배워야 해. ③ 너는 매일 운동을 해야 해. ④ 너는 한국 문화에 대한 블로그를 디자인해야 해. ⑤ 너는 문화에 대한 스타일을 설명해야 해.

03 'What are you good at?'은 상대방이 무엇을 잘하는지 묻는 표현이다. ① 나는 운동을 좋아하지 않아. ② 나는 그림 그리기를 잘 못해. ③ 나는 재능 있는 요리사가 아니야. ④ 나는 훌륭한 선생님이 될 거야.

04 상대방에게 조언을 구할 때는 'What do I need to do?', 'What do you suggest?', 'What should I do?' 등의 표현을 쓸 수 있다.

시험대비 실력평가

p.121~122

01 ④ 02 ② 03 ③ 04 ③
05 You are good at so many things.
06 counseling 07 ⑤ 08 ① 09 ③
10 ③ 11 (A) ⓑ What are you good at?
(B) ⓔ What do you want to be in the future?

01 상대방의 그림을 잘 그린다고 하는 말에 'No, thanks.(아니요, 됐습니다.)'라고 대답하는 것은 어울리지 않는다.

02 피아노를 잘 칠 수 있는 조언을 묻고 있는데, 조언이 아닌 상대방 의견에 동의를 하는 'I think you're right.(네가 옳다고 생각해.)'은 어색하다.

03 fill out: (서식 등을) 작성하다, (정보를) 기입하다, 채우다

04 (B)의 'strengths'는 '장점'이다. ③의 보기는 '힘'의 의미이고, 나머지 보기들은 장점의 의미이다. ① 자신감을 키우기 위해 여러분의 장점에 집중하세요. ② 장점을 이용하는 사람은 창조적이고, 활동적이며 생산적입니다 ③ 빙벽을 오르는 것은 많은 신체적인 힘을 요구한다. ④ 그의 장점은 정직한 점이다. ⑤ 그의 키는 농구 경기에 있어서 그의 장점이다.

05 be good at: ~을 잘하다 so: 매우, 아주

06 counseling: 상담 / 문제 해결을 돕기 위해 누군가에게 주어지는 조언

07 주어진 문장은 '조언 고마워.'란 뜻이다. G는 글을 잘 쓰고 싶어서 B에게 조언을 구하고 있다. 조언을 듣고 B에게 고맙다고 말하는 것이 자연스러우므로 ⑤가 적절하다.

08 글쓰기 기량을 발전시키려고 노력하고 있다는 말을 볼 때 남자아이는 작가가 되고 싶어 한다.

09 ③ What else: 그밖에 무엇을, What do I need to do?: 나는 뭘 해야 하니?

10 ③ Jason은 거의 매일 글을 쓰고 있다.

11 (A)에 대한 대답으로 자신이 잘하는 것에 대해 말했으므로 능력을 물어보는 질문이 어울린다. (B)는 미술가가 되고 싶다고 말했으므로 미래에 무엇이 되기를 원하는지 묻는 질문이 어울린다.

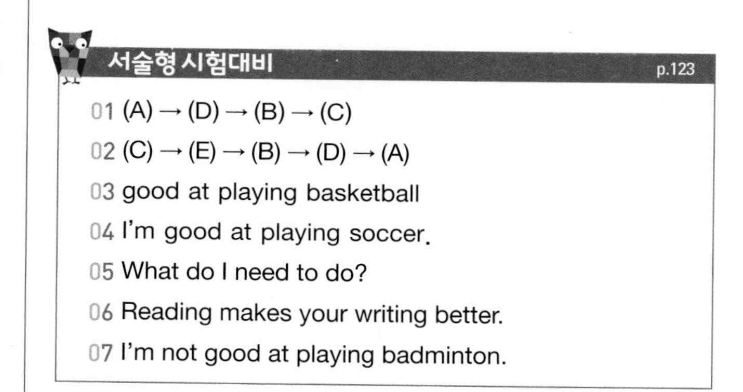

서술형 시험대비

p.123

01 (A) → (D) → (B) → (C)
02 (C) → (E) → (B) → (D) → (A)
03 good at playing basketball
04 I'm good at playing soccer.
05 What do I need to do?
06 Reading makes your writing better.
07 I'm not good at playing badminton.

01 (A)에서 조언을 구하는 질문을 하자 (D) 다양한 종류의 음식에 대해 배워야 한다고 대답한다. (B) 또 다른 것은 뭐가 필요한지 다시 질문하자 (C) 미술 공부도 해야 한다고 말하며 창의력이 중요하다고 덧붙인다.

02 (C) 잘하는 것이 무엇인지 묻자 (E) 사람들을 돌보는 것을 잘한다고 말한다. (B) 그러면 간호사가 되는 것이 어떻겠냐고 제안하자 (D) 좋은 생각이라고 말하며 상대방의 의견에 동의한다. 이어서 간호사가 되려면 뭘 해야 하는지 묻자 (A) 인간의 몸에 대해서 배워야 한다고 대답한다.

03 남자아이가 농구를 잘하지 못한다고 말하면서 '너는 잘하니?'라

고 묻고 있으므로 상대방이 농구를 잘하는지 묻는 질문을 한 것이다.

04 'Okay, then let's play soccer.(그래, 그러면 축구를 하자.)'라고 하는 것으로 보아 남자아이는 축구를 잘하는 것으로 추측할 수 있다.

05 'What do I need to do?'는 상대방에게 조언을 구할 때 하는 질문으로, '내가 뭘 해야 하니?'의 의미이다.

06 reading은 동명사 주어이다. make+목적어(your writing)+목적격보어(better): ~을 …하게 만들다

07 be not good at: ~을 잘하지 못하다, ~에 능숙하지 못하다

교과서

Grammar

핵심 Check p.124~125

1 (1) to be (2) to return (3) to clear
2 to try
3 (1) if (2) rains (3) will come

시험대비 기본평가 p.126

01 (1) be → to be (2) to not lose → not to lose
(3) aren't → are, 또는 unless → if
(4) won't → don't
02 ②
03 (1) to give (2) to join (3) to do (4) do
04 (1) to try (2) If

01 (1) expect의 목적격보어로 to부정사가 적절하다. (2) to부정사의 부정은 'not to 동사원형'으로 쓴다. (3) unless는 'if ~ not'의 의미이므로 뒤에 나오는 aren't를 are로 고치거나 unless를 if로 고쳐야 한다. (4) 조건의 부사절에서는 실제로는 미래의 일을 나타내더라도 will을 쓰지 않고 현재시제를 쓰므로 won't를 don't로 고쳐야 한다.

02 조건의 부사절에서는 미래의 의미를 갖더라도 will을 쓰지 않고 현재시제를 쓴다.

03 (1), (2), (3) ask, want, tell의 목적격보어로 to부정사가 적절하다. (4) 사역동사 make의 목적격보어로 원형부정사가 적절하다.

04 (1) expect의 목적격보어로 to부정사가 적절하다. (2) '만약 ~한다면'이라는 뜻의 조건을 나타내는 부사절을 이끄는 접속사 If가 적절하다.

시험대비 실력평가 p.127~129

01 ⑤ 02 ③ 03 (1) to be (2) to study (3) smile
04 ② 05 ④ 06 ① 07 ②
08 ③ 09 ① 10 if
11 (A) to get (B) to do 12 ②
13 (1) I don't want you to tell anybody about that.
(2) The doctor advised me to stop eating junk food.
(3) If it rains tonight, I will stay at home.
(4) Unless you know the answer, ask me.
14 ② 15 ② 16 ② 17 ④
18 Crossword puzzles are fun to do if you enjoy words. 또는 If you enjoy words, crossword puzzles are fun to do.
19 (1) My family expects me to come home by 9 p.m.
(2) His illness forced him to cancel his visit.
(3) Yesterday my boss even had me walk his dog.
(4) We don't have enough people to get the work done.
(5) If Mina teaches me English, I will help her with math.
(6) If you keep looking ahead and dreaming big, your future will be bright.
(7) I forget things unless I mark them down.

01 advised의 목적격보어로 to부정사가 적절하다.

02 ask의 목적격보어로 to부정사가 적절하다.

03 (1), (2) tell, want의 목적격보어로 to부정사가 적절하다. (3) 조건의 부사절에서는 미래의 의미를 갖더라도 will을 쓰지 않고 현재시제를 쓴다.

04 unless = if ~ not

05 order의 목적격보어로 to부정사가 적절하다.

06 조건절이 미래의 일을 나타낼 때에도 조건절의 시제는 현재형을 쓴다. If Hanbin joins our soccer club, I will play soccer with him.

07 make는 목적격보어로 to부정사가 아니라 원형부정사를 쓴다.

08 ① I asked the man to take my suitcase to the room. ② He advised me to see a doctor right away. ④ His mom allowed them to watch TV after dinner. ⑤ They made me say the same thing over and over again.

09 ② If you go to the aquarium, you can see a lot of fish and sea animals. ③ If you don't have lunch, you will feel hungry soon. ④ I don't know if she will come home next weekend. ⑤ The work will not be done unless you do it now. 또는 The work will be done if you do it now.

10 첫 번째 문장에서 wonder의 목적어로 명사절을 이끌고 두 번째

문장에서 조건절을 이끌 수 있는 if가 적절하다.

11 advise와 allow는 목적격보어로 to부정사를 쓴다.

12 ②번은 know의 목적어로 명사절을 이끌고 있으며 나머지는 모두 조건절을 이끄는 if이다.

13 (1), (2) want와 advise는 목적격보어로 to부정사를 쓴다. (3) 조건의 부사절에서는 미래의 의미를 갖더라도 will을 쓰지 않고 현재시제를 쓴다. (4) unless = if ~ not

14 tell은 목적격보어로 to부정사를 쓴다.

15 조건의 부사절에서는 미래의 의미를 갖더라도 will을 쓰지 않고 현재시제를 쓴다.

16 make는 사역동사이므로 목적격보어로 동사원형이 나와야 하며 나머지는 모두 목적격보어로 to부정사가 나와야 한다.

17 그의 차가 세차를 하는 것이 아니라 세차되는 것이므로 수동의 뜻을 갖는 과거분사 washed를 쓰는 것이 적절하다.

18 조건을 나타내는 말 앞에 접속사 if를 넣는다. if절이 앞에 올 경우, if절 뒤에 쉼표(,)를 써야 함에 주의한다.

19 (1), (2) expect, force의 목적격보어로 to부정사가 적절하다. (3) have는 사역동사이므로 목적격보어로 동사원형이 나와야 한다. (4) get의 목적격보어로 the work가 무엇을 행하는 것이 아니라 행해지는 것이므로 get the work done이 적절하다. (5), (6) 조건의 부사절에서는 미래의 의미를 갖더라도 will을 쓰지 않고 현재시제를 쓴다. 이때 주절의 시제는 미래시제를 쓰는 것에 주의한다. (7) unless = if ~ not

서술형 시험대비

p.130~131

01 (1) to go (2) to focus (3) to stop (4) not to go (5) to keep

02 (1) If Juhee comes to my birthday party
(2) If you do volunteer work for a month
(3) Unless you take the subway

03 (1) I want Jimin to come to school early.
(2) The teacher told the students to respect each other
(3) How much would it cost to have the camera repaired?
(4) Her little black dress and pretty hat made her look chic.
(5) If you don't hurry, you will miss the train.
(6) You will achieve everything you want if you work hard.
(7) If you don't have anything to wear, wear my coat. 또는 Unless you have anything to wear, wear my coat.

04 to start

05 (1) not to forget (2) to join (3) to leave (4) to exercise (5) to become

06 (1) joins, will give (2) will give (3) give, will make

07 (1) If (2) Unless

08 (1) If I don't come out at six tomorrow, please wake me up.
(2) Unless I answer my phone, call my sister.
(3) We will get there tomorrow if we walk all night.
(4) I want my mom to buy me a new cell phone.
(5) She asked me to become friends with her.
(6) She encouraged her son to go to college.
(7) Have him come here at five.

01 (1) allow (2), (3) advise (4) warn (5) encourage는 모두 목적격보어로 to부정사를 쓴다.

02 조건절에서는 현재시제로 미래시제를 대신한다.

03 (1), (2) want, tell의 목적격보어로 to부정사가 적절하다. (3) 사역동사 have의 목적격보어로 the camera가 수리하는 것이 아니라 수리되는 것이므로 repaired가 적절하다. (4) make는 사역동사로 목적격보어로 동사원형이 나와야 한다. (5), (6) 조건의 부사절에서는 미래의 의미를 갖더라도 will을 쓰지 않고 현재시제를 쓴다. 이때 주절의 시제는 미래시제를 쓰는 것에 주의한다. (7) unless는 'if ~ not'과 같은 뜻이다.

04 would like는 목적격보어로 to부정사를 쓴다.

05 warn, want, order, advise, expect의 목적격보어로 to부정사가 적절하다.

06 (1) 아직 일어나지 않은 미래의 일에 대한 조건을 나타내는 것이므로 조건절에는 현재시제를 쓰고 주절에는 미래시제를 쓴다. (2) 접속사 if가 명사절을 이끌고 있으므로 미래시제를 써야 한다. (3) unless도 'if ~ not'의 뜻으로 조건절을 이끄는 접속사이므로 조건절에는 현재시제를 쓰고 주절에는 미래시제를 쓴다.

07 명령문, + and ~: '~해라, 그러면'(= If ~), 명령문, + or ~: '~해라, 그렇지 않으면'(= Unless ~ = If not ~)

08 (1), (3) 조건의 부사절에서는 미래의 의미를 갖더라도 will을 쓰지 않고 현재시제를 쓴다. (4), (5), (6) want, ask, encourage는 목적격보어로 to부정사를 쓴다. (7) have는 사역동사이므로 목적격보어로 동사원형을 쓴다.

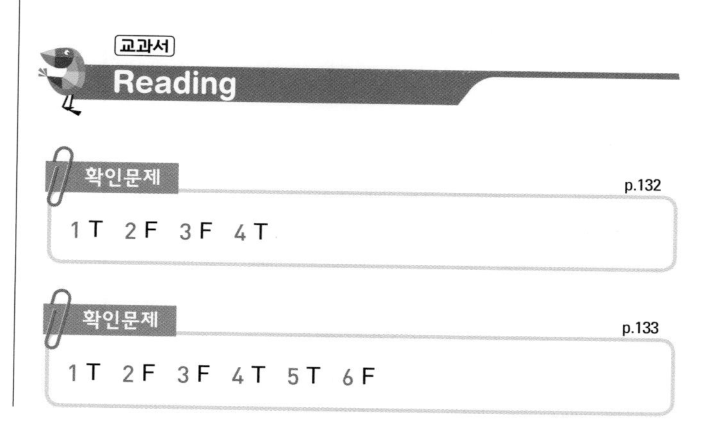

교과서

Reading

확인문제

p.132

1 T 2 F 3 F 4 T

확인문제

p.133

1 T 2 F 3 F 4 T 5 T 6 F

교과서 확인학습 A

p.134~135

01 of the Future 02 be on the market
03 that 04 will print out
05 take space trips
06 under the sea, in floating cities
07 above 08 surprise
09 in the future 10 As, will appear
11 What kind of job 12 be like
13 looked ahead, chose jobs
14 Let's read 15 that Sujin made
16 was made from
17 upcycling designer
18 waste materials 19 in new ways
20 the amount of waste
21 To become, creative
22 Have you ever heard
23 works for, that makes
24 special software
25 specially for patients 26 are good at
27 to use 28 big data specialist
29 works on 30 For example
31 taxi use patterns, late–night travelers
32 analyzed, to create 33 working with
34 collecting data from
35 allows us to learn
36 develop, problem–solving skills
37 yourself, prepare for
38 keep looking, dreaming

교과서 확인학습 B

p.136~137

1 Jobs of the Future
2 2020s: Self–driving cars will be on the market.
3 2030s: People will have robots that do everything for them.
4 2030s: 3D printers in every home will print out almost everything.
5 2050s: People will take space trips.
6 2050s: People will live under the sea or in floating cities.
7 Look at the pictures above.
8 Do these ideas surprise you?
9 You can see that our lives will be very different in the future.
10 As our lives change, many new jobs will appear.
11 What kind of job do you want?
12 What will your future life be like?
13 The following people looked ahead and chose jobs that will be important in the future.
14 Let's read about their jobs!
15 Do you see the flower pot that Sujin made?
16 It was made from old street flags.
17 She is an upcycling designer.
18 She works with waste materials to make new products.
19 Her products show people that old materials can be useful in new ways.
20 Upcycling can reduce the amount of waste in the future.
21 To become an upcycling designer, you should be creative and learn about art.
22 Have you ever heard of 3D modelers?
23 Taeho, a 3D modeler, works for a company that makes artificial hands and legs.
24 Taeho uses special software to print out new hands and legs.
25 They are made specially for patients.
26 If you are good at computer programming and art, you can be a 3D modeler.
27 Taeho wants more people to use 3D printed products in the future.
28 Jihye is a big data specialist.
29 She works on many projects.
30 For example, last year, she made bus routes.
31 To find the best night routes, she needed to collect smartphone use data and taxi use patterns from late–night travelers.
32 Then she analyzed this information to create the most useful routes.
33 Now Jihye is working with an online shopping mall.
34 She is collecting data from customers to find out the best styles for them.
35 She knows big data allows us to learn more about our daily lives.
36 If you want to become a big data specialist, you should develop your math and problem–solving skills!
37 Think about yourself and prepare for your future.
38 If you keep looking ahead and dreaming big, your future will be bright.

시험대비 실력평가

p.138~139

01 ③ 02 (A) appear (B) What (C) ahead
03 under the sea, in floating cities
04 ④ 05 what → that 또는 which
06 ①, ②, ④
07 (A) a 3D modeler
(B) works for a company that makes artificial hands and legs
(C) should be good at computer programming and art
08 ①, ④ 09 customers
10 will keep → keep 11 ② 12 ③
13 ②
14 ⓐ excited ⓑ interested 15 a dream 16 ④
17 ⑤ 18 people 19 ③ 20 ④
21 to learn 22 She made bus routes.
23 at a software company 24 realized
25 She chose her job because she is interested in math and science.

01 ⓐ와 ③번: ~함에 따라(비례), ① ~ 때문에(이유), ② [보통 as ~ as ...로 형용사·부사 앞에서] ~와 같은 정도로 (앞의 as: 지시부사, 뒤의 as: 접속사), ④ ~으로, ~이라고(전치사), ⑤ ~와 같이; ~하는 대로(양태·상태)

02 (A) 우리의 삶이 변화함에 따라 새로운 직업들이 많이 '생겨날 것'이라고 해야 하므로 appear가 적절하다. disappear: 사라지다, (B) 전치사 'like'의 목적어를 써야 하므로 What이 적절하다. (C) '앞을 내다보고' 미래에 중요하게 될 직업을 선택했다고 해야 하므로 ahead가 적절하다. look ahead: (앞일을) 내다보다, look behind: 뒤돌아보다; 회고하다

03 사람들은 육지뿐만 아니라 '바다 밑'이나 '수상 도시'에서 살 수 있을 것이다. not only A but also B: A뿐만 아니라 B도

04 ④ 당신은 미래에 우리의 삶이 매우 '달라진' 것을 볼 수 있다고 했다.

05 선행사인 a company가 있기 때문에 관계대명사 that이나 which로 고치는 것이 적절하다.

06 ⓑ와 ③, ⑤는 부사적 용법, ① 형용사적 용법 ②, ④ 명사적 용법

07 (A) 3D 모형 제작자이다. (B) 인공 손과 다리를 만드는 회사에서 일한다. (C) 컴퓨터 프로그래밍과 미술에 뛰어나야 한다.

08 ⓐ와 ①, ④번: 전문가, ② 비전문가, 아마추어, ③초보자, ⑤ 문외한

09 온라인 쇼핑몰의 '소비자들'을 가리킨다.

10 조건의 부사절에서는 현재시제가 미래시제를 대신한다.

11 수진은 거리의 낡은 깃발들로 화분을 만들었기 때문에, 폐기물을 가지고 새로운 제품을 만드는 '업사이클링 디자이너'라고 하는 것이 적절하다. ① 꽃집 주인[직원], ③ 쓰레기 수거인, ④ 재활용 프로그래머, ⑤ 쓰레기 봉투 디자이너

12 낡은 재료가 새로운 방식으로 유용해질 수 있다는 것을 보여주고 있기 때문에, 표어로는 '쓰레기를 낭비하지 마라'가 적절하다. ① environmental pollution: 환경오염, ⑤ disposable product: 일회용품

13 ② '화분 제작에 걸린 시간'은 알 수 없다. ① 낡은 거리 현수막, ③ 업사이클링 디자이너로서 폐기물을 가지고 새로운 제품을 만든다. ④ 낡은 재료가 새로운 방식으로 유용해질 수 있다는 것, ⑤ 창의적이어야 하며 미술을 배워야 한다.

14 감정을 나타내는 동사는 수식받는 주체가 감정을 느끼게 되는 경우에 과거분사를 써야 하므로 ⓐ excited와 ⓑ interested가 적절하다.

15 '꿈'을 가리킨다.

16 소인이 언제 일을 시작했는지는 대답할 수 없다. ① She is a computer programmer and works at a software company. ② She develops new software for computers. ③ People from different countries. ⑤ She studied computer science and developed her problem-solving skills.

17 우리의 삶이 변화함에 따라 새로운 직업들이 많이 생겨날 것이라는 말이 뒤에 이어지고 있으므로, 당신은 미래에 우리의 삶이 매우 '달라질' 것을 볼 수 있다고 하는 것이 적절하다. ③ similar: 비슷한, 유사한, ④ common: 흔한, 공통의

18 '사람들'을 가리킨다.

19 3D 프린터가 '거의' 모든 것을 출력해 낼 수 있다고 했을 뿐이므로, '모든' 것을 출력할 수 있는 3D 프린터가 인간도 출력할 수 있다는 진수의 생각은 올바르지 않다. ④ adventurous: 모험심이 강한, 모험을 즐기는

20 ⓐ the best styles for them: 그들(소비자들)에게 맞는 최적의 스타일, ⓒ prepare for: ~을 준비하다

21 allow+목적어+to부정사: ~가 …하도록 허락하다

22 작년에 그녀는 버스 노선을 만들었다.

23 소프트웨어 회사에서

24 come true = be realized: 실현되다

25 수학과 과학에 관심이 있기 때문에 그녀의 직업을 선택했다.

서술형 시험대비

p.142~143

01 ahead
02 In the 2030s, people will have robots that do everything for them and 3D printers in every home will print out almost everything.
03 Are you surprised at(또는 by) these ideas?
04 ⓐ old street flags ⓑ the flower pot
05 new → old, old → new
06 (A) an upcycling designer
(B) works with waste materials to make new products
(C) should be creative and learn about art

07 (A) works (B) that (C) at
08 artificial
09 using → to use
10 (A) looking (B) dreaming
11 (1) In order to find (2) So as to find
12 She knows big data allows us to learn more about our daily lives.
13 (1) She needed to collect smartphone use data and taxi use patterns from late-night travelers.
(2) She analyzed this information.

01 미래에 무슨 일이 일어날지를 고려했다, foresee: 예견하다, 내다보다, look ahead: (앞일을) 내다보다
02 2030년대에 사람들은 그들을 위하여 모든 것을 하는 로봇을 갖게 될 것이고 모든 가정의 3D 프린터가 거의 모든 것을 출력해 낼 것이다.
03 be surprised at/by: ~에 놀라다
04 ⓐ: '낡은 거리 깃발들', ⓑ: (수진이 만든) '화분'이 각각의 예에 해당한다.
05 거리의 낡은 깃발들로 화분을 만든 것이기 때문에, '낡은' 재료가 '새로운' 방식으로 유용해질 수 있다는 것을 보여준다고 하는 것이 적절하다.
06 (A) 업사이클링 디자이너이다. (B) 폐기물을 가지고 새로운 제품을 만든다. (C) 창의적이어야 하며 미술을 배워야 한다.
07 (A) Taeho와 a 3D modeler는 동격이므로 works가 적절하다. (B) 뒤에 불완전한 문장이 이어지므로 관계대명사 that이 적절하다. 관계부사 where+완전한 문장, (C) 컴퓨터 프로그래밍이나 미술에 '뛰어나다면'이라고 해야 하므로 at이 적절하다. be good at: ~에 능숙하다, ~을 잘하다, be good for: ~에 좋다
08 artificial = man-made: 인위적인, 인조의
09 want+목적어+to부정사: ~가 …하기를 원하다
10 keep ~ing: 계속해서 ~하다
11 in order to 동사원형 = so as to 동사원형 …하기 위하여(목적)
12 'to'를 보충하면 된다. allow+목적어+to부정사: ~가 …하도록 허락하다
13 (1) 최적의 심야 노선을 찾기 위하여, 그녀는 심야에 이동하는 사람들의 스마트폰 이용 정보와 택시 이용 패턴을 수집할 필요가 있었다. (2) 가장 유용한 노선을 만들기 위해 그녀는 그 정보를 분석했다.

영역별 핵심문제

p.145~149

01 consultant 02 ⑤
03 (1) decorate[to decorate] (2) allowed (3) apply (4) float 04 ① 05 ⑤ 06 apply
07 ② 08 ②
09 you need to develop your problem-solving skills
10 ⑤ 11 ③, ⑤ 12 (B) singing (C) sing
13 ⑤ 14 ③
15 (1) If you don't take a shower first, you can't go into the pool.
(2) If you want to become an upcycling designer, you should be creative and learn about art.
(3) The grandfather wanted his grandson to visit him this weekend.
(4) I asked him to call me back tomorrow.
(5) I need you to do me a favor.
16 ② 17 not to fight, will be punished
18 ④
19 (1) unless you miss the bus
(2) if you tell a lie
20 If you go to Europe, you can see many old structures.
21 ⑤ 22 ②, ④ 23 ③
24 upcycling
25 Sujin(She) made it from old street flags.
26 ① 27 ③, ⑤ 28 ②
29 collecting data, to find out
30 (A) big data (B) our daily lives

01 주어진 단어의 관계는 동사와 그 동사의 행위자의 관계이다. design: 디자인하다, 설계하다 designer: 디자이너, 설계자 consult: 상담하다 consultant: 상담가
02 collaborate: 협력하다
03 (1) decorate: 꾸미다, 장식하다 / 크리스마스 트리 장식하는 것 좀 도와줄래? (2) allow: 허락하다 / 누구도 여기서 담배 피는 것이 허락되지 않는다. (3) apply: 지원하다, 신청하다 / 나는 해외 자원 봉사 프로그램에 지원하게 되어 정말 기쁘다. (4) float: (물 위에) 뜨다, 떠다니다 / 그것들은 물에 집어넣으면 뜰 것이다.
04 route: 경로, 노선 / 두 장소 사이의 길
05 그림을 잘 그린다는 말과 보드게임을 잘한다는 말이 but으로 연결되는 것은 어색하다. I am good at drawing pictures. → I am not good at drawing pictures.
06 apply: 지원하다, 신청하다 / 어떤 것을 하기를 원한다고 말하는 서류를 제출하다
07 남자아이와 여자아이는 같은 행사가 아니라, 남자아이는 만화행사, 여자아이는 게임 행사에서 도움을 주기를 원한다.
08 상대방에게 조언을 구할 때 'What do I need to do?', 'What do you suggest?', 'What should I do to ~?', 'How can I ~?' 등을 사용할 수 있다.

09 develop: 발달시키다, 발전하다 problem-solving: 문제 해결의

10 주어진 문장은 밴드에서 록 음악을 연주할 계획이라고 말하는 내용이다. 이어서 노래를 잘하는 여자아이에게 밴드에서 노래하라고 제안하는 'Why don't you sing for us? (우리를 위해 노래해 주는 게 어때?)'라는 문장과 어울리므로 ⑤가 적절하다.

11 (A)에 대한 대답이 'You're good at dancing, aren't you?(춤 잘 추잖아, 그렇지 않니?)'이므로 자신이 무엇을 잘하는지에 대해 상대방에게 물어보는 것이 적절하다

12 be good at (동)명사: ~을 잘하다, Why don't you 동사원형 ~?: ~하는 게 어때?(제안하기)

13 ① We expect you to win the singing contest. ② The son asked his mom to give him more pocket money. ③ I want Juhee to come to my birthday party. ④ He ordered us to finish the project by Monday.

14 조건의 부사절에서는 미래의 의미를 갖더라도 will을 쓰지 않고 현재시제를 쓴다.

15 (1), (2) if는 조건을 나타내는 접속사로, 'if+주어+동사'로 쓰인다. if절이 앞에 올 경우, 부사절 뒤에 쉼표(,)를 붙인다. (3), (4), (5) want와 ask, need는 '동사+목적어+목적격보어(to부정사)'로 쓴다.

16 주어진 문장과 ②번은 조건을 나타내는 부사절을 이끌고 있다. ①, ③, ④번은 '~인지 아닌지'의 뜻으로 명사절을 이끌고 있다. ⑤ 가정법에 쓰인 if이다.

17 tell은 목적격보어로 to부정사가 나오며 싸우지 말라고 하는 것이 적절하므로 to부정사 앞에 not을 붙인다. If절에서는 현재시제를 쓰지만 내용상 미래의 일이므로 주절에는 미래시제를 쓴다. 또한 벌을 받는 것이므로 수동태로 써야 한다.

18 have는 사역동사이므로 목적격보어로 원형부정사가 나온다.

19 if는 조건을 나타내는 접속사로, 'if+주어+동사'로 쓰인다. if절이 앞에 올 경우 부사절 뒤에 쉼표(,)를 붙인다.

20 'If+주어+동사'로 쓰며 부사절 뒤에 쉼표(,)를 붙인다.

21 2050년대에 사람들은 '바다 밑'이나 '수상 도시'에서 살 것이다. ① be on the market = be offered for sale: 판매되고 있다, ④ take a trip = go on a trip: 여행을 가다

22 ⓑ와 ①, ③, ⑤: …와 비슷한(전치사), ② (…을) 좋아하다(동사), ④ [외관·형태·성질 등이] 같은(형용사)

23 '다음의 사람들은 앞을 내다보고 미래에 중요하게 될 직업을 선택하였습니다. 그들의 직업에 관하여 읽어 봅시다!'라고 했으므로, ③번이 적절하다.

24 부산물, 폐기물, 쓸모없는 혹은 원치 않는 제품들을 새로운 물질이나 더 좋은 품질의 환경적 가치를 가진 제품으로 변형시키는 과정, upcycle: (재활용품을) 더 나은 것으로 만들다 (= upgrade + recycle)

25 'Sujin(She)'을 주어로 해서 고치는 것이 적절하다.

26 3D 모형 제작자가 되기 위해서는 컴퓨터 프로그래밍과 미술에 뛰어나야 하므로, '보람'이가 적절하다.

27 ⓐ와 ③, ⑤번: 경험 용법, ① 결과 용법, ② 완료 용법, ④ 계속 용법

28 앞의 내용의 예가 나오고 있으므로 For example이 가장 적절하다. ① 그러므로, ④ 게다가, ⑤ 게다가, 더욱이

29 현재 그녀는 온라인 쇼핑몰의 소비자들에게 맞는 최적의 스타일을 '찾기 위하여' '데이터를 수집'하고 있다.

30 지혜에 따르면, '빅데이터'는 우리에게 '일상생활'에 관하여 더 많이 알게 해 준다.

단원별 예상문제

p.150~153

01 advice 02 out 03 ②
04 (C) – (B) – (A) – (D) 05 float 06 ③
07 (A) amazing (B) start 08 improve
09 ① 10 ② 11 (A) who (B) decorates
12 ③ 13 ③ 14 ④
15 (1) go → to go (2) to do → do
16 (A) old (B) waste (C) useful
17 (A) reduce (B) waste 18 ④ 19 ④
20 ⑤ 21 Self–driving cars
22 artificial hands and legs 또는 new hands and legs
23 ④
24 (1) 심야에 이동하는 사람들의 스마트폰 이용 정보와 택시 이용 패턴 수집
(2) 온라인 쇼핑몰 소비자들에게 맞는 최적의 스타일을 찾기 위한 데이터 수집
25 ②
26 We[I] need to keep looking ahead and dreaming big.

01 주어진 보기는 명사와 동사의 관계이다. analysis: 분석 analyze: 분석하다 advice: 충고, 조언 advise: 충고하다

02 help out: 도와주다, 거들다 / 내가 할 수 있으면 거들고 싶다. print out: 출력하다 / 이 문서를 출력해 주시겠어요?

03 space: 우주 / 과학자들은 사람들을 우주로 보냈다.

04 (C) 학교 재능 발표회에서 무엇을 할지 질문하자 (B) 아직 결정을 안 했다고 대답하면서 자신이 무엇을 잘하는지 상대방에게 질문한다. (A) 이에 대한 대답으로 춤을 잘 추지 않느냐고 말하자 (D) 자신은 노래를 잘한다고 대답한다.

05 float: (물 위에) 뜨다, 떠다니다 / 물 위에 머무르다

06 주어진 문장은 독서가 글쓰기를 더 좋게 만든다는 내용이다. 'You need to read a lot of books.(책을 많이 읽어야 해.)'의 내용과 연결되는 ③이 적절하다.

07 (A) amazing: 대단한, 멋진, It은 your paper(너의 글)를 받는 대명사로, 그 글이 대단한 것이므로 능동의 형태가 어울린다. (B) Why don't you 동사원형 ~?: ~하는 게 어때?

08 improve: 개선하다, 향상시키다 / 어떤 것을 더 좋게 만들다

09 Well, I need to study art history. → Well, you need to study art history.

10 주어진 질문에 ②번 다음에서 Sure.라고 답하고 있으므로 ②번이 적절하다.

11 (A) 주격 관계대명사의 자리이다. 선행사가 students로 사람이므로 who가 어울린다. decorate: 꾸미다, 장식하다

12 푸드 스타일리스트가 되기 위해서 가장 중요한 것은 무엇인지 언급되어 있지 않다. ① 소녀는 미래에 무엇이 되고 싶어 하는가? ② 소녀는 푸드 스타일리스트가 되기 위해서 무엇이 필요한가? ③ 푸드 스타일리스트가 되기 위해서 무엇이 가장 중요한가? ④ 푸드 스타일리스트는 무슨 일을 하는가? ⑤ 남자의 직업은 무엇인가?

13 allow의 목적격보어로 to부정사가 적절하다.

14 ① The father told his daughter to do her homework. ② I want Seri to watch the movie with us. ③ If something happens tomorrow, call me immediately. ⑤ I didn't expect you to get home so fast.

15 (1) request의 목적격보어로 to부정사가 나와야 한다. (2) let은 사역동사이므로 목적격보어로 동사원형이 나와야 한다.

16 (A) 거리의 '낡은' 깃발들로 만들어진 것이라고 해야 하므로 old가 적절하다. (B) '폐기물'을 가지고 새로운 제품을 만든다고 해야 하므로 waste가 적절하다. (C) 낡은 재료가 새로운 방식으로 '유용해질' 수 있다는 것을 보여준다고 해야 하므로 useful이 적절하다.

17 업사이클링은 '쓰레기'의 양을 '줄일 수' 있기 때문에, 환경 보호에 좋다고 말할 수 있다.

18 업사이클링은 미래에 쓰레기의 '양을 줄일 수 있다'고 했다.

19 ⓐ: 관계대명사 that, ⓑ: 목적어를 이끄는 접속사 that

20 ⑤ (새롭거나 뜻밖의 대상과) 접하다[마주치다], ⓒ와 나머지: 생기다, 발생하다, ① show up: 나타나다, ② emerge: 모습을 드러내다, 생겨나다, ③ come along: 생기다[나타나다], ④ turn up: 나타나다

21 2020년대에는 자율주행차들이 시장에 나올 것이다. be on the market: 판매하고 있다

22 '인공 손과 다리' 또는 '새 손과 다리'를 가리킨다.

23 태호가 누구와 함께 일하는지는 대답할 수 없다. ① He is a 3D modeler. ② He works for a company that makes artificial hands and legs. ③ He makes artificial hands and legs. ⑤ We[I] need to be good at computer programming and art.

24 (1) 지혜가 작년에 했던 작업, (2) 지혜가 현재 하고 있는 작업을 쓰면 된다.

25 ⓐ와 ②, ③, ⑤: 명사적 용법, ① 형용사적 용법, ④ 부사적 용법

26 만약 우리의 미래를 밝게 만들고 싶다면, '우리는 계속 앞을 내다보고 꿈을 크게 꿀 필요가 있다.'

서술형 실전문제 p.154~155

01 planning

02 What am I good at?

03 ②I'm good at took care of people. → I'm good at taking care of people.

04 (1) her son to clean his room for himself
(2) him to stop smoking to live a life without pain
(3) John to pass the entrance exam

05 (1) What do you want me to do for you?
(2) Can you ask my prince to come to this tower?
(3) If you want to save us, throw a rope down to us.
(4) If Seri watches the movie with us, I will buy her some popcorn.

06 Unless, won't go

07 What will your future life be like?

08 No, it won't.

09 new jobs

10 (A) collect (B) daily (C) yourself

11 smartphone use data and taxi use patterns from late-night travelers

12 (A) a big data specialist
(B) math and problem-solving skills

01 be going to 동사원형: ~할 예정이다(= be planning to 동사원형)

02 What am I good at?: 나는 무엇을 잘하지? 'You're good at dancing, aren't you?(너 춤 잘 추잖아, 그렇지 않니?)'로 대답하기 위해서는 자신이 무엇을 잘하는지 질문하는 것이 적절하다.

03 능력을 말할 때 'be good at ~'을 사용해서 '~을 잘한다'는 의미를 나타낼 수 있다. 전치사 at 다음에는 명사나 동명사를 쓴다.

04 ask, warn, expect 등은 목적격보어로 to부정사를 쓴다.

05 (1) want (2) ask 등의 동사는 목적격보어로 to부정사가 나와야 한다. (3), (4) if는 조건을 나타내는 접속사로, if절이 앞에 올 경우 뒤에 쉼표(,)를 써야 한다. 또한 조건의 부사절에서는 미래시제 대신 현재시제를 쓴다.

06 unless=if ~ not

07 'like'를 보충하면 된다.

08 해설| '2040년대'가 아니라 '2050년대'에 사람들은 우주여행을 할 것이다.

09 미래에 우리의 삶은 오늘날의 그것과 같지 않을 것이다. 우리의 삶이 변화함에 따라 많은 '새로운 직업들'이 있게 될 것이다.

10 (A) '수집할' 필요가 있었다고 해야 하므로 collect가 적절하다. correct: 바로잡다, 정정하다, (B) '일상' 생활이라고 해야 하므로 daily가 적절하다. dairy: 낙농장, 유제품의, (C) 주어와 목적

어가 같으므로 재귀대명사 yourself가 적절하다.

11 '심야에 이동하는 사람들의 스마트폰 이용 정보와 택시 이용 패턴'을 가리킨다.

12 (A) 빅데이터 전문가이다. (B) 수학과 문제 해결 능력을 계발해야 한다.

창의사고력 서술형 문제 p.156

|모범답안|

01 What do I need to do to be / You need to[You should/Make sure you] study many recipes. / What else do I need to do?

02 (1) Mom expects me to get good grades.
(2) Mom expects my sister to become a scientist.
(3) Mom expects my dad not to smoke.

03 (A) a computer programmer (B) new software (C) from different countries (D) math and science (E) computer science

01 What do I need to do?: 저는 뭘 해야 하나요?, 저는 어떤 것을 해야 할까요? what else: 그 밖에 무슨 recipe: 요리법 dish: 요리

단원별 모의고사 p.157~160

01 ③

02 (1) collaboration (2) Creativity

03 (1) (a)ppeared (2) (a)pplied (3) (c)ounseling (4) (l)ook (a)head

04 ③

05 ⑤

06 creativity

07 You need to learn about many kinds of food.

08 (A)at (B)of (C)about (D)about

09 develop

10 What skills do I need to develop?

11 ③, ④

12 I am not good at drawing pictures.

13 ②

14 ①, ②

15 (1) to win (2) not to be late

16 (1) The mother wanted her son to clean his room.
(2) I expect Juho to exercise more.
(3) The doctor advised me to stop eating junk food.
(4) If you show us your hand, we will open the door.
(5) If you don't sleep enough, you will be very tired.

17 (1) to go (2) rains

18 ③

19 If you keep looking ahead and dreaming big

20 ④

21 creative

22 ②

23 ①, ④

24 the following people

25 ④

01 amount: 양, 총액 / 많은 양의 정보가 있었다.

02 (1) collaborate: 협력하다 collaboration: 공동 작업, 협동 (2) creative: 창의적인 creativity: 창의력, 독창력

03 (1) appear: 나타나다, 보이기 시작하다 (2) apply: 지원하다, 신청하다 (3) counseling: 상담 (4) look ahead: (앞일을) 내다보다, 예견하다

04 talent: (타고난) 재능, 재주 / 어떤 것을 잘하는 타고난 능력

05 (A)의 대답으로 'A food stylist decorates food to look good for pictures or movies.(푸드 스타일리스트는 사진이나 영화에서 음식이 맛있어 보이도록 장식하는 일을 합니다.)'로 푸드 스타일리스트가 어떤 일을 하는지 얘기하고 있으므로 ⓒ가 어울린다. (B)와 (C)는 푸드 스타일리스트가 되기 위한 조언을 구하고 대답을 하고 있다. What do I need to do?: 뭘 해야 합니까?, 어떤 것을 해야 할까요? what else: 그 밖에 무슨

06 creativity: 창의력, 독창력 / 새로운 것을 생각해 내거나 만들어 내는 능력

07 need to 동사원형: ~할 필요가 있다 kind: 종류

08 (A) be good at: ~을 잘하다 (B) take care of: ~을 돌보다 (C) How about 동명사 ~?: ~하는 건 어때? (D) learn about: ~에 대해서 배우다

09 develop: 발달시키다, 발전하다 / 좀 더 진보된 상태로 되거나 변화되다

10 need to 동사원형: ~할 필요가 있다 skill: 기술

11 ⓐ looking ⓑ are needed ⓔ apply

12 be not good at: ~을 잘하지 못하다, ~에 능숙하지 못하다 draw: 그리다

13 persuade의 목적격보어로 to부정사가 적절하다.

14 빈칸이 있는 절은 현재시제이고 주절은 미래시제이므로, 빈칸은 시간이나 조건의 부사절이 되어야 한다. until은 '~(할 때)까지'라는 뜻의 시간을 나타내는 접속사이다.

15 encourage와 order는 목적격보어로 to부정사를 쓰고 to부정사의 부정은 not을 to 앞에 쓴다.

16 (1) want, (2) expect, (3) advise 등은 모두 목적격보어로 to부정사가 나와야 한다. (4) unless는 'if ~ not'이므로 unless를 if로 고쳐야 한다. (5) 조건의 부사절에서는 미래의 의미를 갖더라도 will을 쓰지 않고 현재시제를 쓴다.

17 (1) tell은 목적격보어로 to부정사를 쓴다. (2) 조건의 부사절에서는 미래시제 대신에 현재시제를 쓴다.

18 주어진 문장의 this information에 주목한다. ③번 앞 문장의 내용을 받고 있으므로 ③번이 적절하다.

19 keep ~ing: 계속해서 ~하다

20 지혜는 빅데이터가 우리에게 '일상생활'에 관하여 더 많이 알게 해 준다는 것을 알고 있다.

21 be동사의 보어이므로, create의 형용사 'creative'를 쓰는 것이 적절하다.

22 ⓐ와 ②번: 쓰레기(명사), ① …을 낭비하다(동사), ③ <기회 등을> 놓치다(동사), ④ 낭비(명사), ⑤ 쓸모가 없어진(형용사)

23 ⓐ와 ①, ④번: 관계대명사(뒤에 불완전한 문장이 나옴.), ②, ③, ⑤번: 접속사(뒤에 완전한 문장이 나옴.)

24 앞을 내다보고 미래에 중요하게 될 직업을 선택한 '다음의 사람들'을 가리킨다.

25 2060년대에 우리의 삶이 어떤 모습일지는 대답할 수 없다. ① Self-driving cars will be on the market. ② People will have robots that do everything for them and 3D printers in every home will print out almost everything. ③ In the 2050s. ⑤ Because our lives will change.

교과서 파헤치기

단어 TEST Step 1 p.02

01 사고 02 명성 03 아름다움, 미(美)
04 순간, 잠깐 05 마음, 정신, 영혼 06 모으다, 수집하다
07 나이가 지긋한 08 살아남다, 생존하다
09 존경하다 10 (그) 다음의 11 친선 대사
12 조각상 13 깨닫다, 알아차리다
14 눈 먼, 장님의 15 국제적인 16 살아 있는, 존속하는
17 세계적인 18 먹이를 주다 19 항목, 물품
20 약 21 기부하다
22 운이 좋게도, 다행스럽게도 23 (음식을) 제공하다
24 양로원 25 자원봉사의; 자원 봉사자
26 집 없는, 노숙자의 27 칭찬하다 28 임무, 사명
29 들어 올리다, (자금을) 모으다 30 예우하다, 존중하다
31 전환점 32 속담, 격언 33 호의, 친절
34 지지하다, 원조하다 35 늘, 내내
36 넘어지다 37 나누어 주다 38 죽다, 사망하다
39 ~ 덕분에 40 ~을 치우다, 청소하다
41 ~을 돕다 42 ~을 찾다 43 ~을 돌보다

단어 TEST Step 2 p.03

01 respect 02 blind 03 saying
04 serve 05 worldwide 06 beauty
07 mission 08 moment
09 goodwill ambassador 10 favor
11 following 12 statue 13 hold
14 accident 15 raise 16 elderly
17 realize 18 collect 19 nursing home
20 spirit 21 fame 22 honor
23 alive 24 turning point 25 support
26 praise 27 luckily 28 grass
29 medicine 30 survive 31 donate
32 homeless 33 volunteer 34 feed
35 pass away 36 fall down 37 take care of
38 hand out 39 thanks to 40 give a hand
41 in need 42 clean up 43 all the time

단어 TEST Step 3 p.04

1 fame, 명성 2 blind, 눈 먼, 장님의 3 accident, 사고
4 collect, 모으다, 수집하다 5 praise, 칭찬하다
6 realize, 깨닫다, 알아차리다 7 support, 지지하다, 원조하다
8 respect, 존경하다 9 donate, 기부하다
10 turning point, 전환점 11 honor, 예우하다, 존중하다
12 mission, 임무, 사명 13 statue, 조각상
14 survive, 살아남다, 생존하다 15 volunteer, 자원 봉사자
16 nursing home, 양로원

대화문 TEST Step 1 p.05~06

Listen & Talk 1 A

can / help me move / What are, going to / going to donate

Listen & Talk 1 B

wrong with / broke it / happened / a hurry to catch, fell down / terrible, Is there, can do / can you help me carry

Listen & Talk 1 C

can you help, wash them / but, can't, to feed / Why don't you ask / ask you a favor / What / Can you help, wash / have to walk / Thank you

Listen & Talk 2 A

What kinds of volunteer / don't we clean up / right, Let's

Listen & Talk 2 B

As you know, was, Why don't we raise, at, on May, bring your items, donate, give all the money to, give a hand, in need

Listen & Talk 2 C

cleaned up, we going to / don't we visit, nursing home, clean it up / bad idea, to do something fun, Why don't we hold / What / can serve / how about playing / can play the cello / sounds like

Do It Yourself A

want to do on that day / Why don't, volunteer activities, help others, make, better / sounds great, is / who has volunteered a lot / has volunteered, help us find / usually search for, don't we check / good idea

대화문 TEST Step 2 p.07~08

Listen & Talk 1 A

B: Mia, can you help me move these books?
G: Sure. What are you going to do with them?
B: I'm going to donate them to a children's library.

Listen & Talk 1 B

B: Hey, Minji! What's wrong with your leg?
G: I broke it last week.
B: Really? What happened?

G: I was in a hurry to catch a train. But I fell down in the street.

B: Oh, that's terrible! Is there anything I can do for you?

G: Well, can you help me carry this bag?

B: Sure.

Listen & Talk 1 C

B1: Wow! These dogs are so dirty. Jay, can you help me wash them?

B2: Allen, I'm sorry, but I can't. I have to feed the cats now. Why don't you ask Nicky?

B1: Okay! Nicky, can I ask you a favor?

G: Sure, Allen. What is it?

B1: Can you help me wash these dogs?

G: Sure. But I have to walk these dogs first. After that, I will help you.

B1: All right! Thank you.

Listen & Talk 2 A

G: What kinds of volunteer activities can we do?

B: Why don't we clean up our town's streets?

G: All right! Let's do it.

Listen & Talk 2 B

G: Good morning, students! As you know, there was a big fire in Mapletown. Why don't we raise money and help the people there? Come to our special event at the school grounds on May 3! Please bring your items and donate them. We will sell your items. Then, we will give all the money to Mapletown. Please give a hand to people in need.

Listen & Talk 2 C

B1: Next Wednesday is Volunteer Day. We cleaned up the park last time. What are we going to do this time?

G: Why don't we visit a nursing home and clean it up?

B2: That's not a bad idea. But I want to do something fun. Why don't we hold a party for the people there?

G: That's a good idea. What can we do at the party?

B1: We can serve some food.

B2: And how about playing some music? I can play the piano.

G: And I can play the cello.

B1: It sounds like a good plan.

Do It Yourself A

G1: We have a class activity day next Friday. What do you want to do on that day?

B: Why don't we do some volunteer activities? We can help others and make our community better.

G1: That sounds great, but choosing a good place is not easy.

B: We need someone who has volunteered a lot.

G1: I know Sumin has volunteered a lot. Sumin, can you help us find some good places?

G2: Sure. I usually search for information on the internet. Why don't we check the volunteering website for teens?

B: That's a good idea.

본문 TEST Step 1 p.09~10

01 Spirit, Audrey 02 During, little, were
03 that, find was 04 felt scared, time
05 Luckily, thanks to
06 groups, helped, was
07 Later, became, worldwide
08 Her name
09 When, up, beauty
10 because of, such as
11 which, wore, even 12 still love, style
13 turning point, life
14 went, international, festival
15 donated money, went
16 Thanks to, more, than
17 realized, fame, others 18 went to, in
19 There, brought, to
20 shocked because, lives
21 After, volunteered, other
22 visited, hand out, support
23 to, passed away, following
24 praised, beauty, real, heart
25 To honor, statue
26 respect, keep, alive
27 favorite saying, mission
28 *As, get, remember*
29 *One, yourself, other, others*

본문 TEST Step 2 p.11~12

01 Spirit of Audrey
02 During, little, were hungry, sick
03 The only, that, was
04 felt scared all the time
05 Luckily, thanks to, others
06 One of the groups that, was

07 a worldwide movie star
08 Her name was
09 grew up, a symbol of beauty
10 because of, such as
11 which she wore, is famous
12 still love her style
13 a turning point
14 an international music festival
15 donated money, to UNICEF
16 Thanks to, collected more, than
17 realized that, help others, a UNICEF Goodwill Ambassador
18 went to Ethiopia
19 brought, to hungry children
20 was shocked because, lives
21 volunteered in other countries
22 to hand out medicine, support
23 to, passed away, following year
24 praised, real beauty was her heart
25 To honor, made a statue
26 who respect, keep, alive
27 favorite saying, her mission
28 *As, get older*
29 *One, yourself, the other, others*

본문 TEST Step 3 p.13~14

1 오드리의 정신
2 제2차 세계 대전 동안, 한 어린 소녀와 그녀의 어머니는 굶주리고 아팠다.
3 그들이 찾을 수 있었던 유일한 음식은 풀뿐이었다.
4 어린 소녀는 내내 겁에 질려 있었다.
5 다행히도, 소녀는 다른 사람들의 도움 덕분에 살아남았다.
6 그녀를 도왔던 단체 중 하나는 유니세프(국제 연합 아동 기금)였다.
7 후에, 소녀는 세계적인 영화배우가 되었다.
8 그녀의 이름은 오드리 헵번이었다.
9 그녀가 자랐을 때, 헵번은 아름다움의 상징이 되었다.
10 그녀는 〈마이 페어 레이디〉와 〈로마의 휴일〉과 같은 흥행 영화들로 인해 매우 인기가 있었다.
11 그녀가 영화에서 입었던 아담한 검은 드레스는 심지어 오늘날까지도 유명하다.
12 많은 사람이 여전히 그녀의 스타일을 사랑한다.
13 1987년 가을은 헵번의 인생 전환점이었다.
14 그녀는 마카오의 한 국제 음악 축제에 갔다.
15 많은 사람이 축제에서 돈을 기부했고, 그 돈은 유니세프로 보내졌다.
16 그녀의 명성 덕분에, 유니세프는 어느 때보다도 더 많은 돈을 모았다.
17 헵번은 자신의 명성이 다른 사람들을 도울 수 있다는 것을 깨닫고, 유니세프 친선 대사가 되었다.
18 먼저, 헵번은 1988년에 에티오피아로 갔다.
19 그곳에서, 그녀는 굶주린 아이들에게 음식을 가져다주었다.
20 그녀는 그들의 삶이 매우 어려웠기 때문에 충격을 받았다.
21 그 후, 그녀는 다른 나라들에서도 봉사하였다.
22 1990년, 그녀는 의약품을 나눠 주고 깨끗한 식수 프로그램을 지원하기 위하여 베트남을 방문하였다.
23 그녀의 마지막 여행은 1992년 소말리아에 간 것이었으며, 이듬해 그녀는 사망하였다.
24 많은 사람이 그녀의 아름다움과 스타일을 칭송했지만, 헵번의 진정한 아름다움은 그녀의 마음이었다.
25 그녀를 기리기 위해, 유니세프는 '오드리의 정신'이라는 동상을 만들었다.
26 그녀를 존경하는 사람들이 그녀의 사명을 이어 나가고 있다.
27 그녀가 가장 좋아했던 구절은 그녀의 사명을 보여 준다.
28 나이가 들어갈수록, 당신에게 손이 두 개가 있다는 것을 기억하라.
29 한 손은 자신을 돕기 위한 것이고, 다른 한 손은 타인을 돕기 위한 것이다.

본문 TEST Step 4-Step 5 p.15~18

1 The Spirit of Audrey
2 During World War II, a little girl and her mother were hungry and sick.
3 The only food that they could find was grass.
4 The little girl felt scared all the time.
5 Luckily, the girl survived, thanks to the help of others.
6 One of the groups that helped her was UNICEF.
7 Later, the girl became a worldwide movie star.
8 Her name was Audrey Hepburn.
9 When she grew up, Hepburn became a symbol of beauty.
10 She was very popular because of her hit movies, such as *My Fair Lady* and *Roman Holiday.*
11 The little black dress which she wore in a movie is famous even today.
12 Many people still love her style.
13 The autumn of 1987 was a turning point in Hepburn's life.
14 She went to an international music festival in Macau.
15 Many people donated money at the festival, and the money went to UNICEF.
16 Thanks to her fame, UNICEF collected more money than ever before.

17 Hepburn realized that her fame could help others, so she became a UNICEF Goodwill Ambassador.
18 First, Hepburn went to Ethiopia in 1988.
19 There, she brought food to hungry children.
20 She was shocked because their lives were very difficult.
21 After that, she volunteered in other countries.
22 In 1990, she visited Vietnam to hand out medicine and support clean drinking water programs.
23 Her last trip was to Somalia in 1992, and she passed away the following year.
24 Many people praised her beauty and style, but Hepburn's real beauty was her heart.
25 To honor her, UNICEF made a statue, *The Spirit of Audrey*.
26 People who respect her keep her mission alive.
27 Her favorite saying shows her mission.
28 *As you get older, remember you have two hands.*
29 *One is for helping yourself, and the other is for helping others.*

구석구석지문 TEST Step 1 p.19

Presentation Time

1. a great person
2. priest, also
3. built, for
4. took care of, taught classes
5. From, that, should help, in need

After You Read B

1. How, during
2. tell me about
3. terrible, were hungry, sick
4. survived thanks to, others
5. begin to work
6. changed my life
7. that, could help other people
8. After that, did, do
9. visited some countries, volunteered there

Culture Link

1. Talking Books
2. program that makes, blind
3. was started
4. record your voice
5. are given, for free

구석구석지문 TEST Step 2 p.20

Presentation Time

1. Lee Taeseok was a great person.
2. He was a priest and also a doctor.
3. He built hospitals and schools for the people of Tonj.
4. He took care of them and taught classes.
5. From this person, I learned that I should help people in need.

After You Read B

1. Reporter: How was your life during World War II?
2. Can you tell me about it?
3. Audrey: It was terrible. My family and I were hungry and sick.
4. We survived thanks to the help of others.
5. Reporter: How did you begin to work for UNICEF?
6. Audrey: In 1987, a musical festival in Macau changed my life.
7. I learned that my fame could help other people.
8. Reporter: After that, what did you do?
9. Audrey: I visited some countries in Africa and Asia and volunteered there.

Culture Link

1. Talking Books Program
2. This is a program that makes audiobooks for blind people.
3. It was started in 1931 in the United States.
4. You just read books and record your voice.
5. These audiobooks are given to blind people for free.

단어 TEST Step 1

p.21

01 발표 02 전망
03 휴식을 취하다, 느긋이 쉬다 04 매우 멋진
05 (여행 중) 머무른 곳, 멈춤, 정거장 06 만화책
07 상태, 상황 08 견학 여행, 현장 학습
09 놀라운, 멋진 10 미술관 11 역사
12 목적, 목표 13 놀이공원 14 외국의
15 길거리 음식 16 하이킹하다, 도보 여행하다
17 똑바로, 일직선으로 18 휴가, 공휴일, 휴일
19 국제적인 20 마을
21 미술 전시회 22 역사적인, 역사상의
23 장소 24 자연의 25 그림
26 상품, 물건 27 계획하다; 계획 28 래프팅, 급류 타기
29 가을 30 거친, 파도가 심한 31 풍경, 경치
32 대학교 33 박물관, 미술관
34 방문하다, 찾아가다 35 동시에, 한꺼번에
36 걸어서, 도보로 37 ~할 수 있다 38 내리다, 하차하다
39 더 이상 ~하지 않는 40 여러 가지의, 다양한
41 (~에) 집중하다, 초점을 맞추다 42 ~ 앞에서
43 버스로

단어 TEST Step 2

p.22

01 comic book 02 scenery 03 international
04 straight 05 condition 06 presentation
07 museum 08 amazing 09 art museum
10 view 11 stop 12 rough
13 field trip 14 hike 15 relax
16 history 17 village 18 foreign
19 university 20 purpose 21 autumn
22 visit 23 historical 24 site
25 holiday 26 amusement park
27 street food 28 goods 29 art show
30 natural 31 rafting 32 awesome
33 painting 34 plan 35 focus on
36 on foot 37 get off 38 a variety of
39 by bus 40 in front of 41 no longer
42 be able to 동사원형 43 at the same time

단어 TEST Step 3

p.23

1 condition, 상태, 상황 2 awesome, 매우 멋진
3 goods, 상품, 물건 4 scenery, 풍경, 경치
5 amusement park, 놀이공원 6 autumn, 가을
7 relax, 휴식을 취하다, 느긋이 쉬다
8 stadium, 경기장, 스타디움 9 foreign, 외국의
10 history, 역사 11 purpose, 목적, 목표
12 rough, 거친 13 rafting, 래프팅, 급류 타기
14 stop, (여행 중) 머무른 곳
15 field trip, 견학 여행, 현장 학습
16 museum, 박물관, 미술관

대화문 TEST Step 1

p.24~25

Listen & Talk 1 A

What are you, this weekend / going to go / What, you planning to do / I'm planning to

Listen & Talk 1 B

have, this, have any / going / What, planning to, with / I'm planning, with them / about, plans for / going, stay home, relax / good idea

Listen & Talk 1 C

Where, field trip / We are going to / interesting, planning to see / are, right now. I'm planning to see, Where, going / We are going to, amusement, excited to ride / sounds fun, good trip

Listen & Talk 2 A

How, get to school / by bus / How long, take to get / It takes

Listen & Talk 2 B

pictures, beautiful, Where, take / were lots of, should / to, How, get, from / Get on, get off, see, in front of / long, take to get / takes minutes / next weekend

Listen & Talk 2 C

How do I get to / go there by bus or on foot / How long, take to get / by, on foot / will walk, Can you tell, how to get / Go straight, turn, on your right / Go, for, turn left

Do It Yourself A

What, planning to do this / to go to / Are you, to see / will, I'm planning to visit / How long, to get / an hour and 40 minutes by / much faster than, have, good trip

대화문 TEST Step 2

p.26~27

Listen & Talk 1 A

B: What are you going to do this weekend?
G: I'm going to go to Jeju-do.
B: What are you planning to do there?
G: I'm planning to go hiking on Hallasan.

Listen & Talk 1 B

B: We have a long holiday this month. Do you have any plans?

G: I'm going to visit my grandparents in Jeonju.

B: Oh, really? That's nice. What are you planning to do with them?

G: I'm planning to go to Hanok Village with them. How about you? What are your plans for the holiday?

B: I'm going to stay home and relax.

G: That's also a good idea!

Listen & Talk 1 C

B: Hi, Nuri. Where is your class going for the field trip tomorrow?

G: Hello, Mike. We are going to the art museum.

B: Sounds interesting. What are you planning to see there?

G: There are three art shows right now. I'm planning to see Vincent van Gogh's paintings. Where is your class going?

B: We are going to the amusement park. I'm excited to ride a roller coaster!

G: That sounds fun. Have a good trip!

Listen & Talk 2 A

G: How do you get to school?

B: I go to school by bus.

G: How long does it take to get there?

B: It takes 15 minutes.

Listen & Talk 2 B

B: Wow, these pictures are so beautiful. Where did you take them?

G: At Riverside Park. There were lots of flowers. You should go there!

B: I want to. How do I get there from our school?

G: Get on bus number 135 and get off at the Riverside Stadium stop. You can see the park in front of the bus stop.

B: How long does it take to get there?

G: It takes 30 minutes.

B: Thanks. I'll go there next weekend.

Listen & Talk 2 C

B: Excuse me. How do I get to Hanguk University from here?

W: You can go there by bus or on foot.

B: How long does it take to get there?

W: It takes five minutes by bus and 20 minutes on foot.

B: Oh, then I will walk there. Can you tell me how to get there?

W: Go straight for two blocks, and then turn left. You will see Hanguk University on your right.

B: Go straight for two blocks and turn left. Thank you!

Do It Yourself A

G: What are you planning to do this weekend?

B: I'm planning to go to a baseball game in Daegu.

G: Are you going to see the All-Star Game?

B: Yes. It will be fun. Also, I'm planning to visit my friend there.

G: Nice. How long does it take to get there?

B: It takes an hour and 40 minutes by express train.

G: Wow, it's much faster than I thought. I hope you have a good trip!

B: Thank you.

본문 TEST Step 1 p.28~29

01 Best Moment, Field
02 How, trip, tell us
03 Market Heaven
04 traditional markets
05 Then go, in
06 one, most famous markets
07 what, famous for
08 selling, variety of, different
09 interesting, all, international goods
10 kinds of, such as
11 Then, walked to
12 Many bookstores, used books
13 excited because, found
14 nice, relax, read
15 Full, Natural Beauty
16 place like, nature
17 First, went to
18 cave, in, condition
19 amazing, natural beauty
20 Near, turned off, minute
21 became, able, focus on
22 most amazing experience
23 Our next stop
24 went rafting
25 excting, rough, view, same
26 City of Firsts
27 where, first, is
28 How about
29 answer, is
30 place, many, firsts
31 To get, went
32 next to, station
33 learned about, history
34 walked around, Western-style
35 view from, awesome
36 great, historical sites
37 places sound great
38 all, done, on, presentations

본문 TEST Step 2 p.30~31

01 The Best Moment, Field Trip
02 How were, last week, Please tell us
03 Market Heaven
04 traditional markets 05 Then go to
06 one of the most famous markets
07 what it is famous for
08 is famous for, a variety of goods
09 It, to see all the international goods
10 also ate many kinds of, such as
11 Then, walked to
12 sell used books
13 really excited because, found
14 to relax, read 15 Full of Natural Beauty
16 no place like, beautiful nature 17 First, went to
18 in good condition
19 so amazing, natural beauty
20 cave tour, turned off, for a minute
21 were able to focus on
22 the most amazing experience
23 Our next stop 24 went rafting
25 exciting to ride, at the same time
26 Firsts 27 where, is 28 How about
29 The answer 30 many of Korea's firsts
31 To get there, went 32 next to
33 the history of *Jajangmyeon*
34 the first Western-style park
35 view from, awesome
36 to see the historical sites 37 sound great
38 on your presentations

본문 TEST Step 3 p.32~33

1 수학여행에서의 가장 좋았던 순간
2 교사: 안녕하세요, 여러분! 지난주 수학여행은 어땠나요? 얘기해 봅시다!
3 부산, 시장 천국
4 전통 시장을 좋아하세요?
5 그렇다면 부산에 있는 국제시장으로 가세요.
6 그곳은 부산에서 가장 유명한 시장 중 하나입니다.
7 그곳이 무엇으로 유명한지 아세요?
8 그 시장은 여러 나라에서 온 다양한 제품들을 파는 것으로 유명합니다.
9 그곳에서 세계 곳곳의 제품들을 모두 볼 수 있어서 흥미로웠습니다.
10 우리는 또한 김밥, 어묵 그리고 호떡과 같은 여러 종류의 길거리 음식을 먹었습니다
11 그러고 나서 우리는 보수동 책방 거리로 걸어갔습니다.
12 그곳의 많은 서점에서는 중고 책을 팝니다.
13 우리는 몇 권의 오래된 만화책을 발견해서 정말 신이 났습니다!
14 카페에서 휴식을 취하며 그 책들을 읽는 것이 좋았습니다.
15 강원도, 자연의 아름다움으로 가득한 곳
16 아름다운 자연에 관한 한 강원도만 한 곳이 없습니다.
17 우선, 우리는 백룡동굴로 갔습니다.
18 이 1.8킬로미터 길이의 동굴은 여전히 잘 보존된 상태입니다.
19 그곳의 자연의 아름다움을 보는 것은 매우 놀라웠습니다.
20 동굴 관광의 끝 무렵, 안내인이 동굴 안의 불을 잠시 껐습니다.
21 모든 것이 매우 어두워져서, 우리는 그곳의 소리에 집중할 수 있었습니다.
22 그것은 여행에서 가장 경이로운 경험이었습니다!
23 우리의 다음 여행지는 동강이었습니다.
24 우리는 래프팅을 하러 갔습니다!
25 급류를 타면서 동시에 경치를 즐기는 것은 흥미진진했습니다.
26 인천, '최초의 것'들의 도시
27 한국 최초의 기차역이 어디인지 아세요?
28 첫 번째 자장면은요?
29 그 답은 인천입니다!
30 이곳에는 한국의 최초의 것들이 많이 있습니다.
31 그곳으로 가기 위하여, 우리는 인천역으로 갔습니다.
32 자장면 박물관은 역 옆에 있습니다.
33 우리는 그곳에서 자장면의 역사에 대하여 배웠습니다.
34 다음에는, 한국 최초의 서구식 공원인 자유 공원을 거닐었습니다
35 공원에서 바라본 경치는 정말 멋있었습니다!
36 공원에서 이 도시의 역사적인 장소들을 바라보는 것은 아주 좋았습니다.
37 교사: 와, 이곳들은 멋지게 들리네요!
38 여러분 모두 발표를 훌륭하게 잘했어요!

본문 TEST Step 4-Step 5 p.34~37

1 The Best Moment of the Field Trip
2 Teacher: Good morning, everyone! How were your field trips last week? Please tell us about them!
3 Busan, Market Heaven
4 Do you like traditional markets?
5 Then go to Gukje Market in Busan.
6 It is one of the most famous markets in Busan.
7 Do you know what it is famous for?
8 It is famous for selling a variety of goods from different countries.
9 It was interesting to see all the international goods there.
10 We also ate many kinds of street food, such as *Gimbap*, fish cake, and *Hotteok*.
11 Then we walked to Bosu-dong Book Street.
12 Many bookstores there sell used books.
13 We were really excited because we found some old comic books!

14 It was nice to relax in a café and read them.
15 Gangwon-do, Full of Natural Beauty
16 There is no place like Gangwon-do for beautiful nature.
17 First, we went to Baengnyong Cave.
18 This 1.8-kilometer-long cave is still in good condition.
19 It was so amazing to see its natural beauty.
20 Near the end of our cave tour, the guide turned off the lights in the cave for a minute.
21 Everything became very dark, so we were able to focus on the sounds there.
22 It was the most amazing experience of the tour!
23 Our next stop was Donggang.
24 We went rafting!
25 It was exciting to ride on the rough water and enjoy the view at the same time.
26 Incheon, A City of Firsts
27 Do you know where the first train station in Korea is?
28 How about the first *Jajangmyeon?*
29 The answer is Incheon!
30 This place has many of Korea's firsts.
31 To get there, we went to Incheon Station.
32 The Jajangmyeon Museum is next to the station.
33 We learned about the history of *Jajangmyeon* there.
34 Later, we walked around Jayu Park, the first Western-style park in Korea.
35 The view from the park was awesome!
36 It was great to see the historical sites of this city from the park.
37 Teacher: Wow, these places sound great!
38 You all have done a wonderful job on your presentations!

구석구석지문 TEST Step 1

p.38

After You Read D

1. live in
2. There is, railway
3. no longer used
4. take pictures of, scenery

Think & Write Step 3

1. Autumn Walk
2. Last autumn, went to, with
3. rode, to the middle of
4. Then, hiked to
5. At the top, autumn scenery, took, pictures
6. It, amazing, exciting to see

Culture Link

1. Eco
2. take trips, without hurting
3. it, to protect nature
4. Volunteer
5. go on trips, special purposes
6. to do volunteer work
7. local communities, during
8. History Trip
9. On this trip, historical sites, learn about
10. During, can understand, lives, in the past

구석구석지문 TEST Step 2

p.39

After You Read D

1. I live in Hang-dong, Seoul.
2. There is an old railway.
3. It is no longer used.
4. You can walk there and take pictures of beautiful scenery.

Think & Write Step 3

1. Autumn Walk in Naejangsan
2. Last autumn, I went to Naejangsan with my family.
3. I rode a cable car to the middle of the mountain.
4. Then , I hiked to the top.
5. At the top, I saw beautiful autumn scenery. I took many pictures .
6. It was amazing and exciting to see beautiful autumn leaves.

Culture Link

1. Eco Trip
2. Some people take trips in nature without hurting the environment.
3. They think it is important to protect nature.
4. Volunteer Trip
5. Some people go on trips for special purposes.
6. They travel to do volunteer work.
7. They help local communities or wild animals during their trips.
8. History Trip
9. On this trip , people visit historical sites and learn about history.
10. During this trip, people can understand the lives of people in the past .

Lesson 7

단어 TEST Step 1

p.40

01 양, 총액　02 진로, 직업　03 공동 작업, 협동
04 자율주행차　05 모으다, 수집하다
06 나타나다, 보이기 시작하다　07 상담가
08 발달시키다, 발전하다　09 감정
10 분석하다　11 (물 위에) 뜨다, 떠다니다
12 상담　13 인공적인, 인조의
14 개선하다, 향상시키다　15 통역사
16 힘, 강점, 장점　17 심야의
18 지원하다, 신청하다　19 (타고난) 재능, 재주
20 환자　21 쓰레기, 폐기물　22 전문가
23 협력하다　24 경로, 노선　25 꾸미다, 장식하다
26 창의력, 독창력　27 줄이다, 감소시키다
28 우주, 공간　29 손님, 고객　30 문제 해결의
31 다음[아래]에 나오는[언급되는]
32 (폐품 등을) 다시 쓸 수 있게 만들다
33 (책, 영화 등의) 논평가　34 창의적인
35 무엇보다도　36 ~을 돌보다　37 (앞일을) 내다보다,
38 예견하다　39 ~을 잘하다　40 그 외에, 그 밖에
41 이루어지다, 실현되다
42 (서식 등을) 작성하다, (정보를) 기입하다, 채우다
43 일기를 쓰다　44 출력하다

단어 TEST Step 2

p.41

01 advice　02 career　03 skill
04 reduce　05 talent　06 reviewer
07 counseling　08 specialist　09 collaborate
10 apply　11 decorate　12 interpreter
13 analyze　14 emotion　15 consultant
16 artificial　17 float　18 strength
19 collaboration　20 following　21 improve
22 late-night　23 creative　24 patient
25 amount　26 problem-solving
27 allow　28 reason　29 customer
30 route　31 develop　32 appear
33 creativity　34 space　35 keep a diary
36 look ahead　37 print out　38 take care of
39 what else　40 fill out　41 come true
42 be good at　43 first of all

단어 TEST Step 3

p.42

1 late-night, 심야의　2 analyze, 분석하다
3 route, 경로, 노선　4 improve, 개선하다, 향상시키다
5 specialist, 전문가　6 patient, 환자
7 float, (물 위에) 뜨다, 떠다니다
8 artificial, 인공적인, 인조의　9 strength, 강점, 장점
10 counseling, 상담　11 talent, (타고난) 재능, 재주
12 creativity, 창의력, 독창력
13 develop, 발달시키다, 발전하다　14 career, 진로, 직업
15 apply, 지원하다, 신청하다
16 reviewer, (책 • 영화 등의) 논평가

대화문 TEST Step 1

p.43~44

Listen & Talk 1 A

Let's play / not good at / What are you good at / good at playing / let's play

Listen & Talk 1 B

are, going to do / decide, What am, good at / good at dancing, aren't / good at singing, singing / planning to play / Why don't you / love to

Listen & Talk 1 C

need to fill out / career counseling / wrote, and / be, P.E. teacher, watching, writing, strengths, What am I good / lots, First of, are good at, aren't you / I'm good at playing baseball / other strengths / work, other people, at listening to / You're good at / Thanks

Listen & Talk 2 A

want to be, What, need to do / need to, develop, problem-solving skills

Listen & Talk 2 B

amazing / Thank, for saying, trying, to improve, writing skills, writer / want, like, What do I, to / a lot of, Reading makes your writing better / else, need to / every day, don't, keeping / Thank, for, advice

Listen & Talk 2 C

Thank, for / problem / who want to be food, about your job / decorates, to look / to be a food stylist, What, need / need to learn, kinds / What else, need to do / too Creativity / Thank, for

대화문 TEST Step 2

p.45~46

Listen & Talk 1 A

G: Let's play basketball.

B: Well... I'm not good at playing basketball. Are you?

G: Yes, I think I am. What are you good at?
B: I'm good at playing soccer.
G: Okay, then let's play soccer.

Listen & Talk 1 B

B: Jessica, what are you going to do for the school talent show?
G: I didn't decide yet. What am I good at?
B: You're good at dancing, aren't you?
G: Not really. But I think I'm good at singing. I like singing very much.
B: Really? Actually, I'm planning to play rock music with my band. Why don't you sing for us?
G: Sure, I'd love to.

Listen & Talk 1 C

B: Mom, I need to fill out this form for tomorrow's career counseling program. Could you help me?
W: Sure. Let me see. You already wrote your dream job and hobby.
B: Yes, I want to be a P.E. teacher, and my hobby is watching sports games. But writing my strengths is hard. What am I good at?
W: Well, I think you have lots of strengths. First of all, you are good at playing baseball, aren't you?
B: Oh, yes. I'm good at playing baseball.
W: And you have many other strengths.
B: You're right. I also work well with other people. And I'm good at listening to people.
W: Right! You're good at so many things.
B: Thanks, Mom.

Listen & Talk 2 A

B: I want to be a scientist. What do I need to do?
W: You need to study science. And you need to develop your problem-solving skills.

Listen & Talk 2 B

G: Jason, I read your paper. It was so amazing!
B: Thank you for saying that. I'm trying hard to improve my writing skills. I want to be a writer someday.
G: Really? I want to write well like you. What do I need to do?
B: You need to read a lot of books. Reading makes your writing better.
G: What else do I need to do?
B: Well, I write almost every day. Why don't you start keeping a diary?
G: Thank you for your advice. I'll start today.

Listen & Talk 2 C

G: Hello, Mr. Watson! Thank you for doing this interview.
M: Sure, no problem.
G: This interview is for students who want to be food stylists. Can you tell me about your job?
M: Sure. You may see pictures of food in books or on TV. A food stylist decorates food to look good for pictures or movies.
G: I want to be a food stylist like you. What do I need to do?
M: You need to learn about many kinds of food.
G: What else do I need to do?
M: You need to study art, too. Creativity is important.
G: All right! Thank you for your time, Mr. Watson.

본문 TEST Step 1 p.47~48

01 Jobs of, Future
02 be on, market
03 robots that, everything
04 every, print out almost
05 take space trips
06 under, floating cities
07 Look at, above
08 Do, ideas surprise
09 lives, different, future
10 As, change, appear
11 What kind, job
12 will, be like
13 following, looked ahead, chose
14 Let's read, their
15 pot that, made
16 made from, flags
17 upcycling designer
18 waste materials, products
19 that, useful in, ways
20 Upcycling, reduce, waste
21 become, creative, learn
22 Have, ever heard
23 works for, makes artificial
24 special software, print out
25 made specially, patients
26 good at, modeler
27 use, printed, future
28 big data specialist
29 works on, projects
30 For example, last, routes
31 collect, use, late-night travelers
32 analyzed, create, useful
33 working with, online
34 collecting, from, find out
35 allows, learn, daily

36 specialist, develop, problem-solving
37 Think, yourself, prepare for
38 keep looking ahead, dreaming

본문 TEST Step 2 p.49~50

01 of the Future 02 Self-driving, be on the market
03 that, everything
04 will print out almost everything
05 take space trips
06 under the sea, in floating cities
07 Look at, above 08 these, surprise
09 our lives, in the future
10 As, change, ill appear
11 What kind of job
12 What will, be like
13 The following, looked ahead, chose jobs, be important
14 Let's read 15 flower pot that Sujin made
16 was made from, flags
17 upcycling designer
18 waste materials, products
19 can be useful in new ways
20 reduce the amount of waste
21 To become, upcycling designer, creative
22 Have you ever heard, modelers
23 works for, that makes artificial
24 special software
25 specially for patients
26 are good at, be a 3D modeler
27 wants, to use, in the future
28 big data specialist 29 works on
30 For example, bus routes
31 taxi use patterns, late-night travelers
32 analyzed, to create, useful routes
33 working with
34 collecting data from, find out
35 allows us to learn, our daily lives
36 specialist, develop, problem-solving skills
37 Think, yourself, prepare for
38 keep looking, dreaming, be bright

본문 TEST Step 3 p.51~52

1 미래의 직업
2 2020년대: 자율주행차들이 시장에 나올 것이다.
3 2030년대: 사람들은 그들을 위하여 모든 것을 하는 로봇을 갖게 될 것이다.
4 2030년대: 모든 가정의 3D 프린터가 거의 모든 것을 출력해 낼 것이다.
5 2050년대: 사람들은 우주여행을 할 것이다.
6 2050년대: 사람들은 바다 밑이나 수상 도시에서 살 것이다.
7 위의 그림들을 보세요.
8 이 생각들이 놀랍습니까?
9 당신은 미래에 우리의 삶이 매우 달라질 것을 볼 수 있습니다.
10 우리의 삶이 변화함에 따라 새로운 직업들이 많이 생겨날 것입니다.
11 당신은 어떤 직업을 원하세요?
12 미래의 당신 삶은 어떤 모습일까요?
13 다음의 사람들은 앞을 내다보고 미래에 중요하게 될 직업을 선택하였습니다.
14 그들의 직업에 관하여 읽어 봅시다!
15 수진이 만든 화분이 보이시나요?
16 이것은 거리의 낡은 깃발들로 만들어진 것입니다.
17 그녀는 업사이클링 디자이너입니다.
18 그녀는 새로운 제품을 만들기 위해 폐기물을 가지고 작업합니다.
19 그녀의 제품들은 낡은 재료가 새로운 방식으로 유용해질 수 있다는 것을 사람들에게 보여줍니다.
20 업사이클링은 미래에 쓰레기의 양을 줄일 수 있습니다.
21 업사이클링 디자이너가 되려면 당신은 창의적이어야 하며 미술을 배워야 합니다.
22 3D 모형 제작자에 관하여 들어 본 적이 있으신가요?
23 3D 모형 제작자인 태호는 인공 손과 다리를 만드는 회사에서 일합니다.
24 태호는 새 손과 다리를 출력하기 위하여 특별한 소프트웨어를 사용합니다.
25 그것들은 환자를 위하여 특별히 제작됩니다.
26 만약 당신이 컴퓨터 프로그래밍이나 미술을 잘한다면, 3D 모형 제작자가 될 수 있습니다.
27 태호는 미래에 더 많은 사람들이 3D 프린터로 출력된 제품들을 사용하기를 원합니다.
28 지혜는 빅데이터 전문가입니다.
29 그녀는 많은 프로젝트에서 일합니다.
30 예를 들어, 작년에 그녀는 버스 노선을 만들었습니다.
31 최적의 심야 노선을 찾기 위하여, 그녀는 심야에 이동하는 사람들의 스마트폰 이용 정보와 택시 이용 패턴을 수집할 필요가 있었습니다.
32 그런 다음 그녀는 그 정보를 분석하여 가장 유용한 노선을 만들었습니다.
33 현재 지혜는 온라인 쇼핑몰과 작업하고 있습니다.
34 그녀는 소비자들에게 맞는 최적의 스타일을 찾기 위하여 그들로부터 데이터를 수집하고 있습니다.
35 그녀는 빅데이터가 우리에게 일상생활에 관하여 더 많이 알게 해 준다는 것을 알고 있습니다.
36 만약 당신이 빅데이터 전문가가 되고 싶다면, 수학과 문제 해결 능력을 계발해야 합니다!

37 자신에 대하여 생각해 보고 미래를 준비하세요.
38 만약 당신이 계속 앞을 내다보고 꿈을 크게 꾼다면, 당신의 미래는 밝을 것입니다.

본문 TEST Step 4-Step 5

p.53~56

1 Jobs of the Future
2 2020s: Self-driving cars will be on the market.
3 2030s: People will have robots that do everything for them.
4 2030s: 3D printers in every home will print out almost everything.
5 2050s: People will take space trips.
6 2050s: People will live under the sea or in floating cities.
7 Look at the pictures above.
8 Do these ideas surprise you?
9 You can see that our lives will be very different in the future.
10 As our lives change, many new jobs will appear.
11 What kind of job do you want?
12 What will your future life be like?
13 The following people looked ahead and chose jobs that will be important in the future.
14 Let's read about their jobs!
15 Do you see the flower pot that Sujin made?
16 It was made from old street flags.
17 She is an upcycling designer.
18 She works with waste materials to make new products.
19 Her products show people that old materials can be useful in new ways.
20 Upcycling can reduce the amount of waste in the future.
21 To become an upcycling designer, you should be creative and learn about art.
22 Have you ever heard of 3D modelers?
23 Taeho, a 3D modeler, works for a company that makes artificial hands and legs.
24 Taeho uses special software to print out new hands and legs.
25 They are made specially for patients.
26 If you are good at computer programming and art, you can be a 3D modeler.
27 Taeho wants more people to use 3D printed products in the future.
28 Jihye is a big data specialist.
29 She works on many projects.
30 For example, last year, she made bus routes.
31 To find the best night routes, she needed to collect smartphone use data and taxi use patterns from late-night travelers.
32 Then she analyzed this information to create the most useful routes.
33 Now Jihye is working with an online shopping mall.
34 She is collecting data from customers to find out the best styles for them.
35 She knows big data allows us to learn more about our daily lives.
36 If you want to become a big data specialist, you should develop your math and problem-solving skills!
37 Think about yourself and prepare for your future.
38 If you keep looking ahead and dreaming big, your future will be bright.

구석구석지문 TEST Step 1

p.57

After You Read D

1. reviewer, writers articles
2. chose, because, watching movies
3. To get, improve, writing skills
4. many different types

Culture Link

1. Personal, Consultant
2. creates, their customers
3. unique strengths
4. by using, personality, knowledge, skills
5. To get, need to, communication skills

Do It Yourself A

1. looking at
2. are needed
3. help out, good at drawing
4. help out
5. Why don't we apply
6. not good at, good at playing
7. help out
8. Let's, apply to become

구석구석지문 TEST Step 2

p.58

After You Read D

1. Taehun Kim is a movie reviewer . He writers articles about new movies.
2. He chose this job because he loves watching movies .
3. To get this job, he read many books to improve his writing skills .
4. He also watched many different types of movies.

Culture Link

1. Personal Brand Consultant
2. A personal brand consultant creates a personal brand for their customers.
3. They find the customer's unique strengths.
4. Then they build a personal brand by using the customer's personality , knowledge , and skills.
5. To get this job, you need to have great communication skills.

Do It Yourself A

1. B: Hey, Mandy. What are you looking at ?
2. G: Hey, Edward. Look! Some volunteers are needed for the school festival.
3. B: Really? I want to help out. You know I'm good at drawing pictures. I think I can do something for the festival.
4. G: I think you can help out at the cartoon event.
5. B: Right! Why don't we apply together?
6. G: Well, I am not good at drawing pictures. But I'm good at playing board games.
7. B: You can help out at the game event then.
8. G: Okay. Let's go and apply to become volunteers.

적중100

영어 기출 문제집

정답 및 해설

능률 | 김성곤